p232 Inupiat's most noted artists

woppebbode
silkscreened prints
abc.gc.ca/trade/culture/index.html
Calif Academy of Sciences
fiddlers p.?.5
p.266. artists talk about their work
p.46 Vanland.

NATIVE PEOPLES
of ALASKA

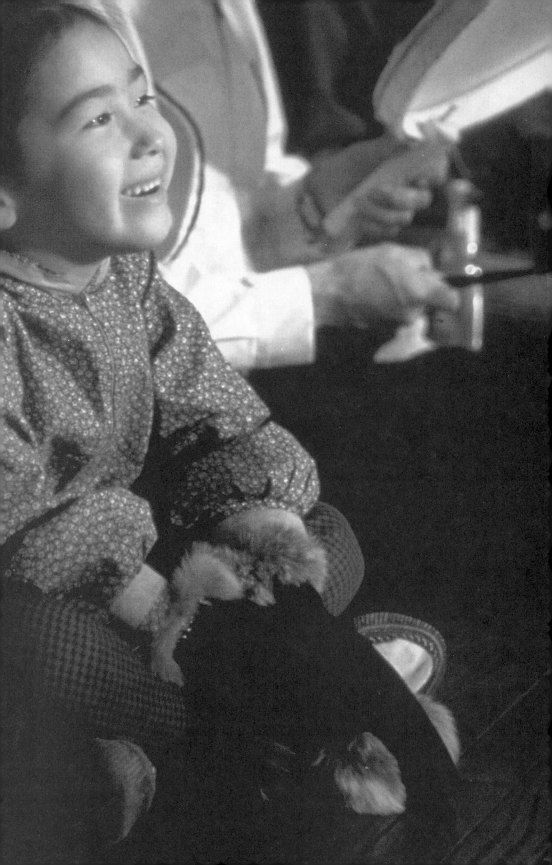

NATIVE PEOPLES of ALASKA

A TRAVELER'S GUIDE TO LAND, ART, AND CULTURE

BY JAN HALLIDAY

WITH PATRICIA J. PETRIVELLI AND THE ALASKA NATIVE HERITAGE CENTER

SASQUATCH BOOKS
SEATTLE

Printed in the United States of America.
Distributed in Canada by Raincoast Books Ltd.
02 01 00 99 98   5 4 3 2 1

Cover and interior design and composition: Hingepin Partners,
Vashon Island, Washington
Fold-out map: Hingepin Partners
Interior maps: Michael Rohani Design; with revisions by Hingepin
Partners

Library of Congress Cataloging in Publication Data
Halliday, Jan.
        Native Peoples of Alaska : a traveler's guide to land, art, and
culture / Jan Halliday with Patricia J. Petrivelli and the Alaska Native
Heritage Center.
        p. cm.
        Includes index.
        ISBN 1-57061-100-9
        1. Indians of North America—Alaska—Social life and cus-
toms—Guidebooks. 2. Eskimos—Alaska—Social life and customs—
Guidebooks. 3. Alaska—Description and travel—Guidebooks. I.
Petrivelli, Patricia J. II. Alaska Native Heritage Center. III. Title.
        E78.A3H33 1998
        390'.089'9710798—dc21   97-51450

Sasquatch Books
615 Second Avenue
Seattle, Washington 98104
(206) 467-4300
books@sasquatchbooks.com
http://www.sasquatchbooks.com

Sasquatch Books publishes high-quality adult nonfiction and children's books related to the Northwest (Alaska to San Francisco). For
more information about our titles, contact us at the address above, or
view our site on the World Wide Web.

Art Credits

Cover photograph: This Yup'ik mask is simultaneously a seabird in flight, holding a fish in its mouth, and its powerful spirit (*yua*), indicated by the face on the back of the bird and by the huge outstretched hands. The mask was collected in 1912 from Goodnews Bay on the coast of the Bering Sea in Southwest Alaska. The mask, so large that the performer needs assistance to hold it up, was among 76 Yup'ik masks that were returned to Alaska in 1995—the first time the masks had "come home" since they were removed from Alaska near the turn of the century. The masks were assembled for *Agayuliyararput*, an acclaimed exhibit of Yup'ik masks and cosmology first shown at Toksook Bay on Nelson Island and then at the Anchorage Museum of History and Art. The exhibit has since traveled to cities throughout Alaska as well as 200 cities in the Lower 48, including New York and Washington, D.C. At the end of the tour, this mask will return to Seattle's Burke Museum of Natural History and Culture, where it is part of the permanent collection. The mask is also pictured in *The Living Tradition of Yup'ik Masks*, by Ann Fienup-Riordan (University of Washington Press, 1996), published to accompany the *Agayuliyararput* exhibit. (Courtesy of the Burke Museum of Natural History and Culture, Catalog Number 4539.)

Cover graphics: *Front cover, top:* The small symbol of a whale inside a circle is taken from an image etched on a seal-oil lamp that was unearthed on Afognak Island in the Kodiak archipelago. The original glyph is over a foot in diameter. The two dots on either side of the whale are raised and are where the cotton-grass wick was placed. The symbol is a trademark of the Afognak Native Corporation's Dig Afognak, which operates archaeological sites in the Kodiak archipelago. (See the Kodiak section of the Southwest Alaska chapter.) *Front cover, bottom:* The graphic used at the bottom of the front cover and on the book title page is the logo for the Alaska Native Heritage Center. It represents Alaska's diverse Native groups. (See the Anchorage section of the Interior Alaska chapter.) *Backcover:* The Raven and Eagle symbol is the trademark of Sitka Tribal Tours. When the two birds face each other in this way, they are called the "Lovebirds." (See the Sitka section of the Southeast Alaska chapter.)

Interior art: *Page ii:* Lena Hensley performing with Inupiat dancers at the Museum of the Arctic in Kotzebue (see the Arctic chapter). Photograph by Chris Arend, courtesy of NANA. *Page 1:* Detail of a totem pole at Totem Bight State Park in Ketchikan (see the Southeast Alaska chapter). Photograph courtesy of Alaska Sightseeing/CruiseWest. *Page 73:* Detail of a contemporary Alutiiq mask by Jerry Laktonen. Photograph courtesy of the artist. *Page 159:* Beaded Mittens. Moosehide, beaver, fur, cloth, beads. Koyukon Athabascan; ca. 1930. University of Alaska Museum Collection; photograph by Barry McWayne; courtesy of the University of Alaska Museum. (See the Fairbanks section of the Interior Alaska chapter.) *Page 221:* Walrus ivory carving. Horned Puffin, by Alvan Olana, King Island, 1981. University of Alaska Museum Collection; photograph by Barry McWayne; courtesy of the University of Alaska Museum. (See the Fairbanks section of the Interior Alaska chapter.) *Page 251:* Sled Bag (detail). Moosehide, cloth, yarn, beads. 18¾ x 20¼. Kutchin Athabaskan. Arctic Village or Fort Yukon, ca. 1905. Donor: Rev. Wilfred C. Files. University of Alaska Museum Collection; photograph by Barry McWayne; courtesy of the University of Alaska Museum. (See the Fairbanks section of the Interior Alaska chapter.) *Page 263:* Detail of a Tlingit ceremonial robe. Photograph courtesy of Alaska Sightseeing/CruiseWest.

CONTENTS

Acknowledgments

This book is the work of many people. Because it was written without any grants or other financial assistance, many people stepped in to help with the huge task of gathering information. First, a special thank you to all the Native peoples of Alaska, the executive board and staff of the thirteen regional Native corporations, and the village corporations and their heritage foundations—for welcoming me into your territories, inviting me into your homes, introducing me to your families, identifying people I should work with, and sharing your stories and favorite places. My heart is full with the memories of this past year.

Pat Petrivelli, of the Alaska Heritage Center, agreed to explain subsistence and the Alaska Native Claims Settlement Act to outsiders (see her two essays in the appendices). I am most grateful, Pat. Also, thank you to Alex Muktoyuk, for sharing his story of walrus hunting on King Island, and to Norma Jean Dunne, for her enthusiasm for this project.

Alaska is a huge state, with villages and towns hundreds of miles apart. Many airlines volunteered to coordinate travel. Thanks especially to Alaska Airlines (and Paradigm Press, publisher of *Alaska Airlines Magazine*); Bering Air; Frontier Flying Service; Lake Clark Air; Yute Air; Gram's Cafe; and pilots John Paul Bouker of Bristol Bay Air, Willie Hall of Kodiak Air Service, Perry Garrison of Yute Air, and Bill Sims of Newhalen Lodge, for flying all those extra miles over unforgettable, breathtaking territory. Special thanks to Chris Beck for all his help in gathering material about Southwest Alaska.

The Alaska Native Tourism Council and Alaska Division of Tourism, with their extensive contacts, helped plan an efficient tour of the state region by region. Convention and visitor bureaus in every town helped identify many of the people whose tours, lodgings, and studios are included in this book. Thank you also to the many non-Native-owned hotels that generously donated lodging, knowing they would not be included in this book.

The directors, curators, and staff of Alaska's museums were most helpful. Thank you all for your personal attention. I wish everyone could tour a museum with the curator of the collection.

Sasquatch Books continues to wade into uncharted territory in the guidebook genre. My appreciation to editors and lifeguards Joan Gregory and Sherri Schultz, who kept us all from drowning in a sca of words.

And finally, thanks to Gail Chehak, President of Indian Art Northwest, for her commitment to cultural tourism and art, and to Chuck Lathrop, my husband, for standing by with caffeine and loving support.

Introduction

Written in cooperation with Alaska Natives themselves, this book is an invitation and a guide to you—to visit Alaska Natives and their lands; to learn about their lives, history, art, and culture from *them*; and to see the wonders of Alaska through *their* eyes. Every activity, tour, business, lodging, and destination recommended in this book is owned or operated by Alaska Natives. Here is local knowledge at its best— tour and trip leaders, hosts and hostesses, guides and artists who are descendants of the peoples who settled in this region 4,500 to 10,000 or more years ago. You could spend your life reading about Alaska Native culture, or even travel the state, without meeting an Alaska Native in person or having these kinds of firsthand experiences.

With the help of the thirteen regional native corporations, the Alaska Native Tourism Council, and Pat Petrivelli of the Alaska Native Heritage Center, we've compiled descriptions of hundreds of activities, destinations, and attractions where you can learn about Alaska's rich Native culture, lands, and art. We tell you who and what to see, where to find the best and most authentic experiences, and how to get there. The range of things to do is extraordinary—from cruising through the Inside Passage aboard a Tlingit-owned ship stacked with kayaks for excursions into smaller bays, to riding a dogsled with Athabascan mushers in the Yukon, to watching the northern lights on a winter night with Inupiat guides in the Arctic, to searching for beluga whales with a Yup'ik family in Southwest Alaska. You can choose whatever activities you are most comfortable doing—whether it's taking a wilderness trip on remote Nunivak Island or poking around museums and art galleries in Anchorage— and enjoy reading about the rest. We are certain that with this book, you will have the most memorable trip to Alaska possible.

Traveling in Alaska

Maps and Travel Information

When incorporating Native travel and art into your trip to Alaska, you'll want to begin with an overview of what the state has to offer in general. We suggest that you begin by contacting the following:

- Alaska Division of Tourism Visitor Information, PO Box 110801, Juneau, AK 99501; (907)465-2010. Open 8am-5pm Mon-Fri. Call for a free 100-page Alaska Vacation Planner, which includes maps and detailed information on travel in Alaska and Canada's Yukon Territories.

■ Alaska Native Tourism Council, 1577 C St, Ste 304, Anchorage, AK 99501; (907)274-5400. Ask for a free full-color brochure of some of Alaska's most popular Native cultural tours and attractions, such as Saxman Village in Ketchikan and Tour Arctic in Barrow. The brochure also lists tour companies, such as Holland America West Tours, Princess Cruises, Alaska Airlines, Knightly Tours, and Auk Nu Tours, that offer experiences with Native cultures as part of their tour packages.

■ For a more detailed map of the state, although it's in bulky book form, we recommend the *Alaska Atlas & Gazetteer*, DeLorme Mapping, PO Box 298, Freeport, ME 94032; (907)865-4171. Available in most bookstores.

■ Convention and visitors bureaus for each city you might be interested in visiting are listed under the chapter headings in this book. All will send you brochures on local lodging, restaurants, car rentals, and bush plane services.

Languages and Terminology

Although there are five distinct cultural regions in Alaska, each with its own language and dialects, most Alaska Natives speak English. Some, such as the Yup'ik people of Southwest Alaska, speak English as a second language, and many have high school and college educations, have served in the U. S. military, and work professionally in various fields.

The question most often asked by non-Natives who wish to be respectful is what term or name to use when referring to Native Americans who live in Alaska. It's a good question and not as sensitive an issue as one might think.

First, a little background: At the time of European contact, North America was divided into more than 500 separate nation-states, each of which had its own language or dialect, just as in Europe. The U.S. government recognized the sovereignty of these separate nations when it signed treaties with each one. At the time most of the treaties were signed, Alaska either was owned by Russia or was an American territory. Thus, most Alaska Natives have a different legal and historical relationship with the U.S. government than do Native tribes who live in the Lower 48.

The term *Alaska Native* is used to recognize the special status of the Native people of Alaska, whether they are of Inupiat Eskimo, Yup'ik Eskimo, Aleut, Alutiiq, Athabascan, Tlingit, Haida, or Tsimshian heritage. A Native Alaskan, on the other hand, is anyone born in Alaska.

The term *Eskimo* has been used historically to identify Alaskan Natives who live in Arctic coastal regions and who share similar languages and cultures. It is acceptable to use *Eskimo,* but the people who live in these regions prefer that you learn and use the terms for the more specific language and culture groupings, such as *Inupiat* and *Yup'ik.*

The term *Indian* is also okay, as long as you think of Indians as diverse individuals with fascinating, complex, and unique heritages. The Ketchikan Indian Corporation and the Metlakatla Indian Reservation in Southeast Alaska would not use the word if it had negative connotations. (We like the theory that the term *Indian* had its origins in the name Christopher Columbus gave the first people he met in the New World: so struck was he by these strong and beautiful people, who apparently lived in paradise on earth, that he called them *In Dios,* which in Italian meant "those close to God.")

American Indian is the term used in legal documents to distinquish Native nations that have a legal relationship with the United States. The term *American Indian* is often used by the press when reporting news about the sovereign nations.

Native American came into common usage as a politically correct term in the United States in the 1970s. It is a respectful way of lumping Indians into one general group, as in "many Native Americans have obtained or are working on college degrees." However, it does not clearly distinguish between Indians and those who consider themselves "native" Americans because they were born in the United States. *Native peoples* has gained more acceptance internationally as a more convenient term than "the indigenous peoples of the Western Hemisphere."

In Canada, *First Nations* is used to distinguish the sovereignty of Native peoples in Canada. In British Columbia, for example, the First Nation of Nuu-chah-nulth comprises nearly twenty reserves on the western shore of Vancouver Island.

Greeting Alaska Natives

When greeting each other, Native people rarely use the words *Alaska Native, Eskimo, Indian, Native American,* or *First Nation.* Instead, they describe themselves according to their tribal affiliation and ancestry. Someone who is Athabascan may tell you more specifically that she is Gwich'in from Arctic Village. An Alaska Native from Sitka who is Tlingit might define himself further by saying, "I'm Kiksadi Tlingit, Raven, of the Frog clan." If he gets even more specific, he may say something like this: "My name is John E. Bartel; my Tlingit name is KUU'-Ush-gun. I was given Paul Willis's name, Ahnn-ka-la-seek, which is from the Eagle (Chh'a'ak') moiety. I am of the Chookeneidi clan. My Sitka house (Naak'a'Hitz'ee) is Iceberg House (Xaatl' Hit) and Iron House (Gaa yeis' Hit). My crest (At.oow) is Bear (Xoot's), Iceberg (Xaatl'), and Porpoise (Ch'eech). I can also use Glacier Bay (Sit eeti Geey) and Woman in the Ice (Kaasteen).

"I was born December 6, 1949, in Sitka, Alaska, to Harry Bartel, half Athabascan and half German, and Agnes Nielsen Bartels (Kahh-dath), all Tlingit. My introduction to totemic art was through my first teacher, my grandfather Peter C. Nielsen (Aak'wa shoox'). His Tlingit name means 'laughing in the lake.'"

Introduce yourself to a Native individual or group as you normally would. If you want to discuss heritage with a Native person—and it often comes up—it's only fair that you know your own. The more you know about the histories of all people, the more you understand what is codified in a simple statement of heritage. For example, when Jan says, "I'm mostly Scot from Northern Ireland," she's saying that she descends from a long line of settlers. When Pat says, "I'm Aleut," she's saying that she descends from people who lived in the Aleutian Islands—1,000 to 1,800 miles from Anchorage—and hunted from kayaks for hundreds of generations prior to Russian occupation. Encoded in these two short introductions is a wealth of history, myth, and legend that has shaped both individuals. What really matters in this exchange is the respect that Pat and Jan have for each other, for their own families, and for each other's extended family history.

How to Pack for Alaska

When traveling in Alaska, a backpack is the best bet for luggage. Buy a good one—the better it's made, the easier it will be to lug across gravel airstrips or down the beach to a skiff. Make sure there's a detachable day pack to carry emergency snacks, water, lunch, rain gear, camera, and bug repellent. Also be sure it has an internal frame so that it will stow easily in a small plane's baggage compartment. You'll be glad you brought your backpack (and sleeping bag) if the rental car doesn't pan out and you have to walk or hitchhike into town, or if the only hotel is full, or if you have an unexpected opportunity to spend a couple of days camping on a remote beach.

Rule of thumb: If there's tundra, there will be bugs big enough to sting through a moose's tough hide. In summer evenings, when the sun sets around midnight or not at all, you have a choice: wear your dopey bug net, or sit in your tent/cabin/room. The best bug net we found is a baseball cap with bug netting that unsnaps, rolls down from the crown over the brim, and ties across your chest and under your arms. Most outdoor outfitters carry mosquito netting; you'll need the smallest mesh size you can find to keep the no-see-ums out. Netting is lightweight, inexpensive, and reusable, and it can be tucked into your day pack. Carrying a little bottle of StingEze, which contains camphor, is a good idea too.

During the summer in Alaska, layers work best. One set of light-weight polypropylene underwear, one wool sweater, one warm vest, and a lightweight windbreaker eliminate the need to drag along all your bulky cool-weather clothing. Sweatpants with elastic at the cuff and knee-high rubber boots (you can pick up a pair at any outdoor store throughout Alaska for under $20) are the norm in villages. Bring plenty of T-shirts, short pants (temperatures in the interior can reach 90 degrees in the summer), casual slacks, sweats, socks, and a rain poncho, and you'll be comfortable most of the time. (However, locals advise not to wear cotton into the wilderness, even during summer months. Cotton has no insulation value when wet and it does not dry quickly. Therefore, wearing it can result in hypothermia, which can kill.) Do not bring anything that needs ironing—or, if you do, wear it wrinkled. No one cares. A swimsuit is a good idea—some villages have public swimming pools. Throw in a pair of shower shoes to wear in the steam bath. Kayak-paddling shoes work well and can be worn with socks (to keep the bugs off your bare feet) around camp in the evening. Sunscreen with a high SPF rating is essential.

You might also want to invest in your own cartridge-inflatable float vest if you're planning to spend much time on boats or float-planes. All watercraft are required to carry Coast Guard–approved flotation devices for passengers, but if you buy your own you can be assured of a comfortable fit (they're flat and can be worn like a normal vest).

Winter comes early to Alaska, and leaves late. If you are travel-ing in the "shoulder season," be prepared for drastic overnight drops in temperature. Never wear a down-filled jacket or vest—if it gets wet, you'll freeze. Cotton kills when it gets wet. And wind (which can plunge the temperature to 80 degrees below zero) blasts right through wool. Wear polypropylene long underwear, with layers of wool on top, and windproof, waterproof outerwear. Use polypropy-lene gloves, covered with mittens. Gore-Tex jackets should be equipped with a ruffed hood (ruffs cut the wind). Ski masks prevent frostbite. Inupiat Eskimos, who live year-round north of the Arctic Circle, suggest insulated, waterproof snow boots worn with polypropylene socks underneath wool socks. Sunglasses or goggles are essential to combat snow glare when the sun returns in February, March, and April (which are also the coldest months in the Arctic). If you have any doubts about what to wear in the winter Arctic, call any of the Inupiat or Yup'ik Eskimo guides listed in this book, and they'll tell you what brands of clothing they prefer. All gear can be purchased anywhere in the United States or through catalogues. Also remember that winter in Southeast Alaska, the Gulf of Alaska, and the Kodiak archipelago is somewhat milder—and wetter; bring rain gear. If you forget anything, Fairbanks, Juneau, and Anchorage all have fully stocked outfitting stores.

Seeing Alaska by Ship, Ferry, or Charter Boat

Dozens of the world's largest luxury liners, accommodating from 500 to 2,000 passengers, visit Alaska every summer. Many depart from Vancouver, British Columbia. Luxury liners feature great food, on-board big-name entertainment, theater, and other diversions.

If you wish to see Native attractions or take Native tours, be sure to ask where the cruise ship calls and how many hours it will be in port. Lists of shore excursions are generally not available until you receive your boarding documents; most excursions are sold on board the ship prior to docking. Some shore excursions, such as Princess Cruise Lines trips into Interior Alaska and the Arctic, can include travel to destinations far from the dock. Tell the cruise ship agent exactly what you want to do, and be persistent about getting all the information you need before signing on.

Smaller ships, which accommodate 50 to 140 passengers, are able to nose into shallower waters and visit villages that do not have deep-water ports or big docks. On these small ships, passengers dress casually, dine family style, and sleep in smaller staterooms. On-board entertainment is often educational and thought-provoking. Most small boats have libraries stocked with videos and good books about the region's natural and cultural history.

Most cruise ships, big and small, visit Alaska during the peak season, between June and August. A few visit through the end of September. Discounts are usually available for early booking, or spring and fall sailings.

Keep in mind that many of the coastline attractions listed in this book are within walking distance of the cruise ship dock. Some tickets to Native tours are not booked on the ships, but are sold independently on the cruise ship docks. Again, be sure to ask how much time the ship spends in each port before you commit to a cruise.

Big ships
- Carnival Cruise Lines, (800)327-9501
- Celebrity Cruises, (800)437-3111
- Crystal Cruises, (800)446-6620
- Cunard Line, (800)221-4770
- Holland America Line Westours, (800)426-0327
- Norwegian Cruise Line, (800)327-7030
- Princess Cruises, (800)568-3262
- Royal Caribbean Cruises, (800)327-6700
- World Explorer Cruises, (800)854-3835

Small ships
- Alaska Sightseeing/Cruise West, (800)426-7702
- Cunard Line, (800)458-9000
- Glacier Bay Tours and Cruises, (800)451-5952 (Native-owned)
- Kenai Fjords Tours, (888)478-3346 (Native-owned)
- Society Expeditions, (800)548-8669
- Special Expeditions, (800)762-0003

Alaska State Ferry

The Alaska State Ferry(also known as the Alaska Marine Highway) is by far the least expensive, do-it-yourself option for getting around. Most towns on the ferry route have few roads, so there's no reason to take your car. The big boats load cars at Bellingham, Washington (between Vancouver, British Columbia, and Seattle), for the trip north. Boats travel through the Inside Passage to ports of call in the Gulf of Alaska, the Kodiak archipelago, and even the Aleutian Islands.

Food is served on board, and overnight cabins are available on all ferries. (They're stark as a shoebox but have private baths, showers, and bunks—and fresh linens on request.) Many people roll out sleeping bags, or rent pillows and blankets, and spend an often damp, but always memorable, night on the deck in reclining lawn chairs. (People try to erect tents on the deck for privacy, but we don't advise it—the wind whips the tent all night long.) If you're sleeping on the deck, take a very warm sleeping bag, a thin sleeping pad, and a wool cap, and wear something to bed to keep the wind from blowing down your neck. If it gets too cold, you can haul your gear into the lounge and sleep on the floor. You won't be alone.

The ferries offer films and documentaries, and during the summer there may be on-board live entertainment. The smaller, inter-island ferries all offer food service, comfortable chairs, and even a shower stall in the restroom.

The Alaska State Ferry schedule is daunting—up to 50 pages long. To decipher it, first look in the table of contents for "Southeast Alaska/Inside Passage," a section about eight pages long. In that section, at the top of the page, look for the month you want to travel. Find the town you plan to leave from. Follow the column down to find the date you want to travel. Dates are coded, but are simple to figure out. For example, in the April section, under the town of Bellingham, "S1, 3:00 p.m." means that the boat leaves the dock Saturday, April 1, at 3pm. Color codes don't mean anything; they just help you read the tiny print across the page. Weird docking times (such as 4am) are not misprints. The ferry travels long distances between towns, is subject to currents and tides, and often arrives and leaves at odd hours.

If a town is listed on the ferry schedule but there are no dates or arrival times in that column, look on the adjacent page for the inter-island ferry schedule.

If you are taking a car in summer, make reservations a season in advance, prepaid by credit card. The back page of the Alaska State Ferry schedule lists information sources in the area serviced by the ferry, including U.S. and Canadian customs, Alaska State Parks, U.S. Forest Service, Alaska Railroad Corporation, and others. Once you've learned to use the schedule, it will be an invaluable guide; carry it with you throughout your trip.

For a free copy of the ferry schedule or for reservations, call (800)642-0066, Monday through Friday, 7:30am to 4:30pm. You can also find information, including the schedule, on the Internet at http://www.dot.state.ak.us/external/amhs/home.html. Credit cards are accepted for reservations. Fares vary according to cars, trailers, number of passengers, and cabin reservations. There's an additional charge for bicycles, kayaks, and canoes.

Private Charter Boats

Private charters are a great way to get to know an area firsthand. This book tells you about many Native-owned charter boat skippers who offer tours—in everything from outboard motor skiffs to cabin cruisers—of the Inside Passage waterways, Resurrection Bay in the Gulf of Alaska, the Kodiak archipelago, the Yukon River, the Noatak and Kobuk Rivers above the Arctic Circle, and other areas.

SOUTHEAST
ALASKA

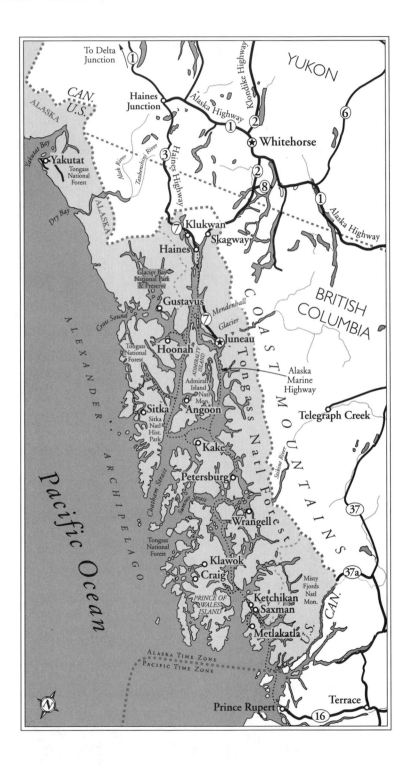

SOUTHEAST ALASKA

The hundreds of forested islands, glacier-carved fjords, churning narrows, straits, and bays of Southeast Alaska are part of the Inside Passage. Protected from the Pacific Ocean's violent storms by barrier islands, the Inside Passage provides safe passage from Puget Sound, in Washington State, all the way to the Gulf of Alaska.

In Alaska, these islands, waters, and shores have been inhabited for centuries by the Tlingit Indians. No one knows for sure whether the Tlingits are the descendants of a first wave of ice-age travelers who crossed from Asia into North America, or of a later wave of immigrants who returned to this rugged area from the interior of the North American continent more than 10,000 years ago. While it is not known when they came here, it is certain that the Tlingits established permanent settlements and summer fish camps, connected by canoe and overland routes, throughout what is now called Southeast Alaska. Their art and architecture reflects the rich tradition of Northwest Coast Indian tribes—large clan houses along the shoreline, constructed of cedar planks covered with pitched roofs, adorned with towering totem poles outside and carved house screens and house posts inside.

Newcomers to Southeast Alaska include the Haida,

who settled on Prince of Wales Island in the 1700s, and the Tsimshians, who settled on Annette Island in the late 1800s—both arriving in huge cargo canoes carved from cedar logs. Today Tlingit, Haida, and Tsimshian people live on many of their original village sites. Some of the sites have grown into large towns, such as Juneau, Ketchikan, and Sitka; some have remained small communities, such as Angoon, Hoonah, Hydaburg, and Kake. All are accessible by jet, small plane, or the Alaska State Ferry. Only one community, Haines, is accessible by road.

One of the most spectacular scenic waterways in the world, the 1,000-mile-long Inside Passage begins in the bays of Southeast Alaska and ends on the tideflats of southern Puget Sound. Carved by glaciers during several ice ages, the Inside Passage encompasses thousands of islands, which shelter watercraft from the rugged Pacific Ocean. The Natives used the swift currents of the Inside Passage, which can run up to 16 knots, and woven cedar sails to propel their huge, cedar-carved canoes. Turning river drainages into the equivalent of our highways, Natives also developed a network of commerce far into the continent's interior.

Visitors should not expect Southeast Alaska's villages and towns to look as they did at the turn of the century, no more than they'd expect to see Oregonians dressed in pioneer garb, making soap over a wood fire. The primary source of income for villagers is logging and commercial fishing; the primary source of food is subsistence hunting and fishing. Natives dress appropriately for those tasks, in rubber boots, sweatshirts, jeans, and raingear. Meanwhile, Alaska Natives dressed in business attire run their corporations from Juneau's modern office buildings. Natives don ceremonial regalia—Chilkat and Raven's Tail blankets, red and blue button blankets, carved headpieces with inset abalone, hats woven from strips of cedar bark—only to drum and sing traditional songs during celebrations.

Alaskan museums, such as the Sheldon Jackson Museum in Sitka and the Alaska State Museum in Juneau, house collections of 18th- and 19th-century (and sometimes older) Native architecture and art, but it is traditional Tlingit, Haida, and Tsimshian art and culture that predominates in Southeast Alaska today. Distinctive totems, many of them newly carved by Native artisans, define the region. Ketchikan alone has more than 70 totems standing in parks, throughout downtown, and inside buildings. Even Juneau's Kmart has totems in the parking lot. Raven and Eagle clan symbols adorn everything from bags of fresh-roasted coffee to beach blankets and T-shirts. Sitka's public radio station, KCAW, is nicknamed "Raven Radio," honoring one of the most important entities in Native culture (and broadcasting Native news daily).

For an easy-to-understand description of Native people and their culture, the Tlingit and Haida tribes recommend **Alaskan Native Cultures, Volume 1,** *which includes historical photographs and explanations of clans, trade, slavery, canoes, traditional art, spiritual life, ceremonies, and contemporary issues. Written by Tlingit, Haida, and Tsimshian Natives; published by and available from the Native-owned Sealaska Corporation, Sealaska Heritage Foundation, One Sealaska Plaza, Suite 201, Juneau, AK 99801; (907)463-4844.*

Southeast Alaska reflects not only Native culture but also the cultural and economic impact of the Russian, British, and American trading of the early 1800s, the gold mining of the late 1800s, and the timber, fishing, and mining industries of the 1900s—all a part of Native history. The Tlingit/Russian town of Sitka, for example, offers both Russian and Tlingit traditional dance performances, tours of a Tlingit/Russian battleground, and both borscht and smoked salmon on local menus.

This vibrant mixture of cultures takes place amid glorious mountains, iceberg-filled bays, emerald green seas, lush Sitka spruce and hemlock rain forests, and abundant wildlife everywhere: returning salmon in clear streams, eagles and bears on the shores, and whales, sea lions, seals, otters, and thousands of seabirds in the straits and fjords.

"Given a choice, salmon will always choose the stronger current, knowing that the current leads the way through a passage. It is the same for a canoe. That's why so many canoes have salmon painted on the bow, to help them find the current, even in the strongest storms. The painting on the stern is something frightening, to scare off monsters, predators, or big swamping waves. Besides, it looks cool."

—Anon

There are dozens of opportunities to learn about Native culture in Southeast Alaska. You will find cultural and ecological tours throughout, guided by Natives— including tours through Saxman's clan house, carving shed, totem park, and Cape George Cannery; flights to Annette Island to visit Metlakatla's historic town and dance house; cruises of the Inside Passage and Glacier Bay on small Tlingit-owned ships; films on Tlingit tradition at the top of Juneau's Mount Roberts tram; ground tours of Tlingit/Russian Sitka with Sitka tribal guides; and wildlife watching and fishing on charter boats owned by Natives. And there are Native fine-art galleries, gift shops, artist's studios, and public art everywhere you look.

Visitor Information Services

For free maps, accommodation lists, and information packets, contact:

- Haines Convention and Visitors Bureau, PO Box 530, Haines, AK 99827; (907)766-2234; e-mail: hainesak@wwa.com.

- Juneau Convention and Visitors Bureau, 369 S Franklin St, Suite 201, Juneau, AK 99801; (907)586-1737; e-mail: jcvb@ptialaska.net.
- Ketchikan Visitors Bureau, 131 Front St, Ketchikan, AK 99901; (800)770-3300 or (907)225-6166; e-mail: kvb@ktn.net.
- Sitka Convention and Visitors Bureau, 303 Lincoln, Suite 4, PO Box 1226, Sitka, AK 99835; (907)747-5940; e-mail: scvb@ptialaska.net.
- Southeast Alaska Visitor Center, 50 Main St, Ketchikan, AK 99901; (907)228-6214. Open daily, May 1–Sept 30; Tues–Sat, Oct 1–Apr 30. This is the best visitors center we've ever seen. There are guidebooks, maps, videos about various regions in the state, exhibits and audiotapes on Native culture, and a great bookstore. Free. Visitors may call ahead and request that packets of information be sent to them.
- Wrangell Chamber of Commerce, PO Box 49, Wrangell, AK 99929; (800)367-9745 or (907)874-3901; e-mail: wrangell@wrangell.com.
- Yakutat Chamber of Commerce, (888)854-6448 or (907)784-3933.
- Yakutat Visitors and Convention Bureau, (907)486-4782.

How to Pack

The Tongass National Forest, which covers most of Southeast Alaska, is a rain forest. Summer or winter, always take rain gear: a hooded slicker, waterproof boots, and nonslip shoes that dry quickly, such as kayaker's sandals. Bring layers of clothing—a T-shirt, shorts, turtle-neck, wool sweater, hat, and lightweight slacks (jeans soak up rain). Silk or synthetic long underwear is a must, even in summer, when you might want to spend time on the deck of a cruise ship or pas-senger ferry.

Getting Around

Keep in mind that when you are coming to Southeast Alaska, you are visiting islands. Juneau, Yakutat, and Haines are the only towns located on the mainland. Of these, only Haines is accessible by road, but the nearest town on that route is Whitehorse, in Canada's Yukon Territory, 250 miles from Haines. Access to all Southeast towns is by jet, small plane (air taxi), ferry, or private vessel.

The only way for visitors to bring their car to towns and villages in Southeast Alaska is aboard an Alaska State ferry. However, since Southeast Alaska is of the few places in the world where you do not need a car, this may be an unnecessary expense. There are only a few miles of roads, and car rentals and taxis are available in every town and village.

The Alaska State Ferry system, appropriately known as the Alaska Marine Highway, is a complex web of routes that service Southeast Alaska and the Gulf of Alaska, with ports as far south as Bellingham, Washington, and as far north as the Aleutian Islands. In Southeast Alaska, smaller ferries, such as the Auk Nu passenger ferry from Juneau to Gustavus, make stops daily or every few days in even the most remote villages, depending on tides and weather.

Alaska Airlines, (800)426-0333, not only flies into Southeast Alaska from all major West Coast cities but also flies between Ketchikan, Wrangell, Juneau, and Sitka. It can save you hours on board the ferry. A flight from Juneau to Sitka, for example, is about 35 minutes; by ferry it's about 18 hours.

Ketchikan- and Sitka-based Taquan Air, (800) 770-8800 or (907)225-8800, has the best safety record of any small airline in Alaska and operates a fleet of turbine-powered Otters and Caravan aircraft on both floats and wheels. Taquan makes short hops between Ketchikan and Prince Rupert, British Columbia, as well as to nearby islands, offering some very impressive tour packages. Taquan Air is Native-owned. For a list of other floatplane and bush plane services, call the visitors center in the town you plan to visit.

The best fold-out pocket map we've found to the Inside Passage is Alaska & Canard's Inside Passage Cruise Tour Guide, which measures about six feet when unfolded. It is published by Coastal Cruise Tour Guides, 158 Thomas, Suite 11, Seattle, WA 98109; (206)448-4488.

Ketchikan and Saxman: *Tlingit*

Ketchikan is easy to explore by foot, and the region's Native heritage is immediately apparent. On Front Street, next to the cruise ship dock, look for the Thundering Wings totem pole, designed by world-renowned carver Nathan Jackson, a Ketchikan resident.

Ketchikan was first called Kichxaan, so named by a Tlingit family who camped near the mouth of the creek each summer to fish. The name means "thundering wings of an eagle." In 1885, Mike Martin bought 160 acres from Chief Kyan, and this land became the township of Ketchikan. The following year the first cannery opened at the mouth of Ketchikan Creek. Gold strikes in Southeast Alaska briefly turned the town into a supply center for miners. By the turn of the century, the little fish camp had four more canneries and dozens of shacks built on wooden pilings and scaffolding on the town's steep hillsides, accessible from the water by ladders and boardwalks. So little land existed between the mountains and the sea that in the old days baseball games were played on the tide flats. When the tide came in, the game was called. By the 1930s, there were seven salmon canneries, a spruce box mill, and logging operations; by 1954, a pulp mill had been built at Ward Cove. A bordello was built on a wharf straddling Ketchikan Creek, and it functioned until the 1950s.

Today, four canneries still operate. A large, picturesque fishing fleet is docked along the waterfront. Ketchikan's functional and pretty little historic downtown, with its restored old hotels and shops, is nestled against the steep, evergreen-covered hillsides and is enhanced with many beautifully carved totem poles. The clapboard-sided buildings that were once bordellos along Creek Street are now shops, restaurants, art galleries, and bookstores. You can follow the Married Man's Trail through the woods along Ketchikan Creek, and continue on to a fish hatchery and the Totem Heritage Center, which houses 33 totem poles that are more than 100 years old. (The center is on the National Register of Historic Places.) Or, from the Creek Street boardwalk, you can take a red funicular up the cliff and inside Westmark Cape Fox Lodge for a grand view of downtown and the Tongass Narrows. At the lodge's front entrance is a stunning *Council of the Clans,* designed by Tlingit/Haida Lee Wallace, a fourth-generation totem carver. Behind the lodge is the Totem Heritage Center.

> *To learn more about totem designs and stories, look for* **The Wolf and the Raven,** *by Dr.* **Viola Garfield,** *anthropology professor, and* **Linn Forrest, U.S. Forest** *Service architect in charge of the Totem Bight restoration project. (University of Washington Press, 1948, 18th printing)*

If you want to see totem poles, this is the place to come. Ketchikan and nearby Saxman, the only towns on Revillagigedo Island, together have nearly 70 totem poles; they can be found in two totem parks, in the totem museum, and standing throughout the area. Ketchikan's appreciation of totem poles goes back to 1901, when a 55-foot totem pole was raised into place in the heart of town. The pole was dedicated to the Kadjuk House of the Raven clan. The Kadjuk totem pole had withstood the weather for nearly 70 years, about the normal life span of a totem before it topples to the ground, when it was removed and installed in the city's Totem Heritage Center. Then, in 1989, Ketchikan commissioned a young carver, Israel Shotridge, to carve a replica of the Kadjuk pole. It now stands on the original site, at the corner of Totem Way and Stedman Street in downtown Ketchikan. At the top of the pole, in the place of honor, is the mythical bird who lives at the top of a nearby mountain. The rest of the pole depicts the story of Fogwoman, who lives at the head of all the creeks, calling the salmon home from the ocean to spawn.

Saxman, three miles south of Ketchikan, is also a historic town, home to a large community of Tlingit Indians whose families moved here in the late 1800s from nearby Cape Fox and Tongass villages. Saxman Native Village, consisting of a community house, Beaver clan house, carving shed, totem park, and gift store, is one of the most visited destinations in Alaska. Cape Fox Corporation also recently opened the historic cannery for guided tours.

Getting There

Everyone who comes to Ketchikan and Saxman arrives by boat or plane. It's a three-day, two-night ride from Bellingham on the Alaska State Ferry, which docks in downtown Ketchikan near the cruise ship dock. A quicker way is a 90-minute jet ride from Seattle, a trip that's one of the more charming ways to enter a town: planes land on a runway on an adjoining island, and from the airport passengers take a small ferry across the Tongass Narrows to Ketchikan. Buses and taxis meet the boat and drive visitors downtown to six square blocks packed with things to do. No need to bring a car here; there are only 30 miles of road. You can walk to just about everything, and take the bus out to the totem park at Saxman or to Totem Bight State Park north of town.

The Ketchikan Visitors Bureau, located on Ketchikan's downtown cruise ship dock, has a free, easy-to-follow walking tour map of the city. Even if you take a Native-guided tour, the informative map is handy to have and makes a nice reminder of your visit. (131 Front Street, Ketchikan, AK 99901; (907)225-6166)

Totem Heritage Center

The 33 totem poles stored at Ketchikan's Totem Heritage Center, which is on the National Register of Historic Places, are so weathered that the original carvings are mere shadows on the cracked surfaces. Drained of color, the totem poles are silver with age and crumbling with dry rot. Most of the poles, 95 to 100 years old, would have disappeared by now if they had been left where they fell in their abandoned villages. Tribal elders, the Alaska Native Brotherhood and Sisterhood, local historians, and the Tongass Historical Museum staff began rescuing the old totems in the 1960s. The Totem Heritage Center, the only major collection of authentic totem poles in the United States, has become an invaluable resource, especially for young carvers inspired by the old masters' work. Photos on the walls, many taken at the turn of the century, show the poles in their village of origin, most within a 50-mile radius of Ketchikan. The collection also includes carved house posts and other wood fragments.

Also available at the center is the Native Arts Program schedule of classes, which are taught by Native artists from throughout Alaska and the Pacific Northwest. Past topics have included Northwest Coast design with illustrious Tlingit artist Nathan Jackson; cedar bark basketry with Tsimshian weaver Irene Bienek; button robe sewing and beadwork with Tlingit Fannie Hanlon; carving-tool making and bentwood box construction with Tlingit Ernest Smeltzer, recipient of the 1996 Governor's Award for the Arts; box drum making with totem carver David Boxley; and spruce root gathering on the Queen Charlotte Islands with Haida weaver Delores Churchill. The center's gift shop is owned and managed by the Ketchikan Indian Corporation.

Totem Heritage Center, 601 Deermount St, Ketchikan, AK 99901; (907)225-5900. Within walking distance of downtown, the center is located in a pleasant park that includes the old salmon hatchery ponds, the new Deer Mountain Hatchery, a footbridge over Ketchikan Creek, and a self-guided nature path explaining the use of the rain forest by Natives. Open daily, May 15–Sept 30; winters, Tues–Fri afternoons. $2 adults; under 12, free; Sun afternoons, all free. Guided tours; wheelchair accessible; exhibits for the blind.

Westmark Cape Fox Lodge

Pick up a walking map at the visitors center on the cruise ship dock and find the Kadjuk totem pole at Totem Way and Stedman Street. From there, cross Ketchikan Creek on the boardwalk to the shiny, cherry red tram. Much like a European funicular, the tram climbs a 130-foot granite cliff and delivers passengers to the Westmark Cape Fox Lodge, a lovely hotel overlooking Ketchikan. Built by HollandAmerica on land owned by the Cape Fox Corporation, the hotel is filled with Native art, including hand-carved house screens, masks, and prints. Next to the stone fireplace in the hotel's great room is a framed ceremonial shirt, made of dark blue wool and decorated with Beaver clan symbols, which dates to the 1880s.

There's an old Tlingit saying that when the tide is out, the table is set. One food is a black seaweed harvested during minus tides. The seaweed is dried slightly, sprinkled with clam juice, and then dried completely in the sun. Crunchy and highly nutritious, it's used in soups or eaten like popcorn. Another sea green is delicious sea asparagus, a plant that looks like a segmented succulent. It's harvested in the spring and steamed.

The views from the 108-room hotel are gorgeous. Below lies the oldest part of Ketchikan: the boardwalk with its turn-of-the-century clapboard whorehouses; the wharf and small harbor sporting one-of-a-kind fishing boats; the cruise ship dock, which sparkles when the big white ships arrive; and the 1950s federal building (inexplicably pink in color). Beyond the town stretch Tongass Narrows and the other islands. Rooms at the back of the hotel open to views of forested mountains. An installation of totem poles, "Council of the Clans," carved by Lee Wallace, stands in a circle outside the hotel's front door. A flier at the desk briefly explains the meaning of each totem.

Like most of the guest rooms, the hotel's Heen Kahidi dining room has a great view of downtown through huge picture windows. The menu features seafood—especially salmon, halibut, fresh Dungeness crab, and shrimp—as well as salads made with field greens and perfectly steamed vegetables. Fish chowders are made with real cream and fresh seafood, and huge slabs of salmon are served with a glaze of brown sugar and browned butter. Wine and beer are moderately priced.

Southeast Alaska Natives carved various kinds of totem poles. One kind commemorated an event, legendary or real. Another was a mortuary pole, with the family clan symbols on the front of the pole and the cremated remains of the deceased sealed in a hole in the back. The ridicule pole was used as a form of public humiliation.

Westmark Cape Fox Lodge, 800 Venitia Way, Ketchikan, AK 99901. For reservations (essential): U.S. (800)544-0970; Canada (800)999-2570 or (907)225-8001. Open year-round. Rooms $109–$159 depending on season. All major credit cards are accepted; no out-of-state checks. Breakfast, lunch, and dinner, with Sunday brunch. Van pickup at the airport; hotel guests pay $5 for ferry crossing.

Ketchikan Walking Tour

Joe Williams (Tlingit) grew up in Saxman, attended public schools in Ketchikan, and studied in New Mexico and Texas before he earned his college degree in Alaska. A member of the Eagle and Killer Whale clans, Williams frequently lectures about Tlingit culture on board cruise ships, with his three sons performing dances in their ceremonial regalia. Williams offers a 90-minute walking tour of Ketchikan, during which he teaches several Tlingit words and phrases; discusses totems, clans, chiefs, and shamans; and intersperses his talk with tidbits about Ketchikan local history.

Call Joe Williams in Ketchikan at (907)225-6754; prices vary according to group size; year-round, by appointment.

Deer Mountain Fish Hatchery

Perhaps it's true that Fogwoman, the mythological woman on the Creek Street totem pole, draws the salmon home to spawn: they always return from the ocean to the creek where they were hatched. A small number of ready-to-spawn salmon making their way up Ketchikan Creek are diverted into the Deer Mountain Fish Hatchery;

the rest of the fish go upstream to spawn naturally. The adult fish can be seen under the concrete raceway at the tribally owned hatchery. Steelhead come up the creek in early spring, chinook (kings) arrive between April and mid-August, coho (silvers) appear throughout the summer, and pinks (humpies) arrive from late July through August. The hatchery also raises thousands of rainbow trout to plant in local lakes. You can gaze into incubation modules and watch fry being fed in the rearing tanks. Mounted specimens of five species of salmon and trophy fish are on the wall. The hatchery's Chinook Theater shows a video about salmon rearing, called *Raised to Run*. Another video about fish culture in Alaska plays continuously. The tribal gift shop sells smoked and canned salmon. The hatchery is a pleasant walk along Ketchikan Creek from downtown (pick up a free walking tour map from the Ketchikan Visitors Bureau, on the cruise ship dock).

Ketchikan Tribal Hatchery Corporation, 1158 Salmon Rd, Ketchikan, AK 99901; (800)252-5258 or (907)225-6760. A short walk from behind Westmark Cape Fox Lodge and an easy hike from downtown. Open daily, year-round. $2 admission includes guided tour.

> **"Clan houses, a representation of the cosmos, always face the water. The fire pit, in the center of the house, is the symbolic center of the universe, and is the intersection to the middle world dominated by man, the underworld, the upper world, the sea world, and sky world."**
> **—Ketchikan Indian Corporation**

Southeast Alaska Visitor Center

Just a step away from Ketchikan's cruise ship dock is this excellent visitor center, operated by the U.S. Forest Service. The Native Traditions Room has a depiction of life in a typical Native fish camp, as well as displays showing how cedar shakes and planks were adzed and replicas of wood implements, including fishhooks and knives. The exhibit includes six audiotapes (a couple of minutes each) of elders describing life in a fish camp. The center also displays portraits of the elders who helped with the five-year planning of the exhibit. Native people are on staff to answer questions. Try to discern the stylistic differences among the Tlingit, Haida, and Tsimshian totem poles—the foyer is the only place in Alaska where all three styles of totems are together.

Southeast Alaska Visitor Center, 50 Main St, Ketchikan, AK 99901; (907)228-6214. Open daily, May 1–Sept 30; Tues–Sat, Oct 1–Apr 30. Free.

Saxman Native Village and Totem Park

In 1894, Tongass and Cape Fox Tlingits from numerous area villages chose a site 3 miles south of Ketchikan for their school and church. Blustery winds, strong tidal waves, a change in salmon migration, and the promise of cannery work, a new church, and a Bureau of Indian Affairs school prompted the move. The Tlingits built a modern town, using house plans provided by the Presbyterian missionaries. The new village was named for Samuel Saxman, a white schoolteacher who disappeared at sea with a Tlingit elder while assessing land for the new village site.

Today, Saxman Native Village, within the town of Saxman, is the leading attraction in Southeast Alaska, drawing more than 65,000 visitors each summer. Buses leave Ketchikan's cruise ship dock every 2 hours for a well-orchestrated tour. Visitors walk in small groups through the community hall, clan house, carving shed, and totem park, which features restored poles and replicas of poles brought from the villages at Cape Fox, Tongass, Cat, and Pennock Islands in the 1930s as part of a U.S. Forest Service program.

No one actually lives in Saxman Native Village, although about 500 people reside in the little town of Saxman surrounding it. A tour by Cape Fox Tours begins with a greeting delivered in Tlingit at the community hall. On stage, masked dancers reenact the story of "The Boy Who Fed the Eagles," accompanied by narration in English. A video briefly introduces Tlingit culture. As visitors leave the hall, they may meet several elders demonstrating crafts. The next stop is an old-style Beaver clan house. Constructed in 1987, it is the first authentic clan house built by Natives in Southeast Alaska in more than 100 years. Robed dancers discuss winter life in the clan house, then perform traditional dances and songs. Visitors are invited to try on carved headdresses and dance robes, and then to join the dancers in a final song.

When you speak to an elder (any gray-haired tribal member) you don't have to speak slowly or simply. While some elders speak Native languages fluently, all are fluent in English and often have, or are working on, college degrees. Elders are treated with deference and respect in the community because it is believed that they have lived long enough to have invaluable perspective, if not downright wisdom.

A clan house is about as different from European housing as is imaginable. The interior of the Beaver clan house smells as fragrant as a new cedar chest. The rectangular room, built around a central square fire pit, is adorned with massive house posts and wall panels carved and painted with clan symbols. In the recent past, a clan house like this one might have lodged up to 50 members of an extended family during winter months, providing warmth and shelter from the wet, windy winters.

After leaving the clan house, visitors walk to a carving shed that is long enough to accommodate a 100-foot cedar log. Some of the best carvers of totems, canoes, and masks in the world (as well as their apprentices) are at work in this shed. Many of the totem poles carved here are commissioned; others are purchased by inspired visitors as the first chip falls, selling for $800 to $2,500 a foot. The carver himself may tell the story about the pole he's working on, a colorful narration that often drives home a moral lesson. Outside, visitors take turns wielding an elbow adz, the primary tool used by Northwest Native carvers. When carvers use the adz, it seems to slide through the wood as if it were butter. It's not as easy as it looks.

Cape Fox Tours, PO Box 6656, Ketchikan, AK 99901; (907)225-4846. Saxman Native Village is open daily May–Sept. (Saxman Totem Park and the Village Store are free and open year-round.) Tickets to Saxman Native Village are available only through Cape Fox Tours. They are sold in advance on board cruise ships and include transportation, which leaves from the Ketchikan cruise ship dock. Tickets are also sold at the Village Store, a gift shop next to Saxman Totem Park. Times of tours always coincide with ship arrivals. A 2½-mile-long walking trail leads from Ketchikan along the road to Saxman; other transportation from Ketchikan to Saxman is by taxi (there is no public bus service to the town of Saxman or Saxman Native Village).

George Inlet Cannery Tour

Pass a roaring waterfall and stroll a short trail to the George Inlet Cannery, where voices of cannery workers once punctuated the air as Indian, Chinese, Filipino, Mexican, Italian, and Puerto Rican laborers toiled day and night to harvest and process Alaska salmon. Built on pilings in 1915, the George Inlet Cannery operated until 1959. Today you can return to that bygone era of fish traps, slime lines, and seiners on a cannery tour developed by Natives to tell the story from a worker's perspective. Watch a film on Alaska's early fishing and canning history, then walk through the old wooden buildings to see five species of salmon along with demonstrations of hauling a purse seine net aboard a fishing boat. There's a peek into a room filled with original canning equipment, including the machine that replaced the laborers who had been employed to gut fish; the slime line, where fish were cleaned, cut, and packed into cans; and the giant retorts (pressure cookers), where the cans were processed. At a re-created fish-trap watchman's shack, a young man talks about his lonely nighttime vigil and the constant threat of fish pirates (thieves who attempted to steal the unmarked, unprocessed catch in order to sell it to a competing cannery). The tour concludes with a young man donning a survival suit and jumping into the sea—a demonstration of the modern gear that has saved hundreds of fishermen's lives.

Book George Inlet Cannery Tours through Gray Line Tours of Alaska, PO Box 5097, Ketchikan, AK 99901; (907)225-5930. May 13–Sept 29. Tours run in conjunction with cruise ship arrivals. Buses pick up passengers on Ketchikan's cruise ship dock. Reservations recommended. Plan 3 hours for the tour.

Taquan Air

Pilot Jerry Scudero (Tsimshian), owner of Taquan Air, has been named Alaska businessman of the year and has received numerous awards for community service. His fleet of floatplanes and bush planes, based in Ketchikan and Sitka, is one of the largest and has the best safety record in all of Alaska. Taquan Air has partnered with guides, excursions, villages, and charter boats throughout Southeast Alaska to provide an outstanding list of "flightseeing" and ground tours. Some packages include a Native cultural component; some just give a firsthand look at remote lands known by the Tlingit, Haida, and Tsimshian people for thousands of years. Scudero is an equal-opportunity employer, hiring both Native and non–Native pilots, guides, and staff.

For a complete brochure of 25 tours, contact Taquan Air, 1007 Water St, Ketchikan, AK 99901; (800)770-8800 or (907)225-8800; e-mail: taquan@ptialaska.net; Web site: http://www.AlaskaOne.com/TaquanAir.

Misty Fjords Flightseeing Tour

Misty Fjords National Monument, four times the size of Rhode Island (2.3 million acres), is a wilderness area that encompasses the entire back side of Revillagigedo Island, Behm Canal, and a sizable chunk of the fjord-trenched, ice-rimmed mainland all the way to the Canadian border. Sheer granite walls tower a neck-straining 3,000 feet above the narrow shoreline. The only way into this roadless area where Tlingits once settled in dozens of small villages is by boat or plane. Evidence of the Natives' rich culture remains in the form of old village sites, burial caves, stone fish traps, and pictographs. Taquan Air's Magnificent Misty Fjords flightseeing trip by seaplane departs from Ketchikan twice daily, year-round. Planes fly over New Eddystone Rock in the Behm Canal at the entrance to Rudyerd Bay, and survey a 1,000-foot waterfall cascading over a stone ridge from Big Goat Lake. The planes land in a remote lake or bay and pause for a quiet interlude in the wilderness before returning to Ketchikan.

A second flightseeing trip is a bit longer, and sweeps you up over the ice field to see the massive glaciers, moving rivers of ice that flow about 11 miles from the mountains until they break apart and splash into the sea.

The third and best option, Misty Fjords Cruise and Fly, combines floatplane and yacht, with a cruise from Ketchikan into Behm Canal accompanied by a naturalist. The boat retraces part of the historic voyage of Captain George Vancouver, who mapped the area for England in 1794. Deer, wolves, moose, mountain goat, brown and black bear, and numerous bald eagles may be spotted. After a seafood chowder lunch, board a waiting floatplane for a panoramic return flight to Ketchikan. In the afternoons, the itinerary switches— you first fly out of Ketchikan, then transfer to the boat for a late afternoon/evening cruise, with a deli sandwich buffet.

Misty Fjords Flightseeing, Taquan Air, 1007 Water St, Ketchikan, AK 99901; (800)770-8800 or (907)225-8800; e-mail: taquan@ptialaska.net; Web site: http://www. AlaskaOne.com/TaquanAir. $129–$185 per person. Misty Fjords Cruise and Fly available four days a week, May–Sept only.

Tongass Historical Museum

At the Tongass Historical Museum is a small "This Is Our Life" exhibit consisting primarily of Tlingit, Haida, and Tsimshian artifacts, basketry, and stone tools. The museum, perched on the edge of rushing Ketchikan Creek, also houses the public library. The totem outside the museum tells the story of Raven stealing the sun, probably the most often told Tlingit tale. There are two ravens in Tlingit myth. One is the great Nass Raven, who lives on the mainland at the mouth of the Nass River, at the border of Southeast Alaska and British Columbia, and who controls the sun, the moon, and the stars. The other is his grandson Scamp Raven, the lovable (and ribald) trickster. In the story carved in the totem outside the museum, Scamp Raven brings light to the world when he steals the box of daylight from his grandfather. The totem pole is a new one, designed and carved by Dempsey Bob (Tlingit) and raised in 1983.

Tongass Historical Museum, 629 Dock St, Ketchikan, AK 99901; (907)225-5600. Open daily May 15–Sept 30, $2; winters, Wed–Sun afternoons, free.

Totem Bight State Park

In 1938, carvers were hired by the U.S. Army Corps of Engineers to create replicas of Tlingit totem poles and a clan house on Mud Bight, the site of an old Tlingit village about 10 miles north of Ketchikan. Original plans were to re-create a number of village houses, but funding dried up before the grand plan was completed. Fragments of old totems were laid beside new cedar poles, and new totem poles were carved with handmade tools. The original poles had been colored with paint made

Born on Quadra Island, British Columbia, in 1917, Esther Shea attended the Sheldon Jackson Indian boarding school in Sitka, then lived in Saxman most of her life, detached from tribal ways. Ironically, at the age of 50 she was asked to return to the Sheldon Jackson school to teach the Tlingit language, which the boarding school had forced her to stop speaking as a child. In 1989, Shea led the first potlatch held in Southeast Alaska in 40 years, inviting the Bear clans of the entire Tlingit Nation to come forward. It was a momentous event for all of the clans, who soon began to hold their own potlatches once more.

from ground minerals and oil extruded from crushed salmon eggs; the new poles were matched to the original and colored with glossy modern oil-based paints.

The totem poles stand along a trail that meanders through the woods overlooking the churning Tongass Narrows. It's a pretty spot, with access to a small beach and a viewing deck overlooking a field filled with totem poles. The clan house, complete with carved house posts, contains a central fire pit and hand-adzed, removable floorboards, underneath which household goods would have been stored. The doorway, facing the water, is so low that an adult must crouch to enter, an effective form of home security.

Totem Bight State Park, Milepost 10 N, Tongass Hwy, Ketchikan, AK 99901; (907)247-8574. Follow trails through the woods to a point of land jutting into the Tongass Narrows. Open dawn to dusk, daily, year-round. The clan house is open Mon–Fri: mid-May–mid-Sept, 8am–8pm; mid-Sept–mid-May, 9am–3pm. Access to the park is free or by donation.

Art Galleries

Northwest Coast art can be found at most of the galleries in Ketchikan, particularly the Village Store at Saxman and the Native-owned gift shop at the Totem Heritage Center, which both carry handsome wood carvings made by local carvers. Keep an eye out for the work of Ernest Smeltzer, a student of carver Nathan Jackson and a recent winner of the Governor's Award for the Arts. Two Native-owned galleries are on the Creek Street boardwalk, directly below Westmark Cape Fox Lodge. Haida carver George Brown sells black argillite (a type of slate) carvings from British Columbia's Haida Gwaii at Hide-A-Way Gifts (18 Creek St, Ketchikan, AK 99901; (907)225-8626); he also carves cedar on-site. Ask for a copy of Brown's father's memoir, which contains reflections on his visit to the Haida Gwaii village the family left in the 1800s. Also see photographs taken in the abandoned villages where relatives once lived in clan houses.

At Alaska Eagle Arts (5 Creek St, Ketchikan, AK 99901; (907)225-8365), look for Diane Douglas Willard's exquisite Haida-style spruce root and cedar bark baskets, and Chilkat and Raven's Tail weaving. The majority of the gallery space is dedicated to owner Marvin Oliver's multimedia work and displays his glass castings, unusual screened prints, vests, denim jackets, T-shirts, cards, and unusual boxed, embossed stationery with a paper fold-out canoe on top of the box. Director of American Indian Studies at the University of Washington and a curator at Seattle's Burke Museum, Oliver (Quinault–Isleta Pueblo) is also on the faculty at the University of Alaska/Ketchikan, where he teaches the history of Northwest Coast art.

Metlakatla: *Tsimshian*

On a warm, windless evening in late July, the Alaska State Ferry *Aurora* quietly passes a small, rocky island iridescent with pink fireweed and glides into the Metlakatla harbor on Annette Island. The boat docks at the foot of Purple Mountain, near the waterfall that streaks down its lavender face and splashes into the bay. In the distance the town's waterfront is defined by a small lumber mill, an old wooden cannery built on pilings over the water, and a weathered boathouse shaped like a dairy barn.

Metlakatla is 15 miles south of Ketchikan— a 15-minute hop on a floatplane that lands between the town's cannery and the boat basin, or an hour's ride on the ferry. From the ferry's upper deck, the land behind Metlakatla looks flat and treeless, as if it has been freshly logged, but it is really a huge wetland as beautiful as any Japanese garden. Created when glaciers scraped across Southeast Alaska during the last ice age, the wetlands, called muskegs, cover hundreds of acres and are prevalent throughout Southeast Alaska. Small, twisted pine trees and clusters of fragrant bog rosemary, leggy buckbean, and evergreen crowberry grow alongside hundreds of lilypad-filled ponds. Most of the trees are lodgepole pines, 400 to 500 years old, their growth stunted by the high acidic content of the bog's deep sponge of sphagnum moss.

Metlakatlan Pat Beal, a retired educator, says that when she was a homesick boarding school kid and was first taught the hymn of praise "America, the Beautiful," she was comforted by the song's "purple mountain majesty," which she thought the composer had penned with Metlakatla's own Purple Mountain in mind.

Rising from the middle of the muskeg behind Metlakatla is Yellow Hill, a geologic mystery of bright yellow, pillow-shaped rock, sanded smooth by winter's hard rain and high winds. Years ago Metlakatla's tribal historian and builder, Ira Booth, constructed a boardwalk through the rocks, across the spongy meadows, and alongside ponds, up to the hill's 546-foot summit. Although the boardwalk has collapsed in many places and treads have rotted away on the stairs, the easy climb to the top is incredibly beautiful in midsummer, when hundreds of wildflowers, such as yellow and red paintbrush and bluebells, nearly engulf the path.

The village site at Metlakatla, on the island's sheltered north end, was once occupied by Tlingit Indians. Although the Tlingits had left long before, their totem poles were still standing near the beach when nearly 1,000 Tsimshian Indians arrived on August 7, 1887, aboard a steamship trailing cargo canoes. They came from British Columbia with Scottish Anglican missionary William Duncan to build a utopian Christian community.

The Tsimshians came from "Old Metlakatla," 90 miles south of Annette Island, near British Columbia's Skeena River. Old Metlakatla, another model town composed of Tsimshians drawn from their villages by the charismatic Duncan, had existed only five years before trouble with church officials, who disliked Duncan's strong-headed ideas, forced the community to move. Duncan successfully negotiated with President Grover Cleveland to secure the entire 86,000-acre Annette Island for the Tsimshians in the newly acquired American territory of Alaska.

> "The canoes pulled behind the steamship were not kayak-sized boats, but large enough to hold 60 men at a time, with 10-foot-high sides. How'd they paddle them? Didn't. They sailed them. With woven cedar sails."
> —Ira Booth, Metlakatla tribal historian

Annette Island wasn't just picked off the map. The Tsimshians had used it regularly as a summer fish camp after the Tlingits had abandoned it. When the Tsimshians moved there permanently, they left behind everything they owned in Old Metlakatla except for a few personal belongings, which were packed in the canoes, and the community-owned sawmill, which was carried aboard the steamship.

The sawmill was soon put to use. New Metlakatla, designed by Duncan and built on boardwalks over the muskeg, was a community consisting of European-style wood-frame houses and the state's largest church, nicknamed the Westminster Abbey of Alaska, which seated over 1,000.

Today the only Indian reservation in Southeast Alaska, Annette Island and its only town of Metlakatla are governed by a mayor and a 12-member council. The village boardwalks are gone, but many of the old buildings remain. The cannery, rebuilt in 1918, still operates, and Duncan's humble little house is a repository of the island's history, with most of the minister's belongings intact. Metlakatla's charm is its patina, not its polish.

Village Tour and Salmon Bake

On this all-encompassing tour, you fly to Metlakatla from downtown Ketchikan over beautiful Nichols Passage on a floatplane; tour the historic working cannery, where you can see fresh salmon, halibut, sea urchins, and other seafood being unloaded and processed (and receive a complimentary can of custom-packed smoked salmon); take a bus around the town with a Tsimshian tribal member guide; see a dance performance by the Fourth Generation Dancers; and have a tasty lunch, featuring salmon cooked over an open wood fire, on the deck overlooking the boat basin.

Metlakatla Village Tour and Salmon Bake, PO Box 10, Metlakatla, AK 99926. Book individual and group tours of Metlakatla through Taquan Air in Ketchikan, (800)770-8800. Daily, May–Sept. Cost is under $100 per person, including round-trip airfare. Tour length is 2½ hours, including 30 minutes of scenic flight time.

Totem Poles

Metlakatla was first occupied by Tlingits. Father William Duncan and the Tsimshians cleaned up the old village site and shipped old totem poles, left behind by the Tlingits, to Sheldon Jackson's new museum in Sitka. Determined to replace their Indian culture with the European model, the Tsimshians carved no new totems. In the 1970s, Tsimshian Jack Hudson rekindled an interest in traditional Tsimshian culture when he taught himself to carve by looking at old photographs and talking with elderly carvers. Still, no totems were carved or traditional ceremonies held in Metlakatla until 1982, when another young Metlakatlan, David Boxley, who had taught himself to carve totem poles at the University of Washington, erected a pole and sponsored a potlatch in honor of his grandparents. Boxley also wrote songs and dances for the ceremonies. Two years later, more than 1,000 people participated in a memorial potlatch held for Boxley's grandfather. Another pole was raised, this time in front of a new, traditional-style longhouse built near the shoreline.

Boxley was raised by his grandfather, a canoe carver who gave up his craft when he moved to Metlakatla. Boxley learned to carve by studying totems in museums. In 15 years, he created 42 poles and hundreds of bentwood boxes, rattles, masks, panels, and prints. Eleven of the thirteen poles in Metlakatla were carved by Boxley, who now lives near Seattle but spends summers at home in Metlakatla.

Resident Artists

Wood and silver carver Jack Hudson (a member of the Wolf clan and a direct descendant of Tsimshian immigrant John Hudson) lives in Metlakatla year-round, teaching carving at the high school and selling his own work at his home gallery, House of the Wolf (on the corner of Leask and Western, Metlakatla; (907)886-1936). His work is in museums and collections throughout Alaska and outside the state. Another outstanding Metlakatla carver is Wayne Hewson (Shim Skeegk, of the

Eagle and Killer Whale clans), who makes and sells exceptional Native regalia, including museum-quality carved cedar headpieces trimmed with ermine and abalone shell. Hewson also painted the clan symbols on the exterior of the new long-house. (Hewson's studio is on Haines St, Metlakatla; (907)886-7051; by appointment.)

Father Duncan's Cottage and Museum

It doesn't look like much from the outside, but the inside of Father William Duncan's original house, where he lived from 1891 until his death in 1918, is a treasure. It feels like a small church, or perhaps someone's attic, with its dormer-style roof, unpainted walls, and fire-places outlined with a simple painted white line. Most of Duncan's furniture, his narrow little bed, his books and personal items, and even a pile of his old shoes are displayed—some items looking as if he had carelessly tossed them in the corner just a few hours earlier. Duncan, the island's only doctor, also served as the community's (harsh) judge and taught school as well. The museum preserves his unusual apothe-cary shop, his classroom, and his cylinder phonograph—a serious tool of early anthropologists and only the second one made and signed by his friend Thomas Edison. Visitors can look through Duncan's scrap-books, which are filled with turn-of-the-century articles, clipped from newspapers all over the world, trumpeting Father Duncan's mis-sionary zeal and the Metlakatla community's hard work.

Father Duncan's Cottage and Museum, Tait and Fourth Sts, Metlakatla, AK 99926; (907)886-4441, ext 232, or (907)886-1122. Call for admission, special shows, and current hours.

William Duncan Memorial Church

William Duncan died in 1918 and is buried on the grounds of the site where the Tsimshians' original church, destroyed by fire, once stood. The two-spired white church on the corner of Fourth and Church Streets is a replica of the second church on the site. Back in British Columbia, in Old Metlakatla, Duncan had enraged Church of England officials by teaching "some rituals and ceremonies to the Tsimshian Indians resulting in the church seizing Tsimshian land and jailing those in defiance," according to newspaper accounts of the time. The rest of the story is chronicled in *The Devil and Mr. Duncan*, available in most Southeast Alaska bookstores. Duncan's journals have been copied onto microfiche by historian Ira Booth; the original handwritten journals are stored in tribal archives. The church, nondenominational until 1945, now houses the local Assembly of God congregation.

William Duncan Memorial Church, 4th and Spring Sts, Metlakatla, AK 99926; (907)886-6577.

Old Cannery

It's modern inside, but the Annette Island Packing Company's old cannery building is a 1918 beauty. Three other historic buildings are on the premises: the old, barn-shaped boathouse, the cannery workers' mess hall, and the bunkhouse that housed Filipino and Chinese cannery workers.

The waters off Annette Island, up to 3,000 feet deep, belong to the Metlakatlans. They use huge fish traps or gill and purse seine nets to catch five different species of salmon. Salmon stocks are replenished at a busy hatchery on the island's south side. The packing company also processes salmon roe, sea cucumbers, sea urchins, herring roe, halibut, shrimp, and bottomfish. The cannery gift shop carries artwork by Jack Hudson, Wayne Hewson, and other local artists as well as Tsimshian art from British Columbia. Look for cedar and pine gift boxes packed with canned and smoked salmon—they're real beauties. One features a replica of the four-clan design that's painted on the front of Metlakatla's longhouse, while another is decorated with a salmon/moon by Hewson. The cannery's labels, also for sale, are exceptional, inexpensive, and easy-to-carry collector's items.

Annette Island Packing Company, 100 Tait St, PO Box 10, Metlakatla, AK 99926; (907)886-4661. The gift shop is open daily May–Sept 15, 10am–5pm; due to safety and sanitation rules, the cannery itself is open for prearranged tours only. Gift boxes may also be purchased in Metlakatla's grocery store and in selected Ketchikan stores.

Watching dancers dressed in traditional regalia sing, drum, and dance can transport you back to an earlier era, especially when they perform in a longhouse or clan house setting. The performance is so heady and exotic that it's easy to forget that the dancers have researched their tribe's past, sewn regalia, learned dances, and even relearned the Native language, all while holding down full-time jobs, attending universities, and raising families. If you are at a loss for what to say to a dancer, ask him or her about the regalia—what the clan symbols sewn on button blankets represent, the number of hours it takes to make a headdress, the origin of a rattle or drum he or she is carrying. One singer we talked with described to us, using operatic terms, the way she uses her voice to fill the room.

Fourth Generation Dancers

The Fourth Generation Dancers consists of 62 members of the Metlakatla community who wear gorgeous handcrafted regalia and have learned and written songs. Their lead singer, Theo MacIntyre, has a voice that could call a kid from Ketchikan—without using the phone. The dancers are completely self-supporting, raising money for travel by holding bake and rummage sales. They dance in the tribe's longhouse, under a black–and–white cedar canoe suspended from the rafters.

The Fourth Generation Dancers perform in the longhouse for tours and at Celebration, an event held every two years in the spring in Juneau.

Metlakatla Village Tour and Salmon Bake, PO Box 10, Metlakatla, AK 99926. Book tours of Metlakatla, which include the Fourth Generation Dancers, through Taquan Air in Ketchikan, (800)770-8800.

Lodging

Visitors not on the Metlakatla Village Tour must obtain a permit if they wish to remain on Annette Island for more than 72 hours, and even then visitors must stay within the town limits or be escorted by a Metlakatla resident, a rule enforced by tribal police. Metlakatla has a fully stocked grocery and sometimes a food booth or two, but no restaurants. Ethel Leask rents two comfortable bedrooms in her pre-fab house, one with its own bath. Continental breakfast and dinner (arrange in advance).

Reservations: Ethel Leask; PO Box 526, Metlakatla, AK 99926; (907)889-5275.

Old Metlakatla and Prince Rupert

Metlakatla's Tsimshian forebears came from an area near British Columbia's port of Prince Rupert, about 90 miles south of Ketchikan (45 minutes by floatplane). Taquan Air offers round-trip flights from Ketchikan to Prince Rupert overnight, and arranges lodging at the Inn on the Harbor. In Prince Rupert, the Museum of Northern British Columbia is housed in a historic 1911 railway station on the waterfront. It has an outstanding exhibit of the cultural history and ethnography of the coast Tsimshians, including their contact with Europeans, early Hudson's Bay forts, William Duncan's first mission at nearby Fort Simpson, and the village of Old Metlakatla. The museum also offers boat tours of Prince Rupert's harbor, where there are ancient rock carvings. Taquan Air gets you there and puts you up in the hotel; you plan your own itinerary.

Canadian Discoverer Tour, Taquan Air, 1007 Water St, Ketchikan, AK 99901; (800) 770-8800 or (907)225-8800; e-mail: taquan@ptialaska.net; Web site: http:// www.AlaskaOne.com/TaquanAir. Daily, Jun 1–Sept 30. Call for free brochure and prices. Museum of Northern British Columbia, 100 First Ave, Prince Rupert, BC V8J

3S1; (604)624-3207; call for admission, tour prices, and hours. For assistance with car rentals and things to do in the Prince Rupert area, contact the Prince Rupert Visitor Information Centre, (800)667-1994.

Prince of Wales Island: *Haida*

Prince of Wales Island, west of Ketchikan, is one of the largest islands in the United States. Slightly smaller than Hawaii's "Big Island," it is largely unoccupied. Most of the 135-mile-long, 2,000-square-mile island lies within the Tongass National Forest, subject to logging by Native corporations and private timber companies. More than 1,000 miles of gravel logging roads wind over the rugged mountain terrain and through the acres of hot pink fireweed that cover logged slopes.

Sometime before the late 1700s, the Haida came to Prince of Wales Island from Haida Gwaii (British Columbia's Queen Charlotte Islands), 90 miles to the south. On Prince of Wales Island, the Haida not only found abundant resources but also discovered abandoned Tlingit villages, where they erected their own clan houses and totem poles. By the early 1800s, the Haida were doing a booming business providing otter pelts for foreign fur traders.

But the advantageous trading with the Hudson's Bay Company and the Russian-American Company did not last long. Sea otters were hunted to near-extinction by 1834. Worse, smallpox and measles claimed not only many tribal members but most of the record-keeping storytellers. Missionaries arriving in 1878 found a desperate group of people battered by their losses: in just one generation, the Haida population on Prince of Wales Island had dropped from 10,000 to about 800.

Known for their intrepid seafaring in some of the world's most perilous seas, the Haida first encountered Spanish explorers nosing about their Haida Gwaii homeland in 1774. Astounded priests aboard the Spanish ship recorded the meeting: Haida oarsmen nonchalantly paddled out to meet the anchored Spanish ship at the height of a furious storm and proceeded to trade. When the British visited the Queen Charlottes in 1787, the northern group had left for Alaska.

Today, Haida and Tlingit descendants live in Craig, Klawock, Hydaburg, and Kasaan on Prince of Wales Island. Craig and Klawock are 7 miles apart; Hydaburg is about 30 miles from Craig over a narrow winding road. Three villages of Haida moved to Hydaburg at the turn of the century, so that all of their children could attend one school. Kasaan is on the Kasaan Peninsula, on the island's east side, and has only recently been connected to Craig and Klawock by road.

The Alaska State Ferry serves Prince of Wales Island, but it lands 30 miles from the nearest town with services. Travelers might want to book an inexpensive and quick flight on Native-owned Taquan Air instead. Flights leave several times daily from Ketchikan to Prince of Wales Island; call (800)770-8800 or (907)225-8800. The narrow pass through the mountains to the west side of the island is flightseeing at its best: seaplanes soar between 3,000-foot narrow sawtooth ridges and jagged needles that are emerald green with moss, then dip so low over the bay as they come in for a landing that passengers can spot huge cloudy rafts of jellyfish in the water.

If you do decide to take your car on the ferry, prepare for a long drive, in the middle of the night, over a rough road prone to mudslides. If you fly, four-wheel-drive rentals are available in Craig. You'll need to reserve one in advance of your trip.

Craig

The heart and soul of Craig, by far the largest town on Prince of Wales Island, is commercial fishing and sportfishing, and that's the primary reason visitors come here. Those interested in culture will want to rent a car in Craig and drive a few miles up a paved road to the village of Klawock to see the Haida totem park on the waterfront, view the historic cannery buildings, and visit the studio of Kathy Kato-Yates (see Klawock section). A large number of Natives, many of them of Haida descent, live in Craig and own local businesses, including a grocery store. The town has most of the basic services, including ATM machines, car rentals, and even espresso.

Native-Owned Lodging

Two Native-owned lodgings are within easy walking distance of the floatplane dock at Craig. The Haida Way Lodge is a modest and well-used motel, a favorite of sport fishermen hauling out at 4am. The other, Sunnahae Lodge, is a small hotel with 10 bedrooms and an attractive dining room decorated with Mission-style furnishings. The Haida Way Lodge rents by the night, but at Sunnahae, lodging is sold only as part of a fishing package that includes a round-trip floatplane flight from Ketchikan, three meals a day, guided fishing aboard a fully equipped cabin cruiser, bait, tackle, rain gear, and equipment. Sunnahae Lodge is owned by State Senator Jerry Mackie. He's swamped during legislative sessions, but during the summer months he's at the lodge and guides many of the guests himself.

Haida Way Lodge, PO Box 690, Craig, AK 99921; (907)826-3268. Located on Front St. Some rooms have Jacuzzis. Also books fishing charters.

Sunnahae Lodge, PO Box 795, Craig, AK 99921; (907)826-4000. Around the block from the Haida Way, on Water St. Three-day fishing packages begin at $1,950 per person. Extended fishing packages are also available.

Klawock

A short drive from Craig, Klawock has been used for centuries as a Native fish camp and permanent village site. To see the most interesting part of Klawock, head for the waterfront and the picturesque old cannery buildings—some of the first canneries built in Alaska, in 1878. Overlooking the canneries is the Klawock Totem Park, where 21 totem poles stand in a circle on a grassy slope. Some of the poles are original, and some are replicated from those found at the abandoned village of Tuxekan on the north end of the island. These totems are very different stylistically from Tlingit totem poles: they feature large realistic figures, such as whales, bears, and birds, all with large staring eyes, perched on top of exceedingly tall poles. Klawock is also a great place to watch eagles, which flock to the beaches when fishermen gut their catches.

Klawock Totem Park, Bayview St, Craig, AK 99921. To find the park, turn from the Craig/Klawock Hwy toward the harbor onto Bayview St.

Taats Art/Designs

Kathy Kato-Yates (Taats), the granddaughter of the chief of the Haida Double-fin Killer Whale clan, Richard Carle, Sr., relies solely on word of mouth for advertising. And the grapevine has brought people from places as far away as Europe and Asia who have heard about her shop, Taats Art/Designs. When we talked with her, 10 young Texans had just left the shop. The kids had saved their money to buy authentic Northwest Coast art, but could afford only her silk-screened postcards. Taats put on her clan robe and cedar hat for them anyway, explaining the meaning of each piece and how it was made. Then she sang them a Haida love song.

Kato-Yates is a versatile artist. She creates deerskin drums, silk-screened prints, and tiny, 1-inch woven baskets with her trademark Russian blue beads sewn onto them. One of the few women carvers in Southeast Alaska, she makes masks and small replicas of the Klawock totem poles from red and yellow cedar that grows on Prince of Wales Island. When the cruise ships first came to town, her biggest sellers were three-dimensional cards made with felt and fur, which in 1989 sold for $4, and are now worth over $100.

Taats Art/Designs, 406 W St, Klawock, AK 99925; (907)755-2409. Open by appointment; Kato-Yates will give you directions to her shop.

Guided Canoe Trip

Fly into Klawock from Ketchikan on Taquan Air and spend the next five days hiking, portaging, and canoeing as you explore lakes, streams, and rivers in the area first seen by Tlingit, then Haida occupants of Prince of Wales Island. Spend the first and last nights at a deluxe island lodge, with homemade meals and hot tub. Backpack-style tent camps and campfire meals are included on the trail. Guides may be Native or non-Native, are insured, and are licensed for the Tongass National Forest. The focus is more on wilderness and fishing than on culture. Group sizes are two to four persons. All equipment is provided. Buy trout fishing licenses in Ketchikan or Klawock.

Guided Canoe Trip, Taquan Air, 1007 Water St, Ketchikan, AK 99901; (800)770-8800 or (907)225-8800; e-mail: taquan@ptialaska.net; Web site: http://www.AlaskaOne. com/TaquanAir. Taquan Air's reservation desk is at the Ketchikan International Airport. Trips offered Jun–Aug, by appointment. Five days/six nights, $1,525 per person.

Hydaburg

Founded in 1911 to centralize schools for three Haida communities, Hydaburg is the largest community (about 500) of Haida Natives in Southeast Alaska. In the middle of town, near the school, is a totem park where poles were rescued from the three abandoned villages (Klinkwan, Sukkwan, and Howkan) and raised more than 50 years ago in a waterfront park. The land was designated the Hydaburg Indian Reservation in 1912, with a trading company, store, and sawmill. Villagers didn't like the arrangement and requested that the land be restored to the Tongass National Forest, with 189 acres reserved for the townsite. Canneries operated here through the 1930s. Although there are no visitor accommodations in Hydaburg, you are welcome to view the totems. The town is 30 miles south of Craig via a narrow, winding road.

Guided Island Van Tour and El Capitan Cave

Tlingit stories passed down for generations have told about hunting parties crawling through deep caves in search of hibernating bears. On the north end of Prince of Wales Island, the legendary caves were recently found, and more than 150 have now been mapped. The largest is El Capitan, with over 2 miles of passageways mapped to date and an enormous hole that plunges 624 feet. Far into the cave, archaeologists have found grizzly bear remains that have been carbon-dated at 12,300 years old. The oldest remains found are those of a marmot estimated to be more than 45,000 years old. The entrance to the cave is 390 feet up the side of El Capitan Peak, via wooden stairs with handrails (331 steps). Cave access is not available without a registered guide, but the U.S. Forest Service offers free 2-hour tours. The problem is getting there. One option is to fly from Ketchikan across Clarence Strait to Prince of Wales Island and take a 185-mile, round-trip guided van tour of Prince of Wales Island. The tour follows the Thorne River and includes several lakes, the settlement of Deweyville, and the El Capitan cave tour. After lunch, return by plane via the spectacular east coast road, by Ratz Harbor and Narrow Point. An alternative is to skip the sightseeing and fly straight from Ketchikan to the base of El Capitan peak.

Guided Island Van Tour, Taquan Air, 1007 Water St, Ketchikan, AK 99901; (800)770-8800 or (907)225-8800; e-mail: taquan@ptialaska.net; Web site: http://www. AlaskaOne.com/TaquanAir. Taquan Air's reservation desk is at the Ketchikan International Airport. Tour offered May–Sept; reservations required; departure times may be arranged. $229 per person for flight, van, and cave tour. Cave temperature is 40 degrees; wear warm clothing, hiking boots, or rubber boots. Bring flashlight and extra batteries; hard hats are provided.

Other Taquan Tours of Prince of Wales Island

Alaska Bush Pilot Tour: Fly out with a bush pilot from Ketchikan on one of Taquan's daily mail, freight, and passenger routes to secluded wilderness areas on the island. Quick landings are made at historic villages, logging camps, remote fishing communities, and lodges. ($79 per person.)

Whales and Wildlife Cruise: Fly to the west coast of Prince of Wales Island for a day's guided eco-cruise aboard a cabin cruiser to see humpback whales, sea otters, seals, birds, and other marine life. ($279 per person; 10 hours; lunch included.)

Island Kayaking, Diving, or Windsurfing: On Prince of Wales Island, kayakers can explore 900 miles of coastline, bays, coves, inlets, points, and hundreds of small islands with some of the richest marine life in Alaska. Diving in cold water is very different from diving in the Caribbean, particularly when whales are in the vicinity. Hand-feed wolf eels and see large octopus, lingcod, and giant green and purple anemones. Visibility ranges up to 60–100 feet except during plankton bloom. Call Craig's Dive Center, (907)826-3481, for guide and equipment rental. Planes depart daily at 7:15am year-round and return in late afternoon. (Prices vary.)

Taquan Air, 1007 Water St, Ketchikan, AK 99901; (800)770-8800 or (907)225-8800; e-mail: taquan@ptialaska.net; Web site: http://www.AlaskaOne.com/TaquanAir. Taquan Air's reservation desk is at the Ketchikan International Airport. Tours vary according to season; call for more information.

Wrangell: *Tlingit*

After flying for nearly half an hour over uninterrupted sweeps of evergreen forest and blue-green water, the jet banks sharply and turns toward what looks like a wall of mountains before it touches down on Wrangell Island at the mouth of the Stikine River. Just before the plane lands, the tiny town of Wrangell appears below. Once an important Russian and British fur trading post (until it became a U.S. military post in 1868), Wrangell now consists mostly of a boat basin, a ferry landing, and a cruise ship dock.

According to their legends, the Stikine Tlingits arrived at the mouth of the Stikine River, near present-day Wrangell, about 1,000 years ago. Having traveled from the interior, they were relative newcomers to the archipelago, which had been occupied for more than 10,000 years by other Tlingit bands. Long before the Russians occupied Alaska, the powerful Stikines controlled the entry (and, therefore, the commerce) to the Stikine River, a rare gap in the otherwise impenetrable wall of mountains that separates Southeast Alaska from British Columbia. The river reaches 330 miles into the interior, and by following it, the Stikine Tlingits could trade goods acquired from Pacific Coast tribes with interior tribes as far east as present-day Alberta and Montana. Thousands of miners followed the same route up the Stikine River into the Cassiar District of British Columbia to mine for gold in the 1870s.

Today, about a quarter of the population of Wrangell is Native, although not all are descended from the Stikine Tlingits. Schools and missions were established in Wrangell between 1870 and 1879, and Natives moved into town from nearby islands. In the 1930s, the Native population changed dramatically when the Bureau of Indian Affairs built the Wrangell Institute, bringing Natives from all over Alaska for job training. Aleut people from the Aleutian Chain and the Pribilof Islands, who had been uprooted and detained during World War II, relocated in Wrangell after they were released from internment camps in Southeast Alaska's abandoned canneries. (To learn more about this episode of Alaska Native history, visit the University of Alaska Museum in Fairbanks.)

As with all towns in Southeast Alaska, Wrangell is small enough that you won't need a car to see the town's major attractions. The Alaska State Ferry docks right downtown, but those flying in by jet will need to call a taxi for the short ride from the airport to town.

Wrangell is most famous for its reconstructed clan house, called Chief Shakes House. Surrounded by totem poles, it sits on the very spot where the original Shakes clan house was built prior to 1700. The Stikine elders and the Native Wrangell Cultural Heritage Committee have also beautified the downtown area with numerous totem poles and a totem park. There's also a small museum containing Indian artifacts. Less known is Petroglyph Beach, on a point overlooking the mouth of the Stikine River; it's well worth the 15-minute walk from downtown.

To get a map of town and directions, stop by the Wrangell Chamber of Commerce, located in a small A-frame on the corner of Outer Drive and Brueger Street near the city dock; (800)367-9745 or (907)874-3901.

Petroglyph Beach

A 15-minute walk from the city dock, north on Evergreen Street, leads to a short trail to Petroglyph Beach. On the beach, turn to the right and look for boulders nesting in beach gravel littered with broken glass. Petroglyphs are best viewed when the rocks are wet—in a rainstorm, after the tide has receded, or dampened with water from a spray bottle. As the rock darkens, faces, spirals, and totemic symbols, chipped in the rock with stone tools, whisper a forgotten language across the centuries.

The meaning of the petroglyphs is unclear. Some appear to be totemic and could illustrate portions of the Raven story, while others seem to correlate with shamanic power signs. No one can say for sure. There is speculation that the glyphs may be the work of two separate cultures—one that may have been here as early as 35,000 years ago, the other a Tlingit community estimated to have been in Southeast Alaska 10,000 years prior to the arrival of the Stikines.

The beach, as unusual as it is, is taken for granted by the public. Sunbathers throw their beach towels casually across the face of the petroglyph-incised rocks and lean against them to read, while kids dig in the sand around them. Washed by high tides, the area was

"Shakes" is an honorary title that was won for Wrangell's high-caste chiefs in a war with the Niska Indians, a Tsimshian tribe from British Columbia. To avoid being taken as slaves after losing the battle, the chief of the Niska gave his "Shakes" name and crest symbol to the victors. The Niska chief's killer-whale crest symbolized the right of Tlingit chiefs to use the title and crest forever. The title was passed down through Tlingit men, uncle to nephew, on the mother's side. The last direct hereditary chief, Chief Shakes VI, died in 1916. One more Chief Shakes was named in 1940. After his death, the title has remained unfilled.

literally used as a garbage dump until a few decades ago. Shell middens—cast-off clamshells thrown into piles by the first inhabitants—lie under a layer of broken glass and pottery sherds dumped in the last century.

Please do not remove or take rubbings of stones. More than 70 petroglyphs were once counted on the beach; in 1974 the count was 46; in 1995 there were about 27.

Detailed descriptions of Wrangell area totems and the stories they tell were written by members of the Cultural Heritage Committee, a Native group, and are reprinted in "The Wrangell Guide," a free publication printed by the Wrangell Sentinel (PO Box 798, Wrangell, AK 99929). The guide is also available from the Wrangell visitors center (on the corner of Outer Drive and Brueger Street).

Petroglyph Beach, Wrangell. Walk from the ferry terminal north on Evergreen St for ¾ mile to a gravel road leading to the beach. Watch for signs. An information kiosk is at the head of the short trail to the beach.

Chief Shakes House

A short wooden footbridge crosses from the end of a street over to a small island in Wrangell's inner harbor. The footbridge ends right in front of Chief Shakes House. Surrounded by rustling cottonwood trees, a lawn speckled with white clover, and about a dozen totem poles, the hand-adzed plank house is painted with a totemic figure that stretches from floor to roof. When the door is unlocked, visitors enter the house through a small hole in the figure's abdomen and step into the darkened single room. The only illumination in the room comes through the smoke hole in the roof over the center fire pit.

Successive generations of chiefs, all with the name of Chief Shakes, lived in the first clan house built on this site after the clan moved in the 1600s to the Wrangell area from their village at nearby Kots-lit-na. The current clan house is a re-creation built in 1939 by the Civilian Conservation Corps as part of their totem restoration project.

All the totems that stand around Chief Shakes House are replicas of originals. Natives inaugurated the new clan house with an authentic potlatch in 1940, one of the first held in Alaska since the ceremony was outlawed by the federal government near the turn of the century.

Interior house posts were raised inside the house in 1979, in the first of a series of new Native carving projects in Wrangell. The posts were copied from the original posts lent by the local Tlingits to the Wrangell Museum.

One of the totems near Chief Shakes House features a realistic-looking black bear perched atop a tall pole. Bear tracks are carved into the pole all the way to the top. According to a story published in the 1940 *Wrangell Sentinel*, the pole commemorates a great flood that was of the same dimensions as the biblical flood: "When the flood came, the Shakes tribe was camped on the Stikine River near Cone Mountain, their summer camp. As the water rose, the people, frightened, fled to higher ground. Fighting their way up the mountains, through the tangled underbrush, they came across two grizzly bears who were also seeking refuge. The bears showed by their actions that they wanted to help the Shakes people, leading the people to safety. The party reached the pinnacle of Cone Mountain, where they stayed until the water receded."

Storytellers say that on the mountain today are impressions of ropes worn into the stone where some of the people tied their canoes to the peak.

A Chief Shakes memorial site is across the harbor from Chief Shakes House on Case Avenue, a short walk around the basin. To find it, look for the three-story-high Wrangell Boat Shop on the Case Avenue waterfront. The memorial is across the street in a grove of trees: a rectangle of grass surrounded by a white picket fence with two carved killer whales erected on corner posts. It looks like a grave site, but no one is buried there; the remains of various Chief Shakes are interred in local cemeteries. The carvings look old, weathered by wind and rain, but were actually made in 1979, the third set of killer whales placed at the site.

Chief Shakes House, Wrangell. Located at the end of Front St. Free. Chief Shakes House is locked except for special events. The grounds are open between dawn and dusk.

Kiksadi Totem Park

About a block from Chief Shakes House is the Kiksadi Totem Park on Episcopal Street. The Sun House, a clan house similar to the Chief Shakes House, was once located on the site of the totem park. The tallest pole, in front, is a replica of the original, carved in 1890, that marks this site as belonging to the Kiksadi clan. Totems in this park were carved by Tlingit carvers Will Burkhart, of Sitka; Wayne Price, of Haines; and Steve Brown, curator of the Native collections at the Seattle Art Museum. Other totem poles are located throughout Wrangell.

Kiksadi Totem Park, Wrangell. On Episcopal St, 1 block from Chief Shakes House. The unfenced park is open year-round.

Wrangell Museum

It's a little museum, full of the stuff of local history, but by far its greatest treasures are the old Chief Shakes house posts, carved about 1740, and other old totems from villages in the area. All are on loan from the Native community. The Tlingit baskets on display were woven in Wrangell and were sold as trade items or given as gifts. The beadwork shows the influence of both intertribal trade and post-contact trade demands. Subsistence technology is represented by halibut hooks, storage containers, gut parkas, fishing harpoons, and hunting points from both Tlingit and northern tribes. The Aleut, Yup'ik, and Inupiat baskets on display were made for trade and sold locally by students attending the Wrangell Institute, a training school operated by the Bureau of Indian Affairs, between 1932 and 1975.

Wrangell Museum, 318 Church St, PO Box 1050, Wrangell, AK 99929; (907)874-3770. Admission $2; children 16 and under free. Open May–Sept, weekdays and Sat afternoons; Sun hours match ferry arrival times. Call for winter hours, tours, and special events.

Alaska Waters Jet Boat Tours

The Stikine River, fed by 20 glaciers, begins about 400 miles inland in the snowcapped Canadian mountains and flows into the Pacific Ocean near Wrangell. Spring brings runs of oil-rich candlefish (eulachon) and salmon, along with one of the largest springtime concentrations of bald eagles in the United States. In the summer, wildflowers cover the grassy flats at the mouth of the river. You can take tours of the river aboard Alaska Waters jet boats, with viewing sights selected by Tlingit elders. Passengers board the boat in downtown Wrangell (reservations necessary) and travel through the Government, Cottonwood, and Andrews Sloughs. After July 1, the water is so clear that the boat lingers so passengers can watch schools of salmon pooling at the mouth of Andrew Creek; then it scoots up-river for a 5- to 6-hour tour. Guides point out an old homestead on the site where the Tlingit, Haida, Tsimshian, and Tahltan Native people once met for potlatches, and the site of the last major battle between the Tlingits from the Wrangell area and the Tsimshians of northern British Columbia. Also included in the tour are more recent historical sites such as Cottonwood Island, where miners set up a "tent city" during the gold rush. The boat zips up to Shakes Slough, a Stikine tributary, and noses through icebergs to Chief Shakes Glacier. There's a stop at Chief Shakes Hot Springs, where guests can relax in either the indoor or outdoor tubs. After the boat ride, join a walking tour in Wrangell to see Native historical sites, including

Petroglyph Beach, a small totem park, and a reproduction of a Tlingit clan house (see "Chief Shakes House").

A second tour heads 35 miles southeast of Wrangell to the Anan Bear and Wildlife Observatory. The site was once used as a summer fish camp by Tlingit Natives and remains an important part of the cultural heritage of the Tlingit people to this day. Anan Creek teems with thousands of fish, which attract bald eagles, seals, and brown and black bears. Tours leave Wrangell for a 1-hour excursion through Eastern Passage to Anan beach. A U.S. Forest Service guide meets passengers for an orientation on bear viewing, then leads hikers down a half-mile boardwalk paralleling Anan lagoon, an area often filled with seals feeding on salmon. The bear observatory is built on a rock bluff above a waterfall—an exceptional place to watch bears snagging fish.

Alaska Waters, Inc., PO Box 1978, Wrangell, AK 99929; (800)347-4462 or (907)874-2378; e-mail: jim@alaskawaters.com. Tours offered May–Sept. Stikine and Anan tours $135 per person; discounts for seniors and kids. Through Alaska Waters you can also rent canoes, rafts, sportfishing charters, and packages that include touring, lodging, and meals.

Kake: *Tlingit*

The Tlingit village of Kake (pronounced "cake") is located between the towns of Juneau and Wrangell on the west side of Kupreanof Island. A 132-foot totem pole, Alaska's largest totem carved from a single tree, marks the village site overlooking Keku Strait. It was carved by Chilkat totem carvers and erected in 1967 on a bluff above the town.

Three new poles, dedicated to the clans of Kake, were erected in the 1990s. A Killer Whale pole, carved by Norman and Mike Jackson, was erected in memory of the Tsaagweidi clan in 1994, during the first potlatch held in Kake in 100 years. Two other new poles, both beautifully carved, overlook Little Gunnuk Creek. One honors the Raven clans, the other the Eagle clans.

What's so bad about losing a language? In English, the French root of the word "dandelion" describes the plant's bright yellow flower. In Tlingit, the word for dandelion describes the way dandelion seeds drift on the wind.

The domain of the Kake Tlingits (the Keex' Kwaan) extended throughout Frederick Sound and most of Kuiu and Kupreanof Islands in central Southeast Alaska. The name "Kake" is derived from a Tlingit phrase that means "the town that never sleeps." It's thought the name was bestowed upon the village following a particularly long potlatch.

During the Russian occupation of Alaska, the people of Kake had a reputation as a fierce and warlike tribe. This perception was underscored when, in 1857, a group of Kake warriors traveled 800 miles by canoe to the Washington Territory on a successful mission to avenge the killing of one of their chiefs. More than one Kake village was shelled to ruins by U.S. gunboats during this time. It was 30 years before the Kake people rebuilt, finally settling at their present village on Keku Strait in the late 1800s. A Bureau of Indian Affairs school and store were built in Kake in 1891; the Quakers established a Society of Friends mission at the turn of the century; and in 1912 the first cannery was built nearby. (The village purchased the cannery in the 1940s.) Today, Kake residents support themselves mostly through subsistence fishing and hunting, commercial fishing, and logging. The village of about 700 people is accessible by the Alaska State Ferry, which makes stops throughout Southeast Alaska. At this time, Kake has partnered with Glacier Bay Tours & Cruises, a subsidiary of Goldbelt, Inc., a Native corporation whose shareholders are Tlingit Indians, to provide tours of the village culminating with a dance performance by the traditional Keex' Kwaan (pronounced "cake-kwahn") Dancers. The tour of the Kake community is included in a seven-day cruise of Alaska's Inside Passage between Ketchikan and Juneau, which also includes Misty Fjords National Monument Wilderness, both arms of Glacier Bay and a jaunt up the Tracy Arm Fjord, and shore excursions in Sitka, Haines, and Skagway.

For more information on the cruise, call Glacier Bay Tours & Cruises, 520 Pike St, Suite 1400, Seattle, WA 98101; (800)451-5952. For more information about tours, call the Organized Village of Kake, (907)785-6471.

Photo Exhibit

In 1913, the Kake clans decided to completely restructure their village after the European model and subsequently destroyed all their totem poles. All that remained were 24 historical photographs, most of them taken in the early 1900s. The photographs were discovered in the state library archives by the Kake Heritage Foundation, enlarged to 3 feet square, and installed in the Kake Tribal Corporation offices. A narrative accompanying each photo explains the history of the village. Visitors are welcome to view them in the corporation offices.

Kake Tribal Corporation, PO Box 263, Kake, AK 99830; (907)785-3221. Located in the Thomas L. Jackson Senior Center. Open year-round during business hours.

Keex' Kwaan Lodge

This pretty new inn, built in 1997, is 5 minutes from the Alaska State Ferry landing, with a gorgeous view of Frederick Sound and Keku Strait. Twelve rooms, all with private baths, are furnished with knotty pine country-style furniture; queen or full-size beds; an extra telephone jack for a computer modem; and cable television. The restaurant, on the first floor, has knotty pine wainscoting, a cathedral ceiling, and big windows that show off the unobstructed view. Breakfast, lunch, and dinner are served. Dinners feature seasonal seafood such as crab, shrimp, halibut, and salmon caught fresh from Kake waters. Local carver Norman Jackson, a Kake Tlingit, provides artwork, including 5-foot totems and masks, for sale in the dining room. A courtesy van is available to take guests to see Kake's famous totem pole, about a half mile from the lodge. Manager Paulette Jackson can also arrange for sportfishing or sightseeing charters with one of the 12 local fishermen who have chartering licenses.

Keex' Kwaan Lodge, 57 Keku Rd, PO Box 207, Kake, AK 99830; (907)785-3434. Open year-round. Rooms $78 single, $98 double. The lodge is owned by the local tribal government, the Organized Village of Kake.

Juneau Metropolitan Area

From the outside, the house looks like any other tract home in a Juneau suburb. But the living room furniture has been pushed aside, making way for a long dinner table. At the back of the house, the kitchen has plenty of room for guests to stand around, with an extra-large pantry stacked with china and dozens of glasses. This is a home where hospitality is taken seriously.

More than 30 guests—many of them heads of Native corporations—munch on appetizers before the main courses of salmon and halibut. Many of the appetizers are traditionally prepared Tlingit, Tsimshian, and Haida seafood: various kinds of smoked salmon, octopus, crab, pickled gumboots (chiton), cockles, herring eggs, dried moose, dried fish strips, and eulachon oil for dipping. Dinner conversation turns from a story of flying a surfing-magazine editor to a remote beach to a discussion of the reorganization of the Bureau of Indian Affairs.

This is a side of Alaska that tourists, dazzled by Juneau's Mendenhall Glacier, the old town's narrow streets, the Alaska State Museum's collection of 19th-century Native art, and the totem poles and souvenir shops, rarely if ever see: Native Alaskans at home and Native corporations at work.

Juneau, the mountain-bound capital city of Alaska, is headquarters for several of the state's most influential Native organizations: the Central Council of the Tlingit and Haida Indian Tribes of Alaska; Goldbelt, Inc.; Yak-Tat Kwaan, Inc.; Huna Totem Corporation; Kootznoowoo, Inc.; Klukwan, Inc.; and Sealaska Corporation and its nonprofit Sealaska Heritage Foundation. Some of the groups are housed in modern office buildings next to the state legislative buildings—all built on tailings from Juneau's AJ Mine, which honeycombed the town's Mount Roberts and filled in enough of the shallow bay for the city to expand.

The city mushroomed after gold was discovered in 1880. In October of that year, an Auk Tlingit named Chief Kowee showed prospectors Joe Juneau and Richard Harris where to find gold. In exchange he received 10 good blankets. Gold meant nothing to Kowee; his people used rare dentalia shells as currency and soft, pliable gold for bullets. But gold meant everything to the white prospectors, and its discovery brought hundreds more gold seekers to the Juneau area. They opened some of the most productive gold mines in Alaska and made the new, saloon-filled town of Juneau their headquarters.

The setting of Juneau is dramatic. Like all towns in Southeast Alaska, it fights for space between the deep fjord and the mountains, which here rise vertically nearly 4,000 feet within a block of downtown. The mountains and 25-mile-deep ice field closing in on Juneau are a boon to hikers but a barrier to highways from the interior; the only way in is by plane or boat.

When the gold miners arrived, the largest permanent Tlingit village was at Auke Bay, 14 miles north of what would become downtown Juneau. Four other villages were located in the area, including a fish camp on the beach, right below the present-day governor's white antebellum mansion. The camp became a full-fledged village in the 1900s when the Tlingits abandoned Auke Bay to live and work in town. The modern office building containing the Haida and Tlingit headquarters sits there now, with a modern clan house adjoining it marked with clan symbols and two totems.

In the Alaska State Library, there's a picture of the Juneau Tlingit village, taken in the late 1800s. In it, modern houses have replaced

> *"As early as 1897, a petition from the Tlingit Orthodox Chiefs to the President of the United States pleaded for relief from barbaric treatment brought on by Presbyterian missionaries and government officials. When the Russian-American treaty was written, the word 'civilized' was not defined and Natives who had previously enjoyed the freedoms of citizenship (under Russia) went unrecognized as American citizens. Their pleas went unheeded."*
>
> *—A Recollection of Civil Rights Leader Elizabeth Peratrovich, the Central Council of Tlingit & Haida Indian Tribes of Alaska*

the old clan houses. Another change is documented in such photographs: blatant discrimination against the Native people. Signs on restaurants proclaim, in big block letters, WHITES ONLY or ALL WHITE HELP.

Probably one of the most important events that happened in Juneau, from the Native point of view, was the passage of an antidiscrimination bill by the State Senate on February 8, 1945. The bill passed only after a nasty debate on the Senate floor, which was finally ended by a stirring speech from Elizabeth Peratrovich, a Tlingit woman from the village of Klawock on Prince of Wales Island. When she had finished speaking, wild applause burst from the gallery and Senate floor alike, and the bill was subsequently passed. Today several Natives win elections and are members of the state legislature. A bronze bust of Elizabeth Peratrovich stands in Alaska's statehouse.

The Native presence, once dismissed, is now everywhere in Juneau—from murals on the walls to public art to totems outside the Kmart. And every two years in June, Juneau is host to Celebration, a weeklong gathering of more than 3,000 Tlingit, Haida, and Tsimshian Natives from all over Southeast Alaska, who come to sing, dance, and celebrate their Native heritage.

Mount Roberts Tramway and Observatory

For a memorable introduction to the land and culture of the Tlingits, ride the Mount Roberts Tramway to the 1,800-foot level of the mountain, once accessible only by a very steep and perilous trail. From the observatory deck is a sweeping view of the glacier-carved waterways the Tlingits once used as their canoe highways, catching the currents and tides to speed their passage between islands. Facilities on top include a nature center; the Rainforest Restaurant & Cafe, a 168-seat casual restaurant with a full bar and espresso coffee bar; the Raven-Eagle Gift Shop; a large souvenir shop; and access to trails. Of particular interest is the award-winning docudrama *Seeing Daylight*, shown free in the tramway's Chilkat Theater every 15 minutes. The message, delivered from the Tlingit perspective, is of a strong culture surviving and adapting through ice ages, the Russian colonial period, the American purchase of Alaska, the gold rush, missionary zeal, and modern-day life. A longer version of the film is for sale in the Raven-Eagle Gift Shop along with Northwest Coast, Athabascan, and Eskimo crafts. In the hallway adjoining the gift shop, look for more expensive fine art, such as a bronze raven wearing a ceremonial Chilkat blanket by artist Roy Peratrovich, Sr.

Goldbelt, Inc., a Native corporation and a major investor in the tram, has commissioned monumental art from some of Alaska's finest

Native artists to be installed in the ground-level terminal and observatory over the next few years.

Mount Roberts Tramway, 490 S Franklin, Juneau, AK 99801; PO Box 21849, Juneau, AK 99802; (888)461-8726 or (907)463-3412; e-mail: junotram@alaska.net. Open year-round; limited winter hours; closed when winds are over 60 mph. Ticket prices vary; combo tickets include tram ride and dinner. Discounted season passes. Special $1 ride one way (downhill only) for hikers. Tramway, observatory, and walkways are wheelchair accessible.

Alaska Native Tours of Juneau

What distinguishes this tour from all others in Juneau is that it's narrated with a Tlingit perspective of Juneau's gold-mining history. As the bus heads through town to the Mendenhall Glacier, past a beautiful mural of the Northwest Creation story of Raven releasing mischief (mankind) from a clamshell, the driver begins to sing a song in Tlingit, softly, like a lullaby. She brakes for an eagle she's spotted, then pulls the bus over to point out salmon running up a stream. Like all of Juneau's many bus tours, this one includes gold-mining history, the state Capitol, totem poles, and a 40-minute break at icy Mendenhall Lake overlooking the glacier, 13 miles from downtown. By tour's end the passengers have learned the healing properties of several indigenous plants, as well as how to speak a few words of Tlingit, and are singing Native songs along with the bus driver, their mouths stained blue by huckleberries they've picked along the way.

Alaska Native Tours, 218 Front St, Room 5, Juneau; inquire by mail at PO Box 22638, Juneau, AK 99802; (907)463-3231. Tickets and tour times available at the cruise ship dock through Last Chance Ticket Broker; advance bookings through Alaska Native Tours. About $15 per person, but prices vary according to length of tour. Bring a coat for the short walk to the glacier.

Mendenhall Glacier Kayak and River Rafting

Mendenhall Lake, at the foot of Juneau's Mendenhall Glacier, is icy cold, churns with glacial silt that's as fine as talcum powder, and covers the house of the mythical Auk Ta Shaa, the Lady of the Lake. Survivors of a visit to her house obtain great wealth.

Like other glaciers in the region, the Mendenhall has repeatedly advanced and retreated, carving out a great valley as it grinds solid rock to silt and sand. With the glacier currently in retreat, Mendenhall Lake, at its foot, grows larger, fed by a river that runs under the ice and by spectacular waterfalls tumbling down the mountains from melting snowpack.

Most people hike up to the visitors center and snap a picture of the lake and glacier from its shoreline. However, more adventurous travelers can take a 4-hour kayak excursion on the lake itself. Accompanied by a guide, you paddle quickly from the shore toward a rookery of kittiwakes (members of the gull family) at the glacier's foot, then glide to a stop on a silt beach on the opposite shore—just a few feet from the icy mists of a raging waterfall. Tlingit women once used glacial sand as a pumice stone and fine glacial silt as something similar to a spa mudpack to keep their skin smooth and unlined.

You can also paddle across the lake on a river raft and, with a guide, drift into the Mendenhall River and ride it through Juneau's residential development (built with confidence in the very valley recently carved by the glacier). The river eventually fans into the broad estuary where Juneau built its airport. With several Class III rapids at high water, it's a short, entertaining raft trip. Rafts pull up for a snack next to a clear, salmon-spawning creek where archaeologists recently uncovered fish traps estimated to be 9,000 years old. Geologists say this spot was once saltwater beachfront, filled over the centuries with glacial deposits of sand and gravel.

Auk Ta Shaa Discovery, 76 Egan Dr, Juneau, AK 99801; (800)820-2628 or (907)586-8687. Kayak and raft trips are sold separately. Both depart twice daily, May–Sept. $89–$95 per person. Cost includes transportation from downtown Juneau to Mendenhall Lake, with a stop for waterproof dry suits and rubber boots. Life vests, waterproof bags, rain gear, and light snacks are provided. The tour company is owned by Goldbelt, Inc., whose shareholders are Tlingit. Tour guides may be non-Native.

Naa Kahidi Theater

The sleek white cruise ship, four stories high and the length of two football fields, moored at Juneau's dock is a startling contrast to the cedar-planked Naa Kahidi Theater on the shore. Built in the style of a clan house of 200 years ago, the darkened theater has planked seats that step down to a central fire pit.

Naa Kahidi is a professional acting company that reenacts Native Alaska's most powerful stories for their dramatic, emotional, and visual appeal. Narration in Tlingit and in English accompanies the animated masked actors who dance the story. Costuming is extraordinary, particularly that of Raven, with his snapping beak and wings made of slats of wood strung over the actor's arms. Naa Kahidi has toured Alaska, the lower 48 states, and Europe, supported in part by the Alaska State

"When I go home from Juneau to my ancestral village, it just smells like home—the kelp at low tide, clean salt water on the cool breeze mixed with the scent of fresh fish and the smokehouse."

—Carol Aceveda, Tlingit

Council on the Arts, the National Endowment for the Arts, and Sealaska Heritage Foundation.

The stories are evocative, so much so that when actors wear carved wooden masks, audience members swear they see the masks' expressions change as the story unfolds. It's also one of the few places in Alaska you'll hear Tlingit spoken. In a quick post-performance poll, the audience gave the theater a solid four stars. Distinctive T-shirts are for sale in the lobby too.

Naa Kahidi, Sealaska Heritage Foundation, One Sealaska Plaza, Suite 201, Juneau, AK 99801; (907)463-4844. Located next to the Juneau library, in front of the Alaska steamship docking area, on S Franklin St. Summers, two or three performances daily, Tues–Sat; winters, the company travels and is available for educational seminars. Admission $15; children under 12, $9. Call first for reservations (at this writing, a reorganization of the theater company is under way); tickets are also sold at the door.

Ravens, big-beaked, black birds twice the size of crows, have a distinctive croak and also make a sound like dice rattling in a cup. Masked raven dancers mime the bird's hopping walk and its glimmering eye. In the flicker of firelight, the dancer spreads his wings, pulls the string on his mask, and slaps the wooden beak open and shut as the drum pounds.

Alaska State Museum

The rich heritage of Alaska's Eskimo, Aleut, Athabascan, and Southeast Coastal people is presented through a selection of tools, clothing, masks, regalia, and other items at the Alaska State Museum. Some of the more fascinating objects in this museum include boats, such as large umiaks and kayaks from Alaska's Aleutian Islands and the Arctic, and ingenious and necessary rain gear—made of transparent seal gut that gleams like alabaster. Modern-day raincoats look dull by comparison.

The museum's largest exhibit is a re-creation of a traditional Tlingit plank house using an elaborate painted screen and four carved house posts depicting the Raven and Frog, both crests of the Gaanaxteidi clan. The posts and screen are on loan from the clan in Klukwan, a Tlingit village near Haines in Southeast Alaska. The house contains a scene from a Tlingit *Kooeex*, or potlatch, using mannequins wearing original ceremonial dress.

A small ceremonial Frog clan hat at the museum, carved from cedar prior to the turn of the century, is an example of unusual cooperation between a museum and the Kiksadi Tlingits, from whom it was collected more than 70 years ago. Like many clan-owned ceremonial items that have left Southeast Alaska, the hat was sold by an individual, without clan permission, to a private collector prior to 1920. When it was offered at a Sotheby's auction in 1981, a consortium of the State Museum, Sealaska Heritage Foundation, and the clan successfully bid $65,000 for the hat; it is worth more than four times that today. The museum protects the hat, while the clan retains the right to use it for potlatch ceremonies.

The arrangement has been mutually beneficial. Elders gave the museum a Chilkat robe worth at least $30,000 because they believe that ceremonial regalia should be stored, shown, and used together. Look here also for a Raven's Tail robe, with its eye-dazzling geometric patterns, woven by a group of Native and non-Native weavers at the museum and lent for ceremonies.

The museum has also preserved several important archaeological artifacts found in waterlogged sites, such as a 700-year-old fish trap and two woven baskets approximately 7,000 years old.

The Athabascan display includes male and female mannequins wearing traditional Denaina beaded outfits collected in the 1880s, and an early birchbark canoe from the Yukon River. Another case contains a set of Athabascan counting cords, sinew strings with special knots, feathers, beads, and tufts of fur, used to help speakers remember stories and historical events. Several Ingalik Athabascan masks are also displayed.

Another item at the museum that you may want to remember, if you are flying north to Kotzebue or Barrow for tours in that region that explain the whaling ceremonies, is a rare bentwood water bucket with carved ivory figures attached. Collected just after the turn of the century, it was used in a whaling ceremony by Inupiat Eskimos to carry a respectful drink of water to the whale after it was killed and beached.

The museum's gift shop carries Alaskan as well as authentic Native art, and offers a thoughtfully chosen selection of books.

Alaska State Museum, 395 Whittier St, Juneau, AK 99801; (907)465-2901; Web site: http://lccl.alaska.edu/local/museum/home.html. Open daily, May–Aug; closed Sun and Mon, Sept–Apr. Admission $3; children 18 and under, free.

Alaska State Library

Books, state and federal publications (34,000 publications ranging from fiction to rare volumes on early exploration in Alaska and the Arctic), historic manuscripts, oral history tapes, maps, newspapers from 90 communities, periodicals, pamphlets, and clippings are held in the Alaska Historical Collections of the Alaska State Library. The photography collection of 100,000 images includes the collections of Winter and Pond, Case and Draper, and Wickersham prior to and at the turn of the century. Items are noncirculating, but there is a comfortable reading room reserved for those who want to use the library's resources. Bibliographic access to published materials is through the online catalog and a card catalog in the reading room.

Alaska State Library, Alaska Historical Collections, PO Box 110571, Juneau, AK 99811; (907)465-2925. Eighth floor, State Office Building. Open Mon–Fri, 1–5pm. Access to the online catalogue is through the state's home page at http://www.educ. state.ak.us/lam/home.html.

Free Documentary Films

Among the videos shown free in the theater at the U.S. Forest Service Information Center are several that are specific to Native life. *Angoon: 100 Years Later* is a documentary about the Tlingit Native village of Angoon (see Angoon section). The video includes footage of a potlatch. Two other films demonstrate how the complicated Raven's Tail blankets are woven and show Native carvers practicing their traditional art.

U.S. Forest Service Information Center, 101 Egan Dr, Juneau, AK 99801; (907)586-8751. In the Centennial Hall. Open daily in summer; Mon–Fri only in winter. Free.

Historic St. Nicholas Orthodox Church

The historic little onion-domed church in downtown Juneau was first built in Siberia, and then was disassembled and shipped to Juneau in freight boxes—along with blueprints, boxes of icons, vestments, and a chalice set. When it arrived in 1893, Auk Tlingits met the ship, carted the boxes up the hill past Juneau's frontier saloons, laid it out, and, with the help of Slavic immigrants, reassembled it on Fifth Street. Today, St. Nicholas is included in the *Princeton Architectural Press Source Book of American Architecture: A Guidebook to the 500 Most Notable Buildings in the United States.*

That the Auks chose the Russian Orthodox religion instead of an American Protestant church is not surprising. Russian missionaries had demonstrated respect for Native cultures, translating scripture and services into Native languages. The first Russian Orthodox Church mission was established in Alaska as early as 1794. Not only did Father John Veniaminov, later canonized as St. Innocent, learn Tlingit (with the help of Natives who helped him sort out the sounds of their language), he devised a Tlingit alphabet (using the Russian alphabet) so that the oral tradition could be recorded.

St. Nicholas Orthodox Church, 326 5th St, Juneau, AK 99801; (907)586-1023. Three blocks north of the Baranof Hotel on Franklin St; call for information on tours. The $1 admission helps maintain the building. Weekend services (6pm Sat, 10am Sun) are sung in English, Tlingit, and Slavonic. The public is welcome to attend.

Tracy Arm Day Trip

Auk Nu Tours offers an inexpensive and spectacular day cruise from Juneau into the narrow, twisting Tracy Arm fjord. The fjord is a corridor of impressive stone cliffs, hundreds of waterfalls, and two glaciers flowing from the massive Juneau ice field into tidewater. The sightseeing boat negotiates icebergs for a close look at the blue glaciers, and lingers for about an hour so passengers can watch huge chunks of ice splash into bottle-green water. Even the sound of the ice is worth the trip: the cracking ice is louder than a gunshot, and huge chunks collapse from the face of the glacier with an explosive splash and wake, sending the whole punch bowl tinkling madly with the sound of colliding ice splinters.

Tlingit tradition teaches that every object of nature, including the glacier, has a spirit; that of the glacier is manifested in the icy glacial wind blowing off the mountain. (Wear a jacket!) Offerings used to be made to the ice spirit to coax the glaciers into retreating; Tlingit stories also tell of a young woman who urged the glacier forward, thus causing the destruction of her village.

Seals give birth to their pups on the floating icebergs in the spring, an easy mark for Tlingit hunters, who once relied on seal for both sustenance and warmth. Naturalists and cultural interpreters are on board the boat to explain all there is to know about glaciers. Hot lunch (soup and chili) and snacks are served throughout the day. Boats return to Juneau by 5pm.

Auk Nu Tours, Seadrome Travel Center, 76 Egan Dr, Juneau, AK 99801; (800)820-2628 or (907)586-8687. The Seadrome Travel Center is at the dock; purchase tickets inside the center in advance or on the day of the cruise. Boats depart daily May–Sept. Prices vary, averaging about $100 per person. Auk Nu Tours is owned by the Native corporation Goldbelt, Inc.

For a full-color catalogue of books and tapes by and about Southeast Alaska Natives, call Sealaska Heritage Foundation (907)463-4844.

Auk Village Recreation Site

By 1900 the winter village at Auke Bay was nearly deserted, the Tlingits having left for Juneau to look for work in the mines. Today, where the village once stood, there is a small public campground, day-park, and harbor. The village site, once standing among tall Sitka spruce with a rocky beach below, is commemorated by a Yax-te totem pole, raised in 1941. The Yax-te, the Big Dipper, was the crest of a Tlingit clan that lived near Klawock on Prince of Wales Island. The crest was given to an Auk chief for his clan's use after a battle, a common way of acknowledging surrender.

Auk Village Recreation Site, administered by the U.S. Forest Service, Juneau Ranger District; (907)586-8800. Located off Glacier Hwy, about 18 miles from town and 1½ miles from the ferry terminal. Primitive campground with 12 spaces; no showers. First come, first served.

Art and Artists

In Juneau, almost all galleries carry Native art. In Southeast Alaska, the primary art forms are totem poles, carved masks, and bentwood boxes based on distinctive formline designs, and from those designs springs art in all media and all price ranges—from silk-screened prints to woven blankets. Prices on hand-carved items can be quite high, but they are generally worth the price; for instance, some Native totem carvers are internationally known and their work highly prized, so they can command more than $3,000 a foot. Chilkat blankets woven of sheep's wool and cedar bark, made by weavers such as Anna Brown-Ehlers of Juneau, can fetch up to $35,000. Silver carved bracelets, such as those made by carver Amos Wallace, are a great value, often around $250. Beware, however, of imitators. If authenticity matters to you, ask the shopkeeper to verify: sometimes shopkeepers neglect to label art or discuss artists until asked specifically if the art was made by an Alaska Native. Don't settle for the explanation that "all Alaskans are native Alaskans." Ask for the name of the artist and his or her tribal, or Native corporation shareholder, affiliation. Dealers passing off non-Native art as the real thing are breaking federal law. (See "Buying Native Art" in the appendix.)

There are four Native-owned galleries in Juneau. The Raven-Eagle Gift Shop is on the second floor of the Mount Roberts Tramway sky terminal. Next to the cruise ship dock and Naa Kahidi Theater is a Native Artists Market, where a different group of artists and crafters is hosted every week; also look here for books and tapes that are difficult to find elsewhere. Totem Twins is at the Juneau International Airport (1873 Shell Simmons Dr, Juneau, AK 99801; (907)789-4672). Mount Juneau Trading Post is in Juneau's historic downtown (151 S Franklin St, Juneau, AK 99801; (907)586-3426). Portfolio Arts (210 Ferry Way, Suite 101 (across from Marine Park), Juneau, AK 99801; (907)586-8111) is owned by non-Native Karen Olanna, widow of Inupiat artist Melvin Olanna, founder of the Shishmaref community carving center north of Nome. Portfolio Arts sells some of Alaska's finest one-of-a-kind Native art, including Southeast, Yup'ik, and Inupiat work. Melvin Olanna's larger pieces are displayed, as is the work of Aleut painter Alvin Amason.

For names of artists, dance groups, singers, storytellers, and lecturers, contact the Tlingit and Haida Central Council (320 West Willoughby Ave, Suite 300, Juneau, AK 99801; (800)344-1432 or (907)586-1432).

Blueberry View Bed & Breakfast

This luxury B&B is called Blueberry View because it sits way up on Douglas Island's Mount Troy, which is covered with blueberry bushes. (Douglas Island is accessed from Juneau by a bridge.) Within a few minutes of the B&B's back door are the Treadwell Mining and Dan Moller Trails; foot-weary hikers can relax afterward in the B&B's huge hot tub outside and look down on cruise ships docking in Juneau. Rooms have private entrances and full baths; some suites have full kitchens. Guests in single rooms are served a deluxe continental breakfast with homemade breads, cereals, and fruit. Those staying in suites are supplied with fixings for an even bigger breakfast. Rooms have cable television with movie channels, a CD stereo system, and a VCR. Guests have access to laundry facilities on the premises. Owner Cheri Renner is Tlingit; her husband, Terry, grew up in Anchorage.

Blueberry View Bed & Breakfast, 2917 Jackson Rd, Juneau, AK 99801; (888)580-8439 or (907)586-3036; Web site: http://www.ptialaska.net/~bluberry. Open year-round. Rooms $65–$150; weekly rates available. Children and families are welcome.

Glacier Bay National Park

Glacier Bay National Park is actually one big bay with two long fjords and small, tree-covered islands. When Captain James Cook sailed into Icy Strait to map the region in the 1780s, there was no Glacier Bay to map. It was completely filled with glacial ice. When Captain George Vancouver mapped the region in 1789, he reported just the slightest new curve in the wall of ice. Remnants of the last ice age 4,000 years ago, 16 tidewater glaciers have been retreating over the last two centuries. Twelve of the glaciers, although shrinking, still actively calve spectacular chunks of ice—some as large as a three-story building—into the tidewater.

Point Retreat in Auke Bay is so-named because explorer George Vancouver turned his boat around at this point when confronted by three huge canoes filled with Tlingit warriors.

Before the ice began to rapidly advance 4,000 years ago, Tlingit Indians inhabited what was a lush river valley here. Today their settlements along the river have been ground to fine dust, the valley widened by glacier advance and retreat and flooded by seawater. Many of the descendants of Tlingits who fled the glaciers during the "little ice age" resettled on Chichagof Island at what is now called Hoonah. When Glacier Bay was made a national park in 1925, any plans the Tlingits had to reestablish settlements along the shoreline were halted. In 1996, however, the Tlingits bid for and were awarded management of the national park's Glacier Bay Lodge, the only lodging in the entire park. Glacier Bay Lodge is accessible by taking the Auk Nu ferry to Gustavus (lodge guests are transported by van from the ferry dock 10 miles to the lodge) or by taking a plane to Gustavus.

Auke Bay Ferry to Gustavus

A high-speed catamaran passenger ferry leaves Auke Bay, 18 miles north of Juneau, once a day for Gustavus and access to Glacier Bay. Gustavus is a very small town with a scattering of bed-and-breakfast lodges in its meadows and woods; at the ferry landing and airport is the town's only road, which leads to the edge of Glacier Bay. The large meadow and marsh where Gustavus now stands was formed when glaciers retreated to the mountains. First called Strawberry Point because of the wild strawberries that grow profusely here, Gustavus was settled near the turn of the century by a handful of cattle ranchers (who soon surrendered their stock to brown bears). Today a growing settlement with a small grocery, gas station, lodges, and cabins for rent, Gustavus is the only settlement near Glacier Bay National Park. Park headquarters and Glacier Bay Lodge are 10 miles from Gustavus on an unpaved road. Buses from Glacier Bay Lodge pick up passengers and transport them to the lodge.

After dropping lodge guests at Gustavus, the ferry heads back into Icy Strait for an afternoon of watching humpback whales, which come here to feed in the summers. The whales breach and slap flippers and flukes as they feed on krill. Pods of orca whales following the salmon show up in June. You may also see Steller's sea lions, seals, and porpoises. Naturalists are on board to explain the natural and cultural history of the region. The boat returns to Gustavus, picks up its boatload of passengers, and departs for Juneau at 5:45pm.

Auk Nu Tours, 76 Egan Dr, Juneau, AK 99801; (800)320-2628 or (907)586-8687. Tours offered mid-May–mid-Sept. Buy your ticket in Juneau; tour buses pick up passengers free at Juneau hotels for the 18-mile trip to and from the ferry landing. Ferry prices are $15 one way, $85 round trip per person. Kayaks, add $40, bicycles, add $10. Wildlife and whale-watching cruise with round-trip ferry fare, $139. Call for schedule. Auk Nu Tours is owned by the Native corporation Goldbelt, Inc.

Wilderness Cruises of Tlingit Waterways

Board a 35-stateroom ship at Juneau, the MV *Wilderness Adventurer*, for a six-night cruise of traditional Tlingit lands and waterways around Juneau that includes Glacier Bay. These small cruise ships, outfitted with racks of two-person kayaks on the stern, stop and circle when wildlife is spotted and anchor in protected coves and fjords so passengers can kayak or walk on shore. Naturalists, Native cultural interpreters, and sometimes Tlingit artists (weavers and carvers) demonstrate and work as guides.

Over a period of three days, the boats circumnavigate huge, forested Admiralty Island National Monument, a place the Tlingits call Kootznoowoo, "The Fortress of the Bears." Kootznoowoo is home to the world's largest concentration of brown bears. The bears are visible on the beaches in May and June, soon after hibernation, when they feed on beach grasses and forage the shoreline. The island also has at least 1,000 nesting bald eagles, which can be seen perched in trees along the shore. The south end of the island is a popular resting area for migrating sea lions.

The itinerary includes kayaking and sightseeing in Glacier Bay National Park, north of Admiralty Island, an awe-inspiring region with some of the longest fjords in Alaska, carved by the advance and retreat of glaciers over the centuries. There's a stop at Glacier Bay Lodge and a full day of wildlife and whale watching at Point Adolphus, in Icy Strait, where humpback and minke whales feed on krill, porpoises slice through the water, and otters float on their backs, munching shellfish. The boats also visit one of the most actively calving glaciers in the region at the end of Tracy Arm fjord.

The ships do not stop at any Native villages or former village sites, but pass by the village of Angoon on Kootznahoo Inlet and Hoonah on Chichagof Island, off Icy Strait. Be sure to examine the framed historic photographs framed on companionway walls, which include the Whale Dance House, Tlingit Dance House, and a Tlingit chief's house photographed in 1901 on Kootznahoo and at Angoon. The ships' libraries have videos and books on natural and cultural history.

All staterooms have private baths and picture windows, and there's a large upper deck for lounging and wildlife watching. Three excellent meals are served each day, with snacks throughout the day (including freshly baked cookies).

More active adventure cruising is available on the MV *Wilderness Explorer*, a smaller ship (18 cabins with bunks) whose tours offer more rigorous kayaking and hiking.

MV Wilderness Adventurer and MV Wilderness Explorer Cruises, book through Glacier Bay Tours & Cruises, 520 Pike St, Suite 1400, Seattle, WA 98101; (800)451-5952. Tours offered May–Sept. Prices vary. Call for fold-out map and brochure. In Dec 1998, the two kayak-loaded ships will be moving their tours to Mexico's Baja Peninsula and Sea of Cortez during the winter months. Glacier Bay Tours & Cruises is a subsidiary of the Native corporation Goldbelt, Inc.

Glacier Bay Lodge

Glacier Bay Lodge is perched near the mouth of Glacier Bay, on its eastern shoreline. In the spring, the beach meadows are dazzling, with purple lupine and chocolate lilies blooming profusely among the beach grasses. In the distance tower the snowcapped peaks of the St. Elias Mountains. The peaks, misted by clouds, can sometimes appear detached from the land; and if cloud conditions are just right, a huge Tlingit cargo canoe, with its high prow and stern, presides in the northern sky over Glacier Bay.

Another canoe is anchored firmly on land here. A huge Sea Otter clan canoe called Yuxwche'ee Yakw sits under a protective shed roof below the lodge. One of the first traditional canoes carved in the region for decades, it was made from a single Sitka spruce log under the direction of George Dalton, Sr. (Stoowu Kaa), a Tlingit elder of Hoonah. Native and non-Native carvers used hand tools and traditional steaming methods to carve and shape the wood. Perhaps it shouldn't be a surprise that not long after this canoe was built, the Native corporation Goldbelt, Inc., took the helm of Glacier Bay Lodge.

Today this area boasts a very large bay and two very long fjords gouged by the retreating ice. Cruise ships and smaller ships alike travel up the fjords to see the 16 glaciers that flow from the mountains into tidewater—a landscape that continues to change as the glaciers withdraw during the current period of global warming.

In the lobby of the handsome wood, glass, and stone lodge, constructed in the 1960s, big cozy couches are grouped in front of a massive stone fireplace; more seating is on the big deck out front. The dining room, filled with Native art, overlooks the bay. Native art is also shown in a small gallery, and there's a small gift shop off the lobby. The National Park Service has its headquarters in Glacier Bay Lodge; a Park Service bookstore, exhibits, and a small theater are upstairs.

The lodge has 54 rooms, all with double beds, private baths, and picture-window views of the rain forest. Three hearty meals are served daily in the restaurant, with a large breakfast buffet on Sunday.

An espresso cart is on the deck; full bar drinks are served fireside or on the deck. Dormitory-style rooms are available too, and a laundry is on the premises.

A wide variety of programs, free through the Park Service, are offered at the lodge: guided trail walks, fireside talks, and slide shows. Guided and unguided kayaking, sportfishing, whale watching, and overnight cruises can all be booked through the lodge. In 1997 the Park Service hired its first Tlingit Park Service guide, a young woman from Hoonah.

The national park's only developed campground (tents only) is tucked into the woods adjacent to the lodge. Dock facilities include limited mooring buoys and water taxi service to the dock. A limited number of vessels are allowed in Glacier Bay by permit, and rules are strictly enforced. Apply for permits by calling Glacier Bay National Park and Preserve, (907)697-2230.

Glacier Bay Lodge, 199 Bartlett Cove, Gustavus, AK 99826; (907)697-2225. Reservations for the lodge are made only through Glacier Bay Tours & Cruises, 520 Pike St, Suite 1400, Seattle, WA 98101; (800)451-5952. Glacier Bay Lodge is operated by the Native corporation Goldbelt, Inc.

Angoon: *Tlingit*

Angoon is a small Tlingit village on the west side of Admiralty Island that has long been home to the Kootznoowoo Tlingit tribe. The village sits on a narrow peninsula guarding an intriguing series of bays filled with tree-covered small islands. It is accessible from Juneau and Sitka by Alaska State Ferry and by bush plane. If you are leaving from Juneau, you can see a film about Angoon at the Alaska State Forestry Center downtown: *Angoon: One Hundred Years Later,* composed of both historical photographs and contemporary footage, explores the events that culminated in the 1882 U.S. naval bombardment of Angoon, during which the entire village was burned to the ground.

The relationship between whites and the Kootznoowoo tribe began well enough. In 1878, the Northwest Trading Company built a whaling station on Killisnoo Island. When a Russian Orthodox church and a Bureau of Indian Affairs school were established at Killisnoo, many Kootznoowoo tribal members moved from Angoon to Killisnoo. The conflict began when a whaling ship's harpoon accidentally misfired and exploded, killing a Native crew member who was also a Tlingit shaman. As was customary for such an important person, Angoon villagers demanded 200 valuable trade blankets for the man's family from the Northwest Trading Company. Instead of complying, the trading company asked the U.S. Navy, stationed in Sitka, for assistance. The Navy sent out the cutter *Corwin*, which shelled Angoon and a summer camp, burning down all the beautifully adorned clan houses, filled with important clan regalia and ceremonial objects, that stood along the Angoon waterfront. Six children also died in the shelling.

Although in 1973 Angoon finally won a $90,000 out-of-court settlement from the federal government, the conflict between the Tlingits and the United States was never diplomatically resolved. Killisnoo was destroyed by fire in 1928.

The film *Angoon: One Hundred Years Later*, produced by the Kootznoowoo Cultural & Educational Foundation, Inc., for the 100th anniversary of the event, asks whether the bombardment was malice or a failure of cross-cultural communication, a deliberate action or an accident. A tour operated by Taquan Air out of Sitka includes a visit with an artist in a present-day clan house in Angoon, built on the site of one that burned down in the shelling.

Admiralty Island (Kootznahoo) Wilderness Tour

You leave Sitka on a seaplane early in the morning and cross Baranof Island and Chatham Strait to Angoon's seaplane dock. With a Tlingit guide, you board a charter boat for a morning of fishing or watching wildlife in Chatham Strait, Kootznahoo Inlet, and Favorite Bay, while your guide shares stories of Angoon's culture and life. At noon you return to Angoon for lunch on your own (the community has several cafes, or bring a brown-bag lunch with you from Sitka). After lunch, the tour continues at the home of JoAnn George, one of Alaska's premier artists. JoAnn, a non-Native, and her husband, Gabriel (a member of the Raven clan), live in Gabriel's grandfather's Killer Whale tribal house. Built in the early 1900s, it rests on the same site where the original clan house burned. There's time to linger in the community (and you are welcome to) before flying back to Sitka.

Admiralty Island Wilderness Tour, Taquan Air, 1007 Water St, Ketchikan, AK 99901; (800)770-8800 or (907)225-8800; e-mail: taquan@ptialaska.net; Web site: http:// www.AlaskaOne.com/TaquanAir.

Sportfishing in Angoon Waters

Gabriel George has fished in Angoon's freshwater streams, inlets, and open water since he was 8 years old and has worked as a fishing guide for the last 10 years. And does he know where the halibut holes are! A few years ago he wowed a television crew with a 340-pound monster halibut. Hooking a big flat one is like trying to reel in a

Volkswagen bus rolling downhill, he says. With George as your guide, you can fish for salmon, halibut, and cutthroat and rainbow trout aboard a 34-foot Northwind. In the works is a log cabin lodge; until it's complete, overnight lodging in Angoon can be arranged if needed.

Gabriel George Charters, PO Box 95, Angoon, AK 99820; (907)788-3232. Day trips only. All gear needed for two to six people is provided.

Kootznahoo Inlet Lodge

State Representative Albert Kookesh and his wife, Sally, both Alaska Natives, own and operate Kootznahoo Inlet Lodge on the Angoon waterfront. Located within walking distance of the community float-plane facility and adjacent to a convenience store, the modern building boasts 12 comfortable rooms, all with private baths and many with kitchenettes (although they really aren't needed, since the lodge supplies all meals). All units have color television and coffeemakers. From the deck visitors can watch the ebb and flow of a tidal current at the mouth of a fast-moving river into Kootznahoo Inlet. A long dock stretches along pilings out front.

Visitors can take boats upstream to fly-fish saltwater rapids and clear-running streams, or catch halibut and king salmon just a few minutes from shore. The lodge also sits at the edge of Admiralty Island's 937,000-acre Kootznoowoo Wilderness. (The Tlingit name *Kootznoowoo* is almost impossible for English speakers to pronounce correctly, which has led to many different spellings—from Xutsnuwu to Hootsnoowoo.) The lodge provides a fleet of boats for fishing, along with Coast Guard–licensed fishing guides, most of whom are commercial fishermen and Alaska Natives. Lodge bookings are structured for fishing packages, but the lodge will also accommodate and make charter arrangements for individual travelers coming to Angoon to sightsee or whale-watch.

Kootznahoo Inlet Lodge, PO Box 134, Angoon, AK 99820; (907)788-3615 or (907)788-3501. The lodge is located on the road to the Alaska State Ferry dock. Open May–Sept. Fishing packages include round-trip airfare from Juneau or Sitka, room and board, three meals a day, four days of guided fishing, and care, handling, and freezing of all fish. Schedule eight people (including yourself) to stay at the lodge, and win a free trip.

Sophie's Bed and Breakfast

Sophie's Bed and Breakfast, owned by Harold and Sophie Frank, is a log home in a wooded area with five private rooms, several dorm rooms, and two shared bathrooms. Continental breakfast is provided. The Franks often host business travelers to Angoon, (907)788-3194 or (907)788-3773. Open year-round; rates vary.

Hoonah: *Tlingit*

Tlingits left the Glacier Bay basin when glaciers suddenly advanced during the "little ice age" in the 1400s. The villages they left behind were pulverized by the grinding ice floes. They resettled on a point of land on Chichagof Island that they called Huna, which in Tlingit means "the place where the north wind does not blow." The name was changed to Hoonah when the post office was established in 1901. The village faces Icy Strait, so named by Captain George Vancouver in the 1700s because the strait was so filled with floating icebergs that he had difficulty negotiating his ship through them. The historic town of Hoonah was destroyed by fire in 1944. Today the rebuilt village is 80 percent Tlingit. Hoonah's location across from Glacier Bay, and the town's well-maintained marina behind the village's breakwater, draw many of Juneau's recreational boaters and sport fishermen during the summer. Kayakers bring their boats and gear over on the Alaska State Ferry from Juneau to poke around in nearby Port Frederick inlet. Although Native corporations have logged the land behind Hoonah heavily in the last two decades, there's still plenty of wilderness to see. Over 200 miles of logging roads lead to numerous rivers teeming with salmon and other species; up to 50 eagles at a time wheel over Hoonah, and whales are frequently spotted in the bay. The Alaska State Ferry docks at Hoonah four times a week during the summer months; air taxis (operated by Wings of Alaska, L.A.B. Flying, and Haines Airways) fly to Hoonah from Anchorage or Sitka.

Janaggen Tours

Faggen Skaslestad was delivered in Hoonah by his Tlingit grandmother, who delivered many of Hoonah's babies in the 1930s and 1940s. He's been a big-game (brown bear and blacktail deer) guide on Chichagof Island for 27 years, but he also leads wildlife photography tours, brown bear viewing tours, and cultural tours of Hoonah. His cultural tours include a natural history walk along Hoonah's shoreline; original Tlingit burial grounds dating back more than 100 years; Pitt Island, covered with totems representing clans and families; the Russian Orthodox church; the Hoonah boat harbor, where you can meet commercial fishermen and tour the fish packing plant; and brown bear viewing at the landfill (don't laugh—you can see huge bears here 20 feet away). Travel is by foot and by van.

Longer tours include guided and fly-fishing, berry picking, camping, and canoeing or kayaking. Itineraries are flexible.

Janaggen Touring and Guiding, PO Box 471, Hoonah, AK 99829; (907)945-3511. Tours offered May–Sept. Call or write for information on 10-day guided hunts.

Whalewatch Lodge and Charters

Floyd and Margie Peterson take visitors sightseeing for whales and other marine life in Icy Strait and at Point Adolphus (one of the best whale-watching spots in Southeast Alaska), or salmon and halibut sportfishing on their 43-foot cabin cruiser. The U.S. Coast Guard–approved boat has two private staterooms, head and shower, galley, and topside seating for eight people. This is a full-service charter, with overnight lodging available at the couple's Whalewatch Lodge, a three-bedroom, two-bath house on the Hoonah waterfront with a wide veranda overlooking Port Frederick bay. The lodge has a furnished kitchen, living room with cable TV, VCR, and radio, telephone, and washer and dryer. Floyd was born in Juneau, is of Tlingit descent, and has been commercial fishing out of Hoonah most of his life, having built his first fishing boat when he was 18 years old. His wife, Marjorie, born in Bethel and of Yup'ik Eskimo descent, has been his deckhand for over 30 years. She cooks meals for guests, serving homemade berry preserves, salmon fillets, and other regional foods.

Whalewatch Lodge and Charters, PO Box 245, Hoonah, AK 99329; (907)945-3327; e-mail: fishers@seaknet.alaska.edu. Open year-round. Rooms $65–$85, including breakfast. Sightseeing and fishing are year-round; high season (the best fishing and whale watching) is mid-April–mid-Sept. Charter prices are based on packages that include sightseeing, fishing, overnight lodging, and meals.

Wind N Sea Inn

Wind N Sea Inn is becoming a bed and breakfast, one apartment at a time, as Hoonah's magistrate, Joyce Skaslestad, and her husband remodel an eight-unit apartment building into overnight lodging. This is shared housing; you rent one of four small bedrooms and share a fully furnished kitchen (continental breakfast is served), bathroom, and living room with other guests. It's all brand-new, with a microwave oven and washer and dryer. Most of the guests who stay at Wind N Sea are professional people: educators, engineers, and medical personnel in Hoonah on business. Groceries are available at the Wards Packing cannery store in town, within walking distance of the inn. Joyce Skaslestad, a Tlingit and a shareholder in the Sealaska and Huna Totem Corporations, moved to Hoonah in the 1960s. She's the great-granddaughter of Chief Kyan (see Ketchikan section).

Wind N Sea Inn, 527 Gaateeni Hwy, #1, Hoonah, AK 99829; (907)945-3451. Open year-round. Room rates vary.

Dancing Bears Bed & Breakfast

Within walking distance of the boat harbor and the center of Hoonah, three bedrooms are available in the upstairs apartment of Vera and Wendy Skaslestad's contemporary (1996) home. Mother Vera is Aleut, from Unalaska on the Aleutian Chain; daughter Wendy is Aleut and Tlingit. Each bedroom has two comfortable pillowtop beds. Two full baths have showers and a whirlpool tub. The common area adjoining the bedrooms has a living room with cable TV, a fully equipped kitchen, and a deck for smokers (no smoking inside). Room price includes continental or full breakfast (waffles, bacon, sausage, and the works) delivered to the kitchen table upstairs. Make reservations early; this place fills up during the summer.

Dancing Bears Bed & Breakfast, 530 Gaateeni Hwy, PO Box 312, Hoonah, AK 99829; (907)945-3500. Open year-round. Room rates vary.

Sitka: *Tlingit*

Sitka, built on the site of an ancient Tlingit village, is one of the most beautiful historic small towns in the United States. On the west side of Baranof Island, facing the Pacific Ocean, Sitka lies in the shelter of an island-filled sound. Its Tlingit names, Sheet Ka and Shee Atika, mean "the village behind the islands" and "people on the outside edge of Shee facing the ocean," respectively. The pretty seascape is dominated by 3,102-foot Mount Edgecumbe, an extinct volcano as perfectly shaped as Japan's Mount Fuji.

The traders of the Russian-American Company were the first outsiders to settle here. Along with their subjugated Aleut teams of otter hunters, they burned down the Tlingit village to establish a fur trading post and renamed the site New Archangel. The Tlingits fought a protracted battle against the Russians, but after their final loss, the Tlingits left the area for a period of about 20 years before returning to work for the Russians and rebuilding their village adjacent to the Russian town. New Archangel was a wealthy, thriving port until 1867, when Russia sold Alaska to the United States. In the early 1800s, more than 1,000 books were donated to the Sitka library by Russian aristocrat Count Nikolai Rezanov. The Russian Orthodox Church, which stepped in with missionaries to smooth relations between the two cultures, operated a college-level boarding school in Sitka with classes in mathematics, history, medicine, Latin, Russian, Native languages, rhetoric, geography, physics, and astronomy. Natives also studied navigation, medicine, anatomy, and surgery in Europe. The town even had its own orchestra. Once larger than San Francisco and considered the hub of culture in the Americas, Sitka was regarded as "the Paris of the Pacific."

Today, Sitka is one of the hippest communities in Southeast Alaska. Its public radio station, "Raven Radio" KCAW-FM (104.7), has been the subject of *New York Times* articles and a *60 Minutes* segment. The Island Institute's annual symposium attracts noted writers and thinkers from around the world. The Audubon Society's Christmas bird count draws an enthusiastic crowd. Other annual events include the Sitka Folk Festival, "Art on the Dock," International Museum Day, and a concert series.

Sitka's unique Tlingit/Aleut/Russian heritage is everywhere in evidence. It's not unusual to find Russian borscht and alder-smoked salmon on the same menu. Public dance performances are in turn performed by Russian dancers and Tlingit dancers; St. Michael's Cathedral, a Russian Orthodox church, has a mostly Tlingit congregation; and businesses, such as the Sitka Rose Art Gallery, are even co-owned by people of Tlingit descent and people of Russian descent. In fact, the whole town appears to be quite harmonious, happily capitalizing, without schlock, on its acrimonious past. Thirty-five years ago, the National Park Service, at the instigation of the Tlingit community, opened a cultural museum and totem park on the site where the Tlingits and Russians had fought their bitter battle. And a few years ago, Tlingit Robert Sam led a campaign to clean up the old Russian cemetery.

Historic Russian Orthodox churches, with their beautiful blue onion domes, candlelit interiors, and icons, are scattered throughout Alaska. For an insightful book about Native spirituality, subsistence, Russian fur traders, the Russian Orthodox Church, the American Presbyterians and their mission schools, read Orthodox Alaska, A Theology of Mission, *Michael Oleksa, St. Vladimir's Seminary Press, Crestwood, NY 10707, 1992; available in most Southeast Alaska bookstores.*

Sitka Tribal Tours

Sitka Tribal Tours offers a 2½-hour bus tour of the last several thousand years of Sitka's Tlingit, Russian, and American history, interwoven with natural history. The tour includes the boat harbor, Mount Edgecumbe boarding school, Sheldon Jackson Museum, and Sitka National Historical Park. Buses turn down Katlian Street along the waterfront to the site of the old village, which once included more than 20 huge clan houses facing the water. Burned down by the Russians, the village was rebuilt, and the clan houses now look like any other small Victorian-era houses. Drivers pick plants along the way and explain their uses, and share stories about their own lives. The tour ends with a dance performance in the Sheetka Kwaan NaaKaHidi clan house (discussed later).

Sitka Tribal Tours, 429 Katlian St, Sitka, AK 99835; (888)270-8687 or (907)747-7290. Tour guides dressed in striking button blanket–style vests sell tickets on the visitors' dock while cruise ships are in port at the west end of Monastery St. Two tours are offered. The longer tour (2½ hours) includes the dance performance and requires a reservation; $28. The 1-hour driving tour costs $10.

Native Natural History Walking Tour

This is a fabulous 2-hour walking tour, designed for families and unlike anything else offered in Southeast Alaska. It begins at Sitka's harbor with a discussion of Sitka's geography, including the Mount Edgecumbe volcano and the barrier islands that protect the harbor from the Pacific Ocean's heavy surf. Islands enabled the Tlingits to harvest food from the intertidal zone year-round. The tour proceeds through Sitka, passing the Russian Orthodox church, the Episcopal church, and the Presbyterian church, while the guides describe the impact of religion on the Tlingits. The thread of natural history picks up again with a stop at Sheldon Jackson College's Sage Aquarium and its touch tanks, where you can handle the sea creatures and plants used by the Tlingits. Then the tour goes along the beach at low tide in front of Sitka National Historical Park, and continues into the forest for discussions of the medicinal uses of plants. In the Southeast Alaska Cultural Center, tour guests meet with artists to learn about the uses of natural materials (including the traditional techniques of mixing paint from minerals, clay, and fish oil), the collection and weaving of mountain goat wool, and the origin of silver carving. Raincoats are provided, along with a long checklist of plants and wildlife that are on the walk.

Tethered live hummingbirds and young abandoned bear cubs were favorite pets of Tlingit children. If the cubs died, their skins were tanned, sewn, and then stuffed with dried plant material—the first "teddy bears."

Sitka Tribal Tours, 429 Katlian St, Sitka, AK 99835; (888)270-8687 or (907)747-7290. Tours offered daily, May–Sept. $18 adults, $9 children.

Sheetka Kwaan NaaKaHidi Community Center

All of Sitka's clans are represented in this traditional-style longhouse, built near the waterfront in front of the old Russian blockhouse. It's a traditional-style longhouse—updated for the 1990s, with lighting, sound, and restrooms, for use as a performing arts theater for the entire Sitka community. Constructed of natural wood and accented with copper, the longhouse has tiered seating for 240 people on three sides of a central fire pit. The building design is similar to those of the huge clan houses that were used in the past to transfer knowledge orally to clan members. The structure was traditionally blessed with sacred songs and prayers in a daylong ceremony when it opened on May 15, 1997. In the corners of the interior walls are brush marks of burgundy paint, where the four Sitka clans marked the building. In the past these markings would have been blood marks streaked by hand near the ceiling. The Sitka tribe has allocated money for artwork that will be painted on the exterior of the building, and plans to add house posts and carved screens in the next few years, along with a wall of historic photographs. A gallery housing fine art for sale is also in the works. The Sheetka Kwaan NaaKaHidi Dancers perform traditional dances here, in conjunction with Sitka Tribal Tours and cruise ship arrivals, throughout the summer. Independent travelers not on tours are welcome to attend as well.

Sheetka Kwaan NaaKaHidi Community Center, 200 Katlian St, Sitka, AK 99835; (907)747-3137.

Sitka National Historical Park and Southeast Alaska Indian Cultural Center

The land for the National Park Service's cultural museum and interpretive center, 107 acres at the mouth of the Indian River, is located on the traditional home of the Kiksadi clan. It was set aside as a public park by President Benjamin Harrison in 1890.

The museum and interpretive center faces a rocky beach that must look just as it did in 1804, when the battle between the Russians and the Tlingits took place at the mouth of the Indian River. Visitors can walk to the battleground and site of the Tlingit fort along a path interspersed with 15 totem poles. (The National Park Service sells a small, well-illustrated guidebook to the totem poles and house posts on the park grounds, called *Carved History*, available in the gift shop for $4.)

The poles are reproductions; most are from Haida villages on Prince of Wales Island. The originals were collected in the early 1900s, with a $50,000 congressional appropriation, for exhibit at the Louisiana Purchase Exposition of 1904. A few were sold in Louisiana; the rest were shipped to Portland, Oregon, for the Lewis and Clark Exposition, and then were shipped to Sitka, Alaska's first state capital, in 1905. The original Haida poles were erected on the park grounds, a lingering affront to the local Tlingit people. The path continues through the woods along the bank of the Indian River, across a stream by way of a wooden footbridge, and down the shore to the site of the Tlingit fort and Russian memorial (2 miles of trail).

In a place of honor at the entrance to the park is a newer pole honoring all the Tlingit clans of the Sitka region, carved by Tlingit carver Will Burkhart and his apprentice Tommy Joseph. Carved from a red cedar tree from Prince of Wales Island, the pole is called "Haa Leelk'whas Kaash da Heeni Dei" in Tlingit, or "Our Grandparents of Indian River." The design is taken directly from stories told by Sitka elders. At the top of the pole is Raven, creator of the people; the next figure is a human wearing a frog hat, symbolizing the Kiksadi clan. He is holding two coho salmon, representing the Coho clan. Below the figure is Frog, followed by Eagle, representing all the Eagle clans. A brown bear symbolizes the Kaagwaantaan and Chookeneidi clans. The totem pole was raised into place in 1996 in the traditional manner, using five ropes pulled by more than 400 people.

The park's museum houses the Brady Collection of totemic art. Some of the most important pieces are on loan from Tlingit clans and individuals. A 10-minute film recaps the 1804 battle between the Tlingits and the Russians.

Look here for a Raven's Tail robe, woven in one of the Native artisans' studios in an adjoining wing. The three large art studios are operated by the Native-owned, nonprofit Southeast Alaska Indian Cultural Center, one of Sitka's major attractions. Master wood carver Will Burkhart, master silver carvers Louis Minard and David Galanin, wood carver Tommy Joseph, drum maker and carver Jennifer Brady-Morales, and others demonstrate their craft in the studios daily during the summer. The public is welcome to observe and ask questions. Apprentices train with the master artists; their first projects are added to the Sitka National Historical Park's permanent collection.

Sitka National Historical Park and Southeast Alaska Indian Cultural Center, 106 Metlakatla St, Sitka, AK 99835; (907)747-6281. Open daily; cultural center may be open winters (call first). Free.

Sheldon Jackson Museum

The Sheldon Jackson Museum, now owned by the State of Alaska and part of the Alaska State Museum in Juneau, has one of the largest collections of Native artifacts in the state (more than 6,000), and it's one of the most interesting small museums in North America. Items such as the Raven helmet worn in battle against the Russians by Tlingit leader Katlian are well displayed on glass shelves, so you can peek at their undersides. The museum also contains hundreds of items from everyday life, such as jewelry, miniature toys, gaming pieces, pipes, paintbrushes, and tools, labeled and laid out in dozens of pull-out glass-topped drawers. Children love this museum. More than 400 objects are available for visitors to touch; some items can be checked out to schools and other institutions.

A passionate collector who saved everything, including scrapbooks of pressed flowers, Dr. Sheldon Jackson traveled extensively throughout Alaska—first as a missionary and then as the state's general agent for education. He collected material from every remote village he visited, trading inexpensive but useful articles—cloth, needles, and kettles—for items used every day and in ceremony. Jackson was an ardent supporter of the Alaska Society of Natural History and Ethnology, founded in 1887. He was one of its first members, its largest financial donor, and one of its largest contributors of artifacts. The first museum he built resembled a plank community house similar to those used by the Tlingits in Sitka. In 1895, wealthy colleagues on the East Coast helped Jackson with funding to build a fireproof concrete octagonal building next to the Sitka Training School (now Sheldon Jackson College). Ironically, while Jackson prized the Natives' tools, household goods, and art, his training school, following the federal mandate of the time, methodically proceeded to replace Native culture and language with Western culture and English. Jackson said in 1887 that the purpose of his collection was "to provide and have on hand for study by the students, the best specimens of the old work of their ancestors." In 1893 he wrote that without preserving artifacts, "in a few years there would be nothing left to show the coming generations of Natives how their fathers lived."

Native artists demonstrate art techniques at the museum throughout the summer. Everything in the museum's small gift shop is handcrafted by Alaska Natives, about half of it by Sitka Native artists. Unique in this gift shop are Sheldon Jackson Museum publications, some of them reprints from the turn of the century, and books about Native art.

Sheldon Jackson Museum, 104 College Dr, Sitka, AK 99835; (907)747-8981; Web site: http://iccl.alaska.edu/local/museum/home.html. Adjoins Sheldon Jackson College campus, off Lincoln Street. Open year-round. Call for hours.

"Raven Radio" KCAW-FM

Sitka's public radio station broadcasts *National Native News* daily at 9am right after the *Raven Morning News*, and replays it at 12:20pm. The station has put repeaters in remote areas such as Kake to make sure that Natives who have little access to daily newspapers can keep abreast of breaking news. On Thursdays at 10:06am, catch *Ut-Ka-Neek* ("This Is My Story"), 2 hours of local Native interviews and Native music. The station has produced *Alaska Natives in Science*, a six-part series on the overlapping of Western science and Native tradition, available for national distribution. This little radio station, on the top floor of an old World War I communication station, raises more money per capita than any other community radio station in the United States—about $75,000 a year. Souvenirs for sale—our favorites in Sitka—include T-shirts and sweatshirts emblazoned with the station's KCAW call letters and a goofy-looking black raven.

KCAW-FM, 2B Lincoln St, Sitka, AK 99835; (907)747-5877. Climb the back stairs outside the building to the second floor during business hours.

> **"People ask me if it isn't odd to be selling my artwork to tourists, but it really isn't. My grandmother sat on the very same sidewalk in front of where my gallery is now and sold moccasins, baskets, and little totems to tourists. People pick up things that are 100 years old and want to know what they were used for. Many things were not used for anything functional but were carved and decorated for the tourist trade. People were going from a subsistence lifestyle to a lifestyle that depended on commodities. They had to pay for them somehow."**
>
> **—Teri Rofkar, owner, Sitka Rose Gallery**

The Sitka Rose

Artist Teri Rofkar, a Tlingit Native, wove one of the several ceremonial Raven's Tail robes on display at Sitka National Historical Park. The Raven's Tail robe is a ceremonial robe that predates the elaborate yellow-and-black Chilkat robes, and Rofkar's was the first such robe woven by a Tlingit in more than 200 years. The weaving took more than 700 hours, not including the six months spent spinning mountain goat wool and the time spent dyeing the wool with wolf moss (a type of lichen), iron, and hemlock bark.

Captain James Cook's journals describe Tlingits wearing stunning black-and-white wool robes. A fragment of a robe found on Kruzof Island (northwest of Sitka) is in New York's American Museum of Natural History. Inspired by her daughter Teri's work, Marie Laws wove a robe herself, a work that took well over 1,000 hours. "What's so great about this," says Rofkar, "is that Mom was from that lost generation that was forced to go to boarding school, where they wouldn't let her learn any of her own mother's skills. She is one of our elders but had to teach herself how to weave."

Rofkar, co-owner of the multicultural Sitka Rose Gallery, also weaves traditional baskets from grasses, cedar bark, and spruce roots gathered from the Sitka area. She teaches, demonstrates, and lectures throughout Alaska and outside the state. Her work is included in the permanent collection of the Smithsonian Institution's National Museum of the American Indian in New York.

Sitka Rose Gallery, 419 Lincoln St, Sitka, AK 99835; (907)747-3030. Open year-round.

Transformations: An Evening of Tlingit Dinner Theater

Robert Sam is an accomplished Tlingit storyteller who has toured the United States and Europe as a performer with Naa Kahidi Theater of Juneau. He's teamed up with his wife, an accomplished potter, to present an unusual evening of dinner theater at the Westmark Shee Atika Hotel. In a darkened room, tables are arranged in a U shape, potlatch style, with ceramic plates and cups decorated to help illustrate the stories Robert Sam tells over dinner. In the "Box of Daylight" story, for example, the plate's designs incorporate pine needles, a raven headdress, a raven border design, a grandfather dressed in a tunic, a sun mask, and the box of daylight. Small basket-shaped cups allow each person seated at the table to take a sip of water at the appropriate moment in Sam's story. Full-course dinners, including Caesar salad, baked halibut, red potatoes, vegetables, breads, and ice cream topped with blueberries, are served during the performance. Robert wears traditional beaded and appliquéd tunics, as well as old pieces that he caretakes for his clan. Replicas of the plates and cups are available by commission or at Studio Sitka Co-op (407 Lincoln St, downtown Sitka).

Transformation Dinner Theater, a production of Ravenware Studio, Robert Sam and Doe Stahr, PO Box 6113, Sitka, AK 99835; (907)747-3108. Call the studio for schedule and for reservations. $40 per person. The dinner theater is also available for private events. Westmark Shee Atika Hotel is at 330 Seward St, Sitka, AK 99835; (907)747-6241.

Native-Owned Lodging

Two elaborately beaded clan robes are framed and displayed behind the Westmark Shee Atika Hotel's registration desk, a nice introduction to the largest hotel in Sitka (100 rooms), built in the early 1970s and owned by Shee Atika Incorporated, a Sitka Native corporation.

Westmark Shee Atika Hotel, 330 Seward St, Sitka, AK 99835; (907)747-6241. A block from the old Russian Orthodox church in downtown Sitka. Open year-round. Rooms $124–$175. All major credit cards and out-of-state checks accepted. The hotel's Raven Dining Room serves excellent seafood and salads; for reservations, call (907)747-6465.

At the Halibut Hide-A-Way, Tlingit Betty Jo Johns rents the one-bedroom apartment adjoining her house. Furnished with a double bed and a couple of futons, the apartment has a fully equipped kitchen and cable television. Pioneer Park is right across the street, with a trail through the park to the beach.

Halibut Hide-A-Way, 1972 Halibut Point Rd, Sitka, AK 99835; (907)747-4751. Three miles from town, toward the ferry terminal. Open year-round. Rooms $65 with tax for one or two people. Reservations advised.

You'll get a bed and a full breakfast with Margaret Gross Hope's family at Bed Inn, her duplex in the residential district, within walking distance of town. There are three bedrooms, each with a double bed. A full breakfast is included in the price.

Bed Inn, 518 Monastery St, Sitka, AK 99835; (907)747-3305. Rooms $50 single, $60 double. No alcohol, no smoking.

Bertha Karras's three-story B&B is on Sitka's waterfront overlooking the Pacific Ocean, the Mount Edgecumbe volcano, the mountains known as the Pyramids, and marine traffic. Summertime guests drink their coffee on the wide deck before a complimentary breakfast of souffles, fruit platters, pancakes, sausages, or eggs Benedict. Karras grew up in Sitka (her husband is Greek) and is an Eagle of the Killer Whale clan. She'll fill you in on Tlingit history and culture.

Karras Bed and Breakfast, 230 Kogwonton St, Sitka, AK 99835; (907)747-3978. Open year-round. Rooms $50–$85 with complimentary breakfast. Reservations advised (this is a very popular word-of-mouth spot).

Haines: *Tlingit*

More than 300 years ago, Tlingit clans from Prince of Wales Island, Kupreanof Island, and British Columbia's Stikine and Nass River valleys moved to the north end of Southeast Alaska's Inside Passage. They established villages near a bridge of land between two rushing glacial rivers, the Chilkat and the Chilkoot. It was a perfect spot for fishing and for building trade routes over the mountains to Athabascan villages in the interior.

The Haines Highway, which follows the Chilkat River from Haines to the interior, was originally a trade route. Whites nicknamed it "the grease trail" because the Tlingits used it to carry dried eulachon (a fish so rich in oil it can be used as a candle) and rendered fish oil over the mountains, where they traded with Athabascan tribes for ivory, beadwork, furs, and lichens used for dyes.

The Tlingits were also skilled navigators who had huge seagoing canoes and trade routes extending as far south as Monterey, California. When Russian and English fur-trading ships began appearing in the 1700s, the Tlingits were the middlemen in trading commodities, guns, iron tools, blankets, and other goods to the northern interior in return for pelts.

White influence came relatively late to the Haines area. In 1879, missionary S. Hall Young and naturalist John Muir chose it as the site for the Presbyterian mission.

In 1903, Fort Seward was constructed near downtown Haines. The fort buildings, including a carpenter and blacksmith shop, mule barn, carriage sheds, and Victorian officers' quarters, arrived by ship in pieces and were erected around a 6-acre parade ground.

Decommissioned after World War II, Fort Seward was purchased by several veterans. The new owners tried to make it into a profitable enterprise, creating everything from a salmon smokehouse to a furniture factory on the site. Carl Heinmiller, a non-Native, hit on a winner when he helped develop the Chilkat Dancers. This group draws on traditional Tlingit stories, dances, and songs and has been performing professionally, in Haines and internationally, for more than 30 years.

Today, the Tlingit village of Klukwan still stands about 22 miles upriver of Haines, a shadow of its former glory. The other original Native villages are gone, but descendents live in the Haines area.

Haines itself is in a strikingly beautiful location. Surrounded by glaciated mountains, it has the aquamarine Portage Cove and Lynn Canal on one side and the long estuary of the swift and shallow Chilkat River on the other. Although Haines is on the mainland and accessible by car, it's 250 miles by road from the nearest town of any size. It is far easier to fly to Haines from Juneau on a bush plane (a 45-minute jaunt) or to ride the ferry from Juneau (a 4-hour trip).

> *"Native people believed that the hole through a shell or stone was a portal for spirit power to enter and exit the 'real' world. So when traders brought Russian blue and red trade beads to Alaska, Natives willingly exchanged items of great value, such as otter pelts, for a few brightly colored beads."*
>
> *—June Simeonoff, Aleut educator*

The main part of town consists of about 4 square blocks. A walk from downtown to the cruise ship dock, a distance of about 5 blocks, passes along the Portage Cove boat basin and by the unmarked mission cemetery. Directly above the cruise ship dock is the Victorian-era Fort Seward, where the Chilkat Dancers perform in the summer. Throughout Haines and on Fort Seward's parade grounds stand totem poles, most of them recently carved.

The upper story of the town's small Sheldon Museum and Cultural Center is devoted mostly to the Tlingits of the Haines area.

Although travelers may be led to a carver's studio in a mobile home, the easiest access to authentic carvers in Haines is through Alaska Indian Arts, Inc., on the Fort Seward grounds.

Old Village Sites

Lutak Road is a scenic route that follows the blue-green Lynn Canal for a few miles north of Haines, past the ferry landing, to the mouth of the Chilkoot River, where it forks and abruptly ends. Near the bridge at the fork in the road is the site of an old camp where Natives caught eulachon and fermented and rendered them in pits. One village lined the banks of the river all the way to Chilkoot Lake, today reached by a short drive on a gravel road that ends at a large campground. On the other side of Haines, on the Chilkat River, the village of Yendestakyeh was located on a wide meadow, adjacent to what is now the Haines airport.

The Tlingit people learned to weave Chilkat blankets from the Tsimshian. The complex blanket, made with dyed goat's wool, took nearly a year to weave. Colors are always yellow and black, with blue accents. The "blue" in older blankets looks more green because the wool was boiled with copper ore and urine. The newer blankets have a more vibrant blue because the wool was boiled with the blue wool from army officers' cast-off coats.

Klukwan, called by the Tlingits "the mother village," exists on its original site (but not in its original form) on the banks of the Chilkat River, near milepost 22 on the Haines Highway. The clan houses, recorded in 1890s photographs on view at the Sheldon Museum, no longer stand, although the 18-foot-wide carved house screen, four carved house posts, 18-foot-long feast bowl, and other items belonging to Klukwan's famous Whale clan house are cloistered in the village away from public view. Other pieces, such as house screens from the Frog clan house, are held in various museums throughout North America. The one-road village, with its weathered old Victorian houses and woodland cemetery, could tell a thousand stories. Don't let Klukwan's modest surroundings mislead you, though. The village's corporation, formed after Alaska Natives received financial reimbursement for lands confiscated in the 1800s, is one of the most profitable in Southeast Alaska. Plans have been under way for several years to build a cultural center here. Until villagers decide what they want to do with the place, tourists must respect their privacy. You may drive through at a reasonable speed, but no photographs, wandering in the cemetery, or knocking on doors, please.

Chilkat Cruises

Klukwan, Inc., Klukwan village's corporation, has recently invested in two sightseeing passenger ferries that cross Lynn Canal many times daily from Haines to Skagway. One of Southeast Alaska's most colorful gold rush towns, Skagway became famous as the base camp for the quickest route into Canada's Klondike. The route into the Klondike goes over Chilkoot Pass, one of the original trails through the nearly impenetrable mountains. It was strictly controlled on both ends until gold rush times by the Tlingits, who carried liquid eulachon oil (a premium, flavored oil rendered from fermented candlefish), beaver hides, salmon, and other prepared goods inland; any other tribes who wanted to use the trail paid a toll. You can follow the 33-mile Chilkoot Trail today, but be prepared: the trail is steep, rough, and buried by heaps of snow even in July. *A Hiker's Guide to the Chilkoot Trail* is available from the Klondike Gold Rush National Historical Park, located in downtown Skagway on 2nd Ave and Broadway (PO Box 517, Skagway, AK 99840; (907)983-2921; or, in Canada, Yukon National Historic Sites, Canadian Park Service, 205–300 Main Street, Whitehorse, Yukon, Canada Y1A 2B5; (403)667-3910).

The round-trip ferry rides from Haines to Skagway are usually booked through the cruise ships as a shore excursion. Individual travelers can buy a round-trip ticket for about $30, depending on the boat. The *Fairweather* holds 250 passengers and takes an hour to cross; the *Sea Lion* catamaran holds 50 passengers and takes 35 minutes to cross. Chilkat Cruises' ferry dock is just south of the cruise ship dock.

Chilkat Cruises, 152 Haines Hwy, Box 509, Haines, AK 99827; (888)766-2103. Tours offered May–Sept, at times coinciding with cruise ship arrivals, which are posted throughout Haines.

Sheldon Museum and Cultural Center

Most of the upper floor of this small, browsable museum is dedicated to local Tlingit culture; items on display include a rare Chilkat pattern board, a partially completed Chilkat blanket, and the raw materials from which it was woven. The Chilkat Tlingits were traders, warriors, and slave traders. The museum has on display a slatted wooden armor vest worn over a moosehide shirt, an outfit that was strong enough to withstand Russian musket fire. There's also a display of coveted Chinese camphor trunks that held Russian trade goods.

The museum is named after Stephen and Elisabeth Sheldon, who moved to Haines in 1911 and whose family donated Stephen's 50-year collection of Native art and artifacts to the community under the care of the Chilkat Valley Historical Society.

Unfortunately, the museum's clan house exhibit can't do justice to the real thing—it gives the false, if unintentional, impression that the Tlingits lived in houses the size of woodsheds, with only meager possessions. A real clan house would be as large as, or larger than, the museum itself, and would be filled with carved house screens, potlatch bowls the size of canoes, carved masks, and other items. Look through the museum's rack of historic photographs, and be sure to see the 1894 John Francis Platt photograph of the interior of the astounding Whale clan house that once stood in Klukwan.

Free monographs about Chilkat blankets, Tlingit history, dances, potlatches, spruce basket making, and other topics are in a rack by the door. The museum's gift shop has a good selection of books as well as Native art from Southeast Alaska, Interior Alaska, and western Canada.

Sheldon Museum and Cultural Center, Main and Front Sts, PO Box 269, Haines, AK 99827; (907)766-2366. Just above the city boat harbor. Open summers daily 1–5pm, with extended hours mornings and evenings when cruise ships are in port; call for winter hours; weekly schedules are posted around town and on the museum door. Admission $3; children under 18, free.

Chilkat Dancers

Potlatches were outlawed in 1910 by the U.S. government, and a whole generation of Indian children were reeducated in boarding schools where they were forbidden to speak their Native language and practice Native dances or songs. Even in the early 1950s, the prevailing attitude of elders was that the old ways should be forgotten in order to spare much-loved children from punishment and ridicule. But after a white man's racially mixed group of Boy Scouts from Haines went to the National Jamboree in Valley Forge, Pennsylvania, to perform dances, wearing crude regalia they'd made after school, the Tlingit kids' grandparents jumped in. The kids were doing it wrong, and the elders couldn't stand to just watch any longer.

The elder Tlingits helped the young dancers obtain permission to use Tlingit, Tsimshian, and Athabascan family-owned dances and songs and showed them how to make authentic regalia. The newly trained and outfitted dance troupe won the dance award at the 1959 Intertribal Ceremonies in Gallup, New Mexico. From that auspicious start evolved a professional dance group, a performing arts hall, a replica of a tribal longhouse on the Fort Seward grounds, and the Alaska Indian Arts carving shed and gallery, which was set up in the fort's old hospital building.

The dance group performs with a mixed group of Native and non-Native dancers, surprising an audience that expects to see all Native dancers. "We don't discriminate on the basis of race," says director Lee Heinmiller, the founder's son and himself non-Native.

About 75 percent of the group is Native. Some of the non–Native dancers are married to Natives or have been adopted by the tribe. All of the dancers are paid performers, and many of them are children. Performances last about an hour, are narrated, and include a dance that uses authentic Chilkat blankets as part of the costuming.

Alaska Indian Arts, Inc., PO Box 271, Haines, AK 99827; (907)766-2160. Performances are held in the Chilkat Center for the Arts Number 1, on Theater Drive, or in the Raven's Fort longhouse on Fort Seward's parade ground. May–Sept; performance schedules, which change monthly, are posted at the theater and at the Haines Convention and Visitors Bureau, 2nd St; PO Box 530, Haines, AK 99827; (907)766-2234. Admission $10; children under 18, $5; children under 5, free. Tickets sold at the door. All shows, including those presold on the cruise ships, are open to the public. Dancers are available for photographs and discussions after the show.

The movie White Fang was filmed by Disney Studios in Haines. The cultural director and lead dancer of the Chilkat Dancers, Charlie Jimmie, is in the film, along with many locals.

Raven's Fort

Raven's Fort, a longhouse and totems, was built in the middle of Victorian Fort Seward's grassy parade ground in the early 1960s. It was paid for by the State of Alaska, in an effort to employ Native carvers who were out of work because of several years of bad fishing. The project was spearheaded by Carl Heinmiller, founder of the Chilkat Dancers, and was similar to the Depression-era Civilian Conservation Corps projects that put carvers to work replicating old totem poles. The longhouse (named Raven's Fort by elders) is used for commercial purposes, not tribal ceremonies. The Chilkat Dancers perform for small groups here, and the evening salmon bake is run by the Halsingland Hotel, housed in one of the old fort buildings nearby.

Raven's Fort, Fort Seward parade ground, adjacent to downtown Haines. For information, call the Halsingland Hotel, (907)766-2000.

Alaska Indian Arts, Inc.

In this workshop at Fort Seward, carvers coat a small totem pole destined for West Virginia with a fragrant mixture of beeswax and linseed oil. Located in the fort's old Victorian infirmary, the shop has a well-used look—open tackle boxes spilling odds and ends; a table strewn with carving tools, templates, and bandsaws; dried yellow flowers stuck in a tin can; and unfinished masks and silk-screened prints hanging on the wall. A realistic bear reaches out of a slab of cedar, and scattered across the floor are old olive oil cans, paintbrushes, and an oily chainsaw, all covered with wood dust and fragrant cedar shavings.

The workshop is open to any Natives who want to learn to carve. In years past, the workshop and the Chilkat Dancers provided the only employment for Natives in the Haines area. Alaska Indian Arts buys some pieces for the art gallery adjoining the workshop (there's great stuff in this gallery, including carved ivory from the Bering Sea region) and acts as a broker between carvers and customers commissioning projects.

Alaska Indian Arts workshop and gallery; (907)766-2160. At Fort Seward, in the old hospital building, next to the Chilkat Center for the Arts. Open year-round, 9am–5pm daily. Free.

Raven's Nest

Michelle Martin, a Tlingit whose ancestors are from the village of Klukwan, was born and raised in the house behind her Main Street shop in Haines. She's of the Raven clan, hence the shop's name. Her wooden sign outside was designed and carved by two of Haines's most well known totem carvers, Clifford Thomas and John Hagen. Inside, she sells artworks and crafts handmade by Southeast Alaska and Athabascan Natives, many longtime friends and acquaintances. There are button blankets and beaded leatherwork by Joyce Thomas, carvings (masks and totem staffs) by Greg Horner and John Svenson, carved silver bracelets and necklaces, moosehide moccasins and boots, and lathe-turned birch bowls.

Raven's Nest, 318 Main St, Haines, AK 99827; (907)766-2808. Open mid-May–late Sept; hours vary with cruise ship schedules; sometimes open until midnight during the summer. Call first.

Aatcha's Shop

June Simeonoff, an Aleut artist and educator who grew up in Old Harbor on Kodiak Island, teaches Aleut basketry, beading, skin sewing, and porcupine quill embroidery in Aatcha's Shop, her small gallery and supply store in Haines. Simeonoff makes beaded elk, deer, and moosehide clothing, and her store also carries Inupiat snow goggles and hunting visors, hand-cut ivory beads, ivory and baleen bracelets and boxes, trade beads, dentalia shells, ermine skins, and mammoth and walrus fossilized bones and carvings. She is a very well known (by collectors) weaver of museum-quality Aleut baskets, and her shop sells small baskets made of very fine, split grasses. Look for her basketry at the Sheldon Museum in Haines, the Alutiiq Museum in Kodiak, and the University of Alaska

Museum's gift shop in Fairbanks. Simeonoff's husband, Charlie Pardue, an Athabascan, makes beaded moosehide gun cases and ivory knife handles.

Aatcha's Shop, 138 2nd Ave S, PO Box 1311, Haines, AK 99827; (907)766-3208. Open long hours in summer, coinciding with cruise ship schedule, and also by appointment; call for winter hours. Mail orders are welcome. Visa and MasterCard accepted. Classes are open to all.

Chilkat Bald Eagle Preserve

The eagle is a major Tlingit totemic symbol (the other is the raven). Each winter, about 3,500 bald eagles journey to the Chilkat River to feed on salmon. The best time to see them is from the end of October through March. Stop along the Haines Highway, especially between mileposts 18 and 22, and park in the turnouts to watch the eagles fight over and gorge on spawned-out fish. Binoculars are useful, and photographers should bring a telephoto lens. Birds perch by the dozens in the cottonwoods along the riverbanks. Look for nests— piles of good-size sticks, 8 feet wide and up to 7 feet deep—wrapped around the tops of hemlock and spruce snags. For a closer look at these big birds, visit the Alaska Raptor Rehabilitation Center in Haines, (907)747-8662.

For more information, call the Haines Convention and Visitors Bureau, 2nd St, PO Box 530, Haines, AK 99827; (907)766-2234.

Yakutat: *Tlingit*

The Yakutat Tlingits live on the shore of a spectacular fjord, protected from the Pacific Ocean by just one narrow cape. Immense, stunning glaciers and more than 200 miles of white sandy beaches surround the small fishing village of Yakutat. It lies near Hubbard Glacier, which in the last century advanced across Russell Fjord, finally galloping so quickly it created an ice dam that trapped whales and seals in a huge saltwater lake (an event some termed "the geologic event of the century"). To the west of Yakutat, the Malaspina Glacier—the size of the state of Rhode Island—flows from the St. Elias Mountains, the highest coastal range in the world (peaks average about 13,000 feet; the glaciers at the other side of the mountain range flow into Glacier Bay). Yakutat is situated at the northernmost end of the Tongass National Forest, a unique preserve of old-growth Sitka spruce forest that covers most of Southeast Alaska. The area is a recreational paradise, with hiking trails, wildlife (black and brown bears, mountain sheep, trumpeter swans), downhill and cross-country skiing (via air taxi), and some of the world's most outstanding surfing (demanding the protection of insulated dry suits, of course). Five clans of Yakutat Tlingits participate in the Mount St. Elias Dance group, and many are shareholders in Yak-Tat Kwaan, Inc., the village corporation. Alaska Airlines makes several flights a day into Yakutat from Juneau. Car rentals are at the airport.

Tsalxaan (Fairweather) Charters

Bertrand Adams, Jr., grew up fishing, long-lining for king salmon in the bays around Yakutat. He's a Raven, a member of the Tluknaxadi clan (the people who lived in the village below Mount Fairweather, 40 miles south of Yakutat). He offers a 4-hour sightseeing tour of the Hubbard Glacier and bays of Yakutat (watching for humpback, beluga, and killer whales, sea otters, and seals along the way) and fishing trips for salmon, halibut, bottomfish, and red snapper along the Yakutat coastline. He visits a number of small coves, island-filled bays, and fjords, all surrounded by Tongass National Forest, Russell Fjord Wilderness, and Malaspina Glacier. His boat is a 27-foot cabin cruiser equipped with galley and head. Snacks and soft drinks are served on board.

Tsalxaan (Fairweather) Charters, PO Box 201, Yakutat, AK 99689; (907)784-3994. Tours offered Apr–Oct. Prices vary.

Yakutat Lodging

At Hanson's Bed and Biscuits, (907)784-3410, Jim and Dixie Hanson have five private rooms and four shared bathrooms in a residential area within walking distance of the waterfront. There's a microwave and a refrigerator in each room, and a grill outside. You'll get a continental breakfast (but no biscuits), too. Open year-round; summer and winter rates; all rooms under $100. Brandon Powell's Mooring Lodge, (907)784-3300, has six fully furnished apartments for rent by the day, week, or month.

Raven's Table

Sam Demmert's Raven's Table is a smokery down by Yakutat's boat basin. Demmert specializes in smoked sockeye salmon and black cod (plain or Cajun style), and fresh frozen, vacuum-packed halibut, salmon, and cod. Customized packing for sport fishermen includes fast freezing, vacuum packing, and storage.

Raven's Table, Yakutat, (907)784-3497. There's no address on the building, but it's on the road to the boat basin. Look for a big beige building; you can't miss it. Open summers, while the fish are biting, 9am–9pm daily.

SOUTHWEST
ALASKA

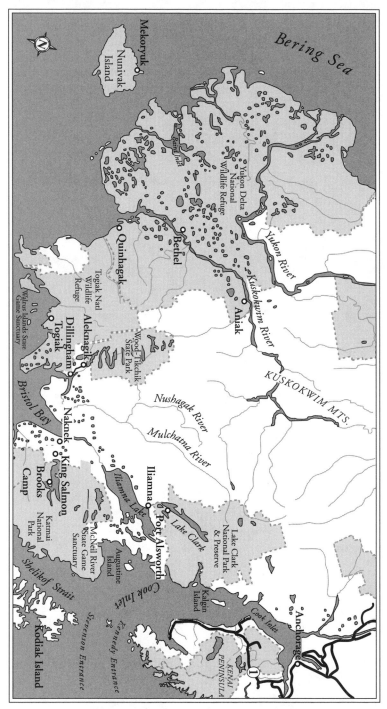

SOUTHWEST ALASKA

The southwest section of Alaska is a vast, nearly treeless land of tundra-covered peninsulas, river deltas, active volcanoes, huge lakes, and islands that extend west into the Bering Sea. The region includes the Yukon and Kuskokwim River Delta, Bristol Bay, the Alaska Peninsula, the Aleutian Islands, the Pribilof Islands, and the Kodiak archipelago. It is home to the Yup'ik Eskimo, Aleut, Alutiiq, and Athabascan people, all of whom established themselves here thousands of years ago, building their lives and cultures around the region's vast resources.

It's no exaggeration to say that most of the land is treeless, but it's by no means barren or desolate. The spongy tundra is a lush tapestry of miniature plants, blanketing the ground in dramatic juxtaposition to the chain of active volcanoes along the Alaska Peninsula.

In the north, two of Alaska's largest rivers, the Yukon and the Kuskokwim, flow from the interior, carrying downed trees into the tundra regions. In earlier times, people living on the river deltas and coastlines used this river driftwood to frame sod houses for shelter against the winds and to build the framework for kayaks and umiaks, once the predominant means of travel in the region.

The world's richest fishing grounds are here, in the waters surrounding the Kodiak archipelago and the

Aleutian Chain, in Bristol Bay and Nushagak Bay, and in the Kuskokwim and Yukon Rivers and hundreds of tributaries. The region teems with salmon that come here to spawn, swimming up the meandering rivers through huge lake systems inland. Caribou and salmon were the primary source of protein for people living along the rivers and lakes. Salmon were also a primary source of food for the marine mammals that coastal Natives hunted for sustenance and warmth—primarily seals, sea lions, and walrus, which pup by the thousands on Bering Sea islands such as the Pribilofs, 300 miles offshore.

All four of the Native cultures that live in Southwest Alaska, as well as the more recent immigrants, are here because of the fish. The region's abundant sea otters and fur seals brought Russian fur traders in the 1700s; the salmon brought American canneries in the 1800s, along with Norwegian, Swedish, Italian, and Irish immigrants who worked in them, and eventually Chinese and Filipino laborers, all of whom affected Native history and culture.

Almost all the Native people in Southwest Alaska today still depend on fishing and hunting for their survival. The Yup'ik Eskimos, who live in villages along the coast and rivers from north of the Yukon River to the Nushagak River, are the most culturally intact Native group in Alaska, probably because their villages, particularly those in the Yukon and Kuskokwim Delta, were mostly untouched by the earliest fur and fish trade. Yup'ik Eskimos today—young and old—still speak Yup'ik dialects, with English as their second language.

The larger towns—Bethel, Dillingham, King Salmon, Unalaska, and Kodiak—are service centers for the smaller villages and have supermarkets, video stores, and gas stations—standard Americana. You'll hear Yup'ik spoken here, but even in the most isolated villages, Native people no longer live in sod houses, wear parkas made of animal or bird skins, or hunt sea mammals from kayaks.

It is possible, however, to see exhibits of traditional culture in the superb Alutiiq Museum in Kodiak, the Samuel K. Fox Museum in Dillingham, and the Yupiit Piciryarait Cultural Center in Bethel. You can take a floatplane to Brooks Camp in Katmai National Park and Preserve to stand on one of the largest unexcavated village sites in the region and learn about the villagers who fled the 1912 eruption of the Novarupta volcano in their kayaks. In Unalaska and Kodiak Island, you can learn about the occupation of the Aleutian Chain and the Kodiak archipelago by agents of the ruthless Russian-American Company and the subsequent slaughter of sea otters in the late 1700s. On the Pribilof Islands, you can learn about the Aleut Natives' role in the seal hunts and about the incarceration of Aleuts during World War II.

Wildlife watching is simply astounding here: thousands of seabirds nesting in huge cliffside rookeries; whales breaching as they feed; seals, sea otters, and walrus hauling out on the islands; and white beluga whales feeding at the mouths of rivers. On land brown bears fish for salmon along the streams, lone moose browse in tall grasses, and huge herds of caribou migrate across the tundra. The region has long been a favorite of fishermen and hunters seeking trophy game, and many Natives have worked for years as guides. They offer overnight lodging and guided fishing and hunting from tented camps, cabins, and lodges in the wilderness, and charters into the open sea—and most are equipped to provide these services for photographers and wildlife watchers as well.

Among the cultural tours offered by Natives is an excursion to meet ivory carvers and basket weavers at their homes on isolated Nunivak Island; and a tour of the town of Unalaska, in the Aleutian Islands, led by a woman of Aleut descent. You can stay overnight in a fish camp at Egegik on the Alaska Peninsula, or spend up to a week assisting with an archaeological excavation of a Russian trading post and 15th-century sod house on Afognak Island in the Kodiak archipelago.

Local art, much of which is produced in remote, outlying villages, is harder to find here than in other regions, with no roads to villages and few centralized sales galleries; generally, the best sources for local art are museum gift shops. Because villagers often fly to Anchorage on business or for health care, and bring their art with them, you can often find their work in Anchorage galleries such as the Alaska Native Medical Center Craft Shop. Look for coiled-grass baskets inlaid with strips of dyed seal gut, ivory and wood carvings, birchbark baskets, masks, skin sewing, miniature kayaks, and kayak paddles.

Planning Your Trip

Southwest Alaska is a vast and diverse region, so before planning your trip, familiarize yourself with the geography using the most detailed map you can find. Read about what the Native cultures were like prior to white contact, and include in your plans a stay with a Native family. This could mean taking a beluga whale-watching trip with a Native tour guide, staying with a family at their fish camp during salmon-harvesting season, or river kayaking with a Native guide to see wildlife and old village sites.

When you visit Southwest Alaska, keep in mind that in spite of what looks like modernity, this is still the bush (if not the last frontier). Your accommodations and services may not be what you expected for the price, but with good reason. All building materials, from each board to the kitchen sink, must be barged a very long way over rough seas from Seattle, or flown in on cargo jet, then barged miles upriver to a village. All the supplies needed for daily living—such as food, laundry soap, gasoline, and toilet paper—get here the same way. And it wasn't so long ago that villages received their electric power from a source no larger than a household generator.

It's function over fashion here, and most people put more money into planes, skiffs, reliable engines, nets, and fish freezers than into superficial items like house paint and new couches. Commercial and subsistence fish harvesting comes first—it pays the bills, funds college tuition for the kids, and puts food on the table. People of all ages work hard, and there's little leisure time during the summer, when the fish are running. The very best way to understand this region is to be with Native people while they work. The summer fishing season is a riveting time in Southwest Alaska: when you visit a fish camp, you'll witness the single-mindedness of fishermen when the salmon return to the streams to spawn. This is not only subsistence fishing to fill the freezer but also the region's biggest cash crop.

How to Pack

Be prepared. Southwest Alaska's summer weather can change abruptly from surprising heat to driving rain or dense fog—leaving you stranded in some very remote locations for hours or several days. Even if you are planning to skip the wilderness experience and stay in town, take a sleeping bag and pad. You may find yourself stuck at the airport—with all the hotel rooms in town full. It's easier to ask for help if you've got your own bedding ready to roll out on a borrowed square of turf. Daytime summer temperatures range from 40 to 85 degrees Fahrenheit.

Most larger villages in the Southwest region have an outfitting section in the local grocery store, where you can buy anything you may have forgotten. Grocery stores in regional hubs such as Dillingham are as well stocked as most urban megamarkets, with impressive selections of canned and dried foods, fresh meat and produce, sporting goods, fishing gear, hardware, pharmacy, and clothing sections. Plan for sticker shock on some items, though: an 8-ounce bottle of shampoo can run $8. Grocers stock bottled water and, in larger towns, offer espresso and deli snacks. Most accommodations, even in the most remote fish camps, provide washing machines and dryers (or at least a clothesline) for guest use.

Getting Around

Although Southwest Alaska covers a huge geographical area, reaching the various communities is no different from reaching any other American town. Regular jet service from Anchorage makes it easy. The bigger passenger planes and jets fly from Anchorage to central locations; from there, bush planes carry you to smaller villages.

Travel between villages is also straightforward and reliable—with one big difference. There are almost no roads between major towns and villages, so all travel *within* Southwest Alaska is by small plane. Jumping in and out of airplanes that fly from village to village is as common as jumping in and out of taxicabs in New York City. In fact, bush planes are called "air taxis." Equipped to land on the beach, water, tundra, and snow, the planes are dispatched in much the same way as a cab; one may land next to your door. Distances between villages are measured in "as the air taxi flies" miles, and the small planes cruise at over 100 mph. (It's a good thing they do—distances between villages can be 200 miles or more.)

Within Southwest Alaska, almost all of the smaller, more outlying villages can be reached by daily scheduled commercial flights on air taxis. Rates are typically $30 to $60 one way. In addition to regularly scheduled flights, a number of air-taxi services sell "seat fares" as an alternative to more costly charter service; these allow an air-taxi company to group a set of passengers on a single plane. Seat fares are fixed-price one-way or round-trip charges, and are usually available to destinations that small numbers of people want to reach on a recurring basis. For example, Lake Clark Air flies three to four times daily during the summer from Anchorage to the Lake Clark and Lake Iliamna area on a seat-fare basis ($275 round trip).

Chartered flights will take you anywhere else you want to go—100 miles up a wilderness river, inside the rim of a volcano, onto the surface of a frozen lake, or to an isolated beach. Air charter fees range from $175 to $450 an hour, depending on the size of the plane. A three-person plane usually costs $200 an hour. The expense of chartering can be reduced if you spread the cost among several people.

The only place with enough roads to make a car rental worthwhile is Dillingham. If you're going anywhere else, make arrangements in advance to be picked up at the gravel airstrip, arrange for a taxi, or hitch a ride. There are plenty of vehicles out there—even in remote villages with only several miles of road, people drive cars, trucks, and the popular four-wheel all-terrain vehicles. In winter, most travel is by snow machine (dog teams are too expensive for most people to maintain).

Most boat travel in the region is by chartered inboard craft with a licensed captain; by skiff; or by raft, kayak, or canoe. Boat rentals (usually skiffs with outboard motors) average about $150 a day; they are readily available along the rivers. Kayakers can bring their own foldable-style boats from Anchorage, but not conventional hard-shell crafts. (Floatplanes can no longer legally tie hard-shell kayaks to the pontoons when carrying passengers.) You can rent kayaks in Kodiak, Dillingham, and King Salmon, and canoes at Brooks Camp.

Visitor Services

Visitors to Southwest Alaska need to be flexible, as travel is often delayed by weather or tides. In Dillingham, for example, boats rest on the mud bottom of the harbor at low tide, waiting for the tide to roll in; until it does, no one goes anywhere. Each year, however, hundreds of independent travelers and guides with clients explore the area's spectacular lakes, rivers, and ocean shorelines.

Because of the extra challenges of getting around and hauling gear, most visitor services in Southwest Alaska are designed for hunters and sport fishermen, who hire private planes to fly them into remote but luxurious wilderness lodges, or to more basic tented fish camps along rivers and lakes. A typical luxury lodge provides a private room with bath and bar, along with three gourmet meals a day, cooked by a staff chef. A fleet of floatplanes are tied up on the beach in front, waiting to fly guests to even more remote fishing and hunting locations. Minimum stay is one week, and the average cost is $3,000 to $6,000 a week. Rafters, hikers, and bear viewers often book directly with outfitters, who put together trips, assemble and haul camping gear, and provide a guide and support team for the chosen adventure.

Native villages, with an average population of 250, are scattered throughout Southwest Alaska—nestled into fjords in the Kodiak archipelago, built at the mouths of salmon-spawning rivers on the Bering

Sea, perched above lakeshores and strung along riverbanks, miles apart from one another. Although Southwest Alaska Natives have hosted and humored anthropologists, archaeologists, missionaries, and schoolteachers for more than a century, only recently have they opened their doors to ordinary travelers who want to learn firsthand about the heritage and contemporary lives of Native people.

Most guest services provided by Natives are midway between the two extremes of luxury lodge and rugged backcountry trip. They are closer to towns and less expensive than, say, a week of fishing for trophy rainbow trout. (Still, any vacation in Southwest Alaska is going to be more costly than in most other places in the United States—this area is *remote!*) Several Native regional and village corporations are investing in luxury hotels and lodges, and individuals own bed and breakfasts and wilderness camps. In recent years, Native tourism has begun to include ecological and cultural tourism along with superb fishing and hunting trips.

For a brochure about the region, contact Southwest Alaska Tourism, 3300 Arctic Blvd, Suite 203, Anchorage, AK 99503; (907)562-7380.

YUKON AND KUSKOKWIM RIVER DELTA REGION

The Yup'ik Eskimos were one of the last peoples living in North America to come into daily contact with Europeans, largely because their homeland, the Yukon and Kuskokwim Delta, had few resources that could be easily extracted. Outsiders were far more interested in the fur seals of the Pribilof Islands, the sea otters of the Kodiak archipelago, the gold washed onto the beaches of Nome, and the old-growth forests of Southeast Alaska than they were in the flat, virtually treeless, marshy tundra of this delta region, which stretches for hundreds of square miles, swept by high winds, rain, and sleet, or blizzards.

Yup'ik families have inhabited the delta for at least 2,000 years, sustained by the abundant supplies of wildlife, tundra greens, and berries. They used driftwood borne along by the rivers—downed trees carried from the interior to the delta—for fuel, frameworks for boats and sod houses, and materials for carving elaborate masks used in dances and ceremonies. Travel was by skin-boat kayaks and umiaks.

In the 1880s, more than 12,000 Eskimos lived in the vast delta. The Moravian Church missionaries tried to change the Yup'ik culture, a practice that was encouraged by federal government policy (which sought to assimilate Native people into Western culture) and abetted by the measles and flu epidemics brought by Nome gold prospectors. Although the Moravians succeeded in changing Yup'ik spiritual practices and westernizing their clothing, house styles, and even haircuts, the Yup'ik people have persevered. They continue to speak their Native language, and many live primarily by subsistence hunting, fishing, and gathering.

Yup'ik communities are private. Going to a village without an invitation from an individual or family is tantamount to entering a private home without knocking. The region has received greater than usual attention recently, due in part to a national exhibition tour of Yup'ik ceremonial masks (similar to the mask pictured on the cover of this book). The tour generated an overwhelming public response, throwing the spotlight on the region's communities. At the same time, foreign fishing interests and sport fishermen have put increasing demands on the salmon runs that Yup'ik people depend on for subsistence (this in addition to state regulations that limit Native fishing and hunting). Such pressures have made many Yup'ik even less happy than before about outsiders coming uninvited into their private communities.

You are welcome, however, to visit the three-room Yupiit Piciryarait Cultural Center in Bethel, the region's largest town, to see changing exhibits; and to travel up the Kuskokwim River to visit the Interior Rivers Arts & Crafts Cooperative in Aniak. Both the museum gift shop and the cooperative can tell you about Yup'ik and Athabascan artists in the area, and may be able to direct you to Native-owned cultural or natural history tours that have opened since this book went to press. Several tours already are offered outside of Bethel: on Nunivak Island, 155 miles west of Bethel and the mainland, and from the Yup'ik village of Quinhagak on the Kanektok River, about 80 miles south of Bethel. Both tours are described below.

To get the most out of your trip, try to learn about the Yup'ik subsistence lifestyle before visiting the region. The book *Always Getting Ready (Upterrlainarluta): Yup'ik Eskimo Subsistence in Southwest Alaska*, by James H. Barker (University of Washington Press, 1993), is photojournalism at its best, with striking black-and-white photographs of Yup'ik Eskimo families gathering edible plants; hunting geese; setting nets for salmon; cutting and drying salmon at a fish camp; bringing in firewood by dogsled; collecting eggs; and hunting and butchering seals, walrus, and beluga whales. Most of the photographs were taken in villages and fish camps in the Yukon and Kuskokwim River Delta, and all were taken with the permission of the Natives. The title of the book comes from elder Agnes Kelly Bostrom, who is quoted as saying, "All through the year we are getting ready; getting ready for fishing, for berry picking, for potlatches, getting ready for winter. We are always getting ready to go somewhere to get foods. And because we are so religious, you know, we are always getting ready for the next life."

Getting There

Alaska Airlines, (800)426-0333, offers regularly scheduled service to Bethel on Era Aviation commuter service from Anchorage. Air-taxi service to 48 villages in the region is available through Kusko Aviation, (907)543-3279; Yute Air, (907)543-3003; and others.

Bethel: *Yup'ik*

The town of Bethel, at the mouth of the Kuskokwim River, 40 miles inland from the Bering Sea, was first established by Yup'ik Eskimos. They called it Mamterillermiut, which, loosely translated, means "the people with many fish caches." Salmon have been caught and smoked over cottonwood and alder fires here for more than 2,000 years.

Bethel, The First 100 Years: Photographs and History of a Western Alaska Town, *by journalist Mary Lenz (City of Bethel Centennial History Project, 1985), is a superb book that's chock-full of historic photographs, a well-written narrative, and interviews with Yup'ik elders and family members. Available from the Yup'ik Museum and Gift Shop in Bethel, (907)543-1819.*

In the 1830s, Russian explorers reached the Kuskokwim Delta the hard way—starting from Bristol Bay, paddling up the Nushagak River, then tramping across the tundra to the Hoholitna River and following it to the Kuskokwim River. By 1880, the Alaska Commercial Company, always looking for advantageous places to trade goods for furs, had established a store at Mamterillermint. It was one of three trading posts on the Kuskokwim River; another was located about 200 miles upriver at Fort Kolmakovsky, first established in 1841 by the Russian-American Company, to trade with both Eskimos living on the lower river and Athabascans living upriver. In 1885 the Moravian Church built a mission across the river from Mamterillermiut. The villagers eventually packed up and moved next to the mission, which was built on the river's eroding sandy banks. Converted Yup'ik and

Moravian founders of the new town named it Bethel after a Biblical town mentioned in Exodus. The eroding river continues to plague Bethel.

Today, Bethel is the largest town in Southwest Alaska, and it is a commercial and governmental center for the 56 Yup'ik villages located in the Yukon and Kuskokwim River Delta. Although Bethel has a busy airport served by two passenger airlines daily, as well as a port and air-taxi services, most local travel is on the rivers. In the summer, residents travel by boat; in the winter, by snow machine, truck, and dogsled over the 48-mile ice-covered river, which is maintained by the city.

For additional information on the Bethel region, contact the Bethel Chamber of Commerce, PO Box 329, Bethel, AK 99559; (907)543-2911. Located downtown, 3 miles from the airport, on 4th Avenue.

Yup'ik Museum and Gift Shop

Formerly housed in a log cabin, the Yup'ik Museum and Gift Shop is now inside the Yupiit Piciryarait Cultural Center, a modern building that includes the public library, meeting rooms, and a gift shop. The three-room museum's prize is a wood-frame boat covered with caribou skin, about 6 feet wide and 15 feet long, lashed together with sinew. Exhibits change frequently: one month there may be beadwork, clothing, and historic pictures of the region; another month there may be a kayak exhibit on loan from Anchorage. Because the Yup'ik people discourage archaeology, particularly any disturbance of grave sites, there are few old artifacts on display in this museum. A handful of Yup'ik masks are in the collection, however. Most masks made before the turn of the century were burned at the conclusion of a ceremony; those that survived were salvaged by collectors and sent to museums outside the region. The work of contemporary Yup'ik mask makers is available in the small gift shop, along with beadwork, ivory carvings, and other items made in surrounding villages.

Yupiit Piciryarait Cultural Center, AVCP Inc., 420 Chief Eddie Hoffman (State) Highway, PO Box 219, Bethel, AK 99559; (907)543-1819 or (907)520-5312. Open Tues–Sat afternoons. Admission by donation except for special exhibits.

Cama-i Dance Festival and Other Events

Dancers from all over Alaska come to Bethel each March to share traditional and not-so-traditional dances at the Cama-i Dance Festival. In May the city sponsors guided bird watching; in November there are craft sales; December brings the fur festival; and the NAPA Sled Dog Race and K300 Sled Dog Race take place in January.

Aniak: *Yup'ik*

Trees begin to appear about 100 miles up the Kuskokwim River—beautiful white birch interwoven with cottonwood and evergreens. The village of Aniak, in the thick of the trees, is on the south bank, 200 miles upstream (about 90 air-miles). The largest town between Bethel and Nome, Aniak is a service center for upstream villages. It was homesteaded, and a general store built, on an abandoned Yup'ik village in 1914. The Native community was reestablished in the 1920s when Willie Pete and Sam Simeon, two Yup'ik Eskimos, brought their families to settle in the town. A school opened in 1936. Today the population of nearly 600 people is mostly Eskimo, with a few Athabascan families.

Molly Hootch Hymes, a resident of the Yup'ik village of Emmonak, was the first name on the list of plaintiffs suing the state to provide high school education in the villages instead of removing students to boarding schools. The lawsuit resulted in the Molly Hootch Act and a state-supported high school in every village.

Interior Rivers Arts & Crafts Cooperative

The visitors center in Aniak is home to Interior Rivers Arts & Crafts Cooperative, which sells art and crafts representing 100 members from 14 villages along the upper Kuskokwim, in the mid–Yukon River area. The building, with its attached greenhouse and deck, is surrounded by a garden filled with wildflowers (if the snow machines haven't wiped them out in the winter). It's a nice place to linger over a cup of coffee. Artist Gwenn Pineda, Interior Rivers' coordinator, lives in the visitors center. If you'd like to visit Aniak, she'll arrange lodging in one of the three B&Bs, show you the artworks, and help you find your way around the village.

The art includes large masks; grass and birchbark baskets and bound boxes; hand-carved wooden bowls; wildlife paintings by Edward Hofseth; hand-beaded necklaces, barrettes, and hair ties; holiday wreaths handcrafted from wilderness plants; ivory carvings; miniature (6- to 8-inch-long) Iditarod sleds made of wood; beaded moosehide gloves trimmed with fur; hand-painted wood; and baby slippers lined with soft rabbit fur.

Those who can't make it to Aniak should look for the Interior Rivers Arts & Crafts Cooperative at the Alaska Federation of Natives' annual October meeting, and the Fur Rondy (both in Anchorage), and at Bethel's main events throughout the year. You can also call Pineda and ask her where she's scheduled to show artwork. A catalogue is in the works.

Interior Rivers Arts & Crafts Cooperative, PO Box 207, Aniak, AK 99557; (907)675-4523. Open year-round. Call for hours.

Nunivak Island: *Cup'ik*

A volcanic island located in the Bering Sea, Nunivak lies 155 miles west of Bethel and about 30 miles off the Alaska coastline northwest of the mouth of the Kuskokwim River. The highest peak on this treeless, tundra-covered island is Roberts Mountain, about 1,675 feet. Nunivak is part of the Yukon Delta National Wildlife Refuge; its rocky sea cliffs are a haven for seabirds and sea mammals, and the island is home to white and red fox, mink, a herd of reindeer, and about 500 musk oxen.

Nunivak Island has been inhabited for at least 2,000 years by the Cup'ik ("choo-pick") Eskimos, also known as the Nuniwarmiut. Russians reported in 1821 that more than 400 people were living in 16 villages on the island; according to a local elder in his 100th year, there were more than 700 Natives, living along the banks of almost all the island's rivers, when he was a boy. A tuberculosis epidemic in the early 1900s reduced the island's population considerably. Reindeer were introduced in 1920 by a trader; the village council manages the herd today for commercial meat production by the Bering Sea Reindeer Products Company. Musk oxen, a prehistoric species, were brought to the island from Greenland in 1934, in order to save the animals from extinction. (There are no predators of musk oxen on the island.) Local women knit or weave their own products from the oxen's underwool.

Many sites on Nunivak Island were named by Cup'ik ancestors. Maps of the island written in Cup'ik and recording these names are available in Mekoryuk for about $12.

Today about 200 Cup'ik Eskimos inhabit Nunivak, most practicing a subsistence lifestyle by fishing, seal hunting, and managing the reindeer and musk ox herds. The 45-by-75-mile-long island boasts crab and halibut fishing offshore, abundant seals, and freshwater rivers filled with fish. Whales and walrus migrate past the island each spring and fall. The only village on Nunivak Island, Mekoryuk, owns a bed and breakfast that houses six guests at a time. Several cabins are also available; one is equipped with a microwave, refrigerator, and hot plate. Visitors are also welcome to camp near town or stay in rooms for rent in private homes. There are daily flights to Nunivak from Bethel. Travel on the island is by boat in the summer and by snow machine over land and over the Bering Sea ice (around the island) during the winter.

For more information about visiting Nunivak, contact Mekoryuk City Hall, PO Box 29, Mekoryuk, AK 99630; (907)827-8314.

Nunivak Island Experiences

Abe David, a Cup'ik Eskimo, licensed commercial airplane pilot, and lifelong resident of Nunivak, offers guided tours of Mekoryuk and the island throughout the year. Tours are customized to the visitors' interests and times of arrival. In Mekoryuk, David provides a tour of the village, with introductions to local ivory and whalebone carvers, basket weavers, and spirit-mask makers; a visit to a fish camp on the Mekoryuk River; and a trip out to nearby cliffside rookeries to look for puffins and other seabirds. Those with more time can join David and his family (wife Mona and their three children) at their fish camp on the island's southern end. You travel to the camp by skiff through barrier islands on the east coast of Nunivak Island; once there, you can enjoy camping, hiking, and beachcombing on long, sandy beaches, or fishing for halibut and salmon from David's skiff. Because Eskimo families are involved in subsistence hunting most of the year, activities depend on the season: ice fishing for grayling in winter, catching king crab in March and April, watching walrus migrate north on floating ice in April and May (David will take visitors out in his skiff to photograph them), butchering reindeer in early and late summer. Options also include winter camping, and photography by snowmobile. David is licensed to transport people around the island, and hunters as well as kayakers use his services.

Nunivak Island Experiences, PO Box 82, Mekoryuk, AK 99630; (907)827-8512. Tours offered year-round. Fully licensed and insured. Call for a brochure.

Amos Services

Howard T. Amos, a lifelong native of Nunivak Island, offers year-round tours of Nunivak Island. Photo safaris of musk oxen, and of Pacific walrus on the ice-pan, take place January through April via snowmobile on the southern and western coasts of the island. From March through May observe traditional seal hunting on the sea ice and hunt musk oxen with a guide (the state issues permits to control the musk ox population). From May through August, go by boat to visit the seabird rookeries on the western side of Nunivak, visit summer subsistence fish camps, and walk the beaches on the south end. There's year-round fishing for halibut, silver salmon, and Dolly Varden; ice fishing for saffron cod and arctic grayling; and always time for visiting with Native artists.

Amos Services, PO Box 47, Mekoryuk, AK 99630; (907)827-8621. Tours offered year-round. Call for rates, lodging, and travel arrangements.

Quinhagak: *Yup'ik*

The Yup'ik name for the village of Quinhagak is Kuinerraq, meaning "new river channel." The village site has been dated to 1,000 A.D. and was one of the first villages along this part of Alaska's coastline to have much contact with whites. The village is located about 80 air-miles south of Bethel. In 1867 the Alaska Commercial Company used the natural harbor as a supply dock for goods bound for Kuskokwim River trading posts. The Moravians built a mission here in 1893, and in the next few years added a store, post office, and school. Reindeer were introduced in the early 1900s to encourage the nomadic Yup'ik Eskimos to become herders and remain in villages where children would go to schools run by the missions. Today, most of the 600 villagers live by subsistence hunting and fishing and by commercial fishing for salmon, pollock, and herring roe. Goods are delivered here by air cargo, with large barges bringing supplies several times a year.

Kanektok River Safaris

The Kuinerrarmuit (people from Quinhagak) offer two opportunities for you to spend time with them and enjoy two of their rivers in the wilderness, the Arolik and the Kanektok. To experience the aesthetic qualities of these pristine, slow-moving rivers, plan to spend five to seven days floating downstream—about the time it takes to really shrug off the cares of the outside world and begin to see the river from the perspective of the people who know it intimately.

The Arolik River float begins 35 miles upstream in the narrows of the Arolik Gap. Rafters and gear are taken upriver by tribal members driving 18-foot jet boats, then dropped off with raft, camping gear, and food for the five- to seven-day float downstream. Fly-fishing for trophy rainbow trout is usually the main activity of visitors taking this float trip. There's no white water, and the shallows of the river make for great wading and fly-fishing. En route upstream, guides point out great fishing holes and camping spots while sharing with you, at their discretion, some of the local lore of the area. You can float downstream on your own or ask for a Yup'ik Eskimo guide to accompany you.

The braided Kanektok River tumbles from Kagati and Pagati Lakes, in the Ahklun Mountains of the Togiak National Wildlife Refuge, and meanders west through the tundra into the Bering Sea. Near its mouth is Quinhagak, with a small dock and boat harbor that face the wide mudflats of Kuskokwim Bay. The village is about 45 minutes south of Bethel by air taxi.

Those who want a more pampered but equally promising fishing opportunity can stay overnight in camp on the Kanektok River and fly-fish for trophy rainbow trout, sea-run char, arctic grayling, and five species of Pacific salmon from 5am into the midnight twilight during the long summer daylight hours. The Kanektok River camp, with floored Weatherport tents for sleeping and dining, traditional steam bath/sauna/shower, and 18-foot Suzuki outboards, is 3½ miles upstream from the river's mouth, in the heart of the best fishing on the river. One guide and skiff are assigned for every two guests. Camp cooks feed you three meals a day with fresh produce and meat flown into camp from Bethel and Anchorage.

You fly in the same way the food arrives: Alaska Airlines, (800)426-0333, to Bethel (they can book you through to Quinhagak on Era Aviation). Or you can make the journey from Bethel to Quinhagak on Kusko Aviation, (907)543-3279, or Yute Air, (907)543-3003.

Kanektok River Safaris, PO Box 9, Quinhagak, AK 99655; (907)556-8211; fax (907)556-8814. Kanektok River Safaris is a subsidiary of Qanirtuuq, Inc., the local village corporation. Cost varies according to proposed trip and length of stay. For best pre-season rates, book by May 1. Season is June 15–Sept 5. Rainbow and char fishing are available throughout the pre- and post-salmon season, with the best rainbow and char fishing in July. Maximum number of guests is 12 per week in camp.

BRISTOL BAY REGION

"It was fish that brought us here," says Karen Roberts, a Bristol Bay resident of Yup'ik and Norwegian descent. The nutrient-rich, icy rivers that feed Bristol Bay make this region one of the most prolific salmon fishing grounds in the world. Small wonder that it drew Eskimo, Athabascan, Aleut, and Alutiiq people to settle at the mouths of spawning rivers and around the lakes. They competed for the resource with very bloody battles that pitted Eskimo against Athabascan extended families in the equivalent of European border disputes.

The north end of Bristol Bay is defined by snowcapped mountains. The south end of Bristol Bay washes the shores of the volcanic Alaska Peninsula, which extends into the Aleutian Chain. Between the two mountain ranges lies a virtually flat plain. The landscape here is a combination of huge stretches of treeless, lake-pooled tundra and swaths of short conifers, with leafy willows and cottonwoods and tall grasses along the banks of rivers that ox-bow through the region. Natives found ingenious ways to live here—using kayaks and umiaks for transportation, carving hunting and fishing implements from bone and ivory, living in subterranean sod houses.

Then, in the 1880s, canneries, equipment, and building materials—brought here on three-masted ships—claimed land at the mouth of every river and creek, capturing millions of salmon before they were able to fight their way upstream to spawn. Some say it was legal for the canneries to take control of the rivers and fish in this way. Some canneries had "purchased" land in the new Alaska Territory by paying cash to Civil War veterans in exchange for scrip—which, in turn, had been issued to the veterans by the federal government for land in lieu of cash. Natives, who had lived at the mouths of these same rivers for more than 6,000 years and depended on dried fish to get them through the difficult winters, had no legal claim to the land or the fish; all resources were up for grabs and the canneries seized their opportunity, bringing shiploads of immigrants to work as fishermen and on the slime line in the processing plants. Even today, the Bristol Bay story is still about the intermingling of cultures—all equally obsessed, during the summer months, with commercial and subsistence fishing.

The few towns and villages along the rivers that feed Bristol Bay haven't silvered with age like the mining ghost towns of Colorado. The historic buildings—which were simple wooden structures to begin with—are peeling, flaking, and melting into the ground among the more modern ones. The towns may seem scruffy and sore-looking, not on a par with the grandeur of the spectacular wilderness surrounding them. The character of the place does not reveal itself immediately; it comes to you in increments.

But the place grows on you as you engage in its typical activities: spending time with a Yup'ik harpooner tracking a pod of beluga whales through the tidewater; watching a woman pick fish from a net; spending an afternoon in a skiff with a squirming group of young cousins, each with a sticky candy bar in hand, squeezed between camping gear and, oddly, a full-size white refrigerator, headed up the Nushagak River to camp and fish; or forking into a dish of lip-smacking-good smoked salmon chunks, shiny with oil, handed to you across the table while a fisherman tells you his tale about nearly drowning in Bristol Bay when his boat rolled over and sank.

The character of Bristol Bay further reveals itself when you join a family to do simple things, such as gathering salmonberries and blueberries in the tundra, or walking through head-high grass that bows in the wind atop a 6,000-year-old village site above a gravel-washed beach. If you come in winter, and some do, you might ride a snow machine uplake to fish through the ice and, on your return, be sent off alone to the *maqi* (steam bath) with an armload of towels, a bottle of shampoo, and a dipper fashioned from a piece of driftwood and a 2-pound coffee can. The longer you stay and the more people you meet, the deeper the hook sinks into your heart. Ask anyone who lives here.

In Dillingham you'll be able to kayak through traditional hunting and fishing grounds with Yup'ik guides; see collections of grass baskets, parkas, masks, and fishing and hunting implements at the Samuel K. Fox Museum; stay overnight with a Yup'ik family or at the Bristol Inn, owned by the local Native corporation; visit a summer fish camp; and tour the Peter Pan cannery. On the south end of the bay, you can visit Katmai National Park and the site of one of the largest villages in the region, stay overnight in Native-owned lodgings, visit a summer fish camp on the Alaska Peninsula, and fish the Naknek River with Native guides.

Getting Around

PenAir, the largest Alaska-owned air carrier, offers air service on twin-engine prop-jets between Anchorage, Dillingham, and King Salmon, with local charter service in smaller planes to most Bristol Bay villages. Book PenAir flights with Alaska Airlines, (800)426-0333, and gain Alaska Airlines mileage points. Or book direct on PenAir, 4851-A Aircraft Dr, Anchorage, AK 99502; (800)448-4226. Alaska Airlines jets also fly directly from Dillingham and King Salmon. For local PenAir charter flights from King Salmon to Bristol Bay, the Alaska Peninsula, and the Lake Clark/Lake Iliamna area, call (907)246-3372. For local charter flights from Dillingham to Bristol Bay villages, the Alaska Peninsula, and the Lake Clark/Lake Iliamna area, call (907)842-5559.

Reeve Aleutian Airways, Inc., has daily service to Dillingham, (800)544-2248 or (907)842-1603.

Yute Air, based in Dillingham, has daily scheduled service between Anchorage, Dillingham, and King Salmon, as well as single and multi-engine small aircraft with wheels and skis, and seaplanes for village commutes, drop-offs, and flightseeing trips; PO Box 890, Dillingham, AK 99576; (907)842-5333.

Local charters into the wilderness and between Native villages in the Bristol Bay region include Bay Air, (907)842-2570, Bristol Bay

Air, (907)842-7182; Mulchatna Air, (907)842-7166; Shannon's Air, (907)842-5609; and Tucker Aviation, (907)842-1023.

In Dillingham, both Ernie's Cab, (907)842-2606, and Gwennie's Cab, (907)842-6900, are Native owned, with van service from the airport. You can also call North Star Taxi, (907)842-7171; for car rentals, call D&J Rental, (907)842-2222.

Visitor Services

- Choggiung Ltd., PO Box 330, Dillingham, AK 99576; (907)842-5218. Information on camping and land use permits in the Dillingham/Nushagak area.

- Dillingham Chamber of Commerce, PO Box 348, Dillingham, AK 99576; (907)842-5115. Information on Dillingham and north Bristol Bay Native villages. Call for a color brochure.

- King Salmon Visitor Center, PO Box 298, King Salmon, AK 99613; (907)246-4250. Information on Katmai National Park and Preserve, the Alaska Peninsula and Becharof National Wildlife Refuges, Aniakchak National Monument and Preserve, Lake Clark National Park and Preserve, and the Alagnak River, a designated National Wild and Scenic River. Also, lists of accommodations and services in the town of Naknek, King Salmon, and other villages in the south Bristol Bay region.

- National Park Service, Alaska Public Lands Information Center, 605 W 4th Ave, Anchorage, AK 99501; (907)271-5555. Ask for brochures and maps of Katmai National Park and Preserve, Aniakchak National Monument and Preserve, and Lake Clark National Park and Preserve.

- Roberts Alaska Tours, PO Box 606, Dillingham, AK 99576; (907)842-5496. Karen Roberts assists visitors with booking customized wilderness, adventure, and Native cultural tours in the Dillingham area, including flightseeing to Katmai National Park and volcanoes on the Alaska Peninsula.

- University of Alaska, Marine Advisory Program, PO Box 1549, Dillingham, AK 99576; (907)842-1265.

Dillingham: *Yup'ik*

A commercial fishing port and the largest town in the region, Dillingham sits at the head of Nushagak Bay, at the mouth of the Wood and Nushagak Rivers. Beluga whales and their calves feed at the mouth of the Wood River; the Nushagak River is a teeming spawning ground for five species of salmon. Dillingham is at the bottom rung of the spectacular stair-step lakes of Wood–Tikchik State Park (the state's largest park, featuring 12 lakes connected by short rivers) and is adjacent to the Togiak National Wildlife Refuge, both huge draws for sport fishermen.

Dillingham's commercial center encompasses about six square blocks, offering just about everything you need: groceries, sundries, clothes, videotapes, a library and museum, a hospital, a school, a couple of hotels and restaurants—even a flower shop and an espresso bar. An old Russian Orthodox cemetery sits on a knoll overlooking the city's commercial dock and Nushagak Bay. In the parking lot in front of the cemetery, Natives stand at cutting tables, slicing up subsistence catches of salmon; behind them, yellow and blue ship containers the size of semi-trucks are stacked 30 feet high.

"It was fish that brought us here. All of us: Yup'iks, Aleuts, Norwegians, Swedes. They still do. There's hardly anyone living here or visiting here who isn't here to fish."
—Karen Roberts

Near Dillingham are the Native villages of Togiak, Twin Hills, Manokotak, Aleknagik, Ekuk, Portage Creek, Ekwok, New Stuyahok, Koliganek, and Clarks Point. Most village sites were established by Yup'ik Eskimos more than 6,000 years ago. Captain James Cook nosed into the coastal region in 1778; he never landed, but he named Bristol Bay. The first Russians are thought to have ventured into the Bristol Bay region in the 1790s. They established Alexandrovski Redoubt on the shore opposite the present townsite in 1818, primarily to hunt fur-bearing sea mammals. The first commercial salmon cannery in Bristol Bay, the Arctic Packing Company, was built in 1883–84 near the Yup'ik village of Kanulik at the mouth of the Nushagak River; by 1910 there were ten canneries on Nushagak Bay, four within present-day Dillingham.

Peter Pan Seafoods cannery, rebuilt after a devastating fire in 1910, is one of the oldest structures still standing in Dillingham. Its picturesque net loft, where multi-strand nets are strung for fishing, is part of the original 1901 cannery; it is constructed of straight-grained old-growth planks brought from the Pacific Northwest on three-masted sailing ships. The rafters still hold original masts from the fleet of distinctive wooden boats equipped with sails that were used for salmon fishing here until the 1950s, when they were replaced by motorized craft. Several of these old boats, weathered with salt and age, are beached in the tall grass that surrounds the cannery. An exhibit of old tools, which includes a foghorn, a canvas fire bucket, and picking hooks, provides a contrast to exhibits at the nearby Samuel K. Fox Museum, which demonstrate how Yup'ik Eskimos fished prior to white contact. Today, Natives fish commercially on their own gillnetter fishing boats alongside non-Natives in Bristol Bay and the Bering Sea.

The first "Dillingham" townsite was at the village of Kanakanak, about 7 miles from present-day Dillingham. The Bureau of Indian Affairs built a school there around 1900 to educate the children of both Eskimos and settlers. It was used as a hospital and Native orphanage during the devastating 1918 flu pandemic. Dillingham's present-day hospital, a striking white building with a red roof, was built on the site of the old schoolhouse.

Dillingham is a jumping-off point for excursions to Wood-Tikchik State Park, Togiak National Wildlife Refuge, Walrus Islands State Game Sanctuary, and world-class sportfishing.

Where's the Art?

The Bristol Bay region has a long, powerful tradition of Native art and craft. Sadly, this flame has been all but extinguished over the last three generations (Western priests and missionaries, for example, discouraged Native cosmology, ceremony, regalia, burial practices, art, songs, and dances). Several Native corporations are now working to rekindle traditional skills. Except for a handful of very finely made artworks such as coiled-grass baskets, evidence of a resurgence is not yet visible in local museums or galleries, but interest is growing. Meanwhile, a remarkable record of past traditions, particularly Yup'ik masks, exists in museums around the world, including those in Fairbanks, Anchorage, and Juneau.

In Dillingham, walk through the Samuel K. Fox Museum to learn about some of the traditional Yup'ik art forms, many of them functional objects such as fur parkas, mukluks, and coiled-grass baskets. Some work is for sale in the lobby of the Bristol Inn. At the airport, at the end of a line of hangars, The Crackerbox, (907)842-4440, offers locally made dolls, slippers, baskets, masks, and carved ivory. Nick Smeaton sells small carved ivory pieces at Bobbi's Treasure Chest downtown (across from City Hall), (907)842-5729. You'll find crafts from outlying villages at the traditional arts and crafts show held the first week of March as part of Dillingham's annual Beaver Roundup.

The Yup'iks call their two-room steam bath a maqi (pronounced "mahk-hay"). Heated by a cast-iron stove and filled with steam from water being poured onto hot rocks, the maqi resembles a steam bath more than a Finnish sauna. Dippers are made from 2-pound coffee cans with attached driftwood handles. Bathers cool off in an enclosed cold room that doubles as a dressing room. There are switches made from the stems and leaves of aromatic artemisia (a powerful medicinal plant with a fragrance similar to chrysanthemums, also known as "stinkweed" or wormwood). In the old days, bathers also used feathered goose wings for switches.

If you can't make it to Dillingham, try the Alaska Native Medical Center Craft Shop in Anchorage (see the Anchorage section of the Southeast Alaska chapter), and ask clerks to point out work from Southwest Alaska. To learn about ceremonial masks from the Bering Sea region, we recommend an exceptional book, *The Living Tradition of Yup'ik Masks: Agayuliyararput = Our Way of Making Prayer*, by Ann Fienup-Riordan (University of Washington Press, 1996), available from the Anchorage Museum of History and Art in downtown Anchorage.

Roberts Alaska Tours

Karen Roberts, a Bristol Bay Native Corporation shareholder of Yup'ik Eskimo descent, grew up in Dillingham and can provide anything from a day trip to a customized month-long itinerary in the Bristol Bay region. Her contacts include over 60 wilderness lodges, outfitters, and tour guides. Tours can combine wilderness adventure with local Yup'ik culture; the tour content depends on what's happening, who is available, and how much time and money you have. You might visit an Eskimo doll-maker, take a mail flight to a Native village, travel to a Yup'ik summer fish camp, or go bear watching at Katmai National Park. The Ultimate Undiscovered Alaska Tour of Bristol Bay and the Aleutian Chain is an eight-day, seven-night marathon that might include flightseeing over the Wood-Tikchik lake system (10 lakes, connected by rivers), salmon fishing on the Nushagak River, touring Dillingham's Peter Pan cannery, and visiting the boat basin while fishermen prepare for the commercial harvest of king salmon. Roberts's friends own kayaks that can be leased and delivered by truck to Lake Aleknagik, or she can set you up with a Native boat owner to see beluga whales and their newborn calves at the mouth of the Wood River. Roberts speaks limited Yup'ik, but she's a cousin to many bilingual Yup'ik speakers in the region and includes friends and relatives in her personal tours.

Yup'ik Eskimos wore socks woven from ryegrass and put grass padding inside their mukluks for extra warmth.

What would it be like to take a personal day tour with Roberts? She might arrange a trip to Igushik (pronounced "ee-goo-shik") beach, a Yup'ik fish camp on the south shore of the Togiak National Wildlife Refuge. Each summer, villagers from Manokotak ("man-oh-koe-tack") move from their village on the Igushik River to cabins near its mouth in order to fish for salmon. You and Roberts take a six-seater village commuter plane to Igushik, flying low over depressions in the tundra where sod houses once stood, then landing on the beach at Igushik. There you see a row of weathered cabins strung along the shoreline for more than a mile. Between them are wooden racks where translucent strips of red salmon dry in the wind, carrying a faint scent of wood smoke from the smoldering fires that discourage insects. Green nylon fish nets lie in neat piles among patches of wild iris and waist-high blue geraniums. Kids dodge wad-dling puppies on the worn trails in the high grass; chattering barn swallows sweep into birdhouses nailed under the eaves of cabins and steam baths. In the lull between tides, people repair houses and clean up after meals; a few women wash clothes in wringer washing ma-chines in the open air and hang them on clotheslines strung between upright driftwood posts. You say hello and ask about the fishing. You borrow a four-wheeler and drive it on the beach, over the ropes hold-ing set-nets (nets that are anchored in place on the beach) in place. The second time the plane lands to pick up a load of passengers (the last trip before the tide comes in and floods the runway), you find a seat and are back up in the air. If the fog socks you in, Roberts comes up with something else for you to do. Trust her.

Roberts Alaska Tours, PO Box 606, Dillingham, AK 99576; (907)842-5496.

Samuel K. Fox Museum

Sam Fox is probably best known for his small carved figures, such as Yup'ik drummers and singers; his miniatures of kayakers, dogsledders, and whimsical fur-clad people; and his large masks. A native of Goodnews Bay, a coastal village between Dillingham and Bethel, Fox is a member of a family with a long tradition of carving ceremonial masks from driftwood. With his wife and six children, he came to Dillingham in the early 1970s to teach carving to schoolchildren. For his work in ivory, wood, soapstone, and other natural materials, Fox was well respected and liked; he served as an important link between contemporary and traditional Yup'ik culture. Tragically, he died in an accident in 1983. Now the Samuel K. Fox Museum, which adjoins Dillingham's public library, houses his work among 3,000 other pieces, including hundreds of Yup'ik Eskimo artifacts and historical photographs. Because of limited space, only a portion of the collec-tion can be shown at one time. Expect to see a photographic timeline of Dillingham's history. An original 1909 map of the region, which includes the Native names of villages and rivers, pinpoints the location of more than 30 canneries and salteries that once dominated Nushagak Bay. (You can walk the beaches circling the bay and find old remnants of the canneries. In fact, these beaches are probably among the few in the world that yield mastodon tusks, rusted cannery boilers, *and* the remains of '57 Chevies.) There's a model of an

Eskimo blackfish trap made of spruce splints, which were used in fenced-in shallows of lakeshores; ivory bird spears, throwing boards, and fishing weights; and stone seal-oil lamps, bone awls, and other household objects.

The museum also houses the Lois Morey collection of Alaska Native baskets, which includes a large exhibit of coiled-grass baskets decorated with colorful geometric patterns, made with strips of dyed seal gut from the Togiak area. Baskets in this region are made from coastal ryegrass harvested after the first big frost. The handles on the basket lids are sometimes animal figures carved from ivory. A 1983 monograph on ryegrass basket making, available from the museum, lists Bristol Bay basket makers in the appendix.

Don't miss the unusual collection of labrets, made of granite, jadeite, quartz, slate, glass, lignite wood, walrus tusk, and fossilized mammoth ivory, which used to be inserted in pierced skin, usually just below the lower lip (the practice was out of fashion by 1900). Seven skin parkas and pairs of mittens and mukluks, designed and hand-sewn by Bertha Olsen, are under glass, along with the tools used in skin sewing. The museum's brochure is written in both Yup'ik and English. The adjoining library's Alaska Native section has a good selection of books recently published on the Bristol Bay region.

Samuel K. Fox Museum, PO Box 273, Dillingham, AK 99576. Call the Dillingham Public Library, (907)842-5610, for hours or to make an appointment to see the collection.

Crystal Creek Lodge, the only lodge on Nunavaugaluk Lake, provides guides, a helicopter, floatplanes, jet boats, fly-tying benches, a fully equipped tackle room, a bar, a spa, and gourmet meals. The 10-hour fishing day begins with breakfast at 7; guests fly out to fish at 8. The charge for such pampering? For seven days and six nights, $4,950 per person. There's no Native culture in sight here, but Choggiung, a Native corporation, owns the land the lodge sits on, and shared lodge profits benefit Native shareholders. Crystal Creek Lodge, PO Box 92170, Anchorage, AK 99509; (800)525-3153 or (907)245-1945

Togiak Kayak Tours

For thousands of years, traveling by kayak or canoe was the best way into the interior from the seacoast. Today you can kayak with Yup'ik Eskimo guides whose ancestors invented the kayak and who first explored and settled along the banks of the remarkable rivers that enter Bristol Bay and the Bering Sea.

Kayak trips begin at Crystal Creek Lodge, a luxury fishing lodge adjacent to the Togiak National Wildlife Refuge, where you pack your gear and catch a floatplane into several wilderness base camps. The Togiak National Wildlife Refuge is a huge tundra plain forested with spruce and cottonwood; just outside the boundary of the refuge is Wood-Tikchik State Park, a series of 12 large lakes that stair-step down through the mountains all the way to Nushagak Bay. Trips are for six days and five nights, and are fully outfitted for groups of six. Two guides with Alaska wilderness experience accompany each group; one is selected for fishing expertise, the other for local knowledge about the land and the culture of the people who inhabit it.

Make reservations through Crystal Creek Lodge, PO Box 92170, Anchorage, AK 99509; (800)525-3153 or (907)245-1945; Web site: http://www.crystalcreeklodge.com. Open Jun–Aug. Under $2,000 per person, including airfare from Anchorage, guides, gear, meals, and overnight lodging at the Bristol Inn. The type of guide may vary depending on availability; the guide is usually Yup'ik but may instead be an experienced fly fisherman, a recognized nature photographer, or an expert on sub-Arctic plant life. Those interested in having a Yup'ik guide should request one when making reservations. For more information, call Choggiung Ltd., (907)842-5218.

Willow Creek Kayak Rentals

Surprisingly, in this area where kayaks were used for centuries, there's hardly a kayak to be found for rent. Although kayaks and their larger cousin, the umiak, are the most seaworthy boats ever invented, most Natives quickly gave them up for more efficient motorized skiffs and commercial fishing boats.

Although recreational kayaking is catching on in Alaska, it may be difficult to transport your kayak or canoe (unless it's collapsible) into the region—boats are just too unwieldy on a small plane, and tying them to the pontoons of a floatplane carrying passengers is illegal. The Mayer family, who live fairly close to Lake Aleknagik, rent one- and two-person fiberglass kayaks as well as spray skirts, camp stoves, cook sets, and waterproof dry bags. They'll advise you on the best places to kayak in the region; they'll even truck you and your kayak to nearby Lake Aleknagik and the Wood River, both accessible by gravel road. You can hardly lose here. Lake Aleknagik is one of 12 lakes, most of them connected by short rivers, in Wood-Tikchik State Park. Gravel bars and firewood for camping are always "just around the next bend" in the Wood River, and you can camp on gravel bars without permission from landowners. The Mayer family will also assist with the logistics of getting groceries, local transportation, and floatplane reservations. Bring your own sleeping bags, or purchase them at local outfitting stores in Dillingham.

Willow Creek Rentals, PO Box 196, Dillingham, AK 99576; (907)842-2808. Single kayaks, $50 a day; double kayaks, $65. Gear includes tarp, spray skirt, pump, paddle float, personal flotation vest, and Werner Camano touring paddles. Gear rentals include three-person tents, stoves, cook sets, and dry bags. Prices are reduced for extended trips.

Sportfishing on the Nushagak River

Muscular king salmon enter the Nushagak River to spawn each June, a biological imperative that has created a hot fishing spot and spawned a number of sportfishing camps along the river's grassy banks. For years, guys with tents and boats have simply set up camp and used Bristol Bay rivers without regard for property rights. They sometimes left behind garbage and sewage in otherwise pristine areas, earning them a bad name with the locals, who have to clean up the mess. The fish camps on the Nushagak River, however, sit on Native corporation–owned land; offering the best fishing on the river, they encompass the area on both banks from the river's mouth to about 60 miles upstream. Guides pay lease fees to the Native corporations for the use of these prime fishing spots; in return, river quality, camp cleanup, and the fish run are monitored. It's a win-win situation for everyone, although there's the usual griping about paying for what used to be free. Camps on the Nushagak River vary in luxury. Guides meet their clients at the Portage Creek airstrip, haul gear down the hill from the airstrip to the river, and take visitors to their camps in outboard skiffs. Camps usually consist of temporary Quonset-style sleeping tents with cots, a cook tent, and outhouse. Every day, guides negotiate the braided river to take clients to the best fishing spots. Some camps keep floatplanes on the river to fly fishermen from camp to other great fishing holes in the region.

The Native corporations that own land on the river are the Bristol Bay Native Corporation, Choggiung Ltd., Ekwok Natives Ltd., and Stuyahok Ltd. You can obtain a list of complying fish camps in the Portage Creek area, near the river's mouth, from Choggiung Ltd., PO Box 330, Dillingham, AK 99576; (907)842-5218. Prices average about $400 per day per person.

Eskimo Fishing Adventures

The Larsons, a blended family (Yup'ik Eskimo and northern European), operate a first-rate sportfishing camp on one acre of a Native allotment. It's upstream and apart from the other camps in a little-used braid of the Nushagak River. The site, overlooking the confluence of a shallow slough and the faster-moving river, is a lovely, quiet spot among dwarf spruce trees and tundra abloom with wildflowers. From the camp picnic table you can watch a family of beavers hauling sticks through the water to their den a stone's throw away, and it's silent enough to hear the slap of their tails on the water before they dive.

Like other camps, this one is made up of four Quonset-style white tents with boardwalks between them. The cook tent is well equipped, featuring a full-size gas range and two large refrigerators, hot and cold running water, and even a washer and dryer. Best of all, there's a large steam bath with lots of headroom, electric lights, hot and cold running water, and stacks of fresh bath towels. The steam-bath stove, fired by propane, flicks on with a switch and is hot within minutes. Over the next few years, the tents may give way to a 1920s-era building that the family dismantled piece by piece last year in Dillingham.

Guided fishing is the main idea here, but tour options include the natural and local history of the river. Owner Adolph (Shep) Larson's grandfather owned the first store in Dillingham in the early 1900s. Larson has been set-netting since he was 9 years old, was a member of a 1955 Army cross-country ski team, and is a graduate of Northeastern Oklahoma State University, an educator, a basketball coach, and a heavy-equipment mechanic. These are nice folks, good cooks (try their spicy fat-free, hormone-free moose sausage), and great company.

Eskimo Fishing Adventures, PO Box 264, Dillingham, AK 99576; (907)842-5678; e-mail: alaskaefa@aol.com. Tours offered June–Aug. $275 per day per person. Reduced rates for groups, families, or longer stays. Guides pick you up at Portage Creek airstrip. Flights to Portage Creek from King Salmon or Dillingham can be arranged for you. You bring fishing gear, rain gear, boots or waders, shoes to wear around camp, warm clothes and jacket, and a sleeping bag. Cots are provided for up to 16 guests. Write or call for free color brochure.

In Togiak's Head Start classes, lessons are taught in Yup'ik, at the request of the parents. Caribou and moose, commercially processed to meet FDA regulations, are served for meals. Adults sit with the kids at tables and do work such as beading, skin sewing, and basket weaving so the kids can watch—the best way to learn. "We're not so much concerned with the end product as we are with the process," says one of the teachers.

Walrus Islands State Game Sanctuary

Located 70 miles west of Dillingham, Walrus Islands State Game Sanctuary is a haven for one of the largest concentrations of walrus in the world. From 6,000 to 8,000 male walruses return to this area each spring to spend the summer hunting, snorting, and sleeping cheek by whiskered jowl, while females and pups follow the retreating sea ice to the north.

Walrus have long been a reliable and prized source of food and ivory for the Yup'ik people residing along the Bering Sea coast. Hunting was halted shortly after statehood by state fish and game managers. In 1995, however, after years of pressure, an agreement was reached allowing an annual harvest of 10 walrus each fall by local Native hunters. The walrus meat is shared in local villages, rekindling an ancient, nearly lost tradition.

Hardy travelers can visit Round Island, the primary walrus haulout spot, during the summer months. Overnight stays require a permit and sufficient skill and equipment for primitive camping. These small, rugged islands are home to Steller's sea lions, foxes, and many bird species. Whales are often seen on the trip to and from the islands. Getting there requires major effort and expense from Dillingham, including a flight to the village of Twin Hills and a boat trip about 45 miles out to sea. Weather can also be very tricky, and facilities are minimal at best. Adventurers will love it.

Arrange permits and trips to Round Island through one of three services: Roberts Alaska Tours, PO Box 606, Dillingham, AK 99576; (907)842-5496; Choggiung Ltd., PO Box 330, Dillingham, AK 99576; (907)842-5218; or the Dillingham Chamber of Commerce, PO Box 348, Dillingham, AK 99576; (907)842-5515.

Triple H Lodge and Wood River Culture Tours

The Hoseth family (Tom and Debbie, Carolyn, and Byrdie—three generations of Yup'ik Eskimo heritage, all born and raised in the area) host visitors at their cabins on the Wood River during the fishing season. The Hoseths pick visitors up at the Dillingham airport and drive them 25 scenic miles over a gravel road through the tundra and spruce forest to a point near Lake Aleknagik; then everyone boards a skiff for a 15-minute boat ride downstream to the camp.

At the camp, the wood-frame cabins are equipped with kitchens and baths, but regular meals are prepared and served in the home of Mike and Byrdie Hoseth. Activities include guided scenic boat outings in open or covered skiffs and fishing for rainbow, grayling, Dolly Varden, northern pike, and salmon. You can also watch, or help, the family pick salmon from gillnets, and learn local methods of preparation and smoking; go berry picking and plant gathering or beluga whale watching; visit a Native village; or tour Dillingham with a family member. You'll also be able to sample traditional foods: moose, caribou, salmon, smoked fish, and seal oil.

Triple H Lodge, PO Box 95, Dillingham, AK 99576; (907)842-5540. Mid-June–mid-Sept. $325 per person per day. Price drops to $250 per person for two, $200 per person for three, and $180 per person for groups of four to eight. Prices include round-trip transportation from Dillingham, daily activities, boats and guide fees, three meals a day, overnight accommodations, fishing equipment, and freezer wrap. Write or call for a brochure.

The Bristol Inn

The largest building in Dillingham, except for the historic Peter Pan cannery on the waterfront, is the Bristol Inn. A fairly new two-story structure with a square cupola, it houses both the hotel and office space. It's billed as a luxury hotel, and for Southwest Alaska, it is. (It wasn't that long ago that luxury, in the bush, was a room that didn't leak and that kept the bugs out.) Thirty rooms have double or queen-size beds and private baths, telephones (free local calls), and cable television. There are kitchenette suites for longer stays, an ice machine, guest laundry facilities, complimentary continental breakfast in the lobby, a fax/copy machine for business travelers, and freezer space for freshly caught fish. The offices in the building are truly handsome. The owner and hotel host is Choggiung Ltd., the village Native corporation, located in a large office suite on the second floor. Hotel guests are welcome to stop in and say hello; it's a nice opportunity to see a Native corporation at work.

Across the street from the hotel is a historic red-shingled schoolhouse with its bronze bell still on top; a block away is a picturesque Russian Orthodox cemetery overlooking Nushagak Bay. It's an easy walk to the grocery, bank, espresso shop, and boat basin. Behind the hotel is the Samuel K. Fox Museum, located in the city's library building. Items from the museum collection, such as ivory carvings and grass baskets decorated with dyed seal gut, are displayed for sale in the Bristol Inn lobby.

The Bristol Inn, PO Box 330, Dillingham, AK 99576; (907)842-2240 in state; (800)764-9704 out of state; e-mail: chognt@nushtel.com. Open year-round. Rooms $147 double; group rates. Most major credit cards accepted.

Maaluq Lodge

Luki Akelkok, Sr., grew up in the village of Ekwok ("eck-wok"), the oldest village on the Nushagak River. Sixty miles upriver, Ekwok takes its name from a Yup'ik word that means "the end of the bluff." It was a prime spot for berry picking and was used until the late 1800s as a temporary fish camp during spawning season. The village became a permanent settlement in the 1890s. The first school here was built by the Bureau of Indian Affairs in the 1930s. Mail was delivered by dogsled until the 1940s.

Akelkok learned to fish from three older generations of Yup'ik fishermen and hunters, and he's been fishing on the river all his life. His Maaluq Lodge, just downstream from the village, offers a large basic cabin with nine beds, a hot shower, and a kitchen with refrigeration. The guys from the Lower 48 who come here regularly to fish have given Akelkok and his staff bragging rights about the food—three big meals a day.

Akelkok and his wife also run a bed and breakfast (which includes lunch and dinner too) that's open year-round. Their guest house has several bedrooms plus one large room with six beds, and two baths with shower. For meals, guests join the Akelkok family in their house. Akelkok also guides hunting trips in the region.

Maaluq Lodge, PO Box 42, Ekwok, AK 99580; (907)464-3317. The bed and breakfast is open year-round; rates vary. For the fishing cabin, the one-month fishing season is mid-June–mid-July. Reservations are essential. Fishing trips are $325 per day per person; minimum stay one day, maximum seven days. Price includes a full day of fishing (four skiffs are available), tackle, accommodations, three full meals a day, guide fee, fish cleaning, and boxing and freezing of up to 70 pounds of fish. You fly from Anchorage to Dillingham, then take a village commuter plane to Ekwok. Akelkok or a member of his staff picks you up at the Ekwok airstrip. You bring fishing gear, rain gear, boots or waders, warm clothes and jacket, shoes to wear around camp, and a sleeping bag. Call for details about guided hunting trips.

King Salmon

King Salmon began as an Air Force base, built quickly during the early 1940s to shore up defenses after the Japanese attacked the island of Attu, in the Aleutian Islands. In 1996, the Air Force "pickled the base": the facilities have been kept ready for rapid reactivation, but nearly all the personnel and hardware have been removed. While still looking much like a military base, over the years King Salmon has evolved into a small community. The area is a government service center that includes offices of the Lake and Peninsula Borough, the Federal Aviation Administration, the National Park Service, and the U.S. Fish and Wildlife Service. King Salmon has a visitors center, several small hotels and restaurants, a grocery store and services, riverfront lodges, charter fishing services, and private homes. During the summer, on your flight from Anchorage to King Salmon, you'll probably encounter commercial fishing and cannery crews coming from the Lower 48 to work in Bristol Bay.

Visitors come here primarily to sportfish on the Naknek River or in the streams of the Becharof National Wildlife Refuge; to fly to the Alaska Peninsula to see the huge volcanic crater at Aniakchak National Monument and Preserve; or to catch a floatplane to Katmai National Park and Preserve's Brooks Camp to watch bears feeding on salmon. The parks and wildlife refuges are located on what is called the Alaska

Peninsula, the landform shaped like a dinosaur tail that sweeps west across the Pacific Ocean, breaking into the Aleutian Chain.

Floatplanes to Brooks Camp are docked in the Naknek River, less than a mile from the King Salmon airport. Smaller planes heading for villages take off from the King Salmon airport.

The town of Naknek, a mix of Native and non-Native families, is 15 miles by road from King Salmon, accessible by taxi. The nearest Native villages are Egegik, South Naknek, and Levelock, all accessible by air taxi.

King Salmon Visitor Center

When you arrive in King Salmon, head straight for the visitor center, adjacent to the air terminal. Packed with information and one of the best places to find books about the region, the center explains the geography of the area and provides detailed information on the Becharof National Wildlife Refuge, Katmai National Park and Preserve, Aniakchak National Monument and Preserve, Lake Clark National Park and Preserve, and the Alagnak River, a designated National Wild and Scenic River.

The center's map of Aleutian and Alaska Peninsula volcanic eruptions might be its most impressive exhibit. Most of the world's active volcanoes line up on the Aleutian Chain like fireworks tubes buried in the sand, waiting for some internal spark to set them off. An alarming 24 major eruptions have occurred in the last 200 years. Near here, villagers fled Old Savonoski, Katmai, and Douglas in what is now Katmai National Park when the Novarupta volcano erupted on June 6, 1912. Pete Kayagvak, an Old Savonoski village chief who spoke Aleut, Russian, and English, gave a description of the cataclysmic event that is quoted at the center: "The Katmai mountain blew up with lots of fire, and fire came down the trail from Katmai with lots of smoke. We go fast Savonoski. Everybody get in *baidarka* [kayak]. Hulluva job. We come Naknek in one day, dark, no could see. Hot ash fall. Work like hell." The eruption of Novarupta caused Mount Katmai to collapse, burying the old Katmai Pass trade route—a shortcut across the Alaska Peninsula from Shelikof Strait to the Bering Sea—under hundreds of feet of ash. You can take a tour bus to the Valley of Ten Thousand Smokes from Brooks Camp, the primary visitors' destination, which offers the only services (overnight lodging, restaurant, small store) in the entire park. Katmai National Park brochures and maps are free at the visitors center.

On loan from the Anchorage Museum of History and Art are a mannequin wearing a seal-gut parka (made in the late 1800s) that is sewn together with caribou sinew twisted into thread, and a colorfully painted version of the traditional hunting visor, made by contemporary artist Patrick Lind (Aleut) and decorated in the traditional manner with whale baleen, walrus ivory, beads, and feathers. These distinctive visors blocked sun, shed sea spray, and funneled sound so that sea-mammal hunters could hear more clearly.

The center highlights the history of fishing in Bristol Bay, including an exhibit on the first fish canneries in the area, a display of old cannery labels, several videos about commercial fishing, and a small collection of carved-bone spear points and hooks. The book selection is extraordinary, particularly the Native section. Look especially for *Baidarka*, by George Dyson (Alaska Northwest Publishing Co., 1986), about the skin boats used by Natives to travel the thousands of miles of open ocean to the Arctic and as far south as northern California, and *The Aleutian Kayak: Origins, Construction and Use of the Traditional Seagoing Baidarka*, by Wolfgang Brinck (Ragged Mountain Press). A few baskets and other crafts from outlying villages are sold in the adjacent air terminal at Chinook Gifts.

King Salmon Visitor Center, PO Box 298, King Salmon, AK 99613; (907)246-4250. In summer, open 8am–5pm daily; in winter, 9am–5pm Mon–Fri. The center sends out a full list of sportfishing lodges, overnight lodgings, campgrounds, supply stores, and transportation in the King Salmon/Naknek area on request.

Bristol Bay Charter Adventures

These knotty pine cabins and bathhouse, built like row houses on the Naknek River, are just about the nicest anywhere, with green metal roofs, porches, built-in tables in front of large windows overlooking the river, kitchenettes, and lofts. A generator provides electricity to fire a spacious sauna (and you can jump off the dock into the clear Naknek River to cool off between rounds). Owners Deidre and Patrick O'Neill meet your plane at King Salmon, stop at the grocery so you can buy supplies and get your fishing license, drive you to the end of the road (about 20 minutes from the airport), load you into their skiff, and head downriver to their isolated cabins. You can rent one of their motorized skiffs, or hire Patrick to take you upriver into the narrow canyons in his jet boat, for trout fishing or sightseeing. The O'Neills will also arrange trips to Brooks Camp or wilderness flyouts (and drive you to a floatplane on the Naknek River).

The O'Neills look European, but both their grandmothers were Native; hers was Athabascan from the Lake Clark/Lake Iliamna area, and his was Yup'ik Eskimo from the village of Levelock. Their maternal grandfathers were Irish and Finnish, respectively; both grandfathers came to Bristol Bay from San Francisco on three-masted ships to work in the canneries. The O'Neills' fathers are both Native; hers just retired as a superintendent of schools, while his is a commercial fisherman. "We both grew up in Native surroundings, eating fish, caribou, and moose, but really what makes us more Native than Irish or Finn is the Native way of relating to family—even your third cousin is a close relation whose birthday is celebrated," says Deidre. Patrick has fished with his dad since he was 7 years old and has run his own boats since he was 19.

Bristol Bay Charter Adventures, PO Box 185, King Salmon, AK 99613; (907)246-3750 in summer; to book in advance during winter months, PO Box 4281, Soldotna, AK 99669; (907)262-2750. Tours offered June–mid-Sept. Rates average $65 per person per night (the cabins sleep four and six); boat rental is $125 a day (only two people allowed in each boat, to ensure safety).

Shawbacks Ponderosa Inn

Forget landscaping. This boxcar-shaped hotel, painted white with a red roof and sun-bleached antlers nailed to the porch posts, sits right on the tundra behind the Shawback family's main enterprise—Bristol Bay Contractors, located just outside of King Salmon. The hotel is screened from the construction yard by trees, but expect to see a few heavy-equipment parts here and there. Rooms are modern, clean, and carpeted, with large private baths. A screened porch houses a pool table; the family room has a big-screen satellite television and tables for card games. The dining room, filled with picnic tables, serves three hearty meals a day, all-you-can-eat cafeteria-style, including a fresh salad bar and desserts. Best deals here are the fishing packages that include a ride to and from the Ponderosa's private dock on the Naknek River. Skiffs, equipped with motor and fish net, are rented separately, by the day. You can fish on your own all day until nearly midnight for big rainbow trout, king and silver salmon, Arctic char, grayling, and Dolly Varden. The room rate includes freezer space and shipping boxes for fish. Laundry facilities are on the premises. Mary Shawback, a small determined woman with a big blue truck, is a longtime resident of the region (she grew up on Lake Iliamna) of Athabascan/Russian/Irish descent, and she set-nets for her quota of subsistence salmon on the beach every summer at Naknek. Recently she turned all business operations over to her sons, but she still lives in her summer house near the Ponderosa; in winter she heads to her condo in Anchorage.

Shawbacks Ponderosa Inn, King Salmon, AK 99613; (907)246-3444. The Ponderosa is about a mile from the King Salmon airport on the road to Naknek. Rooms $80 single; with meals, $110. Fishing-package rates range from $400 (for a single room for three *days and two nights) to $2,000 (for two people staying eight days). Fishing-package rates include room, fish boxes, freezer space, and transportation. Boat rentals are extra, from $85 a day.*

Cottonwood Lodge

The word *lodge* is used quite loosely in this region; it can mean luxury lodge, cabin, or tent camp. This particular lodge is a comfortable, Weatherport tent camp. The Quonset-style tent has a floor and lots of headroom, and it sleeps six or more people on cots or mattresses. The Herrmann family, of Aleut and German descent, have set up camp on their Native allotment (160 acres) on King Salmon Creek, a tributary of the Naknek River.

Cooking facilities include a four-burner butane stove with oven and icebox. Bathroom facilities are an eco-friendly portable outhouse and a permanent, traditional steam bath equipped with soaps, shampoos, and towels, located just 100 feet from the pristine creek. The family takes you and your groceries to their lodge in their four-wheel-drive truck. As an added bonus, ask them to share their one-of-a-kind slide show of old-time fishing during the days when all the fishing in Bristol Bay was from sailboats owned by the canneries. Most of the slides are from the 1940s and 1950s. Two mountain bikes are available on request; the family will also arrange for fishing trips on the Naknek River or side trips to Katmai National Park and Brooks River for fishing and bear viewing.

Born and raised in the Bristol Bay region, Helen and Henry Herrmann have both fished commercially and lived a subsistence lifestyle. Daughter Adelheid is a former state representative and coordinator for the Fisheries Economic Development Commission. They're easy going, good-humored folks with a lifetime of fishing stories to share.

Cottonwood Lodge, PO Box 63, Naknek, AK 99663; (907)246-4495. The family lives in Naknek; the camp is near King Salmon. $200 per person per day, including room, board, and round-trip transportation from King Salmon to the camp. You bring your own sleeping bag and fishing gear (you can purchase sporting goods at Naknek Trading Company and the Alaska Commercial Company in Naknek).

Katmai National Park and Preserve

When the Novarupta volcano erupted in 1912 with a force 10 times greater than Mount St. Helens, the villagers living nearest the volcano, including those residing in Kukuk, Katmai Village, Kajuyak, and Old Savonoski, were forced to flee in their baidarkas from falling ash. A large number of earthquakes began shaking the area a week before the eruption; two days prior to the big blow, Natives reported hearing odd noises—with sound waves that could be *felt* 130 miles away. When Novarupta exploded, the entire dome of the adjacent Mount Katmai was undermined and collapsed under its own weight, creating a crater lake more than 1,000 feet deep. The northern approach to Katmai Pass, used by the ancients as well as traders, explorers, and gold prospectors in the last century, was buried under more than 700 feet of ash.

Devastating as these events were, villagers planned to move back to their homes after the smoke cleared. Two events stopped them. Only six years after the eruption, a flu epidemic decimated the population. The same year, the U.S. government created Katmai National Monument, which would later expand and become Katmai National Park and Preserve. The monument closed off 1,700 square miles of prime lake- and riverfront land surrounding the volcano, and with that land went the possibility of Natives ever returning to their old villages. The creation of the national monument caused a permanent dislocation of the Natives who had called this area home for more than 50 centuries.

Although Katmai National Park and Preserve eventually grew to more than 2,400 square miles, the only major destination in the park with any visitor services, or for that matter any trails, is Brooks Camp, a pleasant wooded spot on an isthmus between Lake Brooks and Naknek Lake that includes a visitors center, cabins, campground, and restaurant.

When Katmai National Monument was created in 1916, villagers left behind 37 sacred spirit masks in a mountain cave. Although villagers were not allowed to return to live in the national monument, many went back to hunt and fish. Sometime after 1918, the masks disappeared. Over the years, eight of the masks, lifelike faces carved from wood, have found their way to safekeeping in the Alaska State Museum in Juneau. Several are on display there. The location of the other 29 masks remains a mystery.

These days, most visitors come to Brooks Camp because it's a prime bear-watching spot. When you step off your floatplane, you're ushered into the visitors center for a lesson on bear safety. Then you cross a footbridge to the area's most popular attraction: bears swiping at salmon leaping over Brooks Falls on their journey upstream.

To see the route Natives once took through the mountains, take the Brooks Camp bus to the Valley of Ten Thousand Smokes. From turnouts along the route, there are good views of the Savonoski River and Old Savonoski village. The bus leaves camp at 9am for the 23-mile trip to Three Forks Overlook, a kickoff spot for short guided walks or more serious hikes. Once there, you can eat your sack lunch in a log cabin and hike 1½ miles to a waterfall before you return to Brooks Camp, or arrange to stay overnight or longer. Some hikers aim for the old Katmai Pass, about a two-day strenuous hike from the Three Forks Overlook. Hiking in this area can be dangerous. Braided rivers flowing through the yellow, red, and brown ash are as narrow as 5 feet across, but can be up to 100 feet deep. (From a Park Service brochure: "It is possible to jump across the [Ukak River] in some places near the bottom of the trail. Hikers should exercise caution when jumping these rivers; a fall into the river gorge would probably be fatal.") The area hasn't yet recovered from the 1912 Novarupta eruption because it has been filled with the infertile ash that flowed from the mountain much like a bag of sugar spilling downhill.

There are a number of intriguing kayak trips possible from Brooks Camp, including journeying through Naknek Lake and down the Naknek River. From Brooks Camp, you can also kayak up to the Savonoski River delta, site of the Old Savonoski village site, abandoned after the Novarupta eruption. The Savonoski River delta is only 20 miles from Brooks Camp, but because of strong river currents, park rangers recommend an 86-mile loop that takes up to ten days. It's for experienced kayakers with good backcountry skills. You begin at Brooks Camp, paddle through the Bay of Islands, and take three or four days to cross Lake Grosvenor to the Savonoski River delta. The loop is no cakewalk—mud and at least knee-deep water on an unmarked portage trail, ravenous bugs, williwaws (severe south and southeast winds with no shelter), fallen trees in the river, and bears on the beach. The trip makes a permanent sod house on the shores of Brooks Lake look like a darn good idea. You may wish to just hire your flightseeing pilot to fly up to the Savonoski River and down to Naknek to see the route that villagers used to escape the volcano, or ride with Alvin and Roger Aspelund on their 40-foot sightseeing boat to the Old Savonoski village site from King Salmon (discussed later in this section).

Katmai National Park and Preserve Headquarters, PO Box 7, King Salmon, AK 99613; (907)246-3305. Or King Salmon Visitor Center, PO Box 298, King Salmon, AK 99613; (907)246-4250. Ask for handouts on hikes, kayak trips, and guides, and request the official Katmai National Park brochure and map. Regularly scheduled flights are made daily to Brooks Camp from King Salmon on Katmai Air's floatplanes (which can be booked through Alaska Airlines); a number of air taxis also serve the area. (Ask the King Salmon Visitor Center to send you a list.) Brooks Camp cabins and Katmai Air charters are reserved through the concessionaire: Katmailand, Inc., (800)544-0551 or (907)243-5448. For Brooks Camp campground reservations and fees, contact the National Park Service, PO Box 7, King Salmon, AK 99613; (907)246-3305.

Brooks Camp

Brooks Camp sits squarely on top of one of the Alaska Peninsula's largest pre-contact villages. The foundations of more than 80 sod houses have been identified here, although only 14 have been excavated. The site "may contain the richest prehistoric and protohistoric cultural resources in perhaps the greatest concentrations known in Alaska," according to D. E. Dumond, a University of Oregon anthropologist who has studied Eskimo and Aleut village settlements for more than 30 years.

The villagers probably settled on this prime spot for the same reason that bears roam here today—prolific red salmon that stay in the river well into the fall, providing a reliable source of food at a time when few options are available. Caribou remains have also been found in the village. From this central, protected location, there was access to the Pacific Ocean through overland passes in the mountains and to Bristol Bay through the waterways of Naknek Lake and the Naknek River—a 60-mile paddle that takes one day in a baidarka if you are charged with adrenaline and have spent a lifetime perfecting paddling skills and strength.

More than 14,000 artifacts have been found on the site so far. The oldest objects found here are an oil lamp made of pecked stone, which used sea-mammal oil as fuel; long, thrusting blades made of polished slate; and smashed scraps of mammal longbones that date to between 2,500 and 1,900 B.C.

In the works are negotiations between the Bristol Bay Native Corporation, the National Park Service, Native descendants of Old Savonoski, and others, in order to both protect and strengthen the site as a profoundly valuable cultural resource, and make its interpretation more detailed and accurate. For now, you'll have to be satisfied with the free presentation, offered daily by Park Service employees, about the people who once lived here. You walk about a quarter mile on a wooded path, warning possible bears of your approach, pausing to imagine what life must have been like here several centuries ago. The talk ends at a facsimile of a traditional sod house, located on a site where a real sod house was excavated in 1957. Houses were entered through a tunnel that trapped cold air; they were illuminated inside by a translucent seal-gut skylight and seal-oil lamps; and the walls and roofs were most likely topped with sod and absorbent sphagnum moss. Today, the model home is protected from the elements by a log cabin built over it.

Regularly scheduled flights are made daily to Brooks Camp from King Salmon on Katmai Air's floatplanes (which can be booked through Alaska Airlines); a number of air taxis also serve the area. (Ask the King Salmon Visitor Center to send you a list.) Brooks

Camp cabins and Katmai Air charters are reserved through the concessionaire: Katmailand, Inc., (800)544-0551 or (907)243-5448. For Brooks Camp campground reservations and fees, contact the National Park Service, PO Box 7, King Salmon, AK 99613; (907)246-3305.

Katmai Spirit Tours

Retired commercial fisherman Alvin Aspelund and his son Roger, a fisherman and airline pilot, offer ecological and cultural tours of Naknek Lake on board their 40-foot catamaran-hulled powerboat. Of Aleut and northern European descent, the Aspelund family picks you up at the King Salmon airport and takes you to their lodge (currently under construction) on a former reindeer station on Naknek Lake. You tour the lake through the Bay of Islands to Katmai National Park and past Brooks Camp to the village site of Old Savonoski on the Savonoski River. The Aspelunds will carry kayaks on board the boat during regular tours, and pick up and drop off kayakers anywhere in Naknek Lake. Theirs is the only service of its kind in the region.

Katmai Spirit Tours, 13610 Capstan Dr, Anchorage, AK 99516; in summer, call Alvin's house in Naknek at (907)246-7688; in winter, call Roger in Anchorage at (907)345-6284. $90 per person for the daylong tour, including breakfast and lunch. Maximum group size is 15 people. The boat is handicapped accessible.

Naknek: *Aleut, Yup'ik, Athabascan*

Naknek, on Bristol Bay, has a very different look and feel from King Salmon. It's accessible from the King Salmon airport by 15 miles of good road. Naknek's roots go back to more ancient settlements and, more recently, to the establishment of major salmon canneries in the late 1800s. The town is adjacent to the site of a 7,000-year-old Eskimo settlement. It has a grocery and outfitting store, a gravel landing strip for small planes, a boatyard, a library, a swimming pool at the school, and a very small museum. It's home to about 620 people, many of whom are Native and non-Native commercial fishermen.

The village was given its name in the early 1800s by one Captain Tebenkov of the Russian navy. Prior to that, the Eskimo village of sod houses on the bluff near here was called Kinuyak and Naugeik. In the 1800s Russians built a fort near the village, and Russian fur trappers lived in the area for many years.

"No one in my family ever talked about ancestry until my husband told his dad he was marrying this little gal who was part Alaska Native. His dad hopped on a plane from Minnesota and came right out here. All he wanted to know was if my 'igloo' had heat."

—Mary Shawback

In 1883, the first salmon cannery on Bristol Bay opened near Naknek, bringing northern Europeans to settle in the area. The first cannery on the Naknek River opened in 1890. Although Alaska had been purchased from the Russians in 1867, the Russian Orthodox Church continued to own most of the land at Naknek, acquired under the United States Homestead Act; the church later sold lots to local residents in the area where the commercial center of town is today. A few historic wood-frame buildings still stand, including the picturesque old Peter Pan cannery between Naknek and the old village site.

The least expensive way to get to Naknek, short of hitchhiking, is to take a taxi from King Salmon, about $16 each way. On the way, ask your driver to point out the "new" village of Savonoski on the south shore of the Naknek River, the first place Native villagers from what is now Katmai National Park relocated after they fled the eruption of Novarupta in 1912. In winter, you can cross the frozen river to Savonoski on a snow machine, but there are only a few buildings left; subsequent generations have moved on to South Naknek, accessible only by plane.

In Naknek itself, at the mouth of the river, there is a wildlife viewing platform built on the cliff, where, in June and July, you can watch fishing boats working in Kvichak ("kwee jack") Bay. Bring binoculars to help you spot beluga whales, harbor seals, and migratory whales. Behind you, in the tundra, you might spot caribou, moose, fox, and bears. Check with locals to find out what time (it depends on the tide) Native set-netters will haul their nets onto the beach and pick fish. You can walk down to the beach and watch.

In town, visit the one-room Russian Orthodox church and the beautiful old cemetery, filled with white crosses and overgrown with wildflowers. An outfitting store is located in one of the old cannery buildings near the grocery store and the historic buildings of the now-closed Peter Pan cannery (the buildings are not open, but you can walk the grounds). Just beyond the cannery is the site of an Eskimo village that dates to 3,000–4,000 B.C. The Bristol Bay Historical Museum, in the old two-room Fishermen's Hall, has a few artifacts from the region; most of what has been excavated from this site is housed in the archives of the University of Oregon Museum of

In the Southwest region, Aleut, the Russian word for "coastal people," was used interchangeably to describe Native people who were of either Aleut or Alutiiq heritage, although the cultures had completely different languages and cultures. Although the name stuck, the people who lived in the villages on the site of what is now Katmai National Park and Preserve, for example, are actually Alutiiq, and some of their descendants today live in South Naknek.

Natural History, donated by a UO anthropology professor who has conducted field research in the region for years.

Accessible by four-wheel drive on the beach (only when the tide is out) is one of the oldest operating canneries in the region, at Pederson Point. Check at the King Salmon Visitor Center to see if anyone is taking visitors on tours out there. You can rent a four-wheel, all-terrain vehicle for $50 a day from Eddie Clark in Naknek, (907)246-3383, or rent a car from Bristol Bay Contractors, (907)246-3360.

South Naknek, historically Alutiiq territory (see the Kodiak section of this chapter), is across the Naknek River and accessible only by boat or small plane. It was first settled over 6,000 years ago, when Natives traveled between Naknek and Katmai using the Naknek River and Naknek Lake as their waterway between the two villages. Many people permanently settled in South Naknek after the eruption of the Novarupta volcano. Russian traders lived here between 1800 and 1867. In 1905, Norwegian Laplanders brought reindeer here to herd. Today the village is mostly Aleut, Yup'ik, and Athabascan. Many villagers are commercial fishermen.

"The canneries owned the fishing boats and controlled everything— the wages, the bank, grocery and supply stores. We all fished at the same time—Natives for subsistence, canneries for profit. My mom knew how to do all that—catch and dry fish, hunt moose and caribou, gather plants and berries, sew skin parkas, and make footwear. Natives got a reputation for being 'lazy' because we refused to give up our subsistence work to earn low cannery wages and buy their store food. The canneries eventually brought in Filipinos and Asians to work for them; now they hire college students."
—Mary Shawback

Bristol Bay Historical Museum

Local families have donated items over the years to the Bristol Bay Historical Society, and today the small collection is housed in what used to be the Fishermen's Hall in Naknek. Among the odds and ends of old cannery-box stencils, sailboat rudders, barrels, fish floats, and handmade frames used to decorate icons in the Russian Orthodox church, there is a collection of very old women's knives (labeled *ulu* in Yup'ik, *vashla* in Athabascan, and *unluka* in Sugpiaq dialects) that have been found in the area. One is a metal blade with a wooden handle, unearthed on Naknek beach below the old village, that dates to the late 1700s. Another, discovered along the Brooks River, is fashioned from green slate and dates to 725–975 A.D.

In a glass case is a parka, designed and sewn by Ahanahook Thompson in the early 1900s, made from otter, seal, wolverine, beaver, and calf skins; and a pair of handsome reindeer hide boots. An old newspaper interview with Thompson is taped to the front of the case. (The "igloo" she talks about in the interview is a sod house, not the ice house common to central and eastern Arctic Canada.)

The reindeer yoke and collar hanging on the wall are a remnant of the reindeer herding that the Alaska Natives used to do in this area, an enterprise launched by the federal government to turn nomadic hunters into herdsmen who would settle in permanent villages, where their children would be required to attend school. (See "The Reindeer Queen" in the Nome section of the Arctic chapter.)

At the museum's counter you can purchase classic Bristol Bay sailboat blueprints ($20) and T-shirts ($20) that help support the museum. Coloring books of paper dolls with traditional clothing, as well as patterns for Aleut headgear (with a dandy little section on design elements), are free, courtesy of the Alaska State Museum.

The Bristol Bay Historical Museum is in Naknek. Staffed by Bristol Bay Historical Society volunteers, it is open only by appointment. Contact Sara Feriante, (907)246-8211; Adelheid Herrmann, (907)246-4495.

> **"One thing about being from this area of Athabascans, Yup'iks, Eskimos, Irish, Finns, Norwegians, and every- thing else—you have family wherever you go."**
> **—Myrtle Anelon**

Al-Lou's Bed & Breakfast

Allen and Mary Louise Aspelund, Bristol Bay Native Corporation shareholders of Aleut, Scot, and Swedish heritage, offer several inexpensive options for an overnight stay in Naknek. These include a fully furnished one-bedroom apartment; a small cabin with kitchen, living room, and bath with showers; or a three-bedroom, two-bath mobile home—all located next to their house, half a block from the school (which has a great indoor swimming pool open to the public) and within walking distance of the overlook, beach, and museum. The couple also operates the Naknek Riverine Lodge, which is right on the Naknek riverfront; it offers three bedrooms (two with private baths) and a bunkroom with shower. The lodge has a fully furnished kitchen and a spacious front room. You can fish for silvers from the shoreline or drive 4 miles to King Salmon to rent a boat to fish the Naknek River; the Aspelunds can help you book guides or trips. Area fishing guides often book their clients into the lodge overnight.

Mary Louise (Lou) Aspelund, who has commercially set-net for 40 years, was born in Port Heiden on the Alaska Peninsula, a village within a few miles of the 6-mile-wide Aniakchak Caldera. The caldera, 2,000 feet deep, was formed by the collapse of a 7,000-foot mountain about 3,500 years ago; its most recent eruption was in 1931, an explosion that rained ash on Port Heiden and surrounding villages more than 40 miles away. Lou's mother was born and raised in Chignik, on the other side of the Alaska Peninsula, facing the Pacific Ocean. Allen Aspelund grew up in Naknek.

Al-Lou's Bed & Breakfast and Naknek Riverine Lodge, PO Box 84, Naknek, AK 99633; (907)246-4270. Open year-round. Apartment or cabin $70 single, in summer or winter; each extra guest $5. Mobile home $70 per person. Riverine Lodge room rates vary.

Violet Willson's Little House

Alaska Native Violet Willson, born on Lake Iliamna, is of Aleut, Dane, and Norwegian descent. Her grandmother was Aleut, from Kodiak Island; her mother was from a village on Lake Iliamna. For years, Willson held one of the best set-net positions on Naknek beach, at the mouth of the Naknek River, until her recent retirement from fishing. Couples and small families are welcome at her new one-bedroom cabin with a peekaboo view of the Naknek River, adjacent to her two-story house. The cabin is immaculate, with a large kitchen equipped with microwave, coffeemaker, and all the fixings for breakfast in the full-size refrigerator: fresh homemade bread, bacon, and eggs. Coffee and tea are provided as well. The bedroom has a large queen-size bed (there's a roll-away in the closet too) and an attached bath with shower. From the cabin, you can walk about 3 miles to the grocery store, to the old Russian Orthodox church and cemetery on the slope above the store, to the museum, and down to the beach to watch the set-netters haul in their catch.

Violet Willson's Little House, PO Box 104, Naknek, AK 99633; (907)246-4486. Open year-round. Cabin $80. No pets.

Egegik: *Athabascan, Aleut*

Egegik is a very small fishing village tucked into a small bay at the mouth of the Egegik River. Although it may not appear to be thousands of years old, Egegik is one of the oldest occupied settlements in the region. Archaeologists estimate that Eskimos fished here for about 6,000 years; in the last century, Athabascans and Aleuts have occupied the site. Contact with Russian fur traders and Russian Orthodox missionaries began around 1818. In 1895, the Alaska Packers Association built a salmon saltery here, where fish were preserved by drying and salting before the advent of commercial canning.

Prior to white contact, Egegik was used primarily as a summer fish camp. Becharof Lake, the headwaters of the Egegik River, dominates the middle of the peninsula. During the winter, villagers lived on the Pacific Ocean side of the Alaska Peninsula, nestled in a glacial meadow at Kanatak ("can-attack"). The village was protected from the Pacific Ocean by rock shoals and overshadowed by the snow-covered volcanic peaks that rose straight up behind it. In the spring, the entire village moved to the Bristol Bay side of the peninsula to harvest the huge schools of fish mingling at the mouth of Egegik Bay. If you've got a good map, such as the *Alaska Atlas and Gazetteer* (DeLorme Mapping, 1992), you'll be able to trace their route over the old Kanatak Pass from the winter village to Becharof Lake and down the Egegik River to the bay. To catch fish they used gill nets made of twine made from split spruce roots, similar in design to the nylon filament net used today by commercial fishermen. They also used fish traps at the mouth of the river. Salmon fillets were wind-dried on racks before they were packed back to the winter village.

Egegik became a year-round settlement after 1900 when a post office and school were established. The population again swelled in 1918 when Natives from other villages moved to the village in an attempt to isolate themselves from an especially virulent influenza epidemic that was sweeping the entire globe. (The flu killed all but three of the 120 Natives who lived at Pilot Point, about 30 miles away. Pilot Point had more canneries, and consequently more contact with the outside world; ships brought cannery workers into the Alaska Peninsula and Bristol Bay from Italy, China, the Philippines, and northern Europe.) Today only about half of the 80 or so houses are occupied during the stormy winters.

Sockeye Adventure

Eddie Clark lives most of the year in Naknek, not far from the gravel airstrip where he keeps his plane. But every summer he and his wife Peggy have taken off for Coffee Point, 40 miles southwest of Naknek on the Alaska Peninsula, to set-net for salmon in one of Bristol Bay's hottest fishing spots. Coffee Point is just down the beach from the fishing village of Egegik. With the Clarks, you'll be able to visit one of the four shore-based salmon processing plants and look for souvenirs at a small local fur and ivory shop in Egegik.

You catch an air taxi from King Salmon, stay overnight with the Clark family, and experience a working set-net operation firsthand. Depending on the tides, you may find yourself up at 4am to observe, the family picking fish caught in the gill net. "Picking fish" is a local colloquialism for disentangling salmon from the net. It's an experience that'll leave you wide awake no matter when you get out of bed to pick—because the silvery fish are huge (up to 50 pounds of dead weight) and the net is wrapped so tightly around them that it looks impossible to liberate them without a knife. You'll want to visit during the king salmon run in June and early July, when more than 1,000 32-foot gillnetters and 30 big fish-processing ships crowd the mouth of the bay.

Sockeye Adventure, Box 167, Naknek, AK 99633; (907)246-3383. In June and July, try their cell phone at (907)4339-3383, but you may have trouble getting through because of the hundreds of fishermen using cell phones on the bay. Prices vary; package options, including day trips, are available. Book your round-trip flight from King Salmon to the landing strip at Coffee Point (specify Coffee Point rather than Egegik, or you'll land on the wrong runway) with PenAir. Cost is about $150 each way. Either the Clarks will pick you up, or the PenAir agent will deliver you to their front door. Bring warm clothes and light rain gear. Bedding and meals are provided.

LAKE CLARK AND LAKE ILIAMNA REGION

On a map, trace the Kvichak River from Naknek on Bristol Bay, through Lake Iliamna along the north shore, and up the Newhalen River to its headwaters in Lake Clark, and you'll see one of the most important spawning-salmon routes in the world. The adult salmon returning to this river system were sought by both Athabascan and Eskimo people. Tales of their battles include supernatural feats by warriors on both sides.

Today, two villages in the Lake Iliamna region have distinctly different cultures. Newhalen, at the mouth of the Newhalen River on Lake Iliamna, is Aleut/Yup'ik; Nondalton, on Sixmile Lake, is an Athabascan village that, in the last century, moved downlake to its present site from the shore of Lake Clark. Between the two villages is the village of Iliamna, the border town between what might be thought of as two separate countries.

To the visitor's eye, there are few differences among the three modern villages. Newhalen keeps pretty much to itself, with no visitor services. Nondalton has a grocery store, one luxury lodge, and a few visitor services. Iliamna has a runway large enough for jets, several luxury fishing and hunting lodges on the lakefront, a grocery store with fishing tackle and an espresso machine, and accommodations for fishermen and hunters. Fishermen and bear-watchers flock to Iliamna from Anchorage to visit the rapids in the Newhalen River, a narrow spot with rock ledges that has long been used by both bears and humans to catch salmon. Lake Iliamna is also home to freshwater seals. If you fly over the lake, you'll spot them hauled out on islands.

Over the hills from Lake Iliamna is another large lake and river system. Lake Clark National Park and Preserve, 1 hour by plane from Anchorage and a short hop from Iliamna on a bush plane, is a wilderness playground for insiders, one of the least known or used national parks in the United States. Nearly 4 million acres are within the boundary of the preserve, which was established in 1980. Its lures are trophy fish, a huge caribou herd (more than 100,000 animals), spectacular open hiking on unmarked ridge and tundra routes, stunning mountain peaks and glaciers, and river running on the Tlikakila, Mulchatna, and Chilikadrotna Rivers, all designated National Wild and Scenic Rivers. The preserve's two steaming volcanoes, Iliamna and Redoubt, which rise more than 10,000 feet, are links to the Pacific Ring of Fire. The majority of residences on the lake are at Port Alsworth, a landing strip at the head of a small bay surrounded by houses and lodges.

"We are nomadic people, and Natives are some of the hardest-working people I've met. A lot of our villages exist where they do now simply because that's where the school is, centralized out of convenience for the educational system. But economically, it makes no sense. Unemployment is very high in the villages. What can 300 people do grouped around a school?"

—Glen Alsworth

Getting There

Access to the Lake Clark/Lake Iliamna region is by air. There are no roads from the outside, and only about 20 miles of gravel road within thousands of square miles of wilderness.

One of the most famous flightseeing routes in Alaska is from Anchorage to Lake Clark National Park and Preserve. On Lake Clark Air (2425 Merrill Field Dr, Anchorage, AK 99501; (800)662-7661 or (907)278-2054), a regularly scheduled service between Anchorage and Port Alsworth, you fly across Cook Inlet and enter the Chigmit Mountain range through a passageway so narrow, steep, and convoluted that passengers swear the plane's wings will touch the mountainsides. The trip is like a good amusement ride: the risks look more frightening than they are. Hundreds of trips by small planes are made through the pass each week without incident. The pass snakes through the Tlikakila River valley to Port Alsworth, where there's a wide gravel landing strip and a little settlement of fishing lodges, private homes, and Park Service headquarters. On stormy days, or when fog clouds the Lake Clark basin, planes fly at a higher altitude and pass through the mountains between the 10,197-foot Redoubt Volcano and Double Glacier.

Lake Clark Air flies out of Anchorage's Merrill Field, which is across town from the Anchorage International Airport. You can take a taxicab between airports; cabs wait at the curb, as they do in any other airport, or look for a list of cab services in the baggage claim area.

You can also fly directly from Anchorage to Lake Iliamna, one of the largest lakes in the United States, on Era Aviation (6160 S Airpark Dr, Anchorage, AK 99502; (800)866-8394 or (907)248-4422), an Alaska Airlines commuter service, offers the only regularly scheduled jet service between Anchorage and Iliamna. The landing strip at Iliamna, a former Air Force base, is larger than the whole town, which has a population of 94. You can also fly to Lake Clark and charter a private plane to take you to Iliamna.

From Iliamna or Lake Clark, you can charter a bush plane or floatplane through a company like Lake Clark Air to take you anywhere you want to go within the inland region. You can flightsee over Lake Iliamna and into the Tazimina Lakes basin, fly through a mountain pass on the Alaska Peninsula to the wilderness beaches of Shelikof Strait, or fly over the south end of Lake Iliamna to Brooks Camp in Katmai National Park. Or you can fly across the tundra to Bristol Bay on the Bering Sea coastline.

On the ground, there are few options for overland travel. A 6-mile gravel road connects Iliamna with a boat landing on Sixmile Lake, a popular launching site for rafters floating down the Newhalen River and fishermen working their way upriver in skiffs to Sixmile Lake and Lake Clark. The only settlement on Sixmile Lake is the Athabascan village of Nondalton (population 178), a 10-minute hop on a private plane from Iliamna over to the Nondalton landing strip. Pay for extra air time and you can flightsee, threading the needle into the Tazimina Lakes basin and then lifting up over the ridge to look for mountain goats before you land in Nondalton.

If you are not an experienced wilderness adventurer, the best way to find your way around in lake country is to let lodge owners, outfitters, and guides arrange transportation and set up trips for you.

Port Alsworth: *Athabascan*

Port Alsworth is a very small village (consisting of a church camp, fishing lodges, and summer homes) on Lake Clark. From the gravel runway, it's a short walk to the Lake Clark National Park and Preserve Visitors Center. There's a small cafe and several places to buy tackle, soft drinks, and candy bars, but no grocery store. Port Alsworth is the rendezvous point for wilderness treks in Lake Clark National Park.

Lake Clark National Park and Preserve Visitors Center

If you are planning a trip to Southwest Alaska to learn about Native culture, the Lake Clark National Park and Preserve Visitors Center is an excellent first stop for an orientation and an overview of the region. National Park Service historian John Branson offers excellent slide shows; one is on life at the turn of the century in the Lake Clark/Lake Iliamna area after reindeer herding was introduced, while another includes views of the Bristol Bay coastline.

In the brochure for Lake Clark National Park and Preserve is a black-and-white photograph, taken in 1902, of Denaina Athabascans standing in front of a log house in a village called Kijik. The village site and those around it were recently designated a National Historic Landmark. The Kijik (sometimes spelled Kijak) Archaeological District is a 2,000-acre area along the shore of Lake Clark. It includes 15 well-preserved Denaina Athabascan Native settlements, one abandoned as late as 1910. Settlements are clusters of 15 to 20 sod houses about half a mile apart. One theory is that they were abandoned when supporting timbers rotted out, and were then reestablished nearby; another theory is that when people became sick, the villagers picked up and moved to new quarters on clean ground. The lakeshore villages were established in the late 1700s, after Russian explorers, traders, and missionaries came upriver from Bristol Bay to Lake Clark. Prior to Russian influence, Denaina Athabascan settlements were more inland, where they were concealed from Yup'ik Eskimo attack. The desired resource on the Kijik River may have been an unusually late salmon run. Fresh, spawning fish could be caught under the lake ice as late as December. After 1900, descendants of Kijik residents moved downlake, then to Nondalton and other villages in the region.

Unfortunately, there are no tours of the archaeological site, although it is regularly patrolled; but you can place these Denaina settlements in context with respect to the Athabascan territory that once surrounded Cook Inlet by looking at the map in *Tanaina Plantlore: An Ethnobotany of the Denaina Indians of Southcentral Alaska*, by Priscilla Russell Kari (National Park Service, 1987), available at the visitors center. An instructive guide, the paperback book is illustrated with lovely color photographs of plants the Denaina used for food, medicine, basket weaving, and building materials. There are also photographs of a traditional steam bath chinked with moss; mountain ash switches, which were used in steam baths to increase circulation; a smokehouse thatched with birch leaves; birchbark baskets; and game lookouts fashioned from spruce limbs.

Lake Clark National Park and Preserve Visitors Center, Port Alsworth, AK 99653; (907)781-2218. Call for hours.

The Farm Lodge

Glen (a Bristol Bay Native Corporation shareholder of Aleut descent) and Patty Alsworth own and operate The Farm Lodge, as well as Lake Clark Air. From the gravel runway that passes right by the front of the lodge, you walk over a path between a large vegetable and flower garden to a two-story modern house and a row of new cabins on the lakeshore. A mowed lawn stretches from the front porches to the beach, where floatplanes are lined up in a row.

The Farm is a full-service lodge, offering guests flyout fishing, flightseeing, customized float trips, camping, hiking, and hunting. The lodge itself is particularly attractive for family stays. The comfortable cabins have roofed porches that overlook the lake. Each sleeps four in made-up bunks and has a bathroom with shower, fresh towels, soaps, and shampoo. Your stay includes three huge meals a day (with fresh vegetables from the garden and homemade breads at every meal) in the family's large dining room. Services include on-premises babysitting, laundry, sack lunches, and parties for special occasions. Also available are boat rentals, tie-downs for aircraft, and tent camping (you can rent camping gear from the Alsworths). If you'd like to fish, Glen and Patty suggest you bring fishing gear and hip boots or chest waders. There are no grocery stores (you have to fly to Nondalton or Iliamna for groceries or bring them with you), but there is a small cafe near the Lake Clark National Park and Preserve Visitors Center. The only maintained trail in the park is an easy 3-mile trail to Tanalian Falls that begins behind the cafe.

On the wall of the lodge dining room is a wolf pelt shot and tanned by Glen's mother, a model of a baidarka (kayak), and a beautiful pair of beaded mukluks from Mary's high school days. Glen's parents, Mary and Leon (Babe) Alsworth, homesteaded "The Farm" in the 1940s. Mary was Aleut, and for years she ran the post office and weather station at Port Alsworth. Glen is mayor of the Lake and Peninsula Borough, a region that stretches from Lake Clark to the tip of the Alaska Peninsula.

Aleuts may have entered the region, first occupied by Yup'ik Eskimos and Athabascans, with Russian fur traders. Glen was surprised to learn that the language he heard his mother speak and thought was Aleut was actually Russian. "You have to remember, it was only 130 years ago that this area was ruled by Russia," he says. Aleuts, enslaved by the Russians, were forced to learn Russian; then, when the United States purchased Alaska, Aleuts had to learn English. The generation of Glen's grandparents spoke three languages.

As a kid, Glen ate fish-head chowders and rich soups with a broth base made from cracked moose bones. "We baked fish heads in the oven on a cookie pan, and picked the meat for chowder," he recalls. Glen says he can recognize people of Aleut descent wherever he meets them. "You can take an Aleut out of the village," he says, "but you can't take the village out of the Aleut. Being Aleut is a matter of character, not necessarily looks; it's more what isn't said than what is." That said, you'll be lucky to get a chance to talk with Glen, who is an extremely busy man.

The Farm Lodge, PO Box 1, Port Alsworth, AK 99653; (907)781-2211. Cabins $85 per person, including three meals; $65 per person for breakfast only. Meals are also available on a per-meal basis. Discounted group rates. Boat rentals are $150 per day, or $300 per day with a guide. Camping is $10 per night per tent. Call for a full-color brochure.

Iliamna: *Athabascan, Aleut, Yup'ik*

Iliamna, on the west shore of Lake Iliamna, is a former Air Force base with a jet-size gravel landing strip scraped across the tundra. From Bristol Bay, salmon enter the Kvichak River and swim upstream to spawn in 78-mile-long Lake Iliamna, the Newhalen River, Sixmile Lake, and finally into Lake Clark. From Iliamna you can fly across the mountains to the spectacular wilderness ocean beaches of Katmai National Park and Preserve, or go up the Newhalen River by skiff to Lake Clark National Park and Preserve. The nearest Native villages are Newhalen, Nondalton, Kokhanok, and Igiugig.

> **"Around here we say the fog is the breath of the fish—when the fog comes in, we know they're on their way."**
> **—Lisa Reimers**

Until the early 1980s, some Iliamna families had no running water, no electricity, and no television. Families used gas and kerosene lanterns for light, and oil ranges and woodstoves for heat; they drew their water from the lake. Today there are large diesel generators at nearby Newhalen that supply electricity for both villages, a noninvasive hydroelectric project on the Tazimina River, and satellite dishes and modern buildings in the village.

If at all possible, take a flightseeing trip across Lake Iliamna and through the mountains to Shelikof Strait to see the ocean beaches, bears, and glaciers of the outer Katmai coast and to get a sense of the region and the challenge of living here. For an introduction to the culture of the region, tour with Myrtle Anelon, owner of Gram's Cafe.

Gram's Cafe

Gram's Cafe, winner of the Alaska Federation of Natives' small business award, is owned by Elia and Myrtle Anelon. Elia is an Aleut/Eskimo who grew up in Newhalen near the mouth of the Newhalen River; Myrtle is of Athabascan and Irish descent. She is a member of the Lake Clark Trefon family—Athabascans who hosted the first "tourists" coming to Lake Clark from Cook Inlet at the turn of the century. Her Irish dad was one of the early traders in the area. According to Myrtle, he "one day paddled up to Lake Clark and found my mom, Alexandria." He asked her parents for permission to marry their young daughter, waited until she grew up, and then brought her to live in Iliamna and taught her to speak English. "She was so homesick, he had to send her home for a year to wait for her to grow up a little more," says Myrtle. The cabin where they raised 17 children together is still standing by Lake Iliamna, not far from Myrtle's cafe and lodging.

Frieda Slye makes dolls and teddy bears from sealskin. You can find her at the Iliamna post office, or drop into the little shop in her house at 205 Lakeview Dr, Iliamna, AK 99606; (907)571-1203.

Myrtle Anelon is president of the Iliamna Native Corporation and was a health aide for 26 years; she traveled by snowmobile and monitored the radio to assist people with health problems in this remote wilderness. She also worked as the village postmaster for 21 years. Now in her mid-50s, she's proprietor of Gram's Cafe, which she operates together with other members of her family. Gram's offers many of the same services as larger lodges on the lake: world-class fishing, bear viewing, rafting on the Newhalen River, jet-boat tours of Lake Clark National Park, flightseeing, and guided and unguided caribou and moose hunts. They also rent vehicles and boats by the day or by the hour.

Several things distinguish this lodge from others in the area, though: you can stay just one night, instead of the usual weeklong package rate; the restaurant is open to the public; and Myrtle guides tours of the area. With her, you tour the region in a van and skiff to meet friends and relatives, including an uncle who worked in his youth as a packer, carrying up to 100 pounds of goods on his back over the portage from Lake Iliamna to the Newhalen landing. You'll see historic photographs of the Trefon family; learn about subsistence hunting, fishing, trapping, and reindeer herding; visit salmon spawning grounds; and explore the modern Native villages of Newhalen (Aleut/Yup'ik) and Nondalton (Athabascan).

The cafe, with picture windows overlooking Lake Iliamna, is paneled in knotty pine with white wainscoting and chintz curtains. The cafe has a new kitchen and a full-time, year-round chef.

Snowshoes, ulu knives, and whale baleen decorate the room. A pot of fresh coffee and freshly baked cookies are on the table. Lodging consists of three furnished houses for rent and a new single-story motel-type unit of rooms (nicely furnished, with floral chintz bedspreads and curtains; some have private baths, and some have kitchenettes). The traditional steam bath, in a small building on the property, is available to guests.

Gram's Cafe, PO Box 248, Iliamna, AK 99606; (907)571-1463. Open year-round. Rooms $85–$250, including buffet breakfast. Special rates for groups. Sack lunches and buffet dinners are available daily. Car rentals include an 11-passenger van, a pickup, and a four-wheeler. Motorized boats are $100 per day plus gas; all are also rented hourly. Services vary from flightseeing (maximum three people, $100 an hour) and bear viewing to guided fishing trips for $2,500 a week. Freezers are available for meat, fish, and berries. Free airport pickup and delivery. Write for a brochure.

Pinned to the bulletin board of Gram's Cafe in Iliamna is a clip from The Sun, a supermarket tabloid, showing a picture of a military jet flying over the writhing head and neck of a Loch Ness–type monster. The article claims the encounter took place in April and that "local Indians have for years worshipped the huge Lake Iliamna monster." They goofed. The lake is frozen over in April, and most Native residents of villages on the shores of Lake Iliamna are members of the Russian Orthodox Church and other Christian-based religions.

Roadhouse Inn

Ethel Adcox, an Athabascan who grew up on the east shore of Lake Iliamna at Pedro Bay, calls her bed and breakfast the Roadhouse Inn, a name that recalls the first "roadhouses" established on the lakeshore at the turn of the century. Hers is an immaculate split-level house overlooking Lake Iliamna. It is actually a full-service inn, with three meals served family style each day, free snacks, two common rooms with satellite television, and a small gift shop. The gift shop stocks Alaskana, T-shirts and hats, and extraordinary, exquisite fur coats made by one of Adcox's best friends, Violet Blatchford, a Yup'ik Eskimo furrier whose contemporary fur parkas have been sold all over the world. The Blatchford family is well known for their skin sewing and ivory carving. The inn has four cozy rooms, each with double and twin beds and three shared baths. The Adcox family seems to have thought of everything for their guests. For fishermen there's a mudroom, a room for storing tackle, and a fish freezer. For business guests, there's office space and a fax machine. The house is divided to provide nooks for quiet activities, such as reading or writing letters.

Roadhouse Inn, PO Box 206, Iliamna, AK 99606; (907)571-1272; fax (907)571-1557. Open year-round. Rooms $110–$135 per person, depending on season, and include three meals a day, snacks, airport pickup and delivery, and fish storage.

Airport Hotel

This small, very basic 1960s hotel sits right next to the airport and is owned by Anesia Batchelder, who was born and raised in the Aleut/Yup'ik village of Newhalen, and her husband, Lem. All the rooms are upstairs, and each is furnished with two single beds. Large shared baths with showers, one for men and one for women, are down the hall. Downstairs, fishermen, hunters, and backcountry hikers can rest their weary bones in one of the comfortable couches and chairs grouped around a warm stove. The kitchen offers breakfast, lunch, and dinner; at the latter meal, you may enjoy chicken-fried steak or pork chops plus all the extras and dessert. The hotel has established relationships with float outfitters, fishing guides, and air taxis as well as a four-wheel all-terrain vehicle rental service (it offers a special price of $10 an hour for hotel guests, which is a real bonus because you need one to run around the airport fence to one of the best fishing holes in Alaska on the Newhalen River). There's also freezer space for up to five fish per day, cutting tables, and canning equipment for do-it-yourself fish canners.

At the Iliamna Trading Company store (a modern grocery, hardware, and sporting goods store), you may find a few grass baskets made in the region, for sale on consignment. Also look here for Joni Paule's beaver and fox hats and mittens. Paule is a transplanted Sioux from the Midwest; she works winters on her trapline on the Mulchatna River.

Airport Hotel, PO Box 157, Iliamna, AK 99606; (907)571-1276. Open year-round. Salmon- and float-fishing trip packages for one to seven days include such things as special rates for round-trip airfare from Anchorage, ground transportation, meals, guides, flyouts, rafting, and camping equipment.

Nondalton: *Athabascan*

This small Athabascan village on Sixmile Lake, the gateway from Iliamna to Lake Clark National Park and Preserve, didn't get electricity until 1986, but it has a good gravel runway and offers shelter from the storm. In addition to a grocery store and the Coffee Cup Cafe (which offers hamburgers and has the best selection of candy and soft drinks outside of Costco), there is a Native-owned bed and breakfast as well as cabins and boat rentals at Wilderness Lodge (known locally as Fish Camp Mike's). Fewer than 240 people live here, and most are dependent on subsistence fishing and hunting. The Nondalton Dancers, a group of Nondalton young and elderly residents, are working with other Athabascan tribes to learn some of the old dances and songs and to make traditional regalia—no easy task when it costs more than $5,000 to fly the group to Anchorage to participate in regalia and dance workshops and celebrations. Donations for travel are always appreciated.

Salmon Run Lodge

"Diamond Jim" and Lydia Wilson built this five-plus-bedroom house where they raised 10 children. It's a casual place where kids and dogs are welcome and the owners can find you a babysitter if you need one. Daughter Janice Balluta ran the inn until 1997, when she moved back to Anchorage; now Jim and Lydia have stepped back in, with Jim wielding the spatula over fried eggs and ham in the morning. Both are deeply involved in cultural activities, including the village's Nondalton Dancers. Jim will pick you up at the Nondalton airstrip on his four-wheeler or from the Iliamna side of Sixmile Lake at the Newhalen River landing in his skiff.

People are generous. If someone gives you a ride into a village or across a lake in a skiff, he or she can be out more than $3 a gallon for gas. Beverage or food shared with you was barged or flown in. The shelter you stay in—the lumber, the windows, the plumbing—was also barged or flown, piece by piece, to the place where it now sits.

Salmon Run Lodge, PO Box 05, Nondalton, AK 99640; (907)294-2205. Open year-round, except when the owners are out of town. Room rates vary.

THE OUTER ISLANDS

Aleutian Islands: *Aleut*

The Aleutian Chain is the assemblage of more than 200 volcanic islands that stretches from the Alaska mainland more than 1,100 miles across the sea, reaching for Russia. The scenery here is breathtaking. The Aleutians are actually the peaks of a sub-marine mountain range and include 57 snowcapped volcanoes, many of them active. Although the islands are treeless, they are carpeted with wildflowers (buttercups, chocolate lilies, lupine, wild iris, and orchids), lush grasses, and mosses. The cold waters of the Bering Sea and the Pacific Ocean provide a wealth of fish and shellfish and the sea mammals that feed on them, such as seals, sea lions, and sea otters. More than 250 species of migratory birds rest and feed on the islands as well.

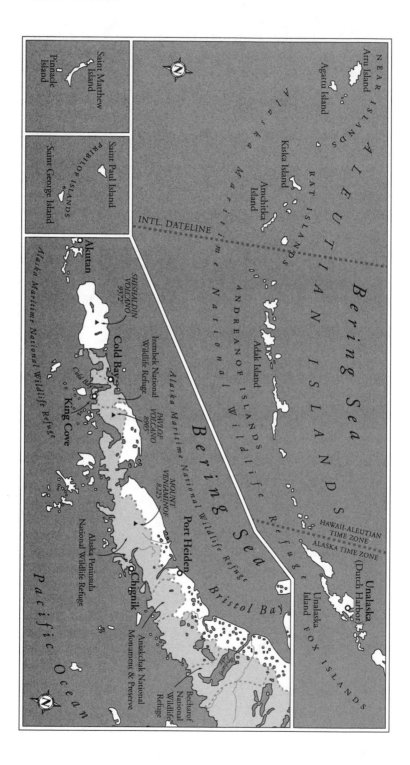

The islands were once home to an estimated 15,000 to 25,000 Unangan people, who lived in villages of sod-covered houses built in protected coves along the seacoasts. The people were nourished by the abundance of marine life and sea mammals (which they hunted from kayaks, which they called *iqyaáx*), bird eggs, and plants. When the Russians arrived in the mid-1700s, they renamed the Unangan people Aleuts, and brought them epidemics, violence, starvation, and slavery. By the early 1800s, the Native population had dropped to less than 1,000. During World War II, the Aleuts were treated no more kindly by the U.S. military, which evacuated them after the Japanese bombed Unalaska/Dutch Harbor and occupied Attu and Kiska Islands. The Aleuts were given just hours to pack a suitcase before they were shipped off to Southeast Alaska and interned in concentration camps.

The Russian desire to acquire exotic goods from Chinese merchants drove the quest for sea otter pelts and other furs, for which the Chinese paid top prices. Russians came to the Alaska coastline because they had wiped out their own fur-bearing mammals in Siberia and on their Pacific coast, because mammals here were plentiful, and because they could force Native hunters to labor by taking their wives and children hostage.

Today, descendants of these Aleuts live in several small villages in the Aleutian Islands. Most of the 200 islands in the chain are unoccupied; all are included in the Alaska National Wildlife Refuge, a haven established to protect migratory birds, marine mammals, and their habitats.

The Aleutian Chain is actually divided into six groups of islands; each group is separated by a broad gap of open ocean. The Fox Islands have the largest land mass and are closest to the Alaska Peninsula. They include the island (and town) of Unalaska. Nearby are the poetically named Islands of Four Mountains.

The Andreanof Islands, which include the intriguing Amlia, Atka, Great Sitkin, Adak, Kanaga, and Tanaga Islands, are home to the small Aleut village of Atka, on Atka Island. Atka, resettled after it was nearly destroyed by starvation during the Russian occupation, suffered another trauma during World War II, when the village was evacuated and then burned to the ground by the U.S. military. Islanders returning from internment camps after the war rebuilt the town on its ancient village site. Adak, on Adak Island, is an abandoned Navy base that once held 100,000 men. Recently decommissioned, Adak has been returned to the Aleuts through the Aleut Corporation, which plans to develop its huge airport and deepwater port into a major way station between Asia and the North American continent.

The Delarof Islands are a smattering of tiny islands, more

mountaintops in the submerged mountain range that makes up the Aleutian Chain. From here it's a leap to the Rat Islands and a very broad jump to the Near Islands, closest to Russia.

Unalaska: *Unangen*

Those wishing to visit the islands can fly directly to Unalaska by jet, although air travel is often delayed because of weather. The largest hotel in the Aleutian Chain is the Grand Aleutian Hotel in Unalaska/Dutch Harbor. Although locals have nicknamed the hotel the "Grand Illusion," it's a good thing a Japanese investor built it—there's an Aleut tour here, the only one in the islands, and you'll need a place to stay overnight. You book your plane to Dutch Harbor (officially known as the International Port of Dutch Harbor), but you are actually landing on a little piece of land that straddles Unalaska and Amaknak Islands. Both the island and the town you are coming to are called Unalaska, and you are way out in the Aleutian Islands—780 miles west of Anchorage.

Adak is home to a small museum as well as the Alaska Maritime National Wildlife Refuge office, (907)592-2406. For a peek at what's in store for Adak, take a look at the Aleut Corporation's Web site at http://www. adakisland.com.

Aleuts first settled here because of the natural deepwater harbor, abundance of marine life and birds, and lush tundra with abundant harvests of berries, greens, and medicinal plants. The scenery of Unalaska Island is spectacular: the active Makushin Volcano steams in the distance, and emerald green tundra blankets the angular volcanic escarpments that rise abruptly above the harbor. The Unangan people named their most populated harbor—located, as are most Native villages, at the mouth of a river teeming with salmon—Iliuliuk, a word that Aleuts say means "to live in harmony" or "curved bay."

Archaeological excavations of Aleut sod houses called *barabaras* (pronounced "bar-raw-bar-rahs") in Unalaska have unearthed artifacts from Iliuliuk that are from 6,000 to 8,000 years old. The Aleuts who lived here traveled thousands of miles of coastline in iqyaáx—wood-frame boats covered with three to six sea lion skins, which are still unsurpassed in performance (today's fiberglass kayaks, based on the Aleut design, are simply lower-maintenance versions of the old skin boats).

The first Russian explorers noted the existence of Iliuliuk in 1759. Russian fur trappers followed, brutally enslaving skilled Aleut hunters to harvest fur seals and sea otters, and making Iliuliuk the first permanent settlement in Russian America.

The arrival of Russian Orthodox Church missionaries helped ease relationships between the Aleuts and Russians. Father John Veniaminov (later canonized as Saint Innocent) settled on Unalaska in 1824 and, with Aleut Ivan Pan'kov, a fluent speaker of Russian, wrote a Russian-Aleut grammar, preserving the language for scholars. The Holy Ascension Russian Orthodox Cathedral, constructed between 1894 and 1896, is a National Historic Landmark and is open to the public. The cathedral, built with California redwood shipped to Unalaska by the Alaska Commercial Company, is filled with irreplaceable icons, most of them from Russia and some painted by Aleut artists.

For a look at the Aleut and Alutiiq antiquities held in Leningrad's Museum of Anthropology and Ethnography, see **Aleut and Eskimo Art: Tradition and Innovation in South Alaska,** *by anthropologist Dorothy Jean Ray (University of Washington Press, 1981). Pictured are beautiful woven grass hats, a puffin-skin garment, and ivory figurines worn on Aleut hunting hats.*

Russians also transplanted Sitka spruce to the treeless island in the late 1700s. When the Americans purchased Alaska from the Russians in 1867, many Aleuts from Unalaska were moved permanently to the Pribilof Islands to harvest fur seals for the Americans.

During the gold rush in the late 1800s, the island became a way station for ships, reloading with water and coal stored on Unalaska Island, on their way north to Nome.

When Unalaska's Dutch Harbor was bombed by the Japanese in 1942, the Aleuts were evacuated and moved to internment camps in Southeast Alaska for the duration of World War II. You can learn more about this episode by viewing a film called *Forced to Leave: The World War II Detention of Alaskan Japanese-Americans and Aleuts* at local hotels and the Unalaska public library.

In 1989 the Qawalangin Tribe of Unalaska was formally recognized by the Bureau of Indian Affairs, securing Native sovereignty. The Ounalashka Corporation was established after the passage of the Alaska Native Claims Settlement Act in 1971. Today Aleut schoolchildren on Unalaska learn about their rich cultural past in the classroom and have made wood-frame boats, wooden visors, and grass baskets, all similar to those used by their ancestors, as school projects. Most Aleuts make their living today as commercial crab and cod fishermen; Unalaska's fleet makes one of the largest commercial hauls in the United States.

Plans are under way to build an interpretive center about the World War II events on Unalaska, in partnership with the Ounalashka Corporation, the city of Unalaska, the National Park Service, and the Aleut Corporation. The Ounalashka Corporation has also selected a site for a new museum with a repository to house artifacts being un-earthed in archaeological excavations and Aleut cultural items that have been returned by U.S. museums.

Most of the land is owned by Ounalashka Corporation, which is-sues permits for hiking, overnight camping, and skiing. A.L.E.U.T. Tours offers a 2- to 3-hour tour of Unalaska, including the cathedral and an archaeological dig.

Getting There

Hang on to your seats: Unalaska Island has the shortest runway in all of Alaska—only 3,900 feet, straddling a little strip of land between Unalaska and Dutch Harbor. Landing here is a memorable experi-ence in itself. The Alaska Marine Highway ferry, (800)526-6731, ser-vices Unalaska, as do Alaska Airlines, (800)426-0333; Reeve Aleutian Airways, Inc., (800)544-2248 or (907)842-1603; and PenAir, (800)448-4226. Car rentals are available at the airport from North Port Rentals, PO Box 214, Unalaska, AK 99685; (907)581-1538.

Visitor Services

- Unalaska/Port of Dutch Harbor Convention & Visitors Bureau, PO Box 545, Unalaska, AK 99685; (907)581-2612; Web site: http://www.arctic.net/-updhcvb. Write for a free Unalaska-Dutch Harbor Visitors Guide, PO Box 920472, Dutch Harbor, AK 99692; (907)581-2092.

- Unalaska/Dutch Harbor Chamber of Commerce; (907)581-4242. Call for a business directory and information guide.

Ounalashka Corporation Offices

Housed in the Ounalashka Corporation offices are a cultural library and a temporary museum that's getting bigger every day as artifacts are excavated from a village site at Margaret Bay. A site for the mu-seum has been chosen; groundbreaking is scheduled for 1998.

Most of the land on Unalaska, Amaknak, and Sedanka Islands, in the Fox Island group of the Aleutian Islands, is privately owned by the Ounalashka Corporation. If you want to hike, ski, bike, or camp on the land, you need to obtain a permit. To get one, stop by the cor-poration office on Salmon Way, fill out an application, and pay a small fee (about $5 a day).

Ounalashka Corporation, 400 Salmon Way, PO Box 149, Unalaska, AK 99685; (907)581-1276. In the Margaret Bay subdivision.

A.L.E.U.T. Tours

O. Patricia Lekanoff-Gregory includes World War II sites in her tour of Unalaska. She's a uniquely qualified speaker on the subject of the island's World War II evacuation of Aleuts; both her parents and her grandparents were sent to an internment camp on Burnett Inlet, near Wrangell in Southeast Alaska. (Ironically, many of the incarcerated Aleuts had proven their loyalty to the United States in the past, having enlisted in the U.S. military and fought in the first world war.) Her tour of Unalaska includes World War II sites (Fort Mears, Fort Schwatka, Bunker Hill, Fort Brumback in Summer Bay, Fort Leonard at Eider Point, and a ship bombed by the Japanese, the MV *Northwestern*. The U.S. Naval Station, the only brick house on Unalaska, was built in 1930 and housed officers' quarters and a radio station for the Navy.

Tours start in a historic house named after Henry Swanson, an Aleut man who participated in the last sea otter hunt in the Aleutian Islands, in 1910; the home is a storehouse of history and information about the Aleutian region. Stepping back in time, visitors are taken through the recently restored Holy Ascension Russian Orthodox Cathedral. The Bishop's House, also a National Historic Landmark, is currently being restored. It was built in the 1860s in San Francisco, dismantled, and reassembled in Unalaska for the Russian bishops. Later it was used as the first bilingual (Aleut and Russian) school in the islands. The tour also stops at the Sitka Spruce Plantation National Historic Landmark, planted by Russians in 1905; the archaeological site at Margaret Bay; and out into the tundra to learn about native plants.

A.L.E.U.T. Tours, PO Box 156, Unalaska, AK 99685; (907)581-6001 (phone and fax). Tours are 2 to 3 hours long and are offered year-round. Call for prices.

Pribilof Islands: *Aleut*

The Pribilof Islands, a cluster of five small islands, are about 250 miles north of the Aleutian Islands and about 300 miles off the Alaska mainland. The islands were reported as uninhabited when navigator and fur trader Garasim Pribylov claimed discovery of them. In 1788, the Russians colonized the two largest Islands, St. Paul and St. George, with enslaved Aleuts to harvest fur seals.

Aleut oral history, however, records the discovery of the Pribilof Islands by an Unimak Island chief's son, Igadik. According to this story, Igadik had long watched pregnant fur seals swimming north through Umiak Pass in the spring and returning in the fall with their pups. Caught in a fierce southerly, he ran before the wind in his kayak for several days until the storm died, and became lost in the fog. Paddling blindly toward the sound of barking seals, he came upon their birthing ground. The Aleuts called the islands Amiq, which means "land of mother's brother" or "related land." In 1786, Garasim Pribylov himself followed the sound of barking seals through ocean fog and found St. George Island; one year later, his men found St. Paul. With Aleut slave labor, the Russians killed seals indiscriminately until a ban on killing female seals was imposed in 1848. By 1910, because of open ocean shooting of seals, the population had declined from 4 million to 200,000. In 1911, reindeer were introduced to St. Paul as an alternative food source for the Aleuts.

After Dutch Harbor was bombed by the Japanese in 1942, Pribilof Islanders had 24 hours to pack their belongings (each person was allowed to take one suitcase of personal belongings), and were removed from the island. In their absence, U.S. troops occupying the island ransacked every house and killed all the reindeer on the island.

The Aleuts, considered wards of the Alaska Territory, were interned, presumably for their own protection, at an abandoned cannery at Funter Bay on Admiralty Island in Southeast Alaska. There were no beds, no facilities, and only K-rations for food. In 1943, the U.S. returned the Aleut men to work as laborers in order to continue the "essential" commercial fur seal harvest. Some of the women and children, left behind at Funter Bay, succumbed to smallpox, measles, and malnutrition. In 1944, families were allowed to return to St. Paul and St. George. Since speaking their language was forbidden by the government, the Aleuts began meeting secretly to plan their future. They organized as a tribe in 1948 under the Indian Reorganization Act, and in 1950 won the right to receive benefits from the federal government as quasi–civil servants. Still, Aleuts got considerably less for their labor than other civil service counterparts, and fair wages and honorable dealings were slow in coming over the next 20 years.

The present-day residents of St. Paul and St. George Islands are descendants of the Aleutian Natives who returned to the Pribilof Islands; many of them work as commercial halibut fishermen. Nearly a million fur seals, protected by the Marine Mammal Protection Act, pup on the island's black sand beaches every spring. The island's

When's the best time to visit St. Paul? Fur seal pups and seabird chicks are more independent and visible, and the islands are carpeted with wildflowers, from mid-July through August. Late spring and early summer are the best times to see large flocks of seabirds and "beachmasters" (mature male fur seals) claiming their territory. In late spring and August, birders can expect to sight vagrant Asiatic birds have wandered off their migratory path.

soaring cliffs and flat tundra meadows are nesting grounds for millions of seabirds, and hundreds of birders flock here, checklists in hand, each spring and summer.

Getting There

PenAir, (800)448-4226, serves St. Paul and St. George Islands. Reeve Aleutian Airways, (800)544-2248 or (907)842-1603, serves St. Paul Island; ask about their all-inclusive natural history package tours.

The Pribilof Islands are part of the Alaska Maritime National Wildlife Refuge. Because of the fragile tundra and the islands' use as a wildlife nursery throughout the summer, camping is very limited. Nearly 35 miles of road follows the coastline of St. Paul Island. Car rentals are available from Tanadgusix (TDX) Corporation, (907)546-2312. Almost every visitor to St. Paul Island comes here on a natural history package tour put together by Tanadgusix Corporation and Reeve Aleutian Airways. Independent travelers are welcome on either island, but they should arrange transportation and lodging well in advance. Northern fur seals are protected under the Marine Mammal Protection Act and are sensitive to human disturbance. For those not on the tour below, permits to view the seals must be obtained from the National Marine Fisheries Service.

Although the U.S. purchase of Alaska was known as Seward's Folly, the $7.2 million price was quickly paid for by the royalties the U.S. government gained from the sale of fur seal skins. Seals were commercially harvested in the Pribilof Islands until 1984. The Fur Seal Act of 1966, also known as the "Aleut Bill of Rights," allowed Pribilof Aleuts freedom of movement on and off the islands and fair wages for the first time in their history.

St. Paul Island Tour

Reeve Aleutian jets fly from Anchorage to St. Paul Island, about a 2½-hour flight over spectacular terrain, with a first stop in Dillingham on Bristol Bay. Visitors stay two to seven nights at St. Paul's King Eider Hotel, a historic boardinghouse where Bering Sea fishermen were once billeted and now a well-appointed inn. Twenty-five rooms have twin beds (some have double beds) and a sink, with shared baths down the hall. Meals, with dinners often featuring fresh halibut, are included in the price beginning in 1999.

Tours of the island's rookeries and seal pup nurseries are on comfortable 22-passenger buses equipped with restrooms. Tour guides are naturalists and local residents. Visitors hear about the island's rich if turbulent history, learn about Aleut heritage, and are introduced to Russian Orthodoxy by visiting the ornate interior of Sts. Peter & Paul Church. Near an extinct volcano rimming a crater lake are the whalebone supports of sod houses constructed by the first inhabitants. Guides also explain aspects of the present-day life and economy of the islands.

Wildlife is the focal point of this tour. Blue (or Arctic) foxes arrive here via the Bering Sea pack ice from the northern mainland and can be easily seen. For many, the island's seabird cliffs are an unparalleled experience. The Bering Sea is thought to be where puffins and related species such as auklets, murres, and murrelets first evolved, and the Pribilof Islands hold the greatest diversity of such species in the world. Excellent views and photographic vantage points can be obtained along the coastline. Such exotics as red-faced cormorants, crested auklets, and red-legged kittiwakes are abundant. Dedicated birders come here from mid-May through the end of June and again through August to spot accidental Asian species (birds that have flown off course).

The islands' most famous denizens, though, are its huge herds of Northern fur seals. In late May the first males arrive to stake out territory on the black volcanic rock beaches. By July more than a million fur seals have arrived on St. Paul and on St. George. It's a caterwauling, barking spectacle.

Tours are customized according to interest so that birders and photographers can cut straight to the chase and skip the history tour. St. Paul Island Tours is a subsidiary of TDX Corporation, the native village corporation on St. Paul. TDX Corporation, whose shareholders are Native Pribilof Islanders, owns 95 percent of the land on St. Paul Island. It also owns two hotels: the West Coast International in Anchorage, and the Paramount Hotel in downtown Seattle (see the Outside Alaska chapter).

The illustrated book Slaves of the Harvest begins with the discovery of the Aleutian Islands by Igadik and records the Russian invasion, Aleut indenture, early fur seal harvesting, the U.S. purchase of Alaska, the U.S. fisheries' harvest of fur seals, World War II at Funter Bay, and the struggle for economic equality and political independence. The history was funded with assistance from the Tanadgusix Corporation in cooperation with the Pribilof Islands School District. It's available from the King Eider Hotel, PO Box 88, St. Paul, AK 99660.

St. Paul Island Tours. Book trips through Reeve Aleutian Airways, (800)544-2248 or (907)243-4700; Web site: http://www.alaskabirding.com; e-mail: pribilof@alaska.net. Tours offered mid-May–Aug 30. Approximately $800–$1,593 per person depending on length of stay. Packages are from three to eight days and include round-trip airfare, ground transportation, accommodations, and tours. Meals are all-you-can-eat buffet and are not included in package price.

St. Paul Summer Cultural Events

Visitors may participate in St. Paul Island festivities, including Aleut dances, parades, and Native games, during special days throughout the summer. The island's Fourth of July is a unique small-town community celebration.

St. George Tanaq Hotel

St. George Island, with 170 residents, no restaurants, and only one small hotel, is less visited than St. Paul. However, it's as wild a place as its sister island, with its own unique ecological niche in the Bering Sea and hundreds of seal and bird rookeries, a historic seal processing plant (which may soon be restored as a historic site), and a completely renovated Russian Orthodox church. The St. George Tanaq Hotel, a National Historic Landmark constructed in 1930, has 10 rooms (accommodating 18 guests), four shared baths, and a shared kitchen. It was built by the federal government to house officials overseeing the seal harvest. It's about 5 miles from the airport (there's taxi service to town) and 1 block away from the grocery store. The hotel is owned and operated by the St. George Tanaq Corporation, an Aleut corporation that owns all the land on St. George Island.

If you are visiting the Pribilofs independently, consider buying an inexpensive mountain bike in Anchorage, carrying it as excess baggage on the plane, and donating it for island children to use after your departure.

St. George Tanaq Hotel. Reserve through St. George Tanaq Corporation, 2600 Denali St, Suite 300, Anchorage, AK 99503; (907)272-9886. Open year-round. $89 per person. Government rates. MasterCard and Visa are accepted.

Kodiak Archipelago: *Alutiiq*

One of the most heavily populated areas in Alaska before it was colonized by the Russians in the mid-1700s, the Kodiak archipelago is a beautiful, mountainous island wilderness, deeply cut with fjords and lovely remote bays. Sixteen large islands and many smaller ones cover a 5,000-square-mile area in the Pacific Ocean, just off the Gulf of Alaska.

Dominating the archipelago is Kodiak Island, an emerald green jewel about the size of the state of Connecticut. Its coastline shelters and feeds hundreds of Steller's sea lions, sea otters, harbor seals, whales, and porpoises. Over 200 species of birds can be found here, including hundreds of sea parrots (tufted puffins). The cliffs of Afognak Island, another island in the archipelago, house one of the world's largest rookeries of kittiwakes (a type of gull). The islands are also home to the famous Kodiak brown grizzly bear, nearly 3,000 of which roam Kodiak Island. The Kodiak National Wildlife Refuge was established in 1941 to protect them.

The Kodiak archipelago has been home to the Alutiiq people for nearly 7,500 years. Although the Russians lumped the Alutiiqs together with the Unangan people of the Aleutian Islands and called them all Aleuts (a Russian word meaning "coastal people"), the Unangans and the Alutiiqs were distinctly different, with unrelated languages and cultures.

When Russian fur trappers began arriving in the 1760s, the Alutiiqs had already established settlements, some with as many as 1,000 inhabitants, on the Kodiak archipelago, on both sides of the Alaska Peninsula, on the coastline of the Kenai Peninsula, and on Prince William Sound as far east as Cordova. Russian penetration into Alutiiq territory was successfully resisted for 20 years until villagers were overwhelmed by gunfire at Three Saints Bay in 1784.

Alexander Baranof stepped in to manage the first large Russian fur trading company in Alaska, the Russian-American Company, in 1792 at St. Paul Harbor (today's town of Kodiak). Kodiak served as the first capital of Russian America until the crown-chartered Russian-American Company moved to Sitka in Southeast Alaska. Artifacts from this period of Russian colonization are today housed in the town of Kodiak—in both the Kodiak Baranov Museum, located in a historic otter pelt warehouse built by Baranof, and in the Holy Ascension Russian Orthodox Cathedral.

Traditional Alutiiq clothing was made of sea otter furs, sealskin, and bird skins; many pieces are preserved in Russia's Leningrad Museum and in the Smithsonian Institution.

The Alutiiq people were forced to labor for the Russians, who used methods of conquest, repression, and colonization similar to those used in the British colonies. Alutiiq and Unangan hunters pursuing sea otters traveled in their kayaks as far south as the Russian outpost of Fort Ross, California. Waves of epidemics killed many more Alutiiqs in the following years. Acculturation to American ways came in the 1860s with the construction of salmon canneries and the corresponding influx of fishermen and cannery workers to the villages.

In the 1990s, the Alutiiq people decided to undertake an effort to preserve and revitalize traditional culture—not an easy task after 250 years of acculturation, first by the Russians, then by the Americans. Leading the charge are the Native corporations, which have supported the construction of Kodiak's Alutiiq Museum and Archaeological Repository and hired archaeologists to conduct fieldwork at specified sites throughout the region. There's also been a

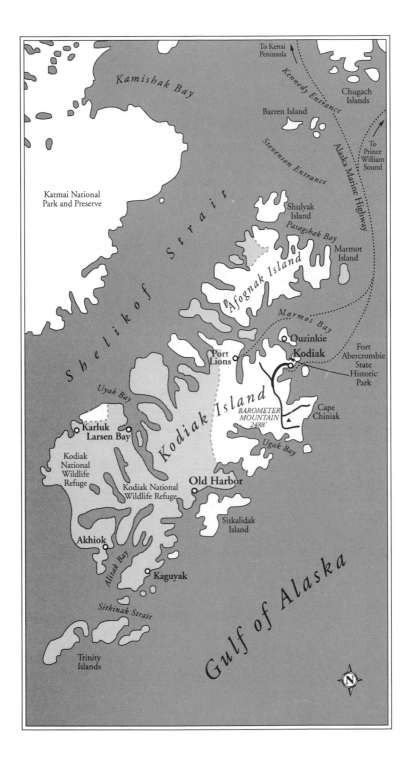

Kamishak Bay

To Kenai
Peninsula

Kennedy Entrance

Chugach
Islands

Barren Island

Stevenson Entrance

To
Prince
William
Sound

Katmai National
Park and Preserve

Alaska Marine Highway

Shulyak
Island

Pasagshak Bay

Marmot
Island

Afognak Island

Marmot Bay

Ouzinkie

Port
Lions

Kodiak

Fort
Abercrombie
State
Historic
Park

Uyak Bay

Kodiak Island

BAROMETER
MOUNTAIN
2488'

Cape
Chiniak

Karluk
Larsen Bay

Ugak Bay

Kodiak
National
Wildlife
Refuge

Kodiak National
Wildlife Refuge

Old Harbor

Sitkalidak
Island

Akhiok

Alitak Bay

Kaguyak

Sitkinak Strait

Gulf of Alaska

Trinity
Islands

N

heightened interest in Alutiiq skin boats and in the visual arts, stimulated several years ago by the Smithsonian Institution's *Crossroads of the Continents* traveling exhibit, which brought Native artifacts back to Alaska from museums throughout the world. Although academic literature hasn't quite caught up with the reemerging cultural identity of the Alutiiq people (you'll see the Alutiiq people referred to as "Aleuts" and "Pacific Eskimos" in many books written before 1990 and on labels in museums), linguists at the University of Alaska are working to reconstruct the Alutiiq language.

The Kodiak archipelago includes six major Native villages, each unique and located in lovely settings on the shoreline: Ouzinkie, on Spruce Island, and Port Lions, Larsen Bay, Karluk, Old Harbor, and Akhiok, all on Kodiak Island. All have Native-owned and operated ecological and cultural tours, charters, and overnight accommodations. You may also participate in an archaeological excavation of an Alutiiq village and a Russian artel (a place where Russians lived and worked together) on Afognak Island, and see the unearthed artifacts and exhibits on Alutiiq culture at the Alutiiq Museum and Archaeological Repository in Kodiak.

How to Pack

If you plan on spending time outdoors, it's important to remember that the Kodiak archipelago has a maritime climate. That means weather can change quickly with the prevailing winds—blanketing the islands with mist, rain, and thick fog at any time. Summer temperatures are comfortable (in the high 50s). Winter temperatures are milder than those in most of Alaska, but winds can be strong, with driving, horizontal rainstorms.

Getting There

Alaska Marine Highway ferries, (800)526-6731, arrive from the mainland at the towns of Kodiak (on Kodiak Island) and Port Lions (on Kodiak Island's northwest coast), and continue on down the Aleutian Chain. Several airlines serve Kodiak: Alaska Airlines (1200 Airport Way, Kodiak, AK 99615; (800)426-0333), which offers flights and package tours to Kodiak; Era Aviation (6160 Carl Brady Dr, Anchorage, AK 99502; (800)866-8394), an Alaska Airlines commuter service; and PenAir (PO Box 890, Kodiak, AK 99615; (800)448-4226).

The main airport is outside the town of Kodiak, about 5 miles from town. This area has only a few miles of road, so renting a car is not necessary. Rentals are available at the airport and in downtown Kodiak, however, and a car can come in handy if you want to have access to hiking trails. From Kodiak, you can visit nearby Port Lions by Alaska Marine Highway ferry and Ouzinkie, on Spruce Island, by charter boat. All other towns discussed in this section are accessible from Kodiak by air taxi.

Visitor Services

- Kodiak Convention & Visitors Bureau, 100 Marine Way, Kodiak, AK 99615; (907)486-4782; Web site: http://www.kodiak.org/kodiak. Open daily mid-June–mid-Sept. Call or write for a free, colorful, well-written guidebook to the region.

- Kodiak Native Tourism Association, (888)288-5736, keeps a current list of Native-owned providers and guides. Attractions include bear viewing, sea kayaking, hiking trails, and places of cultural and historical interest. The association also provides information about hunting, fishing, and camping on the large-scale private Native land holdings throughout the archipelago.

Kodiak: *Alutiiq*

The largest town in the archipelago, Kodiak is a traveler's small-town paradise. Visitors taxi from the airport 5 miles along the scenic road to downtown or enter town directly from the Alaska Marine Highway ferry; from there on, the picturesque town is walkable (although you can rent a car at the airport or downtown). There's a handsome historic Russian Orthodox church, two museums, several galleries, good restaurants, and hotels and inns, all centered around a boat basin filled with fishing vessels and a busy floatplane dock. You can sea-kayak in the town's protected bays, and sightsee with Alaska Natives, on board skiffs and small craft, around the east end of Kodiak Island. Eight Alutiiq Native corporations are headquartered here, and an Alutiiq dance group wearing beautiful regalia performs daily during the summer.

Pick up a guide to native plants at the Alutiiq Museum and head to North End Park on Near Island or to Fort Abercrombie (both near the town of Kodiak), where the plants are labeled along a trail. Signs give both the English and the Alutiiq plant name and explain how Natives raised, gathered, and used them.

The Kodiak Baranov Museum, with many artifacts from the Russian era, is housed in one of the oldest wooden buildings in Alaska. Alutiiq culture and history is presented in the superb Alutiiq Museum and Archaeological Repository; it includes materials unearthed from Kodiak village sites dating back 7,500 years. Visitors can also participate in an archaeological excavation on nearby Afognak Island, a scenic floatplane trip from downtown Kodiak.

Alutiiq Museum and Archaeological Repository

Built in the town of Kodiak with funds from the Exxon Valdez oil spill settlement, and maintained by eight Alutiiq Native corporations, this new museum has superior exhibits explaining traditional Alutiiq culture and history. It is also a repository for artifacts found in the Kodiak archipelago. More than 800 archaeological sites throughout the islands are helping Natives piece together their heritage, nearly lost after the last 200 years of Russian and American occupation. In addition, classes are taught at the museum and at the local community college on almost everything known about Alutiiq ancient life: plant lore, hunting and fishing, food and clothing, prehistoric dolls and toys, and more.

The Alutiiq Museum recommends the following books:

Crossroads of Continents, by William Fitzhugh and Aron Crowell (Smithsonian Institution Press, 1988)

Derevnia's Daughters: Saga of an Alaskan Village, by Lola Harvey (Sunflower University Press, 1991)

The Etholen Collection, by Piro Varjola (National Board of Antiquities of Finland, 1990)

Island of the Giant Bears (a video produced by the National Geographic Society)

Ongoing exhibits, including artifacts from a Russian trading post unearthed in the Kodiak region, explain the Alutiiqs' fate at the hands of the Russian trappers who came here to hunt otters and other fur-bearing sea mammals. Other exhibited artifacts include nets made of nettle fibers, spruce root and grass baskets, grease bowls, stone lamps, ulus, ivory needles, and dozens of other implements.

Also displayed are the Alutiiqs' ingenious waterproof skin boats (called *baidarkas* by the Russians, and today known as kayaks), which were used for centuries by Aleuts, Yup'iks, Inupiats, and Alutiiqs throughout the Arctic, along the west coast of Alaska, and into Prince William Sound. You'll also see a hooded paddle jacket with a spray skirt, called a *kamlaika*, made of stretched seal gut sewn with waterproof stitching. Once essential to Alutiiq life, kayaks and kamlaikas are no longer made or used by Natives; in the last century, they've given them up for more practical motorized boats and microfiber raingear.

In 1999, the Alutiiq Museum will host a major exhibition of the Smithsonian Institution's Fisher Collection. William Fisher was a naturalist at the California Academy of Sciences, specializing in marine biology. In the mid-1870s, he arrived in the Kodiak archipelago to measure the tides for the Coast and Geodetic Survey. Bored with his job, he volunteered to help collect cultural artifacts from the Alutiiq region for the Smithsonian. He collected at a time of major cultural

change, when Kodiak was at the end of the Russian period of occupation and the Natives were being drawn from their traditional mammal hunting into the wage economy of the salmon canneries. Fisher
eventually worked for the Alaska Commercial Company in Kodiak,
married locally, and, from 1879 through 1884, sent crates of carefully
documented wooden masks, dolls, bowls, woven baskets, beaded
headdresses, and other items to the Smithsonian. He
died in 1904, and is buried in the American
Cemetery in Kodiak. The Fisher Collection, one of
the major collections of Alutiiq material culture outside of Kodiak, will be at the Alutiiq Museum for
one year, with lectures and classes on Alutiiq culture
occurring throughout the year.

> *"When we were kids, we played with our grand-father's old wooden kayak paddles. He had six or seven stowed under the house, and we used them to paddle our logs around in the bay."*
>
> *—Andy Christofferson*

The historic photographs displayed in the
gallery and halls of the Alutiiq Museum are part of
the Albatross Collection, a large collection of photos
documenting the Alaska coastline in the 1880s and
1890s, including a Native barabara at Karluk, the
canneries of Karluk spit, a Native of Old Harbor, a Native baidarka at
Old Harbor, and a fish camp. Reproductions can be ordered from the
Still Pictures Branch, National Archives, 8601 Adelphi Rd, College
Park, MD 20740; (301)713-6225.

The museum's gift shop carries contemporary Alutiiq art, including Jerry Laktonen's beautiful full-size and miniature carved and
painted kayak paddles (single, slender blades painted with marine
mammals and fish) and his Alutiiq masks, based on pieces collected in
Kodiak prior to the 20th century. Also prized by collectors (note the
$2,000-plus price tag) are the traditional Alutiiq hunting visors made
of wood and adorned with walrus whiskers, trade beads, and carved
ivory talismans, made by Jacob Simeonoff and Peter Lind. Hats and
mittens made of otter pelts, made by local skin sewers such as Susan
Malutin, are also for sale, along with books, posters, and postcards.

*Alutiiq Museum and Archaeological Repository, 215 Mission Rd, Suite 101, Kodiak, AK
99615; (907)486-7004; e-mail: alutiiq2@ptialaska.net. Open year-round; call for hours.
Special openings with advance notice.*

Dig Afognak

You can join archaeologists hired by the Afognak Native Corporation
to help uncover Katenai village, occupied for at least 7,500 years until
it was abandoned in the 1930s, and an adjoining Russian-American
Company artel dating to the 19th century.

The archaeology camp is on the south side of Afognak Island at the mouth of the Afognak River, about a 30-minute floatplane trip from Kodiak. You stay in a comfortable tent camp tucked in a stand of old-growth spruce, with a traditional large *banya* (sauna/bathhouse) on the shore of the lake, and a staff who cooks and cleans up.

The village site is a short walk from camp, either on a path through the woods or along the rocky beach. At low tide, you can read the geologic history of the islands on the bank along the way. Layers of white ash and sediment mark periodic volcanic eruptions and tsunamis over the centuries. The most recent eruption was in 1912, when Mount Redoubt, on the Alaska Peninsula, erupted and Mount Katmai collapsed, blanketing the Kodiak archipelago with nearly 2 feet of ash. In 1964 the most recent tsunami swept the village of Afognak, on the other side of the bay, with a wall of water, forcing relocation of its inhabitants.

Although spruce trees today blanket eastern Kodiak and Afognak Islands, spruce pollen first appears in archaeological sites only 900 years ago.

By 1996, archaeologists had excavated one Katenai sod house down to the floor, where lidded clay-lined storage containers held the remains of dried fish.

Hundreds of items have been recovered from the Native site, including greenstone adzes, ulus, pendants, gaming pieces, incised stones, thread, and leather scraps—all documented and housed in the Alutiiq Museum's repository in Kodiak. From the Russian site, in 1994 alone, more than 1,000 wound, tubular, and molded glass beads, including light turquoise Canton and green and translucent-lined cornaline D'Aleppo beads were found. Evidence of British Spode and Copeland dishes indicated that the Russian site was in use after 1840, when the Russian-American Company entered an agreement with the Hudson's Bay Company to purchase goods from them. Underneath the Russian site, archaeologists found older items, including a carved bone hairpin and an ivory seal-hunting amulet. Nearby, on the shoreline of Marka and Litnik Bays, is rock art, also of interest to the Alutiiq research team.

Eco-tourists and members of educational groups such as Elderhostel stay for one or two weeks at the camp, working under a makeshift canvas canopy, carefully sifting dirt from an ancient refuse pile. Chatter around the camp can be an inspiring mix of personal stories, science, and speculation about such things as the effect the "little ice age" had on the lives of the Natives, and the fact that far more cod bones have been found in the refuse pit than salmon bones. In the evenings, everyone gathers in the archaeologists' tent to hear visiting scientists (botanists, geologists, limnologists, and ecologists from such varied institutions as Brown University, the Canadian

Museum of Civilization, and Humboldt State University) discuss their particular contribution to the growing knowledge of ancient Alutiiq culture, or to see slides on the island's natural history, botany, and geology. Free time is spent bird watching, fishing, bushwhacking through thick undergrowth to view wildlife, and hiking the beaches.

The banya is stocked with baskets of soap and bottles of shampoo. Steam, emanating from a tub of hot water boiling on top of a huge woodstove covered with slate, permeates the deepest chill and sends most people into a coma-like slumber within minutes of climbing into their sleeping bags.

At the end of your visit, you tour the archives of the Alutiiq Museum and Archaeological Repository with archaeologists to see artifacts gathered from various sites in the region. The difference between the archaeology that is going on here, and other fieldwork in the world, is that the artifacts remain in Kodiak for study, and reports are read with intense interest by the Native community, rather than sitting on some dusty shelf in a distant university. And, under the direction of their Native employers, archaeologists leave gravesites undisturbed.

Alutiiq whale hunters were elite, powerful, intimidating men who were said to possess spiritual and magical powers. They killed whales with poisoned arrows slung by lances. The poison caused nerve damage and paralysis. Harpooned whales were unable to surface for air and drowned. Secured by the harpoon, the carcass was towed to shore. The more decorated a hunter's visor, the higher his status.

Dig Afognak, 215 Mission Rd, Suite 101, Kodiak, AK 99615; (800)770-6014 or (907)486-6014; e-mail: dig@afognak.com. Call for reservations, as mail service to Kodiak is slow. May–Aug. Day trips and week- or month-long stays. Prices vary; average price per person for an entire week is about $1,725, including air, water, and ground transportation within the Kodiak Islands, accommodations, meals, and lectures. $250 deposit holds your space. Group rates. Men and women sleep in separate dormitory-style tents equipped with woodstoves, bunks, and air mattresses. MasterCard and Visa are accepted.

Kodiak Alutiiq Dancers

The Kodiak Alutiiq Dancers, a group of about 35 members from the ages of 6 to 80, perform traditional dances and songs several times a day during the summer. The dancers have created replicas of beautiful traditional garments: blue and white "snow-falling" parkas, ermine headdresses, glass bead headdresses, and spruce root–hunting hats. They perform inside a reproduction of a traditional sod barabara behind the Kodiak Tribal Headquarters, within walking distance of downtown Kodiak and the Alutiiq Museum.

Kodiak Alutiiq Dancers, Kodiak Tribal Headquarters, PO Box 1974, Kodiak AK 99615;
(907)486-4449. Kodiak Tribal Headquarters is a clearly marked modern building at
713 Rezanof Dr, less than 1 mile from downtown. Thirty-minute performances
Mon–Sat, summer only. Call ahead for performance times. Admission charge.

Kodiak Air Service

Willie Hall, an Alutiiq (his Native ancestors are from Afognak Island, and one of his grandfathers was Russian), takes you flightseeing or bear viewing or drops you off to fish or hunt anywhere in the Kodiak archipelago, via his Cessna 206 floatplane. He's a seasoned pilot, surveys salmon by air for the state, and is a herring spotter for a commercial fishery.

The Kodiak archipelago's high-grade slate can be easily resharpened, a quality that makes slate knives especially useful for quickly cutting up fish and butchering whales before they spoil. Archaeological evidence indicates that Kodiak slate may have been traded extensively with tribes living on the mainland.

Kodiak Air Service, 415 Mill Bay Rd, Kodiak, AK 99615; (907)486-4446. Operates year-round. Rates depend on group size and destination.

Wild Spoor

Although he was just a toddler when the 1964 tsunami destroyed Afognak village, Rick Rowland has vivid memories of his family scrambling out of their house for the safety of the hills just before the wave hit. A lifetime resident of the Kodiak archipelago and an avid fisherman and tracker, Rowland offers his services as a guide on Kodiak and Afognak Islands, and on the Naknek River in Southwest Alaska. He provides roomy Weatherport tents, cots, and meals to fishermen, hunters, and eco-tourists interested in seeing and photographing sea mammals, elk, black-tailed deer, brown bears, salmon-spawning rivers, and rare orchids. Rick is a certified merchant marine master pilot.

Wild Spoor, 2107 Lincoln Ave, Anchorage, AK 99517; (888)621-2090; e-mail: infor@wildspoor.com. Seasonal. Rates depend on group size and length of stay. MasterCard and Visa are accepted.

Ouzinkie: *Alutiiq*

Ouzinkie, settled as a Russian retirement community in the late 1800s, is on little Spruce Island, west of Kodiak Island. Narrow Strait, about a mile wide, lies between the two islands. Gillnetters bob against the wharf pilings in a half-moon bay sheltered from weather in the lee of several smaller tree-covered islands. A weathered board-walk, erected after the 1964 tsunami and now brushed by salmonberry bushes, clings to Ouzinkie's waterfront above a rocky shoreline. Behind it is the blue onion dome of the Nativity of Our Lord Russian Orthodox Church, radiant in the afternoon sun against a backdrop of dark green spruce. The interior of the church, where Native Herman Squartsoff conducts services in Slavonic by candlelight, is decorated with icons brought from Russia when the church was erected in 1898.

Spruce Island Charters

Bundle up in warm clothing and join commercial fisherman and Russian Orthodox Church reader Herman Squartsoff in his ocean skiff for a day of fishing for Pacific halibut, cod, rockfish, bass, and salmon, or perhaps for a sightseeing cruise around the bays and islands of the northeastern end of the Kodiak archipelago.

It's a scenic 10-mile drive (you can take a cab) from Kodiak on a gravel road through the hills to the boat ramp on Anton Larsen Bay and Squartsoff's waiting skiff. Within minutes of launching the boat, you are in waters filled with sea life: sea otters bobbing on their backs in rafts of bull kelp, seals popping up alongside the boat. You watch for whales and porpoise in Kizhuyak Bay, then dock at the village of Port Lions. With Squartsoff, you stop in at his brother Melvin's grocery/supply store and have a cup of coffee and a snack while you learn about the tsunami that swept Kodiak in 1964.

Rhonda Panamarioff of Ouzinkie shared with us her recipe for a delicious peroke, a Russian/Alutiiq dish. Fill an uncooked pie crust with layers of sauteed cabbage, rutabagas, celery, and carrots, with rice in between each layer; top with thick, uncooked chunks of king salmon; and cover and bake in a 350-degree oven for an hour. Panamarioff also makes an Alutiiq version of peroshski (deep-fried bread filled with smoked or canned salmon) and cheduk (berries mashed with sugar and table cream or Cool Whip—a dish similar to "Eskimo ice cream," which is traditionally made of berries folded into whipped animal fat).

You bird-watch and fish for most of the day, with a last stop at the village of Ouzinkie, on Spruce Island. Like many Native people in this region settled by Russians, Squartsoff is of both Russian and Alutiiq descent. He was named after Saint Herman, a traditional Russian Orthodox ascetic who lived on Spruce Island in the late 1700s and early 1800s and founded an orphanage for Aleut children.

Spruce Island Charters, Herman Squartsoff, PO Box 189, Ouzinkie, AK 99644; (888)680-2332 or (907)680-2332. Prices vary. All tackle and fishing gear are provided.

Marmot Bay Excursions

Circle Spruce Island, visit Afognak, and linger in Marmot Bay to watch birds, whales, and sea otters aboard Andy and Cheryl Christofferson's 32-foot motor yacht. The boat is equipped for day trips or overnights with bunks, galley, and restroom. There's a flying bridge for wildlife viewing, and a raft and several kayaks for shore excursions. Trips are customized, but may include a walking tour of Ouzinkie with a nature hike to Sourdough Flats, Garden Point, and Pineapple Cove. The boat also stops at Monk's Cove for a shore excursion to the house, church, and small chapel where Saint Herman lived in the early 1800s. The couple will pick you up at the boat basin in Kodiak or at Anton Larsen Bay, or you can take a 10-minute hop on a plane to Ouzinkie (three scheduled flights daily from Kodiak). Andy is a Coast Guard–licensed captain. Fishing charters are also available.

Marmot Bay Excursions, PO Box 129, Ouzinkie, AK 99644; (907)680-2340; fax (907)680-2203. Tours offered May–Oct. Prices begin at $115 per person.

Port Lions: *Alutiiq*

Only about 35 years old, Port Lions was hastily built after the village of Afognak was destroyed by a tsunami following the 1964 earthquake. It's named after the Lions Club International, which helped raise money and build the new town.

Settler's Cove Market

Settler's Cove Market, on the Port Lions waterfront, is a bright haven in the wilderness. The store is owned by commercial fisherman Melvin Squartsoff, who has a pot of coffee on all day long, mans a deli counter with seating for 12, and stocks the store with supplies for fishermen, hikers, and campers (raingear, ponchos, mosquito netting, sportfishing tackle, binoculars, Swiss Army knives, bottled water, film, disposable cameras) as well as essentials needed for bush living (hardware and food). The store is on Port Lions's waterfront; behind it is the old causeway, a half-mile public footbridge that crosses Settler's Cove, a pleasant place to walk and to fish from the railing.

Settler's Cove Market, Port Lions, AK 99550; (907)454-2222. Open year-round, Mon–Sat.

Aamasuuk (King Salmon) Fishing Charters

While other fishermen are chopping holes in lake ice to fish, Aamasuuk Charters, with guide Peter Squartsoff, specializes in open-water, winter sea-run king salmon from January 1 to April 1. Beginning in May, you can troll for kings and long-line halibut and rockfish. In July cohos, pinks, and lingcod are in the waters of the archipelago. Chums and Dolly Vardens, a succulent sea-run trout, are caught with flies and spinning tackle on the rivers. Fishermen stay in a primitive wilderness cabin, fully furnished, accessible only by boat. Squartsoff picks you up in his skiff at the western end of the Kodiak road system on Anton Larsen Bay, about a half hour from the airport. You bring personal gear, sleeping bags, and flies or spinning tackle. Groceries, fishing licenses, tackle, and personal items are purchased at Settler's Cove Market in Port Lions.

Aamasuuk Charters, PO Box 63, Port Lions, AK 99550; (907)454-2333. Seasonal. Cost is $200 per day and includes accommodations, 6 hours of fishing per day, and all bottomfishing and trolling gear. Day trips are $150 per person. All trips have a two-person minimum and a four-person maximum. Aamasuuk Charters advocates catch-and-release fishing. Guests may take home one king salmon per person, and one day's limit of other species.

Whale Pass Lodge

Denise May is of Alutiiq descent, with grandparents from Karluk and Afognak. She and her husband, Bob, lived in tents while they built their three-story family home and guest lodge out of hand-milled Sitka spruce overlooking Whale Pass. The lodge is remote, about 8 miles by water from the Anton Larsen Bay boat landing or Port Lions (you can fly to Port Lions on the mail plane for $30), where they'll pick you up for no extra charge. Whale Pass is a great place to watch birds, whales, and boat traffic moving through the passageway between Kodiak Island and Whale Island into Kupreanof Strait. Bob, a non-Native, is also a fisherman (with a 24-foot aluminum-covered cabin cruiser) and a winter hunting guide who will help you find big game, ducks, and black-tailed deer. He also guides photo shoots for wildlife watchers. The lodge has four guest rooms accommodating seven guests, with three gourmet meals served family style each day. A private living room with a deck overlooking the water is just for guests. A banya (steam bath) is tucked into the spruce woods behind the house.

Whale Pass Lodge, PO Box 32, Port Lions, AK 99550; (800)456-3425. Open year-round. Package rates are available. Discounts for business meetings and parties of four or more.

Larsen Bay: *Alutiiq*

Larsen Bay is a fishing village of about 100 residents on the west side of Kodiak Island overlooking Shelikof Strait. It has two Russian Orthodox churches, one of them a historic building, and one of the oldest operating canneries in the state of Alaska. The town is adjacent to the site of one of Kodiak Island's largest ancestral villages.

It took the Larsen Bay Village Council, headed by Frank Carlson, many years of unrelenting pressure to convince the Smithsonian Institution to return the remains of 756 Alutiiq Natives for reburial. The bones, unearthed in the 1930s by one of the museum's curators, had been held for more than 60 years in crates in the basement of the National Museum of Natural History in Washington, D.C.

The repatriation of human remains to Larsen Bay is extensively documented in **Reckoning With the Dead: The Larsen Bay Repatriation and the Smithsonian Institution,** *edited by Tamara L. Bray (Smithsonian Institution Press, 1994). The book is available at the Shire Bookstore, 104 Center Ave., Kodiak, AK 99615; (907)486-5001. Look here for other titles about Alutiiq and Alaska Native culture and natural history.*

The bone collection was part of curator Ales Hrdlicka's summer research project concerning possible waves of migration into Alaska. His method was to gather as many skulls as he could, date them, and measure them, looking for variations in age and size. He gathered over 4,000 skulls from various sites; Larsen Bay was the largest. Remains were easy to find because the Alutiiq people buried their dead under the floors of small rooms adjoining their sod-covered houses.

The Larsen Bay village site had been occupied for at least 2,000 years. The dislodged remains were from 500 to 2,000 years old, but some—victims of the 1918 flu epidemic—had been buried only a few years before Hrdlicka removed them. Hrdlicka was not a trained physical anthropologist; he didn't ask permission to excavate, nor did he follow even the minimal standards of the 1930s for scientific excavation. Home movie footage of what Hrdlicka called in his diaries "the bone mine" shows young men digging up the old village with spades, pitching dirt and human remains into mining cars on tracks. If no skulls were found, the dirt and other remains were dumped into the bay. Crates of bones and 144 artifacts, including carved wooden eyes that were excavated with the bones, were shipped back to the Smithsonian.

Faced with Native demands that the remains be returned, the Smithsonian continued to argue that the remains were invaluable to science. After a prolonged fight and $100,000 worth of legal assistance from the Native American Rights Fund, the remains were finally returned to the Larsen Bay Village Council in the 1980s. The Smithsonian's action helped prompt the creation of the Native American Grave and Burial Protection Act, passed by Congress in 1990, which ensures that Native American graves have the same protections as do those of other American citizens.

The remains were reburied together at Larsen Bay at a site overlooking the village's nearly 100-year-old salmon cannery, and are marked with a large white Russian Orthodox cross. Dora Aga, a village elder who knew Hrdlicka, told the *Anchorage Daily News*, "He had a rotten attitude. God bless his carcass, wherever he's at."

Visitors are welcome to walk up to the memorial site, visit the historic Russian Orthodox church, and explore the hiking trails located all around Larsen Bay.

Larsen Bay Lodge

This large lodge offers guests the works—halibut charters, flyout fishing in floatplanes, bear viewing, bird watching at the rookeries along the cliffs, and kayaking at the head of Uyak Bay. Owner Mike Carlson hires a staff of eight each summer, including cooks from Costa Rica, and provides everything—from lodging and kayaks to skiffs and fishing gear. The lodge, large enough to accommodate 18, has shared baths, hot tubs, meeting rooms, and a pool table, and is built on the beach overlooking the bay. More private quarters are in two new cabins, also on the beach, with all the amenities. The lodge has been in business for 25 years. It was built by Mike's dad, Frank Carlson, the former head of the Larsen Bay Village Council.

Larsen Bay Lodge, (907)847-2238.

Uyak Bay Lodge

Brad Aga, born and raised in Larsen Bay, and his wife, Tammy, operate a modest guest house year-round, 50 feet from the beach at Larsen Bay. The house has a living room, kitchen, and two shared baths, and all meals are provided. In summer they have two boats available for sightseeing and fishing charters—one a 24-foot skiff, the other a 34-foot commercial fishing boat. In the fall they provide transportation for deer hunting.

Uyak Bay Lodge, PO Box 7, Larsen Bay, AK 99624; (907)847-2350. Open year-round. Fishing charters operate May–Sept.

Karluk: *Alutiiq*

More than 840 archaeological sites have been identified at Karluk (population 65), another of the region's largest villages. The town sits alongside Karluk Lagoon, where the river slows down and prepares to meet the Shelikof Strait, at one of the most scenic and dramatic coastal areas on Kodiak Island. The treacherous strait is named after the murderous Grigorii Shelikhov, an early manager of the Russian-American Company who ordered the massacre of whole villages in the archipelago and Aleutian Islands.

Karluk River and Karluk Lake are well known by elite sport fishermen who seek chinook, sockeye, and coho salmon there. Recently the village has opened its doors to those who want to explore the culture and ecology of the region.

There are a number of Native-owned lodges and tented fish camps in Karluk. Among them are Mary's Bed and Breakfast, (907)241-2203; Karluk Lake Spit Lodge, (907)241-2214; Karluk Cape Lodge, (907)241-2218; Eli's Camp, (907)241-2227; and Larry Sugak's fish camp, (907)241-2230. For information on local land permits, brochures, and airplane connections from Kodiak, call the Karluk Tribal Council at (907)241-2218.

Karluk Lake Bear Viewing

Upstream from the village of Karluk is an enormous, uninhabited lake. Bear researchers and film crews from all over the world come here to photograph and study Kodiak brown bear sows teaching their cubs to fish throughout the summer in a stream trickling into the upper end of the lake. Bears and their cubs nest in wild grasses and blue geraniums in the wide meadows alongside cottonwood-lined streambanks. Bear viewers stay out of their way on Camp Island, out in the lake, in two small wood-frame bunkhouses with an adjoining cookhouse. Right after breakfast a guide takes guests to the mouth of the creek in an aluminum skiff. A short trail through the meadow leads to an open metal bear-viewing platform 30 feet above the creek. At least nine sows visit the stream every day, some with as many as three cubs, sprawling on their backs to suckle.

The Koniag Native Corporation, which owns the majority of the land around Karluk Lake, is committed to protecting Kodiak brown bear habitat. They've limited human access and prohibited bear viewing from noisy float- and bush planes. Only one guide service, Wilderness Air, is allowed to book guests for overnight stays, and only eight guests may visit each day. When you book with Wilderness Air, a portion of your booking fee is paid to Koniag for land use fees.

The floatplane ride over central Kodiak Island to Karluk is thrilling: you skim high emerald green ridges that drop off hundreds of feet into narrow fjords. The village of Karluk and Karluk Lake were some of the first areas uncovered by archaeologists looking for clues about pre-contact Alutiiq culture.

Wilderness Air, PO Box 768, Kodiak, AK 99615; (800)556-8101. $800 per person, including airfare, overnight accommodations, guide services, and meals.

Old Harbor: *Alutiiq*

The village of Old Harbor (population 311) was rebuilt after its destruction in the 1964 tsunami. The largest Alutiiq village in the archipelago, Old Harbor is nestled against tall peaks on the southeast coast of Kodiak Island and has many historical points of interest including nearby Three Saints Russian Orthodox Church (the first version of which was on board a tall-masted ship anchored in Three Saints Bay) and Refuge Rock, the site of a massacre of Alutiiqs by the Russians. Port Hobron, across the narrow strait from Old Harbor on Sitkalidak Island, is a virtual ghost town: the last commercial American whaling station, it closed down in the 1920s. Piers where whales were dragged onto shore are still in place, as are metal vats where blubber was rendered into oil.

The first Russian settlement in the Kodiak archipelago was established near here in 1784 on Three Saints Bay by merchant Grigorii Shelikhov. After 20 years of unsuccessfully attempting to conquer Kodiak Island (see Akhiok, later in this chapter), Shelikhov sailed two ships filled with men, cannons, and muskets into Three Saints Bay, determined to take villagers into captivity as slave labor to help in hunting and skinning sea otters for the lucrative China fur trade. He demanded that ruling families hand over their children as hostages.

According to one story, when Shelikhov made his demands, villagers fled to a sea stack (accessible at low tide by a long spit that joins the rock to the 23-mile-long Sitkalidak Island), as they had in the past when attacked. Thirty houses, filled with stores of food and supplies, were already established there, used in the past mostly to defend against invasion from Tlingit warriors from the south. The Natives quickly threw up more temporary shelters to house more than 3,000 people. But a traitor revealed their hiding spot, and a week later, on August 13, 1784, Shelikhov and his men attacked. Backed by cannon fire, 71 Russians armed with muskets stormed the cliffs. They executed adult males and elders and took 500 women and children to Three Saints Bay as enslaved hostages.

Today the sea stack is called Refuge Rock, but its Alutiiq name is Awa'aq, which means "to become numb" in English. Shelikhov was recalled to Russia after reports reached home of his atrocities (this wasn't the only massacre he commanded). Islanders avoided Awa'aq for two centuries, first because of bodies washing ashore and later because they were still horrified by the loss of so many families who died together there. Islanders kept the location of the rock to themselves until the site was excavated by anthropologists as part of a damage survey after the Exxon Valdez oil spill in 1989. Today the rock is owned by the Old Harbor Native Corporation.

Peterson's Adventures

Jeff Peterson was born and raised in Old Harbor, did commercial fishing there with his dad, and, after a stint in the U.S. Marines, came back to Old Harbor as a village public safety officer. For 10 years he has worked as a guide for fishermen and duck hunters; more recently, he began working with cultural and eco-tourists too. He takes visitors sightseeing to Refuge Rock, Three Saints Bay, and the old whaling station at Port Hobron, and hiking in the Kodiak National Wildlife Refuge. His boat is a 25-foot inboard, closed-cabin cruiser, equipped with a global positioning system and radar.

In summer Peterson specializes in sightseeing tours and fishing; in winter he takes fishermen out to angle for king salmon and halibut (he provides gear), and guides game and duck hunting. Kodiak Island's southeast side harbors large coveys of sea ducks such as king eiders, scoters, goldeneyes, and harlequin ducks, as well as freshwater ducks such as gadwalls, mallards, American widgeons, pintails, teals, and mergansers.

Snacks and lunches are provided for full-day tours, as are fresh seafood dinners at the home of Jeff and his wife, Naomi, in Old Harbor. He also has sea kayaks for rent. Overnight guests can stay at Sitkalidak Lodge, Bayview B&B, or a remote cabin in Three Saints Bay with a woodstove for heat, a wood-fired sauna, and kerosene and gasoline lanterns (water is packed in).

Peterson's Adventures, PO Box 141, Old Harbor, AK 99643; (907)286-2252; pager (907)486-7153. Apr–Jan. Prices are by the day or week.

First Frontier Adventures

Skipper Gary Price and his wife, Wanda, an Alutiiq Native shareholder, have quickly gained a great reputation for putting on first-rate boating, fishing, and sightseeing outings (bear viewing and whale watching included) on board their 53-foot cabin cruiser. The go-anywhere cruiser is Coast Guard–approved to sleep 14 people overnight, making for a comfortable cruise anywhere in the Kodiak archipelago. Wanda and her dad, Sven Haakanson, the mayor of Old Harbor for 30 years, take turns crewing and cooking for guests aboard the boat. The big boat is available for day trips and overnighters; the Prices also operate a smaller jet boat for small groups and will make arrangements for landlubbers overnight at Sitkalidak Lodge (discussed later in this section).

First Frontier Adventures, Inc., PO Box 137, Old Harbor, AK 99643; (907)286-2244.

Al's Charter Service and Bayview B&B

Al Cratty is a commercial fisherman from April through September; during the fall and winter, he's licensed to transport deer hunters on his 47-foot commercial fishing boat, and takes sports fishermen out to sea in his 19-foot skiff to angle for halibut and all species of salmon. Al and his wife, Jonetta, remodeled their split-level home overlooking the bay to accommodate overnight guests. There's one bedroom with a queen-size bed, a living room/dining room with a fold-out bed, a VCR, and a private bath.

Al's Charter Service/Bayview B&B, PO Box 1, Old Harbor, AK 99643; (907)286-2267. Charters offered in fall and winter; B&B open year-round. Room rates vary based on group size. Breakfast is included. Packed lunches and home-cooked seafood dinners are available at an additional charge.

Sitkalidak Lodge

The folks who own this 10-room lodge on the shores of Sitkalidak Strait coordinate travel plans for people who want to explore the south end of Kodiak Island. Tours are customized for individuals or groups of up to 20 for anything from two-day to two-week stays. When a Japanese film crew stayed with them, for example, the lodge owners arranged for a helicopter to access remote areas and a 53-foot charter boat (with accommodations for 20 passengers) to take them out to various sea lion haulouts, to Cathedral Island to see Kodiak Island's largest puffin colony, and to Iliuliuk Peninsula to see brown bears.

The lodge is in Old Harbor, at the edge of the Kodiak National Wildlife Refuge. Unlike the north end of Kodiak Island, blanketed with tall spruce trees, the south end of the island is covered with short willows and cottonwoods and hundreds of wildflowers and wild grasses.

The lodge has four rooms with single beds, five rooms with doubles, and a bunkroom. There's also a cafe, open to the public, that serves three meals a day from a set menu. The Sitkalidak Mercantile and Convention Hall next door houses a general store selling fishing gear, sundries, souvenirs, clothing, and Native art. A recreation room has lounging chairs with a view of the strait, a pool table, a library, and a bar. There's a conference room and, as in many lodgings in Alaska, a room for cleaning and packing fish for shipment home. The lodge will set up charters to see Refuge Rock, visit Three Saints Bay, and tour Old Harbor. Throughout the summer, Old Harbor hosts large groups interested in natural and cultural history, such as Elderhostel. The lodge is co-owned by two couples; one of the owners, Freddie Christianson, is a Native shareholder.

Sitkalidak Lodge, PO Box 155, Old Harbor, AK 99643; (907)286-9246; fax (907)286-2262. Open year-round. Call for rates.

Akhiok: *Alutiiq*

An intriguing network of bays, coves, and lagoons tucked into the cliffs on the south end of Kodiak Island provide 75 miles of protected waters and access to numerous salmon streams in the Kodiak National Wildlife Refuge. This is a spectacular marine wilderness. In May humpback whales linger to feed in Alitak and Portage Bays, migratory and native birds rest and feed on the rocks, and Kodiak brown bears first begin feeding on tall grass, then fish for spawning salmon in the streams through September.

Akhiok Charters

Mitch Simeonoff, who grew up in the village of Akhiok and who has lived on the bays all his life, takes you out in his 30-foot covered boat (equipped with two 200-horsepower Yamaha engines) to explore the bays, watch for wildlife, and visit several areas of cultural interest. A 15-minute boat ride from his dock in Akhiok takes you to a trail to see the Cape Alitak petroglyphs and an old gold mine. He'll also show you the site where Alutiiq Natives banded together, armed with arrows and wooden shields, to discourage Russian fur trader Stephan Glotov from landing on the beach in 1763. (It would be more than 20 years before Russians successfully established a post on Kodiak Island.)

Most people coming here take a day trip with Simeonoff. You fly from Kodiak into Akhiok with the mail (one early-morning flight each day, except Sunday, during the summer) and fly back on a chartered plane in the evening. For bear viewing, you go with Simeonoff by boat to the mouth of Dog Salmon Creek, where you take a smaller skiff upriver to a spot where up to 22 bears fish for salmon. If you want to spend the night, you can stay in Simeonoff's rustic cabin at Cannery Cove, one of the few remaining buildings of the fish cannery that closed in 1929. You bring your own sleeping bag. Food and supplies can be purchased at Ward Cove Packing's cannery store, open year-round. Simeonoff and his family will also provide overnighters with meals; dinners usually feature local seafood such as fresh king and Dungeness crab, halibut, and salmon. Stream sportfishing includes sockeye, king, chum, and coho salmon as well as rainbow trout, Dolly Varden, and steelhead. Halibut, chinook salmon, black bass, and lingcod are caught in salt water. Sea kayaking rentals are also available for beginners or experts. Both Simeonoff and commercial fisherman Gary Rozelle, (907)836-2201, provide drop-off service for deer hunters in the fall. Simeonoff is a shareholder in the Koniag regional and village corporations. His cousin June Simeonoff owns Aatcha's Shop in Haines (see the Haines section of the Southeast Alaska chapter).

Akhiok Charters, PO Box 5008, Akhiok, AK 99615; (907)836-2210. Bear viewing June–Sept. Deer hunting season Aug–Dec. Half-day tours are $75 per person, plus $50 shared boat fee. Overnight guests pay $150 per day per person, which includes boat fee, land use permits, overnight accommodations, and meals.

INTERIOR
ALASKA

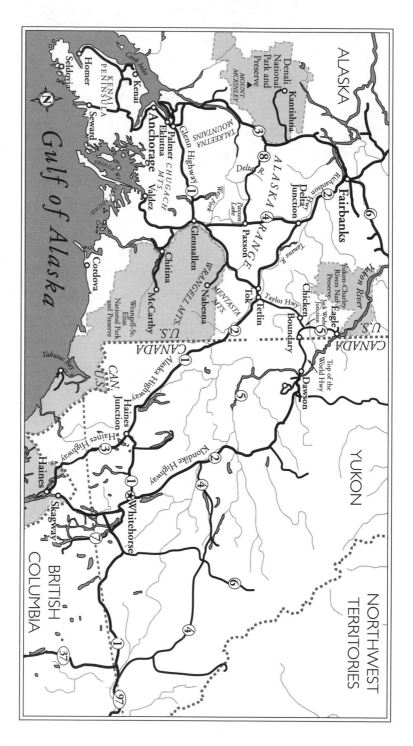

INTERIOR ALASKA

The heart of Alaska has been Athabascan Indian territory for centuries, its peoples more closely related to those of Canada's interior than to the Eskimo cultures that ring them. Occupying central Alaska, a region roughly the size of four Midwestern states, Athabascan territory is defined by geography, from the mountain peaks of the Brooks Range in the north, to the lower half of the Yukon River that sweeps south and divides the interior from Alaska's west coast, to the Kenai Peninsula and Prince William Sound in the south. The Athabascan people were nomadic up until this century, following and intercepting huge migrations of caribou and solitary moose, and returning to fish camps during the spawning seasons of salmon along Cook Inlet and the vast river systems of the interior.

The origin of Athabascan peoples in Alaska, whose territory extends from central Alaska across western Canada, is a continuing puzzle for anthropologists. Archaeological evidence indicates that Athabascans from western Canada migrated into what is now Southwest United States several centuries prior to white contact. In fact, the traditional language of Alaska's Athabascan Indian tribes is related to that spoken by the Navajo of the Southwest. Many words sound identical, although they have different meanings. It's a chicken-and-egg sort of question—did Athabascan culture and language originate in the northern part of the continent and travel south, or vice versa? Or did it travel in a loop, returning to lands it had occupied thousands of years prior?

Traditional Athabascan lands in Alaska include what is today the Arctic National Wildlife Refuge in the north, where polar bears den and thousands of caribou give birth and nurse their calves; most of the 2,000-mile-long Yukon River and its extensive tributaries; all of Denali National Park and Preserve (*Denali* is the original Athabascan name for the 20,320-foot peak later called Mount McKinley); the metropolitan area of Fairbanks and Anchorage; the upper reaches of Cook Inlet; and the Kenai Peninsula, today a popular wilderness playground (and 1.7-million-acre moose sanctuary) in Anchorage's backyard. Major tribes within the Alaskan Athabascan region are the Gwich'in, Koyukon, Ingalik, Tanana, Tanaina, Ahtna, Nebesna, Eyak, and Han; within each of these groups are several major clans.

The traditional lifestyle in this region was nomadic, with extended families living in houses covered with moose and caribou skins—houses that could be moved as hunters followed and intersected migrating game. Travel was by birch canoe and dogsled; clothing was constructed of tanned moosehide and moccasins adorned with porcupine quill embroidery. When fur traders from the Hudson's Bay Company entered the region in the mid-1800s, they brought with them glass trade beads, which became the primary form of Athabascan artistic expression. Beadwork is still practiced today, with some of the finest beadwork in the United States being produced by artists living in the Yukon River villages. The Hudson's Bay Company, whose Irish and Orkney Islander trappers brought fiddles and dance to the region, also spawned a unique musical fusion of British Isles and French Canadian fiddle tunes with Athabascan songs and rhythm—a tradition celebrated annually at the Athabascan Old-Time Fiddling Festival in Fairbanks.

Permanent villages were established early on in the southern part of Athabascan territory, many of them around Cook Inlet. In the north, seasonal camps were essential to survival; permanent villages, such as Fort Yukon, Stevens Village, and Tanana, all on the Yukon River, were not established until the late 1800s and early 1900s, around trading posts and mission schools.

Today, the most populated towns in the region are metropolitan Anchorage and Fairbanks. More than 20,000 Alaska Natives, from all over Alaska, live and work in Anchorage, making it the largest "Native village" in the state. Opening in Anchorage in 1999 is the Alaska Native Heritage Center, with "living heritage" village exhibits that represent the five major Native cultures of Alaska. Other public displays of Native art and culture are at the Anchorage Museum of History and Art and the Anchorage International Airport. Just outside Anchorage is the Athabascan village of Eklutna, with its Russian Orthodox chapel (one of the oldest wooden buildings in Alaska) and colorful spirit houses in the adjoining cemetery.

Three hours south of Anchorage (by car or train) are the spectacular fjords, icefields, and mountain lakes of the Kenai Peninsula. Several Native-owned tour groups operate on the Kenai and neighboring Prince William Sound. You can join one of them to view tidewater glaciers, birds, and wildlife in Resurrection Bay, journey along a trail that crosses an 8,000-year-old Athabascan home site, visit Native villages, and more.

North of Anchorage is Denali National Park, a wilderness where nomadic Athabascan tribes once hunted, following the great game migrations. Today, visitors can stay at Kantishna Roadhouse, an exclusive inn deep in the park. Kantishna is owned by Doyon Ltd., one of 13 regional Native corporations, with 14,000 Athabascan shareholders. Doyon is the largest private landowner in North America, with more than 12½ million acres.

Fairbanks, Alaska's second-largest city, is in the heart of Athabascan country, three hours north of Anchorage by train or by road. In the city itself, the University of Alaska Museum is well worth a visit for its exhibits on traditional and contemporary Native culture and art. Most Fairbanks galleries carry Athabascan beadwork, made by Natives who live in small villages along the Yukon River and its tributaries. Also in Fairbanks is Alaskaland, an Alaska theme park with a model of Yukon villages, as well as opportunities to cruise on a gold rush–era stern-wheeler to a demonstration Athabascan village. Two annual events bring Athabascans and Eskimos together in

Fairbanks: the World Eskimo–Indian Olympics in July, and the Athabascan Old-Time Fiddling Festival in November.

In the vast taiga wilderness (taiga is a Russian word describing the sweep of tundra covered in areas with dwarf evergreen forests) surrounding Fairbanks is a handful of small Athabascan villages and fish camps, several hundred miles apart, perched along the banks of the Yukon, Tanana, Nenana, and other rivers, where villagers live mostly off the land. What was once their exclusive territory has been designated in this century as federally protected wildlife refuges and preserves. Native people are allowed to hunt for their subsistence in these areas, a guarantee from Congress when the Alaska Native Claims Settlement Act legislation was passed. (See two essays on subsistence and an explanation of ANCSA in the appendix.)

Although the unpaved Dalton Highway follows the Alaska oil pipeline from Fairbanks through the taiga all the way to Prudhoe Bay on the Arctic Ocean, there are no roads to villages. All travel outside of Fairbanks, except for tours on the rivers, is by bush plane. Anyone trying to grasp the enormity of this should get up in a plane for a look at the landscape, then visit Athabascan summer fish camps and villages on rivers such as the Yukon, Tanana, and Koyukuk. The lands north of the Yukon and bordering the Arctic National Wildlife Refuge are the traditional home of the Gwich'in, nomadic peoples whose culture centers around the caribou. You can visit

Venetie or Arctic Village, and learn about the Gwich'in's efforts to protect the Arctic National Wildlife Refuge, where more than 160,000 caribou calve and nurse their young each year, from oil exploration and drilling.

ANCHORAGE METROPOLITAN AREA

Anchorage: *Athabascan*

Anchorage, the state's only metropolis, looks just like any other small city: highways, strip malls, residential areas, and a busy downtown with scattered high-rises. It has four-star hotels and restaurants as well as a superb museum and performance center. However, moose graze in the willows between Anchorage's airport and downtown, hundreds of migratory seabirds and ducks feed on the mudflats at low tide, and on a clear day, the snowcapped Chugach Mountains at the city's eastern edge sparkle in the sun.

The apparent absence of Native art in downtown Anchorage is a puzzle to new visitors, especially after they've seen the 90 totems that grace Ketchikan, or the marvelous mural of the Raven creation story on Juneau's waterfront. It's particularly troubling because more than 20,000 Alaska Natives live in Anchorage, and their unique heritage is what draws many visitors to Alaska.

The city of Anchorage is located near the end of the 220-mile-long Cook Inlet, on its southeast shore. The inlet was once surrounded by permanent Athabascan villages, but many of these settlements disappeared or were left with just a handful of survivors after virulent epidemics swept through the region in the 1800s and early 1900s.

Today, Alaska Natives from every corner of the state reside and work in the city of Anchorage. Many Native corporation headquarters, including Cook Inlet Region Inc., are based here, as are the Alaska Federation of Natives, Alaska Village Initiatives, the Alaska Native Tourism Council, and the Alaska Native Medical Center.

Perhaps because of their influence, in just the past decade a significant amount of Native art has been purchased for installation in public spaces. One of the best collections is at the Anchorage airport, where 500 objects ranging from ceremonial masks to beadwork baby carriers are installed throughout the main terminal. Slowly, the city is adorning itself with larger totems, monumental sculpture, and murals. In addition to touring the city's public art and galleries, plan to see the Alaska Native Heritage Center (opening in 1999) and the two Native-owned shops in Anchorage. Outside the city, visit Eklutna Village, with its brightly painted spirit houses.

Getting There

Anchorage is the hub for most flights coming into Alaska from outside the region. The city is about 3 hours from Seattle, the nearest hub in the lower 48 states. For the easiest connecting flights and lowest fares, contact your travel agent. Foreign carriers servicing Anchorage include Aeroflot, Cathay Pacific, China Air, Korean Air, and numerous charters. Many major domestic carriers serve Anchorage as well:

- Alaska Airlines, (800)426-0333.
- America West, (800)235-9292.
- Continental Airlines, (800)525-0280.
- Delta Air Lines Inc., (800)221-1212.
- Hawaiian Airlines, (800)367-5320.
- Northwest Airlines Inc., (800)225-2525; international division, (800)447-4747.
- United Airlines, (800)241-6522.

You can also drive to Anchorage year-round via the fully paved Alaska Highway, which links Alaska with Canada and the lower 48 states.

Visitor Services

Anchorage visitor information centers are located at the Anchorage International Airport and in downtown Anchorage, in a picturesque log cabin at the corner of 4th Avenue and F Street (524 W 4th Ave, Anchorage, AK 99501; (907)276-4118). Call or write for the free "Anchorage Visitors Guide," over 100 pages in full color.

Public Art at the Anchorage International Airport

One of the largest and most accessible showcases of Alaska Native artwork is permanently installed in the Anchorage International Airport, funded by the state's One Percent for Art monies. Instead of awarding a large commission to one or a handful of artists, exhibit curator and folklorist Dr. Susan Fair collected work from individuals throughout the state. The exhibit includes a mural-size painting by Alvin Amason, an Aleut, and 500 exquisite smaller pieces, artfully arranged in glass cases throughout the airport. It's well worth allowing time to examine these closely.

The airport exhibit features a few large pieces that would stand alone in any art gallery, such as Amason's three-piece painting of polar bears, sea otters, and other Alaska wildlife, which is installed over the concourse entry. But most of the collection consists of small items—fishhooks, knives, parka trim—that reflect the art of everyday life. In this case, small is indeed beautiful—and the more you learn about the form and function of these objects, the more beautiful they appear.

> "The construction of material things requires the genius of individual expression, the influence of many people, the intervention of memory and collective tradition, and, often, the need to make an honest living doing what one does best."
>
> —Susan Fair

"Not all of the pieces in the airport collection are what art collectors would buy," says Fair. For example, three Athabascan masks by Philip Arrow are assembled with staples and painted with house paint. They're included because "masks are still being made on the spot, to tell a story at an 'insiders' gathering. They're not necessarily being made to be pretty or to be sold." Even so, the majority of the pieces in the collection are collector's items, dazzling in both conception and execution. One example is Dixie Alexander's Athabascan chief's coat and pouch, made of smoked moosehide and caribou skin, trimmed with beaver fur and black velvet, and richly decorated with glass seed beads, cut and drop beads, silver beads, dentalia shells, and walrus-ivory buttons.

Three major exhibits are located in the airport rotunda; one stunning group, just past the airport's security gate, includes a Tlingit button blanket. Ivory and whalebone carvings are on the C concourse; basketry, masks, and skin sewing are on the B concourse; and dolls, more ivory, and masks are on the A concourse. All pieces are labeled with the artist's birthplace and present home, which gives the work even more meaning for travelers who have been to those places. Some pieces were commissioned by Fair, while others were works in progress, such as an adz that Reggie Peterson Sr. (Tlingit) was making for his own use when Fair visited his home in Sitka. The collection is exceptionally well balanced between male and female artists, as well as among the various cultural areas of Alaska. No heirloom pieces or antiquities were purchased for the exhibit; all work is by contemporary artists, purchased between 1989 and 1992. The works were installed by Wanda Chin, exhibit designer for the University of Alaska Museum in Fairbanks, who has also worked on projects for the Smithsonian and major worldwide traveling exhibitions.

Photographs of objects, artist portraits, working shots of artists, and historic photos of similar works of art are included in the catalogue/guidebook to the airport's exhibit, written by Susan Fair. Titled *Tradition, Innovation, and Continuity: Alaska Native Art in the Public Eye* (University of Alaska Press, 1998), the book is available at most Alaska bookstores, including the one at the airport, and from the publisher, (888)252-6657.

Anchorage International Airport, 5000 W International Airport Rd, Anchorage, AK 99501; (907)266-2437. Open 24 hours a day. You may enter all concourses, whether or not you are a passenger, as long as you walk through the security checkpoint.

Public Art in Downtown Anchorage

Some Native art is displayed in Anchorage, although most of it is tucked away inside public buildings. All art in state-owned public buildings was purchased through the state's One Percent for Art fund, established by the Alaska State Legislature.

If you'd like to see how traditional Alaska Native art complements modern architecture, arrive a bit early at the Alaska Center for the Performing Arts (621 W 6th Ave), in the heart of downtown. Amid the stained glass, vibrantly painted walls, designer rugs, and tapestry are 18 traditional-style masks by some of Alaska's most well known artists: Fred Anderson, Sylvester Ayek, Lawrence Beck, Kathleen Carlo, Nick Charles, Frank Ellanna, Alex Frankson, John Hoover, Edna Davis Jackson, Nathan Jackson, John Kailukiak, Al Kaloke, Hubert Kokuluk, Bert Ryan, James Schoppert, Peter Smith, and Paul Tiulana.

Across the street, in the William A. Egan Civic and Convention Center lobbies (555 W 5th Ave), you can see five wood and whalebone sculptures by Melvin Olanna, as well as *Volcano Woman*, carved of red cedar by John Hoover.

Outside the new Alaska State Courthouse (825 W 4th Ave) stand two 12½-foot cedar totems by Haida/Tlingit carvers Lee Wallace and Edwin DeWitt. Entitled *Attaining a Balance Within*, they depict two stories. One is Raven, stealing the moon and stars; the other is the temptation story of the Eagle boy trying to steal a giant clam (a metaphor for vice), which he's been warned not to touch because the

The voice of Disney's Pocahontas was that of actress Irene Bedard, who grew up in Anchorage, the daughter of an Inupiat Eskimo and a French Canadian/Cree. Chosen by People magazine as one of the "50 Most Beautiful People in the World," she also appeared in Grand Avenue, Crazy Horse, Lakota Woman: Siege at Wounded Knee, and Squanto: A Warrior's Tale.

clam is far stronger than he is. In the courthouse lobby (you'll have to go through security), see Alvin Amason's *Love Me Tender*, a three-dimensional painting of a puffin with a rock-and-roll theme, and new work by Susie Bevins. A few blocks east, step inside the Sheraton Hotel (401 E 6th Ave) and follow the central stairway to the second-floor balcony. Two walls covered in travertine are engraved with *Drummer Sings of Travels with Seals*, by sculptor Larry Ahvakana.

You'll need a car to see James Schoppert's *Transition*, an aluminum sculpture outside the George M. Sullivan Sports Arena (1600 Gambell) and Sylvester Ayek's marble sculpture of a polar bear outside the offices of the Solid Waste Services Administration Building (1111 E 56th Ave).

Alaska Native Heritage Center

At the Alaska Native Heritage Center, which has been in the planning stages for more than a decade and is set to open in the spring of 1999, five village exhibits surround a small lake. Here Natives construct buildings, canoes, and implements used in fishing, hunting, and other activities during the last century. Each of the village exhibits represents one of the cultural groups present in Alaska: the Athabascans of Interior Alaska; the Eyak; the Tlingits, Haida, and Tsimshians of the Southeast coast; the Aleut and Alutiiq of Prince William Sound, the Kodiak archipelago, and the Aleutian Islands; the Yup'ik Eskimo of the Southwest coast; and the Inupiat Eskimo and St. Lawrence Island Yup'ik of the Arctic.

Visitors begin their tour in the circular hall—the Gathering Place—of the Welcome House, a beautiful building reflecting the unique architecture of all five cultural groups. The Gathering Place itself represents a drum circle, a symbol of the life cycle. The drumbeat played here represents the cadence of a mother's heartbeat, and as visitors move through the room they are symbolically reborn into the Native experience of life. In the center is a large exhibit of contemporary rural village life and the subsistence lifestyle followed by most Natives living in Alaska. The Welcome House also contains a gallery, multimedia theaters, artists' studios, the Village Store, a cafe, and a "Travel Native Alaska" kiosk with tourism brochures and maps inviting visitors to the Native villages of rural Alaska.

The center was designed with the help of indigenous culture bearers and Native scholars. A revival of interest in pre-contact skills is under way in Alaska, among them the construction of wood-frame kayaks, umiaks (skin boats), and carved and steamed canoes; totem carving; bentwood box making; basketry; Raven's Tail and

Chilkat weaving; mask making; and bead and porcupine quill embroidery. Works made on site will be available for sale in the center's Village Store.

Creation of the center was approved by a unanimous vote at the 1987 annual meeting of the Alaska Federation of Natives, and fundraising has been ongoing since then. Cook Inlet Region Inc., a Native corporation, donated land; the center's board of directors is drawn from Alaska Native corporations as well as civic and business groups. The majority are Alaska Natives.

Alaska Native Heritage Center (Administrative Offices), 2525 C Street, Suite 425, Anchorage, AK 99503; (907)263-5170. At this writing, the center was set to open in the late spring of 1999, but call to make sure. The center will be located 1 mile northeast of the Muldoon and Glenn Highway intersection, about 12 minutes from downtown Anchorage. Watch for signs to the site. A model of the center and grounds is on display at the Alaska Native Heritage Center administrative offices until the center opens.

Anchorage Museum of History and Art

Alaska's largest museum, in the heart of downtown Anchorage, is a treasure house of Alaska's early history, contemporary history, and fine arts and crafts. The second floor's Alaska Gallery explores Alaska Native culture and the events of the last two centuries that forever changed Natives' lives: the Russian occupation during the late 1700s to 1867, the 1867 Alaska Purchase, the gold rush, the Alaska Railroad era, and the years of missionaries, military presence, and resource extraction, including the construction of the trans-Alaska oil pipeline. The museum has a rich collection of contemporary Native art, a live performance theater where Native dances are performed throughout the summer, a documentary film series, and a lecture series. Traveling exhibits, such as those assembled by the Smithsonian Institution and New York's American Museum of Natural History, both of which have large collections of Native artifacts, are also displayed here.

KNBA (90.3 FM) was the first urban, Native public radio station in the United States. It's owned and operated by Koahnic (an Ahtna Athabascan word meaning "live air") Broadcast Corporation. Call (907)258-8895 for 24-hour programming information. On KAKM television (Channel 7), see Heartbeat Alaska, a program about Native issues broadcast each Sunday at 6:30pm.

Alaska Gallery

The Four Native Cultures permanent exhibit in the Alaska Gallery is a real crowd pleaser, with over 1,000 objects (most of them antiquities) on display. The exhibit begins with a series of miniature traditional Native villages from four major regions of

Alaska. It then sweeps in for a closer look with life-size mannequins of Natives, dressed both in traditional regalia and in everyday garb, inside cutaway sod and plank houses of the kind used in the last century.

Represented here are the Tlingit Indians from Alaska's Southeast coast, Aleuts from the Aleutian Islands, Athabascans from the interior, and Yup'ik and Inupiat (Eskimo) cultures from Alaska's western and northern coastlines. Most of the Four Native Cultures exhibit is based on written ethnographic studies conducted by white anthropologists at the beginning of this century. It is illustrated with artifacts, some predating white contact but most collected during the 1800s and early 1900s—a very narrow but colorful window in time. The main focus of the exhibits is each culture's adaptation to Alaska's natural environment; for example, how the Inupiat people met the challenges of finding and storing fresh water in the Arctic "desert" and of building shelter in a region with no trees. Although everything is captioned, the best way to appreciate this exhibit is to see it twice: first with a museum guide, and then on your own. Free tours are scheduled throughout the day from mid-May through mid-September.

Reprints of "Indian Country: Two Destinies, One Land," a comprehensive seven-part series on Alaska Native self-determination and control over traditional Native lands published June 29–July 4, 1997, are available from the Anchorage Daily News, (907)257-4200. $14 for the series or $2 each, plus postage and handling.

Traditional Art Collection

The museum has a strong collection of Native art, with both traditional work from the turn of the century, and ongoing acquisition of contemporary work. Traditional ivory carvings and woven baskets from all over Alaska are either displayed on the balcony surrounding the atrium or incorporated into the Four Native Cultures exhibit in the Alaska Gallery. The carvings include ivory and bone animal miniatures that were once used as gaming pieces and hunting charms but that in the last century have been created for Alaska's art and souvenir market.

Five distinct styles of traditional woven baskets are exhibited: Inupiat whale baleen baskets, Yup'ik coiled-grass baskets, Athabascan birchbark containers, Tlingit spruce root baskets, and Aleut twined-grass baskets. Displayed throughout the museum are totems, masks, and beadwork. During the summer months, Alaska Native artists often demonstrate and sell traditional crafts at tables on the museum's first floor. (A woman selling ulus, an ancient cutting and fish filleting tool, may not only demonstrate a variety of regional styles but also allow observers to handle an ulu found on St. Lawrence Island, its wood handle and slate blade estimated to be over 1,000 years old.)

Contemporary Art Collection

The museum's collection also houses dazzling contemporary Alaska Native art, including monumental sculpture by such artists as Larry Ahvakana (Inupiat), Bill Prokopiof (Aleut), and Nathan Jackson (Tlingit). Because the collection is so large, such pieces are not all on view at once; rather, items are periodically chosen to fill a gallery, to be set around the spacious first-floor atrium, or to be displayed in a hallway.

Although the artists may not be familiar to you, many of them have had commissioned work installed, and have exhibited, all over the world—from Japan and France to Minnesota and Washington state. Look here for work by Alvin Amason, Susie Bevins, Kathleen Carlo, John Jay Hoover, Bernard Kayexac, Melvin Olanna, James Schoppert, Ronald Senungetuk, Susie Silook, Jacob Simeonoff, Preston Singletary, and Gertrude Svarny, among others. Some of the artists live outside of Alaska, in areas (such as Santa Fe and New York) where fine art made by Alaska Natives is better supported by the international marketplace. Fine arts jeweler Denise Wallace is one example of this phenomenon. Wallace grew up in Seattle but returned through the years with her mother to her grandmother's village of Tatitlek on Prince William Sound. She sells her work, and that of other Alaska artists, out of her Santa Fe studio. Many Alaska Native artists have been invited to exhibit in one-person shows all over the world, hold advanced degrees in fine art from major universities, and are also skilled in traditional forms.

Contemporary Native art often combines traditional art and contemporary techniques as well as methods and materials such as metal casting, fused glass, and lithography. Lawrence Beck, for example, used traditional Inua mask design elements and modern "found" materials (a shiny hubcap, black plastic pancake turners, dental mirrors, safety pins, plastic, and feathers) along with clever wordplay to create a beautiful contemporary mask he named *Punk Nanuk Inua*.

Special Events

Dance groups from every geographic region of Alaska perform in traditional regalia during the Alaska Native Performance Series—30 minutes of dance, song, and storytelling, held in the museum auditorium several times daily from June through August. Free films are also shown daily throughout the summer months, and a lecture series continues throughout the year.

Gift Shop

The museum's gift shop is well respected for the integrity of its buyers. Georgia Blue, a 20-year gallery owner and former member of the

State Arts Council, is assisted by Mary Lou Lindall, a former buyer for Alaska Native Arts and Crafts, also with 20 years of experience. The shop divides its Native art into cases by cultural region and provides biographical information about the artists it represents. Books sold here include esoteric, academic-oriented works that are hard to find anywhere else. The store has an educational mission, but it's also a lovely place to browse.

Anchorage Museum of History and Art, 121 W 7th Ave, Anchorage, AK 99501; (907)343-4326. Open year-round; call for hours. Admission $5; children under 18, free. Group and senior rates. For group tours, call the Museum Education Department, (907)343-6187. The Gallery Cafe offers snacks and lunches during museum hours. The museum atrium and auditorium (230 seats) can be rented after hours for special events.

Heritage Library and Museum

This private collection of Alaskana, open to the public, is owned by the National Bank of Alaska. It includes a large collection of Alaska Native artifacts from all over the state, especially baskets and ivory carvings. Pieces of the collection travel to bank branches throughout Alaska and are installed according to regional interest.

The 2,500-volume reference library, available for public use, features books on all matter of Alaska subjects, including Native culture and art. Archives include photos of the gold rush and of Alaska Natives from Little Diomede and Nome.

Alaska Heritage Library and Museum, 301 W Northern Lights, Anchorage, AK 99501; (907)265-2834. Corner of C St. and Northern Lights, on the first floor of the National Bank of Alaska's corporate headquarters. Open summers, Mon–Fri, noon–4pm. Free. Parking is free in the bank's customer parking lot. Wheelchair accessible.

Alaska Native Medical Center

Don't be shy about visiting the Alaska Native Medical Center, a few miles from downtown, to see one of Alaska's best private or public collections of Native art. This high-tech $167 million facility, which opened in 1997 and looks like a grand hotel, welcomes visitors with large public spaces filled with art from its Heritage Collection.

The seeds of the center's impressive art collection were planted more than a decade ago, when managers of the craft shop at the old medical center heard rumors about plans for a new building, and began purchasing and storing art for display in it. The Seattle architectural firm NBBJ, believing that art would speed the healing process by putting patients at ease, worked with the craft shop staff both to display the collection throughout the hospital and to commission monumental pieces for installation in its public areas. The result is a beautiful, modern medical facility made human and healing by art.

In the medical center's circular meditation room, the wall screens and mosaic floor are by Susie Bevins, while John Hoover's carved *Spirit Birds* soar around the curved walls. On the second floor, see Clarissa Hudson's interpretation of a Tlingit ceremonial robe, carved on cedar panels that wrap a curved wall. Smaller pieces are exhibited in large glass cases installed outside elevator entrances on the five floors of the main building. You can also peer into Tiffany-style display cases recessed in the walls of the stairway to all five floors, as good for your heart as climbing the stairs.

More artwork is across the street in the lobby of the primary care unit; visitors are welcome to walk in and see it. A catalogue describing the Heritage Collection and a self-guided walking tour are in the works.

Off the medical center lobby is the center's craft shop, which sells Native art from all over Alaska. Patients (and their families) from Alaska's bush who come to Anchorage for health care have always brought their art and crafts to exchange for cash. "Patients used to sell their art from their hospital bedside," says craft shop founder Agnes Coyle, a hospital volunteer for 30 years. To assist with sales, volunteers incorporated the first craft shop 25 years ago, lodged in a space in the old hospital that was barely larger than a supply closet. It was always swamped with buyers; insiders have long known that the hospital's craft shop is one of the very best places in Alaska to buy Native art.

Events

APRIL: As part of the Native Youth Olympics, students from 30 villages compete in traditional Native sports events at the University of Alaska/Anchorage Sports Center; (907)272-7529.

OCTOBER: Quyana Alaska, a Native dance celebration with traditional dancers from all over the state, is held in conjunction with the Alaska Federation of Natives' annual meeting; (907)274-3611.

A new shop was finished in 1997 and it is a beauty. Light and bright, it has enough room for the lines of customers who, as in the old shop, line up to choose from the artworks displayed behind the counter: handmade ivory bracelets, coiled-grass and birchbark baskets, carvings, beadwork, mukluks, fur slippers, Eskimo yo-yos, skin balls, masks, and more. It isn't unusual to meet artists in person, standing patiently in line with customers, bringing in one or two objects from a remote village to sell.

This shop is hard to beat: the quality of the art is high, the work is guaranteed to be authentic, the prices are reasonable (just a 20 percent markup), and the proceeds go to good causes. The craft shop offers scholarships to Native students, and its profits helped purchase art for the Heritage Collection.

Alaska Native Medical Center, 4315 Diplomacy Dr, Anchorage, AK 99508; (907)729-1122. Hospital public areas open 24 hours a day; craft shop open Mon–Fri, 10am–2pm, and the first Sat of the month, 11am–2pm.

Alaska Native Arts and Crafts

The windows of this downtown gallery are tinted to protect the delicate artwork showcased inside. Make sure you don't pass this one by in favor of flashier stores; the work here is guaranteed to be authentic. Alaska Native Arts and Crafts began as a clearinghouse in 1938, and is today fully Native-owned and operated. Buyers for the store used to travel out to the villages; today they work with village cooperatives and directly with Native artists, some of them part of the second or third generation of artist families who have sold their work through Alaska Native Arts and Crafts for decades. Many well-known Alaska Native artists, such as Lawrence Beck and Alvin Amason, started here when they were young. The gallery carries the work of ivory and soapstone carver Edith Oktollik; Athabascan Leonard Savage, whose Eskimo-style ivory miniatures of birds are remarkable in their detail; the Topkok family's sealskin and beadwork; and Jack Abraham's traditional and contemporary Yup'ik masks. The gallery owners know their artists, carry high-quality, signed work, and keep prices at reasonable levels. Labels on each piece state the artist's name, home, and ethnic background. The gallery also provides detailed information on how specific kinds of art are produced—the mark of a truly reputable store.

Alaska Native Arts and Crafts, 333 W 4th Ave, Anchorage, AK 99501; (907)274-2932. Open Mon–Fri, 10am–6pm; Sat, 10am–5pm. About a block and a half east of the Anchorage Visitors Center log cabin, between C and D Sts in the Ship Creek Center Mall.

Laura Wright Alaskan Parkys

Laura Wright was an Inupiat clothing designer who, in the 1940s, patented the Laura Wright Alaskan Parky, an Eskimo-style parka with a fur "sunshine ruff" that encircles the wearer's face. The inspiration for Laura's parka design is in a corner of her Anchorage shop: two traditional, hand-stitched, hand-pieced fur parkas. One she wore as a young woman while living near Kotzebue Sound; the other is a child's parka from the Yukon Delta region.

Born in Candle, an Inupiat village near the south end of Kotzebue Sound, Wright and her husband operated a gold mine and raised six children in Haycock. In the 1940s they moved to Fairbanks, where Wright opened her first parka shop. She had already proved herself during World War II when, as a sharpshooter for the Tundra Army, she hit the bull's-eye 49 times out of 50. Her parka designs also proved to be right on the mark. Her original "parky" titillated the media when it was worn by a contestant in the Miss Universe Pageant, and stars such as Elvis Presley, Ricky Nelson, Burl Ives, and Shirley Jones purchased and wore them in the 1960s.

Wright was named Most Outstanding Living Eskimo by the Alaska Federation of Natives, and she was listed in *Who's Who of American Women* in 1967. In 1971 she opened her parka shop in Anchorage, operating it until her death at 87 several years ago. Today her granddaughter Sheila Ezelle runs the shop. Ezelle still produces her grandmother's original winter design, a luxurious insulated parky made of velvet, with a hood trimmed in fox, wolf, coyote, beaver, or wolverine fur. The parkys are stitched on the premises.

Laura Wright's parkys are available in summer and winter weights in a large variety of fabrics, colors, and trims. If you don't see one you like in your size, the shop will customize a parky for you. Prices begin at $90 for summer parkys trimmed with bright colors and start at $600 for winter parkys trimmed with fur.

Laura Wright Alaskan Parkys, 343 W 5th Ave, Anchorage, AK 99501; (907)274-4215; fax (907)277-5021. In summer, open 10am–7pm daily; in winter, open Tues–Sat, 10am–5:30pm. Call first to make sure they're open.

Oomingmak

As isolated villagers are forced by federal regulations and dwindling reserves to rely less on subsistence and barter and more on cash purchases, one of their biggest challenges is finding a source of revenue that doesn't harm the environment. Musk ox farming was an early solution to this ongoing problem of finding a small but steady cash crop. The Oomingmak cooperative provides a sales outlet for knitted products made from musk ox wool.

The shaggy musk ox are survivors of the last ice age. They have a silky, dense underwool (*qiviut*) that protects them from the bitterly cold Arctic winds and that can be shorn and used for knitting. The musk ox were hunted to extinction in Alaska by the mid-1800s. In 1930 a herd from Greenland was introduced to Nunivak Island, then domesticated on farms to provide wool for Cup'ik and Yup'ik village women to knit and sell. Today between 150 and 250 villagers, many of them living in Alaska's coastal villages between Bethel and Nome, are members of the Oomingmak cooperative. They work at home knitting distinctive scarves, hats, and tunics from musk ox wool, which are then sold through the cooperative. The knitwear is very fine and soft, and over the years knitters have developed village "signature patterns," many of them taken from traditional art forms.

The Oomingmak cooperative's only store is in downtown Anchorage. Look for a building with a mural of a musk ox on the exterior. You can also visit the Musk Ox Farm, 50 miles from Anchorage in the scenic Matanuska Valley, Alaska's banana belt of ranches and farms. Tours begin in the farm's visitors center and move to the colonial-style barn and fenced walkways to observe the animals and herders.

Oomingmak: Musk Ox Producers' Co-op, 604 H St, Anchorage, AK 99501; (907)272-9225. In downtown Anchorage. Open 10am–6pm daily in summer; fewer hours in winter. Mail-order catalogue available. Musk Ox Farm, PO Box 587, Palmer, AK 99645; (907)745-4151. Milepost 50.1 on the Glenn Highway. Open daily, May–Sept, 10am–6pm, with guided tours every half hour.

Native-Owned Lodging

West Coast International Inn is a first-class, full-service hotel owned by Tanadgusix (TDX) Corporation, whose shareholders are Aleuts from the Pribilof Islands. The hotel is conveniently located near the Anchorage airport and overlooks the Chugach Mountains and Hood and Spenard Lakes, which together make up the largest floatplane base in the world. Hundreds of colorful small planes are docked on the lakes, within view of the hotel's dining room and deck.

The hotel, managed by West Coast Hotels & Resorts, has 141 well appointed rooms, with three master suites, nine junior suites, and banquet space for up to 320 people. Rooms have free cable TV, pay-per-view movies, coffeemakers, hair dryers, irons and ironing boards, dual-line speakerphones, and voice mail. The fitness room has Olympic free weights, Tunturi bikes, and a sauna.

Pipers Restaurant and lounge, with a deck overlooking the lake, is open throughout the day, and features fresh seafood on its lunch and dinner menus.

West Coast International Inn, 3333 W International Airport Rd, Anchorage, AK 99502; (800)663-1144 or (907)243-2233. Open year-round. Rooms $114 single to $258 suite. 24-hour courtesy van to and from the airport. Guests receive Alaska Airlines mileage for each stay at the hotel.

SOUTH OF ANCHORAGE: KENAI PENINSULA

The mountainous Kenai Peninsula, larger than the state of Vermont and dominated by a 300-square-mile ice cap, juts into the Gulf of Alaska about 130 miles south (by paved highway) of the city of Anchorage. If not for the narrow isthmus connecting it to the mainland, the peninsula would be an island. Its western shore is bordered by Cook Inlet; its eastern shore is bordered by Prince William Sound— which, of course, became internationally known in 1989, when the *Exxon Valdez* ran aground and spilled 11 million gallons of oil into the Sound. Among the results of the spill was a $100 million civil settlement targeted to assist in the restoration of resources damaged by the oil spill. To restore habitat, large blocks of Native corporation land that might have been used for timber harvest or other resource development were purchased for conservation. Research has also been funded to gauge the recovery of species and resources injured by the spill, as well as to recover artifacts from the dozens of archaeological sites that had been pinpointed prior to the spill, but had not yet been excavated. The Alutiiq Museum and Archaeological Repository in Kodiak (see the Kodiak section of the Southwest Alaska chapter) was built with *Exxon Valdez* funds to be a repository for these materials. A similar project is under way in Prince William Sound.

The coastlines of the Kenai Peninsula and Prince William Sound were inhabited at least 4,500 years ago by a Pacific Eskimo culture. In the Izaak Walton State Recreation Area on the Kenai Peninsula's Cook Inlet shoreline, archaeologists have discovered Eskimo fishing settlements that date back 2,000 years. Recovered artifacts indicate that these first Eskimo settlers may have been related to inhabitants of Kodiak Island and the Alaska Peninsula, forebears of today's Alutiiq people. Archaeological evidence also seems to indicate that sometime in the last two centuries, Athabascan Indians occupied most of the Kenai Peninsula and also lived along the southwest coast of Prince William Sound, and that there was considerable intermarriage between the two distinct cultures in this region. When the Russians entered the area in the 1700s, they brought with them Aleut and Alu-tiiq sea otter hunters, many of whom settled in coastal villages.

The cultural diversity of the Kenai Peninsula, which includes Russian occupation and American homesteaders, is best explained by the Pratt Museum in the small town of Homer. In the little town of Kenai, north of Homer, Kenaitze tribal members lead a histori-cal interpretation tour through an old Athabascan village site on Cook Inlet. At Seldovia, south of Homer and accessible by ferry (and less crowded than other towns on the Kenai Peninsula during the busy summer months), you'll want to load up your shopping bag with smoked salmon and the jams and jellies produced and bot-tled by the Seldovia Native Association from wild berries picked on the peninsula.

The town of Seward, once a Pacific Eskimo summer fishing camp on the Kenai Peninsula's south end, is accessible from Anchor-age by train (about a 3-hour journey). In the last century, Seward be-came the gateway from the Pacific Ocean into Alaska's interior after the railway was constructed from Seward to Anchorage. Today the rail line and a paved highway bring hundreds of tourists to Seward and Kenai Fjords National Park, one of the nation's newest national parks. From Seward's waterfront, you can take a sightseeing cruise with Kenai Fjords Tours, owned by Native shareholders of Cook Inlet Region Inc. The tour cruises through Resurrection Bay and into Kenai Fjords National Park to see firsthand the region where early hunters sought prey from their baidarkas (kayaks)—a region teeming with sea lions, seals, whales, and thousands of birds. The tour includes a stop for an all-you-can eat salmon lunch and, if you wish, an overnight stay at the Kenai Fjords Wilderness Lodge, a group of cab-ins tucked into the trees, offering magnificent views of the moun-tains and bay.

Getting There

The Kenai Peninsula is about a 2-hour scenic drive from Anchorage (car rentals are available in Anchorage), or a 30-minute air-taxi ride from Anchorage International Airport. On the Kenai Peninsula is a network of roads to the towns of Kenai, Homer, and Seward. Homer is about 4½ hours from Anchorage. The little town of Seldovia requires taking a boat or air taxi across Kachamak Bay from Homer.

Seward is also accessible by train from Anchorage. The Alaska Railroad (411 W First Ave, PO Box 107500, Anchorage, AK 99510; (800)544-0552 or (907)265-2494) offers one round trip daily dur-ing the summer months to Seward, the gateway to Kenai Fjords Na-tional Park.

The Alaska Marine Highway's car ferry route through South-west Alaska stops on Prince William Sound at Cordova and Valdez, and stops on the Kenai Peninsula at Seward, Portage, Homer, and Seldovia, before crossing Cook Inlet to the Kodiak archipelago and Unalaska on the Aleutian Chain. Boats making the long journey are equipped with staterooms, a dining room, and lounges. Two or three vessels operate during the summer. For a free copy of the ferry schedule or for reservations, call (800)642-0066 between 7:30am and 4:30pm weekdays, or call the ferry's Prince Rupert, British Columbia, office at (250)627-1744 or (250)627-1745. You can also read the ferry schedule on the Internet at http://www.dot. state.ak.us/external/amhs/home.html (although it's easier to just ask them to mail you one). Fares vary according to cars, trailers, number of passengers, and cabin reservations. Credit cards are accepted. Bicycles, kayaks, and canoes are allowed for an additional charge.

Visitor Services

- Kenai Fjords National Park Visitor's Center, 1727 4th Ave, PO Box 1727, Seward, AK 99664; (907)224-3175.
- Kenai Peninsula Tourism Marketing Council, 150 N Willow St, Suite 42, Kenai, AK 99611; (800)535-3624 or (907)283-3850. Call for a free 36-page, map-filled Kenai Peninsula vacation planner with sample itineraries.
- Kenai Visitor and Cultural Center, 11471 Kenai Spur Hwy, PO Box 1991, Kenai, AK 99611; (907)283-1991.
- Seldovia Chamber of Commerce, PO Drawer F, Seldovia, AK 99663; (907)234-7612.
- Seward Chamber of Commerce and Seward Visitors and Convention Bureau, 2001 Seward Hwy, PO Box 749, Seward, AK 99664; (907)224-8051. Two miles out of town on the highway. Write or call for a free brochure.

Kenai: *Athabascan*

The town of Kenai was known prior to 1700 as Skitok (from an Athabascan word that means "where we slide down"). The original village, consisting of semi-subterranean houses, smokehouses, and cache pits, was located on a bluff above Cook Inlet at the mouth of the Kenai River, a prolific salmon-spawning river.

Captain James Cook sailed up Cook Inlet in 1778 and noted villages along the shore; Skitok was colonized by the Russian fur traders in 1791. A year later it became the headquarters on the Kenai Peninsula for the Russians' trade in fish and furs.

The Russians called the Athabascans who lived here Kenaitze, meaning "the people who live along the Kenai River." The Kenaitze, however, called themselves Kahthuht'ana, an Athabascan word meaning "the people of the Kenai." The Kenaitze dialect contains coastal and marine terminology as well as 400 documented Russian words.

The Kenaitze tribe recommends several books, including K'tl'egh'i Sukdu-a: Dena'ina Legacy, the collected writings of Peter Kalifornsky (Alaska Native Language Center, University of Alaska, 1991); Tanaina Plant Lore, Dena'ina K'et'una: An Ethnobotany of the Dena'ina Indians of Southcentral Alaska, by Priscilla Russell Kari (Alaska Native Language Center, University of Alaska, 1991); and Ethnography of the Tanaina, by Cornelius Osgood (Yale University Press, 1966).

The Russians established the Holy Assumption Russian Orthodox Church at Kenai in 1841. In 1869, two years after Alaska was purchased from Russia by the United States, a military post (Fort Kenay) was installed to protect U.S. trade interests. The Fort Kenay log building, reconstructed in 1967, is an exact replica of the original fort. A fish saltery was established in 1878, and 10 years later the first of many canneries was built in Kenai.

The Kenaitze tribe consists of 800 lineal descendants of the people who lived at Skitok, but the town of Kenai has swollen to nearly 7,000 mostly non-Native residents. The village grew rapidly when the first road from Anchorage to Kenai was constructed in the early 1950s, opening the area to homesteaders. It boomed again when oil was discovered in the nearby Swanson River in 1957, the first oil strike in Alaska. Today the town is a major fish processing area and a growing center for oil exploration of Cook Inlet.

Kenaitze Tribe Tours

The Kenaitze tribe, in cooperation with the U.S. Forest Service, offers a special tour into the original Skitok village site. The village site is behind the Kenai Visitor and Cultural Center, located on the Kenai Spur Highway near Cooper Landing. Inside the center, you can pick up a historic timeline of the Kenai region as well as the tribe's self-guided tour of landmarks along the short trail that meanders through the old Skitok village site. Interpretive signs explain mounds, depressions in the ground, and other landmarks you might not otherwise recognize. Building techniques in this area differ from those of other regions; roofs, for example, were covered with hollowed-out cottonwood logs laid like Spanish tiles, and canoes were fashioned from wood frames covered with cured moosehide.

During the summer a representative from the Kenaitze tribe may be available to provide tours of the Skitok site with themes ranging from plant identification to historical information. A small gift shop on the premises sells the work of Kenaitze artists and Native American arts and crafts.

The Ts'itsatna Center, at the tribal office (address listed below), houses over 400 items documenting the Kenaitze's culture, traditions, and language—much of them oral histories and videotapes. Visitors are welcome to stop by and pick up a copy of "Raven's People Today," a brochure explaining the tribe's history and giving directions to their garden, where you may buy a hanging basket filled with native plants and perennials.

The Skitok site is behind the Kenai Visitor and Cultural Center, 11471 Kenai Spur Hwy, Kenai, AK 99611; (907)283-1991. Milepost 54. Open year-round, with extended hours June–Aug. Free. The trail is self-guided, but you may arrange a guided tour in advance by calling the tribal office. Kenaitze Tribe, PO Box 988, Kenai, AK 99611; (907)283-4321. Tribal offices are adjacent to the Russian Orthodox church in Kenai; open year-round during business hours.

Violet Mack Furs

Violet Blatchford is a clothing designer and furrier living in Kenai. The exquisite contemporary fur parkas that she designs, sews, and finishes by hand reflect her traditional Yup'ik Eskimo upbringing, in the 1930s, in the village of Golovin, southeast of Nome. She learned skin sewing, and how to make elaborate ceremonial parkas, from her mother, Jenny Blatchford. Her coats, in both full-length and shorter styles, are fully lined; some have ivory buttons. She also makes baby-size mukluks. Violet may be best known for her souvenir seals, made in various sizes up to a foot long and stuffed with rolled barley, which are finished by hand and sold throughout Alaska in gift stores. For an appointment to commission a coat, call (907)283-4390.

Homer

Homer is located on the southeastern end of the Kenai Peninsula near the mouth of picturesque Kachemak Bay, 227 road-miles south of Anchorage. It's been known historically as Denaina Athabascan Indian territory. Sites on Kachemak Bay, however, have yielded artifacts, dating to 4,500 years ago, that reveal the presence of older cultures believed to be Pacific Eskimo or Alutiiq. One of the sites on the Kenai Peninsula unearthed arrowheads and knives belonging to what archaeologists call the Ocean Bay Culture. More recent artifacts were identified as belonging to a newer culture known as the Kachemak Tradition, which is about 1,000 years old. Similar objects from both these time periods have also been unearthed west of Kachemak Bay in the Kodiak archipelago and on the Alaska Peninsula.

Today only a small number of Natives live in Homer, a town of more than 4,000 people. Homer is not recognized by the federal government as a traditional Indian village; however, the Native villages of Port Graham and Nanwalek, and the Seldovia Village tribe in the town of Seldovia, are nearby—on the shore of Kachemak Bay and Cook Inlet.

Originally from Kotzebue, Dolly Spencer (Inupiat) lives in Homer and often demonstrates or offers doll-making workshops at the Pratt Museum. One of Alaska's foremost doll makers and a recipient of an award from the National Endowment for the Arts, Spencer carves lifelike faces for her dolls from birch and dresses them in fancy parkas made of wolverine, badger, coyote, seal, and caribou skins, often sewn with twisted caribou sinew. For more information, call the Pratt Museum, (907)235-8635.

The town of Homer was first established on the 4½-mile-long Homer Spit as a coal distribution port in the late 1800s. The shipments of coal continued until just after World War I, when export mining operations ceased. Today the town is fueled by commercial fishing and sportfishing, fish processing, and tourists disembarking from the Alaska State Ferry, cruise ships, and charters during the summer months. The city is open to tourists through the winter as well, drawing cross-country skiers, dog mushers, bird watchers, and fishermen. The community is also one of Alaska's most dynamic artists' communities. Native artists can be contacted through the Pratt Museum.

Pratt Museum

This dynamic little museum in downtown Homer, with a peekaboo view of Kachemak Bay, has a big story to tell about the diversity of cultures that have inhabited the Kachemak Bay area in prehistoric and historic times. The museum, which houses an aquarium, marine gallery, and outdoor exhibits such as a homestead cabin, botanical garden, and interpretive trail, is probably best known for its exhibit about the March 1989 *Exxon Valdez* oil spill, *Darkened Waters: Profile of an Oil Spill.*

The museum has created a Native Cultures exhibit filled with marvelous things. While the objects on exhibit have been collected from throughout Alaska, they represent tools, clothing, and ceremonial items believed to have been used on the Kenai Peninsula and in the Kachemak Bay region.

A particularly great place for children, who are often bored by museum exhibits, the Pratt offers a narrative written especially for children (it works for adults as well) that asks them to imagine themselves as a Pacific Eskimo child living out such memorable scenarios as this: "A member of the clan has died and the family is preparing for the burial. This is very important to your people, as your gravesites show. Intrigued by the tiny carved figure, the ulu knife, and the stone point, you realize that they will be buried with the body." Narratives include climbing cliffs to gather seabird eggs in a halibut-skin shoulder bag, wearing clothing made of tanned fish skins, picking rose hips with a favorite aunt and dropping them into a basket, and digging chocolate lily roots with a bone root pick while dressed for rain in a halibut-skin parka. Exhibits include harpoons, clubs, kayak visors with carved seal heads, a kayak and a small umiak, stone lamps, and ivory labrets that were worn as facial decorations. Athabascan culture is represented by such things as a feather headdress; a rattle made of puffin beaks; glass trade beads; otter pelts; stone wedges; a wooden mesh gauge to repair nets, fishing floats, and sinkers; birchbark baskets; and a model of a semi-subterranean house.

Want to learn more about Alutiiq plant lore? **An Ethnobotany of the Peoples of English Bay and Port Graham,** Kenai Peninsula, Alaska, *a publication of the Pratt Museum, is available at the museum or from the Homer Society of Natural History (3779 Bartlett St, Homer, AK 99603; (907)235-8635).*

The first "Tamamta Katurlluta: A Gathering of Native Tradition" was held at the Pratt over Labor Day weekend 1997; a second gathering is slated for September 5–7, 1998, and it will probably continue semiannually. The event began with a kayak landing by Natives wearing traditional Alutiiq and Athabascan regalia. They were greeted on shore by dancers celebrating their arrival and by a blessing of the boats. The festivities were completed by an evening festival of dance, an arts and crafts fair, a potluck featuring Native foods, and the Pratt's exceptional exhibit *Qajaq, Kayaks of Alaska and Siberia.*

The museum offers tours and lectures year-round on natural history, fisheries, local archaeology, Native culture, marine mammals, seabirds, and shorebirds. It also sponsors field trips to observe birds and geologic features. Visiting Native artists from all over Alaska demonstrate traditional skills including doll making, beading, mask making, spruce root basketry, ivory carving, and skin sewing throughout the year.

The best-kept secret in Homer is nestled into a corner of the Pratt—the Museum Store, specializing in high-quality Native art, traditional crafts, and educational items from all over Alaska. Expect to find authentic baskets, beadwork, ulus, walrus ivory and soapstone carvings, masks, dance fans, jewelry, and collector dolls. The store also serves as one of the few outlets for the Native musk ox producers' cooperative (see "Oomingmak" in the Anchorage section of this chapter). There's a small but well-selected book section. A juried art show and sale each summer at the Pratt includes Native artists, many of whom live on the Kenai Peninsula.

Pratt Museum, Homer Society of Natural History, 3779 Bartlett St, Homer, AK 99603; (907)235-8635. Open daily mid-May–mid-Sept, 10am–6pm. Call for a current schedule of events.

Fish River Ulus

Lorita Linder (Inupiat) makes reproductions of traditional women's knives (ulus) and men's skinning knives based on old Inupiat, Yup'ik, and Alutiiq patterns, which differ slightly from village to village all along the coastline of Alaska. Blades are made from high-carbon steel cut from old handsaws; handles are carved from musk ox horn, caribou antler, wood, and ivory. In her collection are several ulus with slate blades that date back 500 to 1,000 years. Linder also makes jewelry using ivory and old beads.

MELD, Alaskan Native Art, Fish River Ulus, PO Box 2237, Homer, AK 99603; (907)235-3964. 1½ miles out Eastend Rd; best to call first for an appointment.

Seldovia

One of the most charming little towns in Alaska, Seldovia is located across from Homer on Kachemak Bay's south shore, accessible by Alaska State Ferry, by tour boats that leave from the Homer Spit from May through September, or by air taxi, 15 minutes from Homer or 45 minutes from Anchorage (for a list of tour operators, contact the Seldovia Chamber of Commerce, listed in "Visitor Services" earlier). The protected site, tucked into a smaller bay near the mouth of the Seldovia River, has been occupied over the centuries by Pacific Eskimos, Alutiiqs, and Athabascans, each of whom had their turn at control. The Athabascans named the area Chesloknu. The Russians brought Aleut sea otter hunters with them in the early 1800s; by the 1860s a mix of Native peoples lived in Seldovia and considered themselves one tribe, with a recognized chief by the time of the 1860 census. More Aleuts relocated to Seldovia after they were evacuated from the Aleutian Islands during World War II (see the Aleutian Islands section of the

Seldovia Native Association Inc. (328 Main St, Seldovia, AK 99663; (907)234-7625) welcomes campers and hikers on their lands, along with berry pickers. The best time to go berry picking is July, August, and September. Contact them for information on renting a rustic cabin or obtaining a berry-picking permit.

Southwest Alaska chapter). The town is picturesque and well preserved: St. Nicholas Orthodox Church, built in 1891, is now a National Historic Landmark open to the public; a wooden boardwalk
built along the waterfront in 1931 is maintained to this day.

Seldovia is legendary for its spruce-clad slopes lushly covered
with varieties of wild berries, including pungent highbush cranberries
that make a light, tart jelly. The Seldovia Native tribe owns most of
the berry-picking land and issues free berry-picking permits to visitors (and buys surplus berries from you to add to those they use in
their commercially prepared Chesloknu Foods jams and jellies, mar-
keted under the name Alaska Tribal Cache).

Chesloknu Foods

A multi-use building on Seldovia's Main Street contains tribal
offices, museum cases of artifacts reflecting the cultures of Seldovia,
and the kitchen where Alaska Tribal Cache's wild-berry jams and
jellies are made. The kitchen is open for viewing daily during the
summers. Jams, jellies, and syrups made from blueberry, huckleberry,
red or yellow salmonberry, and highbush cranberry are sold in the
adjoining gift store. The pretty, teal green labels have the Seldovia
Tribe's attractive logo emblazoned upon them: an Eskimo-style spirit
mask with a puffin in the center. "We do this for a couple of reasons," says tribal economic development director Rod Hilts, "to use
a longtime traditional resource and to share favorite old family
recipes." Customized gift baskets filled with the sweets and a jelly pot
are available, along with a cookbook of 528 local recipes put
together by local Seldovians.

*Chesloknu Foods, 328 Main St, PO Drawer L, Seldovia, AK 99663; (800)270-7810 or
(907)234-7898. The kitchen, museum, and gift store are open 10am–6pm daily
during the summer (the kitchen generally shuts down operation by 2pm). Call or write
for an order form and brochure. The berry products are also sold in gift shops
throughout Alaska.*

Seward and Kenai Fjords

Alutiiq and Russian history intersect, as they did in the Kodiak archipelago in the late 1700s, when Alexander Baranof—Russian fur
trader, explorer, and head of the crown-chartered Russian-American
Company—discovered Resurrection Bay in 1791. He was sailing
from Kodiak across the Gulf of Alaska to Yakutat when an unexpected
storm forced him to seek shelter. He named the protected bay after
the Russian Orthodox Sunday of the Resurrection.

Archaeological excavation reveals that no permanent village existed at Seward, although it is presumed that the seasonal camps along the shore were Alutiiq (or Pacific Eskimo). The town of Seward, poised at the base of tree-covered, 3,033-foot Mount Marathon, was founded by Alaska Railroad surveyors and incorporated in 1912. After the railroad was opened in 1923, Seward became, and still operates as, an ocean terminal and supply center. The gateway to Kenai Fjords National Park, the town of Seward is primarily non-Native. More than 2,000 Natives, many of whom have relocated to Seward from other regions in Alaska, are members of the Qutekcak Native tribe, the Mount Marathon Native Association, and the Grouse Creek Village Corporation. In 1996 Cook Inlet Region Inc., whose shareholders are pan-Alaskan, bought Kenai Fjords Tours, one of the state's most reputable tour companies. It offers daily marine sightseeing trips throughout the summer in Resurrection Bay and along the glacier-fed shoreline of Kenai Fjords National Park.

You can buy a package ticket that includes a day trip aboard one of Kenai Fjords Tours' sightseeing boats in Resurrection Bay and admission to the Alaska SeaLife Center to see Steller's sea lions, seals, puffins, and other marine creatures close up. The boat dock and SeaLife Center adjoin on Seward's waterfront. For details contact the Alaska SeaLife Center (PO Box 1329, Seward, AK 99664; (800)224-2525 or (907)224-3080).

Kenai Fjords National Park

Kenai Fjords National Park was established in 1980, encompassing nearly 580,000 acres of the rugged Kenai Peninsula coastline first claimed by Pacific Eskimos more than 4,500 years ago. The Harding Ice Field dominates the park, capping over 300 square miles with solid ice and snow thousands of feet thick. From this ice field flow about 40 glaciers. Some remain enclosed by rock, while others flow into tidewater. The most famous of these are Holgate, Northwestern, and Aialik Glaciers; more than 200 cruise ships visit the Holgate and Northwestern Glaciers during the summer months. The tidewater is rich with sea life. Steller's sea lions, Dall's porpoise, sea otters, humpback whales, and orcas (killer whales) are easily spotted here. The park has an ongoing relationship with Nanwalek and Port Graham, two Native villages on the lower Kenai Peninsula, west of the park. Both villages are historically Alutiiq, related to the Alutiiq cultures of the Alaska Peninsula and Kodiak Island. The Nanwalek Village Corporation recently sold their land holdings, about 5,000 acres, for incorporation in Kenai Fjords National Park. The Port Graham Native corporation, with both Port Graham and Nanwalek tribal members as shareholders, owns about 33,000 acres inside the park boundaries and helps manage the park via a tribal member from Port Graham who is a member of the National Park Service's resource management staff.

The Kenai Fjords National Park Visitor's Center, the gateway to the park, is located in Seward's small-boat harbor. Check here for maps, literature about the park, and lectures by park rangers.

Kenai Fjords National Park Visitor's Center, 1727 4th Ave, PO Box 1727, Seward, AK 99664; (907)224-3175.

Kenai Fjords Tours, Wilderness Lodge, and Kayaking

Kenai Fjords Tours is a subsidiary of Cook Inlet Region Inc., an Anchorage-area Native corporation. It is one of the best established and most popular tour companies in Alaska, offering several different touring options as well as accommodations at their Wilderness Lodge on Fox Island in Resurrection Bay.

Each day, eight sleek sightseeing boats belonging to Kenai Fjords Tours leave Seward's small-boat harbor. They take visitors on captain-narrated cruises of the spectacular fjords and tidewater glaciers of Kenai Fjords National Park, Resurrection Bay, and the Chiswell Islands, where more than 20,000 puffins nest each spring. Early-season cruises include a tour to view gray whales as they migrate through Resurrection Bay on their way north to feed.

Kenai Fjords Tours offers several different tour options. These include a 7-hour boat tour to an active tidewater glacier, with wildlife watching; a 9½-hour round-trip journey through Resurrection Bay to the spectacular Northwestern Fjord; a half-day wildlife-viewing tour of Resurrection Bay; and an overnight package that includes a cruise of the national park shoreline and glaciers, wildlife viewing, meals, and overnight accommodations. The daylong tours typically include a stop at the lodge for a salmon buffet. There are also tour packages that include cruise and round-trip transportation from Anchorage by bus, train, or air.

The Wilderness Lodge is in a beautiful setting on Fox Island, about an hour by boat from Seward. Eight private cabins, tucked into the woods, have a view of both the mountain-rimmed bay and a small freshwater lake. Cabins are built of knotty Sitka spruce with skylights, wood stoves, and private baths with showers. Each cabin is furnished with two beds. Cabins are illuminated by propane lanterns; there is no electricity. Three meals a day are served family style. Lunch is an all-you-can-eat salmon buffet. A 2½-mile trail behind the cabins leads through the rain forest to a spectacular overlook of Resurrection Bay. Overnight guests get a special rate on 4-hour sea kayak guided tours.

Kenai Fjords Tours also contracts with Sunny Cove Sea Kayaking Company, (907)345-5339, to offer kayak trips from Fox Island. The various packages range from half-day tours that include paddling instruction, to overnight camping trips in Resurrection Bay, to five-day paddle trips in the Northwestern Fjord, where you can paddle among icebergs and seals and watch the glacier calve. Experienced paddlers should look into the outer coast trip. All tours include kayaking equipment and instruction, transportation from Seward, gourmet meals, guide service, and camp setup. No prior kayaking experience is necessary for most tours. You can also customize a tour to include hiking and mountain biking. Prices vary.

Kenai Fjords Tours, PO Box 1889, Seward, AK 99664; (888)478-3346 or (907)224-8934; Web site: http://www.kenaifjords.com. Reservation office located on the boardwalk in the Seward small-boat harbor, and in Anchorage at 536 W 3rd Ave, in the Hilton Hotel. Tours are offered during the annual whale migration, Apr–early Oct.

Chieko Charters

John Kito, of Tlingit/Japanese descent, a school administrator and a shareholder of the Sealaska Native corporation, operates sightseeing and fishing charters from Seward into Resurrection Bay on his 34-foot Bayliner. The boat is equipped with tournament-quality tackle and gear. You can fish for halibut, lingcod, bass, snapper, and several species of salmon, and participate in July's Jackpot Halibut Tournament and August's Silver Salmon Derby. The boat is U.S. Coast Guard–licensed and certified for six passengers.

Chieko Charters, 12601 Beachcomber Dr, Anchorage, AK 99515; (907)345-0422. Slip C-3, Seward dock. Charters from June–Aug.

Harborview Inn

Jolene King, great-granddaughter of Ketchikan's Chief Kyan and a shareholder in the Sealaska, Goldbelt, and Huna Totem Native corporations, owns and operates the Harborview Inn, which offers peek-aboo views of the Seward waterfront. She and her husband, Jerry, vice mayor of Seward and captain of a university-owned research vessel, opened their first B&B in 1989, the year of the *Exxon Valdez* oil spill, to offer tourists a haven when other hotel rooms were filled with oil cleanup crews.

From the inn's large, free parking lot, it's a short walk to the boat basin and the Alaska SeaLife Center. Behind the inn is the trail to the top of 3,033-foot Mount Marathon.

The inn is actually a complex of two buildings housing 23 nicely furnished hotel rooms (the first building was constructed in 1989, while the second was completed in 1998) and a two-bedroom duplex overlooking Seward's waterfront. All the hotel rooms—including the newest, which have Mission-style furniture—offer private baths, data ports, cable television, and phones. The inn's deluxe suite, built with honeymooners in mind, has a stone gas-flame fireplace, king-size four-poster bed, cathedral ceilings, large to-the-ceiling windows, and bath with hydrotherapy tub and shower/steam room. Both units of the duplex have two bedrooms, a living room, a fully equipped kitchen, cable television, and a phone.

Harborview Inn, 900 3rd Ave, Seward, AK 99664; (907)224-3217. Open year-round. Rooms $49–$149 double occupancy, depending on season. Complimentary continental breakfast in the lobby each morning.

Prince William Sound

Prince William Sound, one of the most beautiful marine wildernesses in North America, is poised for dramatic change. When a new road is punched through the Chugach National Forest, the Sound will be an hour's drive from Anchorage—far more accessible than ever before.

Two Native corporations in the Prince William Sound region are considering developing tourism-related enterprises. One is the Eyak Corporation, based in Cordova. Another is the Chenega Corporation, representing the village of Chenega, which was virtually destroyed by the 1964 tsunami that followed Alaska's most devastating earthquake. The new town of Chenega is about 10 miles south of old Chenega, with a new ferry dock, enabling the Alaska State Ferry to stop weekly. To inquire about new sightseeing charters, museums, kayak adventures, and accommodations on the drawing board in this region, contact the Eyak Corporation, (907)424-7161, or the Chenega Corporation, (907)277-5706.

The Chugach Heritage Foundation (4201 Tudor Centre Dr, Suite 220, Anchorage, AK 99508; (907)563-8866), the non-profit arm of the regional corporation for the Kenai Peninsula and Prince William Sound area, offers a variety of publications, posters, and artwork, including books called Chugach Legends *and* Eyak Legends of the Copper River Delta, *and prints—some of them numbered—by non-Native artist Nancy Stonington, depicting the Orca, Morpac, and Uganik canneries of Prince William Sound. Call or write for an order form.*

NORTH OF ANCHORAGE

Eklutna: *Athabascan*

The village of Eklutna—25 miles northwest of downtown Anchorage on Highway 1, at the mouth of the Eklutna River—looks very small, with just a few unpaved roads and a handful of buildings. But nearly 450 people live here, many of them descendants of the Tanaina Athabascan Indians. Just past the last house at Eklutna, visible through a thicket of trees, are the mudflats of Cook Inlet's Knik Arm, where a string of Athabascan fish camps and villages once stood along the shore. Eklutna is the Anglicized version of Eydlytnu, the Athabascan name for the village. Archaeologists date the village to 1650, although the site was probably occupied long before then. Today, Eklutna and thousands of acres surrounding it are protected from outside development by the Alaska Native Claims Settlement Act of 1971.

On display at Eklutna's Heritage House is a hand-cranked Singer sewing machine, over 100 years old, donated by a former student at Eklutna Vocations School. From 1924 to 1945 the Bureau of Indian Affairs operated this school for Native children from all over the state. Children attended the boarding school from kindergarten through high school.

Anthropologists are still trying to trace the origins of the Athabascans who settled in Interior Alaska. One thing is known for sure—their language is so closely related to the Navajo tongue that when Navajos and interior Athabascan speakers compared words, they found that many were the same. Sometimes, though, the same words had very different meanings, a continuing puzzle for linguists and anthropologists trying to trace settlement patterns.

The first known contact between the Tanaina and Europeans was in the 1700s, when sea captains and explorers Vitus Bering and James Cook nosed inland along Alaska's coast, entering into what came to be called Cook Inlet. Russian fur traders and missionaries soon followed. Eklutna's Russian Orthodox St. Nicholas Church, a little log chapel, is the oldest existing building in the Anchorage area, and stands where it was first erected in 1830.

Long a bountiful fishing area that fed many people, Knik Arm was closed to subsistence fishing by the state in 1960, forcing most of the Native people who depended on subsistence fishing to find jobs in Anchorage, Eagle River, and the Mat-Su Valley. A few families have held on, and a handful of Athabascan descendants are responsible for preserving the village's history. The local powwow grounds host Athabascan gatherings several times a year. Most visitors make a stop here to photograph the colorful spirit houses erected over the graves at Eklutna Village Historical Park.

Eklutna Village Historical Park

Two little Russian Orthodox churches, one of them the oldest building in the Anchorage area, and a small graveyard make up Eklutna Village Historical Park, a fenced area within the village of Eklutna.

Half-hour guided tours of the churches and cemetery begin in Eklutna's Heritage House, a former railroad section house that now functions as a very small museum housing a few precious reminders of the past. After a brief introduction, visitors are led to the old and new Russian Orthodox churches, where they are introduced to orthodoxy. In the adjoining cemetery, more than 100 colorfully painted "spirit houses" cover the graves of loved ones. Spirit houses are short-walled structures with rooftops placed over graves and decorated with bright primary colors, a Russian Orthodox adaptation of the Athabascan funeral custom of placing remains in bentwood boxes under the trees. Colors and geometric patterns distinguish different families, a way of marking graves before villagers could read or write Russian. This small fenced section of what is actually a much larger burial ground is visible from the road and has long been a curiosity to tourists, who have stopped here for years to take photographs and walk through the graveyard. Villagers opened the cemetery for guided tours because it was the best way to protect the sensitive area. You may take photographs but are asked to remain on the walkway that surrounds the cemetery.

Eklutna Village Historical Park, 16515 Centerfield Dr, Eagle River, AK 99577; (907)696-2828 or (907)688-6026. Just off the Glenn Highway, 28 miles north of Anchorage, 18 miles south of Palmer. The village is well marked by highway signs. Open May 15–Sept 15, 10am–6pm daily. Admission $3.50; children under 6, free. Discounts for tour groups of 20 or more.

Mike Alex's Eklutna Cabin

The little log cabin across the road from Eklutna's new Russian Orthodox church may look humble, but it's worth a visit to say hello to the descendants of Mike Alex and his wife, Daria. Mike Alex, the last of the hereditary Eklutna Village chiefs, was one of nine children. He was a member of the Cheesi (Clans of the Color Red) and the Nulchina (Clan of the Sky People). Daria was the granddaughter of the chief of the nearby Susitna tribe, also located on Cook Inlet. Daria's grandfather was a shaman who correctly forecast the demise of the Susitna people. As he predicted, nearly all of the 600 to 700 Susitna villagers died from communicable diseases in the early 1900s. Daria's parents were among the few in their community who survived the devastating epidemics that swept Alaska after contact with whites.

Daria and Mike Alex raised their 13 children in this two-room log cabin, which they built in the early 1920s of hand-hewn logs and heated with two woodstoves. The cabin had no electricity until 1967. A foreman for the Alaska Railroad for 30 years, Mike helped feed his kids and other villagers by subsistence fishing at Fire Island in Cook Inlet and at the mouth of the Eagle River, as well as by growing a large garden. He smoked salmon and moose in the smokehouse that still stands next to the cabin.

As chief of Eklutna Village, Mike Alex used his own money to pay Native attorney William Paul to stop the U.S. government from dissolving the village and opening the land for sale to outsiders. In later years, he also stopped the government from assigning Natives allotments around each of their houses, a scheme that would have declared the remaining acreage to be surplus and enabled the state or federal government to sell it to the highest outside bidder, such as a land developer. (A hundred years ago, in the Lower 48, Indian reservations were broken up in this same way. Indian families were each "allotted land"; then the rest of the so-called "surplus land" on their reservations was "opened" to white families for "homesteading." When whites "improved the land" with farm buildings, fences, and crops, they then owned it outright. Most Indian reservation land ownership is checkered with white ownership throughout. In the old days, that meant reservation lands became fenced, denying the Indian families access to large meadows of camas and other food and medicinal plants they depended on for survival. Today, it means that many Indian tribes are trying to buy back reservation lands they lost in the 1800s, at today's prices.)

In the past, villagers hunted together throughout the year, sending game back to the village by dogsled for distribution to the tribe. When Mike was a young boy, he hunted moose with his father on what is now Anchorage's 4th Street. His family also had a summer fish camp at the mouth of Ship Creek, in present-day downtown Anchorage, where they caught and smoked salmon for winter distribution. Mike and Daria Alex's cabin is a National Historic Site. Entry fees help keep the building open for visitors.

Mike Alex's Eklutna Cabin, Centerfield Dr, Eagle River, AK 99577. Just off the Glenn Highway, 28 miles north of Anchorage, 18 miles south of Palmer. The cabin is across the street from Eklutna Village Historical Park. Look for a sign that says Lois' Gift Shop. The cabin is usually open when the historical park is open. Check at the door.

Denali National Park and Preserve: *Athabascan*

What is today Denali National Park and Preserve was actually the traditional hunting grounds for the nomadic Athabascan tribes of central Alaska; it was used for centuries by Native hunters following game migrations. Fish camps, to which the nomads came back year after year, were established along rivers such as the Bearpaw and Kantishna, but no camps were inhabited year-round and none remain today. (Most permanent villages in this part of the interior came into being during the missionary years of the 1800s, although the village of Nenana, discussed later in this chapter, was a known winter gathering place for a number of nomadic Athabascan families.) As anyone else would do in a wilderness, Athabascans named geographic features and other landmarks such as Chitsia ("heart of the moose"), a peak in the Kantishna hills that is shaped like a moose's heart, and Denali ("the great one"), the highest peak in North America, which Americans renamed Mount McKinley. A very few of these names and their origins, gleaned from Athabascan oral history, have been preserved in an academic text, *Place Names of the Kantishna Drainage*, published by the National Park Service. In 1995, Doyon Ltd., the regional Native corporation of the interior, bought Kantishna Roadhouse, a rustic but luxurious hotel near the end of Denali National Park's only road, about 100 miles from the park's gate. While there are several other small hotels inside the park, Kantishna Roadhouse is the only hotel that offers Athabascan cultural presentations for guests each evening, and a gift shop stocked with authentic Athabascan beadwork and baskets.

Getting There

Denali National Park is halfway between Anchorage and Fairbanks. You can drive there over a paved highway, but traffic inside the park is limited to 400 cars a day, selected by lottery. Many people take the Alaska Railroad north, stay in hotels outside the park gates, and take wildlife-viewing bus tours through the park, hoping to get a look through the clouds at 20,320-foot Denali and the surrounding 12,000-foot peaks.

Kantishna Roadhouse

Kantishna Roadhouse is one of the most exclusive and picturesque lodges in Alaska, located deep within Denali National Park. It's built on the same site as the original roadhouse that served miners in 1905, when gold was struck in the hills and Kantishna was named Eureka. There's little left of the town except the historic recorder's cabin on the lodge property. Kantishna's log lodge and cabins, on Moose Creek, are surrounded by a grove of birch trees and are strolling distance from mountain lakes. Cabins and duplexes have spacious rooms, lofts, handcrafted furniture, and warm quilts on twin or queen-size beds. Naturalists lead guided hikes each day, and mule-drawn wagons take guests up to Wonder Lake, where an Athabascan fish camp was documented early in the century, and to Eldorado Creek for daily gold panning. The lodge is equipped with mountain bikes, fishing gear, and pans for gold panning. In the evening, there are interpretive programs ranging from naturalists' talks to music or slide shows to Alaska Native cultural presentations that include storytelling, songs, drumming, and sometimes artist demonstrations. The roadhouse's gift shop sells authentic, high-quality Athabascan beadwork, baskets, and carved ivory from the coast as well as the Doyon Foundation's commissioned, Native-designed Pendleton blankets (see "Athabascan Blanket Collection" in the Fairbanks section of this chapter). All activities, as well as gourmet meals with fresh vegetables and homemade bread, are included in room rates. The hotel is owned by Doyon Ltd., and its shareholders are Athabascan Indians, descendants of the original inhabitants of this region.

Two Old Women *is the retelling of an Athabascan Indian story of two elders abandoned during a brutal winter famine. Rather than succumb, they decide to survive. Written by Athabascan author Velma Wallis and illustrated by James L. Grant Sr., the book won the 1993 Western States Book Award and a 1994 Pacific Northwest Booksellers Award. Wallis's second book,* **Bird Girl and the Man Who Followed the Sun,** *is the interweaving of two classic Athabascan legends set in ancient Interior Alaska. Both available from all Alaska booksellers or by mail from the publisher, Epicenter Press, (425)485-6822.*

Kantishna Roadhouse transports overnight guests between the lodge and the Alaska Railroad train depot, outside the park gates, by bus. Buses pick up at the train depot each afternoon and depart the roadhouse early the next morning.

Those who want to see Kantishna Roadhouse but not stay overnight can take a 12-hour round-trip excursion bus with a trained naturalist. Guests board the bus at Denali hotels early in the morning, tour the park, stop for lunch at the Roadhouse, and return to the hotels each evening. Air charters and flightseeing around Denali are available through the lodge.

Kantishna Roadhouse, PO Box 81670, Fairbanks, AK 99708; (800)942-7420, (907)683-1475, or (907)479-2436; Web site: http://www.doyon.com. The hotel is 92 miles from the entrance to Denali National Park, with views of Denali for the last 30 miles. Full bar; major credit cards accepted; personal checks OK. Open June–mid-Sept. Rooms about $540 for a couple; rates include meals and activities. Average stay is two to three nights.

Fairbanks: *Athabascan*

The taiga is a tree- and tundra-covered plain north of Fairbanks, where cottonwood, willow, and birch trees grow abundantly along the riverbanks, providing materials for shelter, baskets, and even food (willow buds are edible). Rivers provide huge, easily caught runs of salmon and other species, and make transportation easier, especially when they freeze over during the winter, creating wide swaths through the interior into present-day Canada.

In the mid-1800s, fur trappers from the Hudson's Bay Company navigated the Porcupine River from Canada into Alaska, introducing glass beads for trade and Scot and Orkney Island fiddling and dance to Athabascan villages along the way. (Today the Athabascan Old-Time Fiddling Festival, held in Fairbanks each November, is one of Alaska's largest Native events.) The major rivers of the region—the Yukon and Tanana—were the freeways of the interior—and in many ways still are, with villages every couple of hundred miles. Smaller, family-owned Native fish camps consisting of a few cabins, a smokehouse on the bank, a dock, and a fish wheel in the river were interspersed between villages, and those are also still here today. Smaller rivers such as the Chena, which runs through today's city of Fairbanks, were also navigable, with viable runs of salmon and other species. During the gold rush in the late 1800s, more than 200 riverboats plied the Yukon, Tanana, and other rivers.

Look for beadwork, mukluks, ivory carvings, and other arts and crafts at the Festival of Native Arts in Fairbanks each February. Native people from all over Alaska gather to hold dances and craft exhibits. Call the University of Alaska/Fairbanks, (907)747-7181, for this year's date.

One of these riverboat captains accidentally founded the city of Fairbanks due to a navigational error that landed him a spectacular 200 miles short of his destination, on the banks of the Chena River, with $20,000 worth of goods. He sat there a year, trading with Athabascan families living in nearby villages, until Felix Pedro, an Italian immigrant, struck gold nearby—a strike that brought hordes of miners to Fairbanks.

In Fairbanks, Alaska's second largest city, you can learn about Athabascan villages, the Yukon River system, and gold-mining history at the Alaskaland theme park; and visit a reconstruction of an Athabascan village on the Riverboat Discovery tour of the Chena and Tanana Rivers. Those wanting to experience the Yukon River and contemporary village life firsthand can tour, and even stay overnight, with Native families in seven villages on the Yukon and its tributaries outside of Fairbanks. The rivers still feed the people and operate as roads in this mostly roadless area. In summer, people travel between villages by boat; in winter, they travel by dogsled and snow machine.

Alaska Athabascans are well known for their exquisite beadwork. Cut glass beads replaced or augmented embroidery with porcupine quills, bone, and ivory. The University of Alaska Museum, one of the state's largest visitor attractions, does a superb job of explaining all of Alaska's Native cultures in context—from prehistoric natural history to modern-day village life.

Getting There and Getting Around

You can drive from Anchorage to Fairbanks on two paved routes that pass through Denali National Park. The Alaska Railroad, (800)544-0552, makes the Anchorage-to-Fairbanks loop daily. The following carriers have daily service between Anchorage and Fairbanks: Alaska Airlines, (800)426-0333; Delta Airlines, (800)221-1212; Frontier Flying Service, (907)474-0014 or (907)474-0014, e-mail: frontier @polarnet.com, Web site: http://www.polarnet.com/Users/ Frontier; Northwest Airlines, (800)225-2525; and Reno Air, (800)736-6247.

Cab services and car rentals are listed in the *Fairbanks Alaska Visitors Guide*; to receive one, call the Fairbanks Convention & Visitors Bureau, (800)327-5774. Rental agencies do not allow their vehicles to be driven on unpaved roads north of Fairbanks, and most villages are accessible only by air taxi. To get around in the interior, contact one of these air services: 40-Mile Air, (907)474-0018; Frontier Flying Service, (907)474-0481; or Warbelow's Air Ventures Inc., (800)478-0812 or (907)474-0518.

Visitor Services

■ Alaska Public Lands Information Center, 250 Cushman St, Suite 1A, Fairbanks, AK 99701; (907)456-0527. Located on the lower

level of Courthouse Square, at the corner of 3rd Street and
Cushman, this is a great place to get oriented to Interior Alaska.
The center provides trip-planning information for parks, forests,
refuges, and recreation areas, as well as Native culture and
wildlife displays, guidebooks, and maps.

- Fairbanks Convention & Visitors Bureau, 550 1st Ave, Fairbanks,
  AK 99701; (800)327-5774 or (907)456-5774; e-mail:
  FCVB@polarnet.fnsb.ak.us. Write, call, or e-mail for a maga-
  zine-style brochure on the Fairbanks region. A current calendar
  of events and updated travel information is on the Web at
  http://www.polarnet.com/Users/FCVB. For a recorded message
  about Fairbanks's events and activities, call (907)456-4636.

University of Alaska Museum

The superb museum on the University of Alaska campus showcases
Native art, history, and culture. This is one of Alaska's most popular
visitor attractions, and a visit is well worth at least several hours of
your day. The exhibits present Native culture in the
context of the animals, plants, and climatic conditions that shaped each of Alaska's five distinct peoples—illustrated by objects selected from the
museum's 762,000 artifacts (including fossilized
bones of prehistoric animals). The ethnographic collection abounds with exceptional examples of Native basketry, beadwork, ivory carvings, masks, dolls,
and tools used in subsistence activities, dating from
the 1890s to the present.

Bring your binoculars and see caribou, musk oxen, and reindeer from viewing stands, or take a tour at the University of Alaska/Fairbanks Large Animal Research Station on Yankovich Road in Fairbanks. Tours are $5; reduced rates for seniors and children (kids under 6 are free). June 1–Aug 31; call for days and hours of tours, (907) 474-7207.

The Collection

Among the items exhibited at the museum are a small
figure carved from ivory, the *Okvik Madonna*, thought
to have been carved 2,000 years ago; a huge umiak (a
wood-frame skin boat used for whaling and moving
cargo in the Arctic); Athabascan porcupine quill embroidery; and unusual contemporary pieces such as
toys made from tin cans. Glass-topped drawers installed under the exhibits hold even more treasures, such as dolls, dance fans, fur parkas,
and regalia. Clips from films produced by the university's Native Film
Center accompany the exhibits. With the umiak and harpoons, for example, you can see 30-second clips of men whale hunting and butchering, fishing through the ice, and fishing with a lingcod trap.

The museum distinguished itself early on when curators worked
with Natives to identify objects and label them with the names of the

makers, if known. The main gallery, which opened in 1980, was designed in consultation with Native advisors—something rarely done at that time, although it is standard practice today.

Special Exhibits and Events

In keeping with the educational mission of the museum, its special exhibits challenge viewers by confronting them with the jarring realities of American culture. *Forced to Leave: The WWII Detention of Alaskan Japanese-Americans and Aleuts*, for example, chronicles the evacuation of the Aleut people from their homes on the Aleutian Chain and Pribilof Islands during World War II, and their internment in heartlessly managed camps where many died. There's also a film giving an Athabascan view on how the construction of the Alaska Highway during World War II affected Native life. In conjunction with special exhibits, the museum's Geist Lectures feature speakers from all walks of life, from traditional healers to oil-spill cleanup specialists.

You can visit the Carlo-Kendall Studio (946 Chena Pump Rd, Fairbanks, AK 99209; (907)479-5529), where contemporary Native artist Kathleen Carlo carves panels and masks in wood and metal. Call first for an appointment.

During the museum's "Gatherings North" demonstrations, visitors meet Native artists in person. Artists who create work for the museum's gift shop, such as Tsimshian carver Bert Ryan, Athabascan beadworker Shirley Holmberg, and doll maker Colleen Odden, complete projects on site and talk about their work as they create it. Demonstrations are held twice a year: for several weeks during the summer and once in the winter, prior to Christmas.

From June through August, the museum hosts the very popular "Northern Inua," an hour-long performance of Eskimo-Indian Olympic events, songs, and dances, performed twice daily in the outdoor dome tent. (See "World Eskimo-Indian Olympics," later in this section.) Performances alternate with a 50-minute multimedia show on the Arctic's northern lights. You can buy combination tickets for the two programs.

Museum Store

The museum store offers authentic artwork from all across Alaska, including Athabascan beadwork; traditional Kuskokwim (Yup'ik Eskimo) dolls made by Jeanette Ramberg and dressed by Anna Anvil, a Yup'ik skin sewer; and walrus ivory carved into Arctic animals by Inupiat Eskimos living at Shishmaref and St. Lawrence Island. Teachers and kids may be interested in such materials as *A Teacher's Guide to the Athabascans: People of the Boreal Forest*, an instruction book for making Tlingit/Haida button robes, and an activity guidebook written by Native Alaskan educators on the differences between Alaska Eskimo and Indian cultures. You can also buy fur-trimmed Alaskan *kuspuks* (long-waisted dresses with ruffled skirts and hoods, worn in the Arctic by Eskimo women, especially during the summers) made for 11-inch dolls. A handsome Alaska Native language map is a favorite teaching tool. Books, materials, and selected gift items can be ordered from the Museum Store catalogue, PO Box 756960, Fairbanks, AK 99775; (907)474-7505. You can also request the museum's quarterly newsletter, "Reflections," by writing to the Museum Store.

The University

The university itself has come a long way since its founding in 1917 as the Alaska Agricultural College and School of Mines. The curriculum now includes liberal arts, anthropology, archaeology, geophysics, business, and Native language, heritage, and art. Its fine arts program has produced a number of outstanding professional artists. The university is also the statewide educational center for Alaska Natives. Acknowledging the difficult transition for Native students from village to university life, the university has built a $1.8 million Inupiat residence hall, in partnership with the Native Arctic Slope Regional Corporation, for its Native students.

University of Alaska Museum, Fairbanks, AK. 99775; (907)474-7505 for 24-hour information; Web site: http://www.uaf.edu/museum. Admission $5; children under 7, free. Reduced prices for tour groups, seniors, and youth. May and Sept, open 9am–5pm daily; June–Aug, 9am–7pm daily; Oct–Apr, 9am–5pm Mon–Fri and weekends noon–5pm.

Alaska Center for Documentary Film

The Alaska Center for Documentary Film is an arm of the museum that has been recording the changing cultures of Alaska Natives since 1972. Unlike traditional documentaries made by outsiders, these award-winning films are produced in collaboration with Native communities. Many have been shown on public broadcasting stations throughout the United States. The films cover topics such as whale and walrus hunting, fishing, family life, dance, missionary influence, storytelling, and changing times. The center is housed in the university's Rasmuson Library and is open to the public. The library also houses a collection of publications, ranging from monographs to books, about Alaska Native art, lands, and culture. It's a great place to browse. Titles include *Archaeological Whale Bone: A Northern Resource;*

The Far North: 2,000 Years of American Eskimo and Indian Art; Medicine Men of Hooper Bay; and *Archaeological Excavations at Kukulik.*

University of Alaska/Fairbanks Rasmuson Library, PO Box 756800, Fairbanks, AK 99775; (907)474-7481. The library is on the lower campus, below the museum. It's best to ask for directions once you get to the campus.

Alaskaland

The big draw at Alaskaland, a faded 44-acre Alaska frontier theme park containing many original cabins and outbuildings moved from the bush, is the landed SS *Nenana*, a refurbished riverboat that brought cargo, medical supplies, and food to Native villages on the Yukon and Tanana Rivers between 1933 and 1944. Inside the *Nenana* is a miniature, three-dimensional model of 22 villages along the river system where the *Nenana* once stopped, all created using early photographs for reference. At one time more than 200 riverboats plied the Yukon River system, their steam engines fired by cords of wood provided by villagers. Yukon villages today are serviced by bush planes. This is a good place to get oriented to the region if you are new to central Alaska and unfamiliar with the rivers and their colorful history.

Dixie Alexander used more than 500,000 glass beads, all hand sewn on black velvet, to create a mural of the northern lights, leaping silver salmon, and Alaska wildflowers. It hangs in the foyer of the Fairbanks North Star Borough's Carlson Center (2010 2nd Ave, Fairbanks).

When the park closes during the winter, a group of history buffs/model makers work on the village models, incorporating information gleaned from people who lived there during the riverboat years. ("We get a lot of older women, in their 80s, who stop by and tell us how it used to be," says one volunteer.) The boat is named after the village of Nenana, at the junction of the Tanana and Nenana Rivers, where it was constructed.

Alaskaland, PO Box 71267, Fairbanks, AK 99707; (907)459-1087. Located at the intersection of Airport and Peger Roads. Park grounds open 24 hours a day mid-May–Sept 1; shops and entertainment (including the Nenana) open 11am–9pm daily. Admission to both the park and the Nenana is free.

Riverboat Discovery Tour

A reconstructed 19th-century Athabascan village on the Tanana River is the highlight of the Riverboat Discovery tour of the Chena River and its confluence with the Tanana River.

Captain Jim Binkley, whose father was one of the first sternwheeler riverboat pilots during the gold rush era, began taking people on excursions of the Chena and Tanana Rivers in the 1950s. Today he has three sternwheelers; one of them is three stories high, holds 900 people, and features television video monitors in every corner, a souvenir shop, and free sourdough doughnuts and 25-cent coffee. You board the boat just outside of downtown Fairbanks and travel down the Chena River until you enter the Tanana River, a tributary of the great Yukon River, which traverses Alaska. The boat maneuvers between sandbars in a very small stretch of the braided, 500-mile-long Tanana River, which roils with glacial silt. All these rivers provided access and trade routes for aboriginal people (and trappers, traders, and gold seekers), transporting them from the coast, through the tundra, to deep in the interior of the continent.

Although a case could be made that this orchestrated tour is no more than a tourist trap, it has been carefully planned to introduce visitors to Alaska history and heritage: Iditarod dogsled champion Susan Butcher waves to the boat from shore, and the boat slows at an Athabascan fish camp for a demonstration of the workings of a fish wheel. A Native fillets a salmon in seconds, a skill honed in subsistence fish camps when all the fish come at once and, because there is no refrigeration, have to be processed before they spoil.

The highlight of the 3½-hour riverboat trip is a long stop at a re-located Tanana Athabascan village from the 1890s (many of the buildings are original). Passengers disembark for a tour and good-natured demonstrations, conducted by young Alaska Natives, of pre-contact tools and implements. The tour guides are students working on the riverboat for the summer; your particular guide may be a Yup'ik Eskimo graduate of Notre Dame, an Inupiat high school counselor and Brigham Young University grad, or an Athabascan in the Coast Guard.

You learn a lot on this tour—about the original use of chum, or "dog salmon"; about the use of rawhide for lashing; about the floral patterns of beadworking; and about trading for coastal sea urchins. You see a Yup'ik (coastal Southwest Alaska) fur parka made of the pelts of 80 ground squirrels, accented with wolverine tassels, and learn about Siberian husky dogs that pulled dogsleds made of wood with mammoth-ivory runners. You see a skin hut, used by northern nomads, made of caribou hides stretched over bentwood poles, and learn how fire was carried in fungus conks that grow on birchwood.

Artist Dixie Alexander, whose moosehide "chief coats" are in the collections of the Smithsonian Institution, the Western Museum in downtown Denver, and the Anchorage International Airport, demonstrates caribou and moosehide skin sewing and beading from the front porch of a picturesque log cabin at the village. She learned beadworking from her grandmother, Julia Peter, and her mother,

Charlotte Douthit, at their family home in Fort Yukon, 8 miles above the Arctic Circle. The riverboat's gift shop sells out of Alexander's work as soon as it's completed. You can arrange commissions through the riverboat.

Riverboat Discovery, 1975 Discovery Dr, Fairbanks, AK 99709; (907)479-6673. Turn right at Dale Rd exit off Airport Rd and follow signs. Tours offered mid-May–mid-Sept; twice-daily departures. $39.95 adults, $29.95 children.

World Eskimo-Indian Olympics

Every July Fairbanks hosts the World Eskimo-Indian Olympics, a four-day series of traditional Alaska Native athletic competitions and dances. Although today the games are competitive, they originated in the villages to build endurance and teach young people the skills of balance and speed needed to survive in the Arctic.

The Eskimo-Indian Olympics were initiated by two bush pilots in response to the rapid spread of Western culture into rural areas. Both men had observed games and dances in Native villages and thought some attempt should be made to encourage their continued practice. The first Eskimo-Indian Olympics, held in 1961, were a perfect reflection of the Alaskan cultural milieu of the early 1960s: games included a blanket toss, a seal-skinning contest, and a Miss Eskimo-Indian Olympics beauty contest.

Over the years, the Eskimo-Indian Olympics have evolved into a major event whose primary purpose is a social gathering of friends and relatives from all over Alaska, Canada, and the United States. Like the large powwows in the Lower 48, in which dancers compete for prizes based on regalia as well as execution of dances, the Eskimo-Indian Olympics features parka and Indian dress contests; the exquisite beadwork and embroidery sewn on tanned moosehide dresses, and the luxurious fur parkas and mukluks trimmed with geometric patterns, are amazing to behold. Dancers and drummers from remote villages all over the North compete throughout the four-day event. The winning group performs again on the last night of the event. As at powwow gatherings, there are arts and crafts booths, often staffed by the artists themselves or by individuals such as Ann Goessel, an Athabascan shop owner in Fairbanks who represents the work of Alaska Natives from all over the region.

Like the games played at the worldwide Olympics, such as the shot-put and footraces, the Eskimo-Indian Olympics games evolved out of custom. One of the most difficult, and entertaining to watch, is the 2-foot-high kick: keeping both feet together at all times, competitors leap into the air from a standing position and kick a softball-size sealskin ball dangling on a string up to 8 feet off the ground; both feet must touch the floor simultaneously upon landing. Walking on a birch pole slathered with bear grease is good practice for keeping balance in precarious situations, such as checking a fish wheel on the river. The fish-cutting competition, using ulu knives, has its origins in the need to quickly process large catches of fish before spoilage occurs.

Spectators are welcome, although it may appear to outsiders that events could be organized more efficiently, with everything starting on time and scored as a worldwide Olympic event would be. It's important for observers to remember that competition and prizes are not the underlying purpose of the games.

For visitors who can't attend the World Eskimo-Indian Olympics, the University of Alaska Museum offers Northern Inua, an entertaining sampling of events, songs, and dances performed daily from June through August.

World Eskimo-Indian Olympics, (907)456-6646. Held every July; call for information on this year's dates and location, or check with the Fairbanks Convention & Visitors Bureau.

Athabascan Old-Time Fiddling Festival

While the aurora borealis lights up November's night sky, the ballroom of the Fairbanks Westmark Hotel crackles with four days of charged fiddle music—all bowed and plucked by Athabascan Indians and Eskimos from Alaska and western Canada. Fiddle music is a long-standing tradition in Alaska's villages; it was first introduced here in the mid-1800s. Hudson's Bay Company fur trappers and traders, most of them French Canadian Scots and Orkney Islanders, brought their fiddles inland with them when they navigated the length of the Yukon River and its tributaries. A second wave of fiddle music was introduced during the 1886–1910 gold rush, which added to the mix miners' songs, American contra dances such as the Virginia reel, square dances, and fiddle tunes from Appalachia via California goldfields. More recently, musicians learned songs from country-and-western and Cajun recordings and played them on fiddles and guitars ordered from Sears Roebuck catalogues. (At one time, Sears Roebuck accepted pelts along with cash as payment.)

Alaska Native fiddlers compete in contests all over the United States, including the annual National Indian Fiddlers Contest in Tahlequah, Oklahoma. For more information, read **The Crooked Stovepipe: Athapaskan Fiddle Music and Square Dancing in Northeast Alaska and Northwest Canada,** *by Craig Mishler (University of Illinois Press, 1993). Alaska Native songs and fiddle tunes by Charlie Peter and Jimmy Roberts are available on audiocassette from the Smithsonian Institution Museums, Office of Folklife Programs, (800)410-9815 (ask for inventory number F4070).*

One of the largest Alaska Native cultural events of the year, the festival brings planeloads of fiddlers and dancers from the bush to Fairbanks. They wear beaded moosehide vests and moccasins, feathers hang from the necks of guitars and fiddles, and everyone dances the afternoons and half the night away. The event begins midweek with a dance each evening. In cooperation with the Fairbanks North Star School District, fiddlers teach dances to elementary school children—as many as 5,000 participate in morning sessions. The nights get longer as the weekend approaches. Friday's dance begins in the afternoon and doesn't screech to a stop until 3:30am. Saturday's events include a banquet, closing ceremonies, and a Last Chance Dance that starts at 9pm and winds down at 4am. The festival is a nonsmoking, alcohol-free event. Gorgeous artwork such as ivory carvings, masks, beadwork, and snowshoes arrives with the fiddlers and dancers from outer villages, who bring their work to sell at exhibitors' tables set up in the hallway outside the ballroom.

The festival is presented by the Athabascan Fiddlers Association. Sales of souvenirs—hats, pins, T-shirts, mugs, and commemorative booklets—help support the festival, and are available year-round from the Fiddlers Association. The association also sells audiocassettes of Athabascan and Eskimo fiddling, recorded at past festivals, as well as a videotape on the history of Athabascan fiddling.

Athabascan Fiddlers Association, 411 4th Ave, Suite 1, Fairbanks, AK 99701; (907)452-1825. Held each November; a list of nearby accommodations is available from the Fairbanks Convention & Visitors Bureau. Families are encouraged to attend (no one under 18 is admitted to the Saturday banquet or Last Chance Dance, however). Four-day passes and afternoon and evening performance tickets are available in advance from the Athabascan Fiddlers Association. Tickets are sold at the door for higher prices; individual tickets at the door are about $12. Donations are welcome to help pay the expenses of fiddlers and performers who must fly to Fairbanks from their villages. The Westmark Hotel provides rooms at special rates for out-of-town festival guests.

Beads & Things

Beadworker Ann Goessel sells Alaska Native arts and crafts from all over the state, particularly the Yukon, the interior, and hard-to-reach coastal Inupiat villages. She also sells art made by Alaska Natives who have moved to urban Fairbanks and Anchorage. In her 2nd Avenue shop, Beads & Things, she carries fine ivory and soapstone carvings, birchbark baskets, dolls, beadwork, and slippers decorated with beads and with moose tufting. Goessel knows all the artists personally and buys directly from them. The gift shop doubles as a sales outlet and a mail-order service for beadworking materials: hanks of glass beads hang on the wall, and bins are full of bone, shell, and ivory beads as well as crystal beads she's purchased from auctions. She also sells do-it-yourself beadwork kits, complete with needle and thread, featuring Athabascan patterns she designed.

Goessel learned to sew and design beadwork in the 1950s at the feet of her late grandmother in Stevens Village, an Athabascan community on the Yukon River, about 45 minutes north of Anchorage by air. The village had no electricity or running water. When state regulators clamped down on subsistence hunting and fishing, Goessel's grandmother made craft items for sale to supplement the family's growing need for income. By the age of 12, Goessel was making cigarette cases and small purses; as a young mother she, like her grandmother, also exchanged beadwork for cash, food, and clothing for her children. She made many of her contacts with outlying Native artists when she worked as a health and safety education representative for the Tanana Chiefs Conference and traveled to schools and villages in the bush.

In winter, Goessel takes her work on the road to Native conferences in the Lower 48. Her own suncatcher designs, produced by Native beadworkers, were featured in the 1991 Smithsonian Institution catalogue. She has also produced a small craft book, *Ann's Creations*, on Athabascan beadwork.

Beads & Things, 537 2nd Ave, PO Box 1897, Fairbanks, AK 99707; (907)456-2323. Open daily; hours vary depending on season.

Athabascan Blanket Collection

A series of limited-edition blankets, each woven by Pendleton Woolen Mills and numbered and signed by the artist, are available from the Doyon Foundation, a nonprofit arm of Doyon Ltd., whose 14,000 shareholders are Athabascan Indians of Interior Alaska. The blankets are beautiful keepsakes. The images, woven into the Spirit Keeper Series of four blankets, depict a single story known by all three major clans of the Gwich'in Athabascans of northern Interior Alaska.

The first blanket, *Seyelneyoo* (My Relatives), represents the three major clans: Caribou, Bear, and Middle of the Stream. The background is the color of smoked moosehide, with caribou antlers, bear tracks, and turquoise stripes that represent water incorporated into the weave. It was designed by Koyukon artist Kathleen Carlo, best known for her abstract carving of masks and panels combining wood and metal.

The second blanket, *Medzeyh Te Hut'anne* (People of the Caribou), issued in 1997, weaves caribou, stars, and banded hills into bold yellows, blues, and a touch of teal green. It was designed by Athabascan artist James Grant, who was born in Tanana and raised in California. Currently a resident of Fairbanks, he illustrated Athabascan author Velma Wallis's award-winning book *Two Old Women* and is well known for his sculpture in wood, ivory, and ice.

Each blanket is issued in quantities of 1,000. Proceeds from the sale of the Spirit Keeper Series support a mentoring program as well as scholarships and internships awarded by the Doyon Foundation; about 300 students receive scholarships each year. Carlo, a graduate of the University of Alaska/Fairbanks with a bachelor's degree in fine arts, was a past recipient of foundation support for her studies.

Doyon Foundation, 201 First Ave, Suite 300, Fairbanks, AK 99701; (888)478-4755; Web site: http://www.doyon.com. Foundation offices are open to the public Mon–Fri, 9am–5pm. Postcards and posters featuring the blanket designs are available.

Yukon River Native Fisheries

Yukon River salmon swim 2,000 miles or more upriver to spawn, giving them firm, bright orange-red meat and rich flavor. They also have the highest omega-3 fatty acid content of any fish in the world. As an Athabascan staple food that returned year after year to the rivers where it was easily caught, salmon kept the people both well fed and healthy.

Interior Alaska Fish Processors, a non-Native-owned company, buys salmon from Yup'ik and Athabascan villagers operating their summer fish camps all along the Yukon River and its tributaries. Fish are caught in the traditional way, in fish wheels along the riverbanks and in gill nets. The Japanese, connoisseurs of salmon, buy nearly the entire Native catch of Yukon king salmon for sashimi and salmon flakes. The roe is processed by "salmon technicians" into *ikura* and *sujiko* caviar, created when the salmon's orange-red eggs are handled and packed in a specific way. Yukon chum salmon (also called Yukon keta after their Latin name, *Oncorhynchus keta*) travel as far upstream as the kings—almost 1,500 miles—to spawn. Ketas are harvested from mid-June to early July in short, 6-hour openings, iced down, and shipped fresh by air freight to Lower 48 markets. Others are processed immediately into cans or smoked and made into sausages, hot links, and jerky. The company also makes buffalo and reindeer products.

In Fairbanks, the processor's retail store is called Santa's Smokehouse. They offer six different gift packages, including one containing two cans of smoked Cajun-spiced chum salmon, a can of smoked salmon sausage, a jar of berry jelly, snack crackers, an ulu knife, and one caribou antler back scratcher, packed in a wooden box.

Santa's Smokehouse, Interior Alaska Fish Processors, 2400 Davis Rd, Fairbanks, AK 99701; (907)456-3885; fax (907)456-3889; Web site: http://www.alaskasbest. com/fish. Between Wilbur St and Peger Rd. Open year-round: Mon–Fri, 10am–6pm; Sat, 10am–5pm. Call for an order form. Major credit cards accepted.

YUKON RIVER AND BEYOND

The area north of Fairbanks is an almost unimaginably vast tundra marsh with a scattering of very small Native villages several hundred miles apart. Only one road cuts through the tundra, the unpaved Dalton Highway (nicknamed the "haul road"), which follows the trans-Alaska pipeline from Prudhoe Bay south to Fairbanks. Most car rental companies won't allow you to take their cars on the rugged Dalton Highway; it can cost up to $2,000 to be towed back to town if your car suffers a breakdown on this road. So if you plan to drive north, check with your rental agency first.

The trans-Alaska pipeline would never have been built without the settlement of Native land claims, a financial and land agreement that altered the face of every Native village in Alaska (see the appendix "Alaska Native Claims Settlement Act and Native Corporations"). The oil fields and pipeline also set off a raging controversy over the health of the migrating caribou herds, upon which Athabascan and Inupiat villagers depend not only for subsistence but also for their cultural identity. Prior to white contact, Athabascans were nomadic, fishing year-round (through the ice in winter) and tracking game. Villages and fish camps evolved from nomadic camps along the rivers.

Families in seven villages north of Fairbanks offer tours, and some offer overnight stays along the Yukon and its tributaries. Most villages have a population of under 500 and few visitor accommodations other than what are listed here. All travel to the villages is by air taxi.

Getting Around

Ask your host for assistance in making travel arrangements, including flights to the village you want to visit. Villages here have few roads and, subsequently, few car rentals. You'll depend on your hosts for travel in

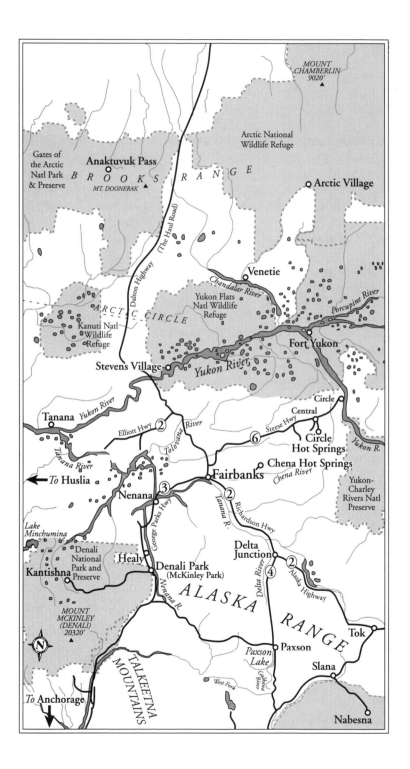

the region. In the summer, travel between fish camps and villages is by skiff, and all-terrain vehicles are used within the villages. In the winter, when the rivers are frozen, travel is by snow machine or dogsled.

Woodyard Fish Camp: *Athabascan*

Yukon River Tours (whose main offices are in Fairbanks) offers a boat tour of Woodyard Fish Camp, a demonstration Koyukon Athabascan fish camp located on the Yukon River. This is an unusual opportunity for outsiders, since most fish camps are not open to visitors. The camp is owned by the Dinyee Native village corporation of Stevens Village and has been hosting tourists since the late 1980s.

The 1½-hour tour leaves from Yukon River Bridge, on the Dalton Highway, 135 miles north of Fairbanks. (This is the only bridge in the state that spans the Yukon.) Visitors board the 49-passenger *Yookene Spirit* and travel 6 miles up the Yukon to the camp, which is in the Yukon Flats National Wildlife Refuge. There they can watch the fish harvest and processing, or enter a cabin to view a small exhibit of Koyukon tools and implements, along with photos of local Native families from the late 1800s to the present day.

The Woodyard Fish Camp was so named because it was one of the stops along the Yukon River where villagers supplied cords of firewood to fuel the steamboats. It is typical of Athabascan fish camps on the Yukon River, where families spend each summer harvesting and processing fish as they have for generations. It's hard work. Fish are taken from a wheel in the river, dropped onshore, and hand-processed quickly to prevent spoilage. They are filleted, cut in strips, and hung neatly over wooden racks inside a smokehouse, where the meat is dried and becomes permeated with smoke from a smoldering alderwood fire. A typical fish camp looks like, and is, a well-established family camp with cabins among the trees.

Bring your own camping gear, groceries, and drinking water, and you are welcome to spend the night in a spacious, floored tent (you need to call ahead to arrange this).

Koyukon Athabascan Indian Fish Camp, Yukon River Tours, 214 2nd Ave, Fairbanks, AK 99701; (907)452-7162. Tours offered June–Aug. $30 per person; overnight $45 for one, $70 for two; reduced rates for longer stays. Tours depart daily from the Yukon River Bridge, 135 miles north of Fairbanks, about a 3½-hour drive. From Fairbanks, you reach the Yukon River Bridge by following the Dalton Highway north. Unfortunately, most rental car companies won't allow you to take their cars on the rugged Dalton Highway (it can cost up to $2,000 to be towed back to town if your car suffers a breakdown on this road), so check with your rental agency first. Another option is to travel with a tour company; contact Yukon River Tours for recommendations.

Nenana: *Athabascan*

The Athabascan word *nenana* means "a good place to camp between the rivers." This village at the convergence of the Tanana and Nenana Rivers, now numbering about 450 people, has long been a gathering place of Tanana Athabascans. In 1903 a trading post was built here to supply riverboats and to trade with the Athabascans. Several years later, St. Mark's Episcopal mission was built upriver (the historic church still stands), and by 1915 the Alaska Railroad had pushed through to Nenana, doubling the trading post's population.

Today there's daily railroad passenger service from Anchorage and Fairbanks, and a bridge across the river connects the village to the George Parks Highway, 65 miles south of Fairbanks. The village is a mix of Athabascan families and non-Natives; many live by subsistence hunting and fishing in the region. Yutlana Barge Lines is one of Nenana's largest employers, supplying villages along the Tanana and Yukon Rivers all summer. Although a Native heritage center is being planned, the primary focus in Nenana is on contemporary village life and the last century of the village's history. The town boasts an Alaska Railroad Museum, the Golden Railroad Spike Historic Park and Interpretive Center, and the historic Episcopal church. A replica of the sternwheeler *Nenana* is moored on the river and open to visitors. Alexander's River Adventure, operated by an Athabascan family whose members have spent their lives on the region's rivers, leaves Fairbanks daily for a tour of the Tanana River and the village of Nenana.

Alexander's River Adventure

Wes Alexander, an Athabascan who grew up on the Tanana and Nenana Rivers, pilots his nine-passenger sightseeing boat around the rivers' sandbars with aplomb. A five-time winner of the Yukon 800 Riverboat Race and a certified master river pilot, he's a pro at reading the river.

Passengers disembark at his family's fish camp on the Tanana River, where Nina Alexander (Wes's mom) and other family members are pulling fish out of the fish wheel, cutting and drying salmon. Nina is a skilled traditional beadworker and takes a break from cutting salmon during the afternoon to share a cup of herbal tea and chat with guests.

Wes offers various package tours, all of which include a stop at the family fish camp, with its 50-year-old smokehouse, its authentic log cabins still used by trappers and dog mushers, and the chance to watch an Athabascan family preparing salmon. Tours range from 4 hours to overnight, priced accordingly. In addition to visiting the fish camp, a tour might include a stop at the village of Nenana, with a guided tour of the Alaska Railroad Museum (housed in the original 1922 depot), the longest single-span railroad bridge in Alaska, and the Ice Classic watchtower and tripod. This device is essential to the most exciting guessing game in Alaska—the contest to predict the exact time the ice on the Nenana River will break up in the spring (the winner takes home up to $100,000). You'll also learn about Athabascan culture, and about what the breakup of the ice means to people who depend on the river for subsistence.

Overnight trips include deluxe tent accommodations at the Alexander fish camp on the Tanana River. There's usually fresh salmon for dinner with all the fixings, a guided nature hike after dinner (remember, it doesn't get dark until after midnight), and a relaxing late evening around the campfire. Wes's wife, Mary, makes all-you-can-eat sourdough pancakes for breakfast.

Alexander's River Adventure, PO Box 62, Nenana, AK 99780; (907)474-3924 or cellular phone (907)322-4247. Length and nature of tours vary; prices range from $99 to $225.

Tanana: *Athabascan*

The Athabascan village of Tanana is at the confluence of the Yukon and Tanana Rivers, 130 miles west of Fairbanks and the nearest road. It's below the narrow Yukon River canyon, a great fishing spot. Mountains rise behind Tanana, which is surrounded by a forest of birch, cottonwood, tamarack, and spruce. The village (population 350) is at the head of the old Tanana Allakaket Winter Trail, used for centuries by dog mushers, which continues over the tundra all the way north to Anaktuvuk Pass in the Brooks Range. Long before white contact, Tanana was a trading settlement for Koyukon and Tanana Athabascans. In the late 1800s, the St. James Mission built a large school and hospital here, influencing many villages along both the Tanana and the Yukon Rivers. Athabascan culture is still strong in Tanana, with subsistence hunting and fishing, potlatches, and dances an important part of village life.

You can fly to Tanana from Fairbanks on Frontier Flying Service, (907)474-0014 or (907)474-0481, or Warbelow's Air Ventures, (800)478-0812 or (907)474-0518 (average round-trip airfare is $130 per person). Once there, you can borrow a car and drive around on 32 miles of maintained road.

Yukon Star Enterprises

Paul and Mary Star meet your plane at the Tanana landing strip and bring you back to their house for coffee. You board a covered skiff that holds seven passengers and embark upon 5½ hours of touring on the Yukon River, with stops at fish camps belonging to the Stars' friends along the way. Overnight stays can be arranged, either in the fish camps (you stay in log cabins or tents, depending on who takes you in), or at the Stars' guest accommodations in Tanana. The Stars live in a frame house, with a sauna and showerhouse in outbuildings. Like many people in the village, they haul their water and live primarily on subsistence fishing and hunting. Overnighters eat three meals a day with the Stars. You can also charter the Stars' boat, with Paul as your captain and fishing guide, for king salmon and catch-and-release pike fishing.

Yukon Star Enterprises, Paul Star, PO Box 126, Tanana, AK 99777; (907)366-7251; e-mail: slfm45a@prodigy.com. Tours offered June–Aug depending on when the ice breaks up on the Yukon River. Cost is $150 per person for a full day, not including airfare to Tanana. Overnight guests pay $75 per couple. Substantial discounts for families.

Fort Yukon: *Athabascan*

In the mid-1800s, trappers seeking the pelts of beaver, lynx, muskrat, bear, and other animals came from Canada into Interior Alaska by way of the Yukon and Porcupine Rivers. Fort Yukon, a trading post set up in what was then Russian territory by Alexander Murray, a trapper for the Hudson's Bay Company, was one of the first English-speaking Native villages in Alaska. As at other trading posts the company established in North America, trappers brought cut glass beads, guns and ammunition, windowpanes, wool, and novelty items from their central warehouses to trade for furs. Fort Yukon became an important trade center for the Gwich'in Indians. Trappers, mostly Orkney Islanders and Scots, brought their fiddles and taught Fort Yukon Athabascans and residents of other villages along the river how to play their music.

Today Fort Yukon fluctuates between 650 and 750 residents. Most are descendants of Gwich'in tribes living in the Yukon Flats, along the Chandalar River, Birch Creek, Black River, and Porcupine River. From January through March, the place is very popular with Japanese tourists, who come here to take dogsled rides on the frozen Yukon River and view the spectacular northern lights. You come here by air taxi from Fairbanks.

Alaska Yukon Tours

You've hit the mother lode of year-round tour possibilities if you hook up with the Athabascan Richard Carroll family in Fort Yukon. Richard Carroll the elder was one of the first Arctic tour guides in the 1950s and owns Porcupine River Lodge. His son Richard was born into the tour business and is a historian. The younger Richard leads everything from 3-hour village tours of Fort Yukon to gold-panning excursions on the upper Yukon River. He also outfits and guides six-day trips on the Porcupine River, following trade routes used by both the Athabascans and the Hudson's Bay Company in the last century.

The tour of the historic Hudson's Bay Company trading fort site and the village of Fort Yukon includes historical narration (Richard's narration is both educational and funny), a dog team ride, and lunch at the Carroll house.

A longer excursion explores 170 miles of the historic Porcupine River trade route by boat, stopping to look at Athabascan hunting and trapping grounds and to visit three abandoned villages. The trip, which goes through the Arctic National Wildlife Refuge, is ideal for photographing wildlife, hiking, and fishing. You fly on a bush plane upriver from Fort Yukon to the Porcupine River Lodge and return by boat. The lodge is a large log cabin with four small frame homes with kitchens. Water is packed in. Meals, camping and fishing gear, and travel to and from the lodge is included in the price: about $3,000 for one or two people, including airfare. In the winter, when the river is frozen over, the same 170-mile route is explored by dog team and snow machine.

Another option is to visit a historic mining district and pan for gold with the Carrolls in their riverboat tour of the Yukon-Charley Rivers National Preserve. This trip leaves from Circle, accessible from Fairbanks by the Steese Highway, which follows the historic gold trails to the Yukon. Along the way, Carroll explains the effects of America's gold fever on Athabascan lives in the region.

Other tours include travel by dog team to a historic trapper's cabin, wilderness day trips, and other customized riverboat and canoe trips in the region. The family also rents riverboats (20- and 24-foot flat-bottomed riverboats with 25- and 40-horsepower outboard motors) for $250 a day, available at Circle, Eagle, Fort Yukon, and the Porcupine River Lodge.

Alaska Yukon Tours, Richard Carroll Family, PO Box 221, Fort Yukon, AK 99740; (907)662-2727. Call for a complete brochure.

Huslia: *Athabascan*

The village of Huslia (population 260), on the banks of the Koyukuk River in the heart of the Koyukuk National Wildlife Refuge, is accessible only by air taxi from Fairbanks or Nome. Take a look at a detailed map and you'll find it way out there, between Fairbanks (about 300 miles from the city) and Nome. The Koyukon Athabascans were active traders with the Kobuk River Eskimos. Russian explorers followed the Eskimo trade route upriver from the Bering Sea coastline to a point 50 miles below the present-day village site in 1843. The Koyukuk, a tributary of the Yukon River, is home to thousands of migrating birds, caribou, bear, wolf, otter, and beaver. The Koyukon have used the Huslia village site for centuries. They continue to exist primarily on subsistence hunting and fishing. It's a rich, full lifestyle that makes living in the city seem both hollow and a blessed relief by turns. Artists here create exceptional beadwork and skin sewn garments to earn a little extra cash for other necessities. The village offers overnight tours to visitors through Athabasca Cultural Journeys.

Athabasca Cultural Journeys

The opportunity to stay in a wilderness camp with an Athabascan family is rare indeed, particularly when you are hosted by people willing to introduce you to friends, relatives, and local artists as well as teach you some essentials about the subsistence lifestyle. Athabasca Cultural Journeys, a village tour, gives you this experience.

A three-day tour with Athabasca Cultural Journeys begins with a flight from Fairbanks to Huslia on a bush plane. Tour guides meet your plane and provide an orientation to you and other members of your group. You then board a skiff for the trip to your camp on the Koyukuk River in the Koyukuk National Wildlife Refuge. Accommodations are in deluxe tent camps. Three meals are served each day (regular Lower 48 fare, with the opportunity to sample moose, caribou, bear, beaver, and fresh fish).

During the course of your stay, you learn to read animal tracks and signs, discover how to set a fish net (and how to cut and dry your catch), and visit archaeological sites and bear hibernation dens. In keeping with Athabascan ways, Native travelers on the Koyukuk will pull their skiffs up on the bank and visit with campers. In the fall, Native guides lead hunting trips.

Athabasca Cultural Journeys, PO Box 72, Huslia, AK 99746; (907)829-2261. Tours offered June–Aug. Cost of three-day stay, including airfare, accommodations, meals, and guides, is $1,650 per person. Groups limited to six people. No credit cards; postal money orders are preferred. Fall hunting trips are priced individually; call for details.

Venetie Tribal Lands: *Athabascan*

This is the only Indian reservation in Alaska other than the Tsimshians' Annette Island in Southeast. The Venetie Tribal Lands cover 1.8 million acres in central Alaska, located north of the Yukon River and bordering the Arctic National Wildlife Refuge, the calving and nursery grounds for more than 160,000 caribou (and the site of one of North America's most heartfelt battles against oil drilling).

The Venetie Tribal Lands include two villages: Arctic Village, in the eastern end of the Brooks Range, the mountains that separate central Alaska from the Arctic slope; and Venetie, on the Chandalar River in Yukon Flats, a huge wetland and haven for migratory birds.

Arctic National Wildlife Refuge: Defending the Nursery

The traditional homeland of the Gwich'in Athabascan Indians, whose language is related to the Apache and Navajo tribes of the southwestern United States, is actually much larger than the present-day reservation. It extends over a vast area of tundra plain in northeast Alaska, including the Arctic National Wildlife Refuge, all the way into what is today Canada's Northwest Territories and Yukon Territory. It covers almost the same land mass through which the Porcupine River caribou herd travels on its migratory route from its wintering grounds to its calving grounds. The Gwich'in have always relied on the herd to meet the nutritional, cultural, and spiritual needs of their people.

Today the Gwich'in communities from Alaska and Canada have united to save the 160,000-member caribou herd, which they feel is endangered by proposed oil and gas exploration in the Arctic National Wildlife Refuge's coastal plain. The communities of Arctic Village, Venetie, Fort Yukon, Beaver, Chalkyitsik, Birch Creek, Stevens Village, Circle, and Eagle Village in Alaska, and Old Crow, Fort McPherson, Arctic Red River, Akalavik, and Inuvik in Canada have taken a unanimous stand against oil drilling in the Arctic refuge. Conservationists call the caribou calving grounds on the Arctic plain "America's Serengeti"; the area is a haven for more than 200 species, including polar bears, who give birth to cubs here during the winter, and musk oxen. Every spring, the Porcupine River caribou herd journeys 1,000 miles from wintering grounds to the

The Kutchin Beadwork Tradition (University of Alaska Press, 1997) is a compilation of beadworkers' comments and the history of Gwich'in beadwork, beginning with regional differences and including work that today exists only in memory. The book is a collaboration between Eunice Carney, a Gwich'in elder and beadworker, and Kate Duncan, an art historian. Phone orders can be charged; (888)252-6657.

coastal plain, where they bring forth nearly 40,000 calves. Thousands of birds migrate from as far away as the Patagonia region of Argentina to nest in the refuge. Already, more than 90 percent of the coastal plain has been made available by Congress to oil interests for development. Only the Arctic National Wildlife Refuge, a last 125-square-mile fragment, has remained untouched.

The Gwich'in have recorded nearly 500 oil spills per year since the 1960s in the Arctic and Prudhoe Bay, just 60 miles west of the refuge. Oil drilling in the refuge would introduce hundreds of miles of roads and pipelines, toxic waste contamination, and heavy equipment into an extremely sensitive wildlife area.

Two videos address these issues from a Native perspective. The award-winning *Voice from the North* is about the Gwich'in, the Porcupine River caribou herd, and the fight to save them. It's narrated partially in Gwich'in dialect and features dozens of beautiful close-ups of tundra wildflowers, animals, the Brooks Range, and the Arctic coastal plain. It's very difficult to comprehend the concept of thousands of square miles untouched by roads until you see them. This film also delivers a Native American perspective of the natural world that has rarely been stated so succinctly.

Not all Natives agree with the Gwich'in position on oil drilling. Some Alaska Native corporations support oil exploration and drilling, and profit from it.

A second video, produced in 1988, records the first gathering of tribes of the region, held to focus attention on the issue of oil drilling in the Arctic National Wildlife Refuge. *Arctic Refuge: A Gathering of Tribes* features music by indigenous people from all over the Americas whose lives would be affected by the destruction of this important migratory wildlife habitat. Musicians include flutist R. Carlos Nakai (Navajo/Ute), Tze'ec (Mayan), Cha–das–ska–dum Which ta-lum (Lummi), and Sarah James (Gwich'in).

The Gwich'in Steering Committee also sells "Caribou Is Our Life" T-shirts, hats, buttons, and posters to help fund its congressional lobbying efforts.

For more information or to order, contact the Gwich'in Steering Committee, PO Box 202768, Anchorage, AK 99520; (907)258-6814. Arctic Refuge: A Gathering of Tribes can be ordered directly from Soundings of the Planet, PO Box 43512, Tucson, AZ 85733; (800)937-3223 or (520)792-9888.

Arctic Village and Venetie Tours

The Gwich'in remained nomadic until 1910, when they built permanent villages to facilitate private traplines for the commercial fur trade. The Arctic Village Council and the Venetie Tribal Government have teamed up with Wright Air Service to bring people to these villages year-round to learn about Athabascan subsistence lifestyles. You fly from Fairbanks over the Yukon River and the Arctic Circle to either Arctic Village or Venetie.

In Venetie, you stay overnight with a dog-mushing family and learn how the dogs are trained to pull sleds, about hunting and trapping, and about modern-day overland travel on snow machines. In winter you can ride on a dogsled, in summers on a cart pulled by a team of dogs. Your stay includes a visit to the Venetie Tribal Office to learn about Native issues.

In Arctic Village during the winter, you stay with a local family to observe the northern lights high in the mountains, learn firsthand about the Arctic National Wildlife Refuge, and cover trails on snow machines. During the summer, you spend the day with tribal members, or spend up to three days and nights (the sun shines 24 hours a day, and most traveling is done at night to avoid the heat) canoeing and hiking in the region, which is puddled with hundreds of large lakes. Trips are led by Native guides with Coast Guard training in Arctic survival, as well as a lifetime of personal experience in the region. You'll meet beadworkers here. Beads were introduced in Alaska in the 1700s by Russian fur traders on the coast, but the nomadic Gwich'in began designing with beads only after the Hudson's Bay Company established trade with them in the mid-1800s. Beads were originally worn on clothing to symbolize wealth.

You must have permission from the Venetie Tribal Council to visit Arctic Village, Venetie, or their surrounding lands. Permission is assumed for those touring with Arctic Village Tours. On tribal lands, alcohol is strictly prohibited, as are video cameras.

For information about Arctic Village Tours, contact Ben Boyd, Director of Tourism, PO Box 82896, Fairbanks, AK 99708; (907)479-4648. Boyd, who is frequently up north, checks his voice mail daily and will return your calls. Tours offered year-round. Prices $150–$400; package rates include airfare, food, lodging, guide, and activities.

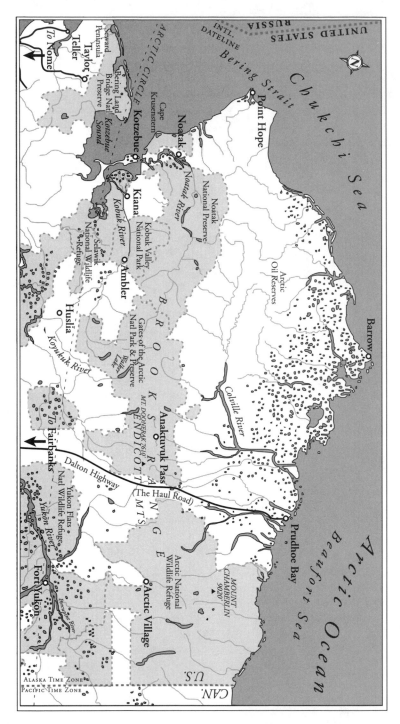

THE
ARCTIC

From the perspective of people living in the Arctic region, the center of the world would be the North Pole, ringed first by ice, then by a wide band of sometimes frozen, sometimes open Arctic Ocean, and finally by a ring of broken coastline. Although the cultures of this circumpolar region occupy geographical regions far from one another, they are similar in many ways, since all have adapted to the rigors of living in the extreme northern climate.

Prior to white contact, Native cultures in northern Canada, Alaska, and northeastern Siberia depended on the sea mammals, land mammals, and birds that migrate to and throughout the Arctic each spring, and on the abundant berries and greens that spring to life in the tundra during the short summer.

The term *Eskimo* is a non–Native word early explorers used to describe all the peoples of northeastern Siberia, Alaska, and northern Canada. There are various interpretations of the word *Eskimo*; the most common is that it derives from the Micmac Indian word *Eskameege*, which means (as translated by French Canadian trappers and whalers in the early 1800s) "to eat raw fish." *Eskimo* is not, however, a word that the Arctic peoples use to describe themselves, nor does it sum up their cultures. Natives prefer *Inupiat* to describe the people of northern Alaska, and

Yup'ik to describe the "Eskimo" people living along Alaska's northwest coast. Of course, these terms are also very general. The Inupiat people of King Island, 95 miles off the coastal town of Nome, for example, called themselves the *Ugiuvokmiut* (the suffix "miut" means "the people of").

Freeze Frame: Alaska Eskimos in the Movies, *by Ann Fienup-Riordan (University of Washington Press, 1995), reveals how non-Natives got such odd ideas about Eskimo culture—from igloos to "Eskimo kisses" —from a century of bad reporting, staged photographs, and skewed movie scripts, cartoons, and commercials.* Anthropologist Fienup-Riordan examines Eskimo stereotypes—*using examples from such diverse sources as the journals of confused 16th-century Arctic explorers, the documentaries of missionaries, and the Eskimo Pie commercials of the last two decades.*

After years of watching film and advertising images of "Eskimos," outsiders may envision an Eskimo as a person wearing a fur parka who lives in an igloo and drives a dogsled over a perpetually snow-covered land. Nothing could be further from the truth, whether you are imagining Eskimos prior to white contact or Eskimos today. The disparity between image and reality can be disturbing to tourists, who sometimes feel cheated when they don't see any igloos perched on the Arctic ice. But the truth of Inupiat and Yup'ik Eskimo life is far more fascinating than movie cliches.

For example, although artifacts from the Arctic have been collected and studied for centuries, it wasn't until the 1981 excavation of Barrow's Mound 44 site that a complete picture of pre-contact Inupiat life was revealed. This narrow window into the Arctic world of 500 years ago is regarded as one of the most important archaeological finds in North America (see the Barrow section later in this chapter). The artifacts and a replica of the sod house uncovered in Mound 44 will be displayed at Barrow's new Inupiat Heritage Center, set to open in 1998. Visitors will also learn how Arctic cultures flourished in one of the coldest, most inhospitable climates in the world.

Visitors to the Arctic can increase their understanding of Eskimo cultures by taking one of the tours described in this chapter. Two of the most popular are offered in Barrow and Kotzebue. These towns, hundreds of miles apart, are regional centers with medical services, provisions, and educational and government services for surrounding villages. And, unlike smaller villages in the region, they have overnight accommodations, including full-service hotels.

One way to hunt seals involves drilling a hole through the solid ice. Over the top of the hole, you suspend a feather that is tied with sinew to a neckbone from a goose. When the seal comes up through the hole to exhale, its breath lifts the feather. The seal hunter must lie on the ice and wait motionlessly for the seal to come up, because the ice carries sound like a drum.

On these tours (both in operation for more than 20 years), visitors can learn about the natural history of the region, enjoy traditional songs and dances, and see demonstrations of many aspects of traditional culture based on subsistence activities. These tours can also show what's involved in constructing and operating a modern town in the Arctic (supplying building materials, food, and dry goods; building on permafrost; providing services such as electricity, heat, and water).

Also listed in this chapter are smaller tours, conducted by Inupiat guides, that independent travelers will enjoy. (Note that tours at Gambell, a Siberian Yup'ik community on St. Lawrence Island, 38 miles from Siberia's Chokotsk Peninsula, are not described here; they are booked through the year 2,000 and asked not to be included in this edition.)

This chapter covers the main population centers of the Alaskan Arctic, including the little village of Anaktuvuk Pass, at the interior gateway to the Arctic in the Brooks Range, Barrow, Kotzebue, Kiana, and the town of Nome, located south of the Arctic Circle on the Seward Peninsula, famous for its gold rush history.

Anaktuvuk Pass: *Inupiat*

The Nunamiut Inupiat (or inland Eskimos) have lived as nomads near this passageway through the Brooks Range for more than 4,000 years, hunting caribou and mountain sheep. They were so isolated that only one generation separates the modern village of today from the hunters who wore fur clothing and lived in skin tents. Their creation story tells of a giant man, Ayagumalhaq, who taught survival skills to the Nunamiut. To ensure that he and his teachings would be remembered, he took off one of his gloves and transformed it into a mountain at the headwaters of the Alatna River. The Natives call the jagged peaks the Arrigich, a Nunamiut word that means "outstretched fingers."

Contact with explorers was first made in 1886, and in the 30 years thereafter, the Nunamiut experienced catastrophic events. First there were epidemics of deadly flu and measles, followed by a cyclical decline of caribou herds between 1890 and 1910 that led to starvation. By 1920, the Nunamiut had completely abandoned their traditional lifestyle. Many moved to the coast to work for whalers or to inland Canada.

When bush planes made access to the region easier, Nunamiut descendants moved back into the region and established a permanent village at Anaktuvuk Pass. You can fly here from Fairbanks or Barrow. Upon arrival, call the Simon Paneak Memorial Museum (see below) for help with lodging and to make travel arrangements with bush pilots. If possible, view the town's Web site (it's excellent) at http://www.nsbsd.k12.ak.us/villages/akp/nunal.htm.

Simon Paneak Memorial Museum

The Simon Paneak Memorial Museum, housed in a log cabin against the backdrop of Soakpak Mountain and overlooking the village, chronicles the historical Nunamiut culture. Elders Simon Paneak, Amos Morry, Arctic John Etalook, Eligah Kakinya, and others left journals, drawings, and recordings of the old ways. Artifacts such as skin clothing, wooden plates, hunting gear, and tool kits have been borrowed from major museums or re-created especially for this small museum. From the porch, visitors can see Anaktuvuk Pass and the headwaters of two major rivers. A small gift shop carries skin masks and skin sewn items, as well as books and pamphlets about the region. The museum sells a small booklet, "Anaktuvuk Pass, Land of the Nunamiut," containing old photographs and a brief history of the people.

Simon Paneak Memorial Museum, PO Box 21085, Anaktuvuk Pass, AK 99721; (907)661-3413.

Barrow: *Inupiat*

Barrow, a predominantly Inupiat Eskimo community of about 4,500, is the northernmost town in North America, located near an exposed point of land jutting into the Arctic Ocean and the Beaufort Sea. The town is a spot of modern shelter in the treeless, Arctic desert (with less than 5 inches of rain and 20 inches of snow annually). In winter, the peninsula is engulfed by Arctic Ocean pack ice, with temperatures that drop to 80 below zero. In summers the ice pack breaks apart and rides away from land on the current; temperatures hover between 40 and 55 degrees, with a rare spike in the 80s, bringing enough heat and sunlight to send the tundra wildflowers into spectacular bloom, ripen the berries, and wind-dry meat.

Barrow is more than 1,000 miles north of Juneau and 725 miles from Anchorage, connected to the outside world by daily jet service and state-of-the-art computers, satellite television, fax machines, and phones. The town was established as early as 1850, when whalers from New Bedford, Massachusetts, worked side by side with Inupiat

Howard Rock was born in 1911 in a sod house in Point Hope. In the 1950s, Rock learned that the Atomic Energy Commission and scientist Edward Teller had proposed to create a deepwater harbor near Point Hope by blowing a hole in the permafrost with an atomic blast. The explosion, which would have been 160 times more powerful than that of the bomb dropped on Hiroshima, would have also allowed Teller to test the effects of atomic fallout on a remote population. Rock assisted villagers from his hometown in making an appeal to Secretary of State Stewart Udall to stop the test. Dan O'Neill's The Firecracker Boys (St. Martin's Press, 1994) is a detailed, and hair-raising, account of the AEC plans for the atomic explosion near Point Hope.

whalers here. Some of them stayed, becoming part of Inupiat society and fathering children. Charles P. Brower constructed the Cape Smythe Whaling and Trading Station in 1886, about 10 years before Presbyterian missionaries established a post in Barrow, named after a secretary of the British Admiralty. The town has been a tourist destination since 1954, when visitors first flew north on prop passenger planes and toured the area in a military chassis (essentially a wooden box punctuated with windows and filled with bus seats) equipped with an enclosed viewing station to keep them safe from roaming polar bears.

As the crusading editor and owner of the Tundra Times, *an Alaska Native newspaper, Howard Rock helped Alaska's Native people press their land claims before the U.S. Congress, winning a settlement of nearly $1 billion and 40 million acres of land. His biography,* Art and Eskimo Power: The Life and Times of Alaskan Howard Rock *(Epicenter Press, 1988), is a must-read for anyone wanting an account of the challenges that have faced Alaska Natives in the last century.*

The original settlement of Barrow was called Ukpeagvik ("a place to hunt owls"), named for the thousands of snowy owls the Inupiat found nesting on tufted mounds in the tundra. Although the Eskimos were nomadic hunters, living in skin tents as they tracked migratory animals, archaeological excavations indicate that they had a permanent settlement at Ukpeagvik for at least 1,500 years. They lived in subterranean and above-ground sod houses, with multiple rooms at various levels, supported with whalebone and driftwood. Traditional Inupiat culture was very complex, with large extended families and an extensive bartering and trading system, messenger feasts, and days-long trade fairs and festivals held throughout the Arctic.

One of the most significant archaeological sites in North America, Mound 44, was accidentally discovered in the old village in 1981. Entombed in their sod house by ice that had rafted over a bluff were two Inupiat adult women, two adolescents, and a child. The bodies were mummified by the dry Arctic air and had been perfectly preserved for more than 500 years. Found in the house were their tools, implements, and clothing, carefully bundled and stored according to the season in which they were to be used. The bodies, along with other remains found in nearby archaeological sites, have been reburied in the Imaiqsaun Cemetery; the artifacts found in the house are exhibited in Barrow's new Inupiat Heritage Center.

The community today is 64 percent Inupiat. Most Inupiat people are bilingual, speaking both their Native dialect and English. Residents live in a dual economy of cash and subsistence; most area jobs are with federal, state, and village corporation agencies and with businesses servicing the local government and oil industry. The majority of Inupiat Eskimos live primarily on subsistence hunting for marine mammals and inland game, together with bartering. For many people, heading to summer subsistence camps (which have no running water or electricity) along the Arctic and Beaufort Sea and out in the tundra provides blessed relief from town.

Whaling remains an essential part of the culture: bowhead, gray, beluga, and orca whales migrate near Barrow. Bowhead whales are hunted from umiaks—huge boats with lashed wooden frames. Umiaks, used by Natives for thousands of years, are still the best boat for the job—covered with sealskins sewn together with a waterproof stitch, and perfectly constructed for maneuvering between the rough edges of the floating ice that chokes the Arctic during whaling season. In the old days, gut sails and paddles supplied the power; today the Inupiat generally use outboard motors, killing the motor and using the quieter paddles only when near prey. Bowhead whales are the most important hunt of all; a successful season is celebrated in June with the Nalukataq Festival. Kivgiq, a three-day celebration held in January or February, includes dance, song, and bartering among villages from all over the North Slope, Russia, and Canada; it is followed by the Piuraagiaqta Spring Festival each April.

Order Barrow, Alaska: A True Story, a videotape about life in Barrow that will help you learn about polar bears, whales, snowy owls, and other wildlife on the North Slope; the Inupiat subsistence lifestyle; traditional Eskimo dances; and local artists and daily life in modern-day Barrow. Available for $24.95 from Touch Alaska, PO Box 881, Barrow, AK 99723; Web site: www.touchalaska.com. A portion of the proceeds go toward funding the Inupiat Heritage Center.

Today Barrow is an ever more popular destination, with year-round tours. Summer tours include bird watching and viewing the wildflowers that cover the tundra. Winter travelers come to stay overnight at the Top of the World Hotel, see the spectacular northern lights, and experience the ice-bound Arctic during the months when Barrow is engulfed by 24 hours of darkness.

Getting There

Alaska Airlines, (800)426-0333, offers daily jet service to Barrow from Anchorage and Fairbanks.

Visitor Services

The North Slope Borough Public Information Office, (907)852-0215, will give you the dates of local events. Brochures about the area, local events, and activities are available from the Top of the World Hotel, (907)852-3900.

How to Pack

See "How to Pack" at the beginning of this book. Weather in Barrow is very unpredictable. Always bring a warm jacket. When the ice is breaking up in the spring, birders planning to walk on the tundra should bring knee-high rubber boots. Average summer temperatures climb to 50 degrees. Winter temperatures average 20 below zero and can drop to 80 below zero.

Tundra Tours

This eye-opening bus and walking tour of Barrow and the Arctic Ocean coastline is a great introduction to the Inupiat Eskimo culture of the last 5,000 years. One of the things that makes the tour exceptional is the way that past and present are constantly juxtaposed by Inupiat guides—a stop at a traditional hunting camp that mirrors Barrow 50 years ago, followed by a stop at the old naval research station and Distant Early Warning System installed during the Cold War. You'll see historical film footage of old Barrow back in the 1930s, and then drive past the glass-enclosed headquarters of the Arctic Slope Regional Corporation, whose shareholders are Inupiat. Caribou and polar bear skin and meat wind-dry on wooden racks between modern houses and satellite dishes; a umiak sits overturned on posts overlooking the Arctic Ocean, which is bobbing with pack ice.

The heart of the tour is an extended stop at the Inupiat Heritage Center (discussed later in this section) to learn about the 5,000-year-old traditional Inupiat Eskimo culture of the entire Arctic Slope, with demonstrations of Inupiat masked and unmasked dancing, drumming, and crafts. Native crafts (mukluks, Eskimo yo-yos, ivory carvings, baleen baskets, and other work) are sold here too, and visitors can meet local artisans. Winter tours include all this as well as a long look at the night sky and the northern lights, accompanied by traditional and modern stories that explain this dazzling phenomenon. All tours include an overnight stay at the Top of the World Hotel.

Tundra Tours Inc., PO Box 189, Barrow, AK 99723; (800)882-8478 or, inside Alaska, (800)478-8520. Tours offered year-round; summer tour mid-May–mid-Sept, winter tour mid-Sept–mid-May. The most economical packages are booked through Alaska Airlines Vacations, (800)468-2248, or Alaska World Tours, (800)733-2930. Included are round-trip airfare on Alaska Airlines, destination transfers, guided tour, northern lights tour (in winter only), Arctic Circle certificate, and overnight stay at the Top of the World Hotel. Tundra Tours is a subsidiary of Arctic Slope Regional Corporation, whose shareholders are Inupiat.

Top of the World Hotel

Built in 1974 and recently completely refurbished, the Top of the World Hotel is a two-story oasis of comfort offering 50 rooms, many of them overlooking the Arctic Ocean and the Chukchi Sea. The rooms are equipped with queen-size beds (twins, singles, roll-aways, and cribs are available), and all feature private baths with separate showers and tubs, refrigerators, 56 channels of satellite television, and direct-dial telephones. Some rooms have kitchens; complimentary tea and coffee is served in the lobby, which is staffed 24 hours a day. The world is indeed getting smaller—the hotel's restaurant is Pepe's North of the Border Restaurant, serving up Mexican and American cuisine. Off the hotel lobby is an informal gift shop where you can purchase locally handcrafted items.

Top of the World Hotel, PO Box 189, Barrow, AK 99723; (907)852-3900. Open year-round. Room rates vary according to package. Independent travelers can book hotel and tours separately.

Inupiat Heritage Center

Nearly 20 years in the planning, the Inupiat Heritage Center—a museum, library, and cultural center—is scheduled to open in 1998, with some of the most exciting exhibits in the state of Alaska. Among the permanent exhibits are a large ethnographic collection acquired by the North Slope Borough, the Mound 44 collection of artifacts found with the bodies of five mummified Inupiat people, and an extensive exhibit on the Arctic weather—polar winds, ice, the cycle of light and dark, and its effect on the climate—that creates phenomena such as the raft ice that trapped the Mound 44 dwellers in their sod house.

How do you keep sand out of the food in a subterranean sod house? The Inupiat people discovered that if you pour seal oil onto the ground and set it on fire, it cools into a hard surface similar to concrete.

An exhibit explaining the importance of the bowhead whale in 5,000 years of Inupiat culture, some of it based on the 19th-century collections and illustrated journals of Edward William Nelson and John Murdoch, is a cooperative effort with the New Bedford Whaling Museum and New Bedford Whaling National Historical Park, both in Massachusetts. Commercial whalers from New Bedford worked with Inupiat whalers in Barrow as early as 1850: as a result of their years together, many Inupiat and New Bedford whaling families have descendants in common.

The Inupiat Heritage Center, which displays portraits of Arctic Slope leaders along with text describing what they accomplished for their communities, is also acquiring the work of the region's most noted artists, among them Samuel Simons, Harry Brower, Simon Koonuk, and Howard Rock.

The center's building includes a "teaching" section where elders and artists will work in residence. Designed in the style of a traditional sod house, with a *qargi* (an open room for storytelling), the center also has a very large room that can be divided into classrooms for lectures and large performances, along with an area for exhibits of traditional skills—large enough to drag a umiak (whaling vessel) inside to repair and re-cover with sealskins prepared in an adjacent skinning room. A small gift shop carries the work of regional Arctic artists.

The beauty of this heritage center is that it was conceived by Inupiat people determined to pass centuries of very specific cultural knowledge to future generations. North Slope elder conferences, held from 1975 through 1989, generated the vision for the center. Many of the people currently involved in the center's completion grew up in Arctic villages in the 1950s, in sod houses with kayaks and dog teams for transportation, and have moved into the 1990s as full participants in the world. Acting director Ronald Brower Sr., for example, an Inupiat artist who lived in a sod house until his family moved into a wood-frame home in Barrow in the 1950s, is a graduate of the University of Fairbanks and the Sorbonne and a Vietnam veteran; was chairman of the North Slope Borough's History, Culture, and Language Commission; and is vice president of the Inuit Circumpolar Conference for the state of Alaska.

Inupiat Heritage Center, PO Box 749, Barrow, AK 99723; (907)852-9165. At the corner of Ahkovak St and North Star St. The center is slated to open in June 1998, but construction delays may postpone the opening. The phone number listed is for Ilisagvik College, part of the management team for the museum; they can provide you with the opening date, hours, and other general information.

Hiking

The North Slope Borough recommends four hiking routes around the Barrow area. (On all four, hikers need to watch for the very small (insects) and the very large (polar bears) local residents.) The first is a walk from town to Fresh Water Lake, an original source of drinking water for the village. On the way you pass Imaiqsaun Cemetery, the final resting place of the famous Mound 44 family, found in the early 1980s, and of a prehistoric girl whose body was recovered from an eroding bluff in 1994. A second walk, which is 13 miles each way over spongy tundra and pebble beach and can take all day, heads along the coast of the Chukchi Sea to the crash site of the small plane in which Will Rogers and pilot Wiley Post died early in this century. A third, full-day hike is along the Arctic Ocean shoreline out to Point Barrow, the most northerly point in the United States and the site of the old village of Nuwuk. Along the way is Ilisagvik College, an old naval research lab that has been renovated into a community college (if you want to stop your hike here, there's a bookstore and cafeteria inside). There's also a subsistence-hunting summer campsite known as Pigniq ("shooting station") where families have gathered for thousands of years to hunt waterfowl, seals, and other wildlife. The fourth hike heads out of town into the tundra on Gas Well Road, also a popular snow-machine, biking, and all-terrain vehicle road. If you are walking, wear waterproof boots, and bring binoculars to spot caribou, Arctic fox, snowy owls, and hundreds of nesting birds among the wildflowers.

Hiking brochures and maps are available at the Top of the World Hotel lobby, which also functions as Barrow's informal visitors center.

Kotzebue: *Inupiat*

The tip of the Baldwin Peninsula, tucked into the east side of Kotzebue Sound, was an ideal spot for an Eskimo village. Qiqitagruk, as it was originally named by Inupiat Eskimos, was the hub of ancient Arctic trade routes long before European contact. The village was located at the mouth of two major rivers, the Noatak and Kobuk, that travel far into the interior. Coastal Eskimos met there and traded with Athabascan Indians far upstream, traveling during the summer by umiak and kayak, and during the winter by dogsled. Today Kotzebue is a service center for 11 Arctic villages in the region.

Hundreds of square miles surrounding Kotzebue are today under federal management. To the north, Cape Krusenstern National Monument, a large coastal plain bordered by the Chukchi Sea and the Arctic Ocean, is filled with lagoons and brackish lakes, forming a vast wetland for nesting migratory birds. The Noatak National Preserve, adjacent to Cape Krusenstern, encompasses most of the 436-mile Noatak River and extends to the high peaks of the Brooks Range. Kobuk Valley National Park includes the most scenic stretch of the Kobuk River,

Kotzebue sits almost directly in the path of what is known as the Bering Land Bridge, a 1,000-mile-wide ridge of dry land that is thought to have existed between Asia and North America during the ice age (it is now submerged). According to the land bridge theory, humans followed migratory animals from Asia across the bridge into North America thousands of years ago. Not everyone agrees, though. Because the continents are only 55 miles apart, some say they could have easily been crossed in umiaks and kayaks. Winter's pack ice shortens the distance between the continents even more; during ice ages, some argue, it could have been crossed on foot.

east of Kotzebue, and the Great Kobuk Sand Dunes (which cover 25 square miles) as well as the drainages of five small rivers flowing into the Kobuk. Southeast of Kotzebue are Selawik Lake and the 2.15-million-acre Selawik National Wildlife Refuge, dotted with hundreds of lakes—a migratory bird refuge and home to caribou, bears, and moose. The Selawik River is a nationally designated Wild and Scenic river that runs through 240,000 acres of designated wilderness. All this wilderness surrounds Kotzebue, a bustling village of 3 square miles on the tip of the Baldwin Peninsula. The village faces Kotzebue Sound; from your hotel window, you can look straight across the Sound and out to the Chukchi Sea, an uninterrupted body of water that reaches all the way to Siberia.

You won't believe your eyes when you land in Kotzebue. You are visiting an Eskimo village north of the Arctic Circle, whatever that may mean to you (many visitors expect to see igloos made of ice and Eskimos dressed in fur parkas). But what you do see, after flying over millions of acres of tundra, is the end of a narrow spit that looks as if it has been leveled with a bulldozer and then constructed on a street grid laid out on poured gravel. Kotzebue is estimated to be the oldest settlement in Alaska, but it is also a modern technological miracle. You land on an airstrip, for example, that floats on a 6-inch layer of Styrofoam-type material over permafrost that is 2,240 feet deep. At first glance, as the plane taxis down the runway, the place more closely resembles an industrial park than a town.

There's far more to Kotzebue than meets the eye, however; to learn about it from the inside out, take Tour Arctic's half-day tour of the town, and spend at least several more days in Kotzebue to grasp the immensity of the surrounding wilderness. In summer many Inupiat families are away, primarily at fish camps on Cape Krusenstern, where salmon and other meats can dry in the open air away from the dust of town. To fully experience Kotzebue, you might want to come back in the winter, when most of the days are passed in darkness and everyone is back at home from summer fishing, hunting, and berry picking. Under the northern lights, the Inupiat use their snow machines to reach outlying villages, traveling up the frozen rivers and over snow trails that have been used by generations of dog mushers.

Getting There

Alaska Airlines, (800)426-0333, provides the only jet service to Kotzebue from Anchorage. It also offers several packages that include round-trip airfare and day tours of Kotzebue, as well as tours that include overnight lodging and sightseeing by bush plane and riverboat up the Kobuk River.

Frontier Flying Service, (907)474-0014, has regularly scheduled service on smaller planes that fly from Anchorage and Fairbanks to Kotzebue. Bering Air, (907)442-3943, has regularly scheduled service to outlying villages.

Visitor Services

The National Park Service Visitor Center (152 2nd St, Kotzebue, AK 99752; (907)442-3890) is open May through September. The center focuses on Arctic natural history and geology and offers brochures in Russian, Japanese, and Braille as well as in English. In winter, when the visitors center is closed, you can pick up maps and brochures and buy books from the National Park Service headquarters, behind the post office (no street address; PO Box 1029, Kotzebue, AK 99752; (907)442-3890). Ask for their Cape Krusenstern, Noatak, and Kobuk Valley brochure and map. The brochure has great photographs of Eskimo seal hunting, the Great Kobuk Sand Dunes, and the migration patterns of caribou herds.

Tour Arctic

Your Native guide begins unraveling your preconceptions about the Arctic the minute you climb on the bus. You're 180 miles from Russia, 4,000 miles from Washington, D.C., 6,000 miles from Greenland, and 1,500 miles from the North Pole; and tonight's sun sets at midnight and rises at 4:30pm, with twilight in between. The Russian explorer Vitus Bering charted this coast in 1729; Russian fur traders, in pursuit of fur seals, followed. The tour bus takes you over unpaved roads past houses with dogsleds on the roof, past the Quaker church established here in 1897, and stops at the Alaska Commercial Company store, a fully stocked supermarket.

Watch carefully before you join the dancers on-stage at Kotzebue's Museum of the Arctic. They aren't doing the Swim or the Hand Jive, and neither should you! Dances are similar to haiku poems; the essence of a story is told in motion to a drumbeat—the first time slowly, the second in faster time. Hand motions, accented with woven fans trimmed with fur, are deliberate; gestures spell out the tale, and body language adds to the telling.

Just when you begin to think that Kotzebue is really a space station supplied by corporations back on Earth, the bus stops at the culture camp, where you learn about some of the tools that people once used to make a living here, such as ice-fishing jiggers—made of whale baleen, bone, bear claws, and sharpened ivory—that were dangled through the ice on braided sinew twine to catch tomcod.

The centerpiece of the Kotzebue tour is the Museum of the Arctic, an impressive gallery of stuffed Arctic mammals, birds, and fish that really comes alive during tours. A stunning slide show illustrates the seasons in the Arctic. As the screen fades to black, a dramatic story begins onstage, illuminated by a single seal oil lamp. The animals that have provided nurture and warmth for generations of Inupiat Eskimos are spotlighted one at a time: bowhead whales, walrus, Dall's sheep, caribou, moose, musk ox, sandhill cranes, shee fish. Then the drums and dances begin. The tour ends with a "blanket toss" on a stretched walrus hide that acts as a trampoline.

Eskimo ice cream is made by warming caribou, sheep, moose, or bear fat and then whipping it by hand as it cools. You can flavor it with seal oil; add meat and raisins, or fish; or sweeten it with sugar or honey and add berries. Other modern additions include rice, nuts, and coconut. Instructions for making Eskimo ice cream and other traditional Inupiat foods, along with anecdotes, stories, and illustrations, are in **Nauriat Niginaqtuat: Plants That We Eat,** *by Anore James (Mianiilaq Association, 1983), available at the National Park Service headquarters in Kotzebue.*

The museum also has a very small display of antiquities, such as old birchbark baskets used for berry picking, behind glass; you pass it on your way out. The museum's gift shop sells handsome birchbark baskets from upriver villages, ivory and whalebone carvings from Shishmaref, a few pieces of fur clothing and mukluks, handcrafted jewelry, and moosehide masks. They will ship your purchases home for you. You can also purchase small items, such as skin-sewn balls and Eskimo yo-yos, directly from the Natives demonstrating crafts in the culture camp.

In conjunction with Alaska Airlines and Bering Air, Tour Arctic offers several tour packages that include airfare. You can take the half-day tour of Kotzebue; add on a night at the Nullagvik Hotel with time for sightseeing on your own; add on a flightseeing trip to the village of Kiana on the Kobuk River; and/or fly south to Nome for an overnight tour to learn about the gold rush.

Tour Arctic, PO Box 49, Kotzebue, AK 99752; (907)442-3301; fax (907)442-2866. Tour Arctic is a division of NANA Corporation, whose shareholders are Inupiat Eskimo. Tours offered mid-May–mid-Sept. $350–$844 per person depending on the package you choose; prices include hotel and round-trip airfare from Anchorage. For your convenience, book through Alaska Airlines Vacations, (800)468-2248. Tour Arctic also offers packages through other tour companies; for a list of suggested tour operators, call NANA Corporation at (907)442-3301.

Noatak River Tours

Because the summer sun doesn't set until after midnight in Kotzebue, time seems suspended when you leave town after dinner with William and Maureen Reich on their tour of the Noatak River. Both Bill and Maureen are Inupiat Eskimos and were born, raised, and educated (and are raising their children) in Kotzebue. They have camped on the river and climbed to the top of Hugos Mountain since they were small children.

The trip up the Noatak usually begins in early evening, after the Reichs finish their workday, and ends around midnight—all in blazing sunlight. Board their Bayliner cabin cruiser and cross Kotzebue Sound to the Noatak River. (The current of the Noatak, which begins 425 miles inland in the Brooks Range, is barely perceptible in a large boat.) The riverbank is thick with tall, lush grasses, and hills rise dramatically from the water's edge. A band of short, dark green evergreens girdles the hills; the rest of the way to the top is exposed bedrock blanketed with wildflowers and ripening berries.

About 22 miles upriver, Bill nudges the boat into the bank at the foot of Hugos Mountain. It's a good straight-up climb, although not perilous. Maureen knows the Inupiat names for edible plants, but refers to an identification guide for the names of flowering species that are inedible but pretty to look at. Up top, from craggy outcroppings and sheer cliffs, the view of roadless tundra meadows and the Brooks Range is spectacular.

For those who prefer not to hike up 869-foot Hugos Mountain, the Reichs will take you 10 more miles upriver by boat, into the scenic lower canyons.

Noatak Tours, PO Box 576, Kotzebue, AK 99752; (907)442-2747; E-mail: wtktours@ptialaska.net. Tours offered June Sept. Hugos Mountain tour $100 adult, $75 child; group discounts available. Six people per boat (Bayliner and outboard skiff). Courtesy van to and from Kotzebue's dock; restrooms on board; refreshments provided. A Noatak River lodge is in the works.

Art at the Maniilaq Health Center

Named after an 19th-century Inupiat healer and prophet, the $51 million Maniilaq ("man-eel-ik") Health Center sits at the edge of Kotzebue's lagoon. Scheduled to open in mid-summer 1998, it will be the town's largest building, serving 11 outlying Native villages in the Arctic region.

The Anchorage architectural firm of Livingston Slone met with the all-Inupiat board (composed of one representative from each village) and with traditional Native doctors to reach agreement on everything from the building design to the furnishings. "The sense of space and arrangement in the Arctic speaks to the same concerns as the Chinese system of feng shui," says architect Tom Livingston. "We learned that Arctic people have respect for smaller, enclosed space, and to waste space (and heat) with something like a cathedral ceiling or an atrium would make people uncomfortable. It would not only not feel safe or comfortable for someone coming for health care from a village where three generations share a small house, it would not be considered responsible."

The one-story building has sloping, shingled roofs in order to make its 80,000 square feet feel homey. As in old-style semisubterranean sod houses and modern Arctic construction, visitors enter the building through a "cold room" vestibule that traps the icy Arctic air at ground level; they then take an elevator up to the first floor. The patterns on the center's floors, such as those in the reception area, are inspired by the geometric designs of parka trim.

Thanks to the state's Percent for the Arts program, the building is filled with art, "making the building, which is fabricated entirely with imported materials, belong to the community," says Livingston. Five Inupiat jurors helped select the artwork, all of which reflects Kotzebue's unique culture and environment. A bronze sculpture of a swimming beluga whale, a ceramic piece entitled *Kotzebue's Wild Garden*, and a print called *Mending the Nets* were installed in the vestibule. A number of glass cases protect and display a permanent collection of smaller items such as Inupiat masks. One case is devoted entirely to objects made of gut and fish skin, another is filled with skin sewing, and yet another displays the handsome birchbark basketry common to this area (you can see some early examples of birchbark baskets used for berry picking at the Museum of the Arctic, discussed earlier under "Tour Arctic"). Nearly all the art is made by living artists; a very few irresistible older pieces are family heirlooms, such as the Chukchi reindeer herder's winter clothing, a woman's fur parka, and children's clothing. A "portrait doll" by dollmaker Dolly Spencer, who carves realistic faces from wood, is a tribute to one of Kotzebue's most famous Eskimo doctors, Della Keats. Spencer, who currently resides on the Kenai Peninsula, is originally from Kotzebue. She continues a dollmaking tradition originated by Lena Sours and Ethel Washington in Kotzebue in the late 1930s.

Maniilaq Health Center, Kotzebue, AK 99752; call information for telephone number. Scheduled to open in mid-summer 1998; will be open 24 hours daily. Visitors are welcome to look at the art and have lunch in the cafeteria.

Arctic Circle Educational Adventures

For more than two decades, registered nurse LaVonne Hendricks, a non-Native who worked for 14 years as a public health nurse serving 26 villages, has run a culture camp on the beach 5 miles outside of Kotzebue. The camp is a gathering of Inupiat elders and children who engage in subsistence fishing, gathering plants, and picking berries throughout the summer. What's unusual about this camp, besides its Arctic location and Inupiat teachers and students, is that the general public is invited to participate and learn.

Traditionally, children learned living skills from everyone in the village—because all worked together to harvest and prepare foods—but especially from their grandparents, who cared for the little ones while their parents labored. Schools, with their emphasis on long, separate hours away from home and with curriculums based on outside-world concerns, sciences, and English-based literature, interrupt and restrict the Inupiat people's family-based education. Culture camps, which are sponsored by tribes throughout indigenous America, bring grandparents and children together to pass on essential cultural knowledge to the younger generation.

The camp offers several options for guests. There are one-day natural history tours of the tundra with an Inupiat guide, as well as a longer overnight stay in the camp, which is a commercial salmon fish camp located right on the beach under 250-foot bluffs. Fish are caught in the Chukchi Sea using 6-inch-mesh gill nets and skiffs equipped with outboard motors. The camp is accessible by a four-wheel-drive road from Kotzebue. Guests stay in very rustic private cabins that are heated with electricity when the generator is on; an outhouse is out back. A modern kitchen, dining room, and hot shower facilities are housed in a separate cabin. Linens, blankets, and towels are provided.

The curriculum for a three-day, two-night stay varies depending on group interest, the weather, and the schedules of local people. Local grandmothers (*annas*) are involved in almost every activity. Up to 40 possibilities are offered, some relatively simple (beachcombing for shells and old ivory, hiking to Loon Lake, and observing the reindeer herd at Sadie Creek) and some more complex (setting fish nets, skin sewing, and learning about traditional Eskimo healing practices). There's also a discussion with the Inupiat called "Walking in Two Worlds," about their pragmatic, pantheistic view of the world, which

In the 1940s, Lela Kiana Oman translated tales she heard from Inupiat-speaking storytellers into English. One of these, The Epic of Quyaq: The Longest Story Ever Told by My People (Carleton University Press, 1995), chronicles the journeys of the young man Quyaq. On a mission to save the human race from evil, Quyaq kayaked four northern rivers, traveled along the Arctic Ocean to Barrow, went to Herschel Island in Canada, and journeyed to a Tlingit village in Southeast Alaska. It's a mythological tale— there's an Inupiat Adam and Eve, a Great Flood, and parallels to such ancient Greek myths as the story of Scylla and Charybdis in Homer's Odyssey. The tale of Quyaq, which originally took over a month to narrate, is estimated to be more than 1,000 years old.

assists them in everything from hunting and gathering to making decisions in corporate boardrooms. The group always visits working summer fish and seal camps on the rivers, and the Museum of the Arctic in Kotzebue. Guests also learn how to harvest plants from the tundra and the beach for use as food and medicine, how to cut salmon Eskimo style so it stays preserved without refrigeration, and how to pick salmon from a net.

Meals consist of local fresh fish, game meats, greens harvested from the tundra and beach, huge salads, and unique Inupiat appetizers such as seal jerky, *maq-taq* (whale skin and blubber), *puniktuq* (dried fish), and smoked salmon jerky. Breakfast is hearty—sourdough pancakes, reindeer sausage, and fresh fish.

The camp is a favorite of Elderhostel groups, but individuals can participate when the camp isn't full. Extended stays can also be arranged.

Arctic Circle Educational Adventures, PO Box 814, Kotzebue, AK 99752; (907)442-3509; Web site: www.alaska.net/~akhal; winters at 200 W 34th Ave, Suite 903, Anchorage, AK 99503; (907)276-0976. Offered late June–mid-Aug or later. Stays are customized, so prices vary.

Nullagvik Hotel

Even if you don't stay overnight in Kotzebue, make sure you stop in at the Nullagvik Hotel's gift shop. It's small, but there are treasures to be found here, most of them locally or regionally made. Look especially for finely crafted birchwood baskets decorated with porcupine quills from upriver villages, and carved ivory from Shishmaref (a small village between Kotzebue and Nome). You may find locally carved jade here, too; the green jade tiles set in the hotel lobby's floor and countertops were quarried from nearby Jade Mountain in the Brooks Range.

This is a full-service hotel, built right on the shore of Kotzebue Sound, with a restaurant, gift shop, and travel agency on the first floor. As are all other buildings in Kotzebue, the hotel is anchored on stilts above the ground to protect the delicate permafrost, and is equipped with vents that disperse building heat—which look like something out of an old sci-fi movie. The hotel was constructed in 1974 and refurbished in 1989. The restaurant and the lounge areas at the end of the hallways have picture windows that face Kotzebue Sound, but the windows in the guest rooms consist of one narrow, insulated pane, designed to keep out winter's bitter cold and summer's round-the-clock sun (you'll be glad to sacrifice the view in order to sleep in a darkened room). The 78 rooms have queen-size beds, full private baths, cable television, and phones. The Nullagvik Restaurant serves American fare (scrambled eggs and bacon, steaks, burgers) as well as reindeer sausage, sourdough pancakes, and fresh Arctic fish when it's in season. The facility is owned and operated by NANA, the Native regional corporation for northwest Arctic Alaska.

Nullagvik Hotel, PO Box 336, Kotzebue, AK 99752; (907)442-3331; fax (907)442-3340. On Shore Avenue. Open year-round. Rooms $95–$145. Major credit cards accepted. Meeting rooms accommodate up to 40 people.

Kiana: *Inupiat*

About 60 miles up the Kobuk River from Kotzebue, the village of Kiana sits on a bluff overlooking the confluence of the Kobuk and Squirrel Rivers. Home to 400 Inupiat Eskimos, the village is 300 miles from the nearest road system. The 347-mile Kobuk River, lined with birch and white fir forests, parallels the Arctic Circle and has been used for centuries as a main inland-to-coast route by the forest-dwelling Kuvuungmiut Eskimos, who also traded with the inland Athabascan Indians. They traveled in skin boats on the river, using dogs to pull the boats upstream. Families would move camp during the summer in pursuit of fish and game, and would set up temporary winter villages.

Traditional Inupiat foods were simple and practical. Greens, oils, meats, and roots were prepared so they could be served to large groups of people while traveling, using few containers or utensils.

Today's villages, such as Kiana, were established in the last century when trading posts, schools, and missions were built in permanent locations. Kiana is the jumping-off point for exploring Kobuk Valley National Park, which is famous for its herd of 400,000 migrating caribou; the Great Kobuk Sand Dunes; pristine wilderness rivers; fishing for trophy shee, arctic char, chum salmon, northern pike, whitefish, and burbot; and, in the winter, cross-country skiing. Bering Air, (907)442-3187, and other services offer daily air-taxi service to Kiana from Kotzebue.

Don's Sled Shop (and Tours)

Don Smith, an Inupiat Eskimo, was born and raised in Kiana and has lived here most of his life, except for a stint in the U.S. Army. Smith grew up in the old village, now razed, when winter travel on the Kobuk River was entirely by dogsled. English is his second language, taught to him in a one-room log cabin illuminated by gas lamps when he was a child. He taught himself to make sleds when he was a young boy. "My dad was not the best sled maker," he says, "and I got tired of fixing them." For years he made sleds from the birch trees that grow along the banks of the Kobuk River, hand-planing the wood into narrow planks.

Today he constructs beautiful sleds from imported hickory, similar to birch in color and pliability. In the workshop next to his home, he steams the wood until it can be shaped, and uses rope and bolts to assemble sleds that average 10 feet long, a process that takes about three weeks. The sleds have a tow hitch so they can be shackled to snow machines or attached to a bridled team of dogs. Ask to see the extra-long sled piled with furs.

During the summer, Smith guides fishermen (he provides rods and reels to catch shee fish, a whitefish that grows up to 40 pounds) and sightseers up the Kobuk River to the Great Kobuk Sand Dunes and the village of Ambler, aboard his six-passenger Boston Whaler skiff. Two small houses adjoining Smith's property are available for overnight stays; both have furnished kitchens. A grocery/outfitting store is within walking distance. Smith also works with Tour Arctic (see Kotzebue section) as Kiana's host and guide, and with Alaska Discovery (a non-Native company that partners with Natives) to transport adventurers upriver. Guests tour Smith's dogsled shop and are welcomed into the log home he built for his family.

Don Smith, Don's Sled Shop, Kiana, AK 99749; (907)475-2186. Tours offered May–Sept. Dogsleds can be commissioned; prices average $100 per foot with a 5-foot minimum, plus shipping costs.

Kobuk River Tours

Lorry and Nellie Schuerch, both of Eskimo descent and lifelong Kiana residents, offer overnight tours of Kiana and the Kobuk River; Lorry has been guiding sport fishermen and hunters since the 1950s. Part of a tour package that includes Kotzebue and the Museum of the Arctic, the Kiana leg includes a scenic 30-minute flight from Kotzebue to Kiana on Bering Air, a tour of Kiana, an overnight stay in the Schuerchs' new riverfront Kiana Lodge, and three meals (a four-course breakfast, a sack lunch, and dinner). One full day is spent touring the Kobuk River in jet boats from the lodge to the Great Kobuk Sand Dunes, which cover 25 square miles.

Guests can also make arrangements to visit the Schuerchs independently. If the lodge is booked, you can stay overnight in remote upriver cabins that sleep four, with propane stove, gas lanterns, and cooking gear, and rent a boat to fish or sightsee on the river. The Schuerchs also offer drop-off service for rafters, kayakers, and hunters.

The lodge is open year-round, and there are compelling reasons to visit during the off season, between September and June. In September, a herd of 400,000 caribou crosses the river at Kiana, an unforgettable sight. In winter—which, residents agree, is the best time of year in the Arctic—guests can use the lodge as headquarters for cross-country skiing (skis are supplied) and snow-machine or dogsled trips into the wilderness. You can go ice fishing for trophy shee on Arctic lakes. The northern lights are resplendent from the lodge, 26 miles above the Arctic Circle and 2 miles upriver from the lights of the village.

The 3,200-square-foot lodge has six guest rooms (two with private baths), a commercial kitchen, laundry, sauna, and an 80-foot deck overlooking the Kobuk River. Jet boats are Coast Guard certified; guides and equipment are licensed. Year-round, there are nine daily 30-minute scenic flights from Kotzebue to Kiana (our personal favorite is the mail plane, where you squeeze into your seat among piles of boxes). In winter, planes land on skis.

Kiana Lodge, PO Box 89, Kiana, AK 99749; (800)478-6149 (Alaska only); (907)475-2149; fax (907)475-2150; Web site: www.alaskaoutdoors.com/kiana/. Rooms $125–$175 per person per day, including three meals; ask about other tours and boat rentals. The Kiana summer tour is sold in conjunction with Tour Arctic packages offered through tour companies. Alaska Airlines Vacations, (800)468-2248, includes the Kiana tour in their packages, which also include round-trip airfare from Anchorage and a stop in Nome.

Guided Raft Trips

With guides from Kiana Lodge, raft on your choice of three pristine Arctic rivers: the Noatak, Kobuk, or Squirrel. The Noatak River raft trip begins at the confluence of the Cutler and Noatak Rivers, 130 air-miles inland from Kotzebue. You land in the heart of the Noatak National Preserve, tucked between the Brooks Range and the Baird Mountains, and spend seven days floating and camping on the Class I and II river, highlighted by a stretch of steep cliffs known as the "Noatak Grand Canyon." The six-day Class I Kobuk float begins in the village of Ambler and runs 100 miles downstream to Kiana through Kobuk Valley National Park, past Jade Mountain, the Great Kobuk Sand Dunes, and the confluence of the Salmon River. You can fish and watch for birds and wildlife. On the five-day Squirrel River trip, you float 60 miles down a gentle Class I river that is home to abundant wildlife, including barren-ground grizzly bears. The Squirrel River originates in the Baird Mountains, is crystal clear, and offers great fishing.

Kiana Lodge, PO Box 89, Kiana, AK 99749; (800)478-6149 (Alaska only); (907)475-2149; fax (907)475-2150; Web site: www.alaskaoutdoors.com/kiana/. Noatak River trip (7 days/6 nights) $2,625 per person; Kobuk River trip (6 days/5 nights) $2,250 per person; Squirrel River trip (5 days/4 nights) $1,875 per person.

Nome: *Inupiat*

Best known in Alaska for its colorful gold rush history, which included a huge tent city on the shores of the Bering Sea, Nome is today a hub that serves 16 villages on the Seward Peninsula. On the north end of the peninsula is the Bering Land Bridge National Preserve, the Alaska side of what is thought to have once been a natural land crossing from Russia to North America. Today the continents are separated by "only" 55 miles of water. Native people living on the coast of Siberia and on Alaska's northern Bering Sea coastline share similar languages, tools, clothing, and spiritual practices. The Inupiat settlements on the Seward Peninsula and offshore islands, estimated by archaeologists to be 4,500 years old, were strategically located to intercept huge migrations of marine mammals and birds.

While you are in Nome, look for the pocket-sized Shishmaref Eskimo Cookbook, with recipes collected and edited by Melvin and Karen Olanna in 1989 to benefit Shishmaref's Rural Alaska Native Vocational Arts Workshop. Included are local recipes for fresh boiled oogruk (bearded seal) intestines, fermented seal flippers, reindeer tongue soup, seal oil doughnuts, and preparing willow bark.

When Europeans first explored the Bering Sea in the 1700s, the Eskimo population numbered about 30,000. Prior to white contact, Native people living on the coast and islands traveled to the Seward Peninsula to trade with people living inland. Then gold was discovered in Nome in 1898. Within two years, more than 20,000 outsiders had arrived in Nome and scattered to the hills to find their fortunes. By 1911, more than $60 million in gold had been mined from the area's beaches, streams, and hills. The rush was mostly over by 1905, and the white population dropped to 5,000. During the gold rush and well into the 1950s, skilled Native ivory carvers and skin sewers came to Nome during the summers to sell souvenirs to the tourist trade, and many eventually moved permanently to Nome for education, health services, and employment. Most Native people, however, still rely primarily on subsistence hunting and fishing: hunting for walrus in skiffs, gathering greens and berries in the tundra, and wind-drying salmon on wooden racks on the beaches. (See the appendix for Alex Muktoyuk's memoir of subsistence hunting for walrus on King Island in the 1950s.)

The Nome countryside is lovely, particularly during the summer when the tundra—rolling hills against a backdrop of granite peaks—is emerald green and covered with wildflowers and berries. In March, Nome is the finish line for the 1,049-mile Iditarod Trail Sled Dog Race, which begins at Knik, near Anchorage, and passes through 20 checkpoints at villages between Anchorage and Nome. The annual race, with as many as 60 dog mushers, begins the first Saturday in March; 9 to 15 days later, mushers arrive in Nome. Although dog mushing was traditionally a common way for Inupiat and Yup'ik people to travel, most of the Iditarod contestants are not Native. (For many Native families practicing a subsistence lifestyle, dogs are too expensive to maintain, so today most winter travel is by snow machine.) Nome, however, celebrates the Iditarod with a full month of events in March that include Native arts and crafts shows, local sled dog races, showings of *The Reindeer Queen* (a documentary video about the owner of the largest reindeer herd in the Arctic), readings and book signings by Alaskan authors (including, increasingly, Native authors), and other events.

Reindeer were introduced into Alaska when the Rev. Sheldon Jackson, general agent of education in Alaska, imported 16 of the animals from Russia in 1891. Mary Antisarlook, who worked as a translator on Alaska's coast, and her husband accompanied Jackson to Russia. The Reindeer Queen, the first documentary to highlight the life of an Inupiat Eskimo woman, incorporates over 100 archival photographs, early motion picture footage, and the memories of elders who knew Mary, who became the owner of the largest reindeer herd in the Arctic. Available from KAKM Video, 3877 University Dr, Anchorage, AK 99508; (907)563-7070.

Getting There

Alaska Airlines, (800)426-0333, offers daily service from Anchorage and Kotzebue. Some packages include Nome, Kotzebue, and ground tours; call (800)468-2248. Flight time is 80 minutes from Anchorage. Yute Air, (888)359-9883, offers one round-trip flight daily from Anchorage. Frontier Flying Service, (907)474-0014, offers one round trip daily from Fairbanks.

Getting Around

During the summer, Bering Air, (907)443-5620, offers sightseeing flights over the Seward Peninsula's beautiful landscape, and over King and Little Diomede Islands (a 2-hour flight in a twin-engine plane to the international dateline, where you can see the Russian mainland). The airline also makes regularly scheduled stops at Seward Peninsula villages and St. Lawrence Island year-round. Cape Smythe Air Service, (907)443-2414, offers sightseeing flights to the Seward Peninsula and to the Bering Sea villages of Gambell and Savoonga on St. Lawrence Island. Olson Air Service, (907)443-2229, also offers sightseeing flights to villages. Five air taxis operate on the Seward Peninsula. Ask the Nome Convention & Visitors Bureau (see "Visitor Services") for a list.

Unlike most rural areas in Alaska, Nome has an impressive road system: several hundred miles, with three main routes. The 72-mile Nome-Teller Road travels north through rolling hills and over crystal-clear streams to the village of Teller, tucked into a protected bay. About 275 people live here year-round. The 89-mile Nome-Kougarok Road travels inland to the mountains, past Pilgrim Hot Springs, to Kougarok, near the border of Bering Land Bridge National Preserve. The 75-mile Nome-Council Road travels along the Bering Sea coastline, then swings inland to Council, on the Niukluk River (two families live here during the winter, 30 to 40 during the summer). The road is scenic, passing the Nuk fish camps along the beach and Safety Lagoon. All the other villages in the area—including Shishmaref, famous for its exceptional whalebone and ivory carvers—are accessible by air taxi. Car rentals are available in Nome (call the Nome Convention & Visitors Bureau for information).

Prior to white contact, Serpentine Hot Springs was called Iyat, an Inupiat word meaning "a site for cooking." Located in a valley surrounded by dramatic granite spires, the area was used by Eskimo shamans because it was thought to be the home of powerful spirits. After Christian missionaries entered the Seward Peninsula, Native healers continued to rely on the waters to promote good health. Today the hot springs are located in the Bering Land Bridge National Preserve (accessible only by air taxi); the public is welcome to throw down a sleeping bag in the old World War II cabin near the springs, and take a soak beneath the rustic shelter. For more information, call the preserve, (907)443-2522.

Visitor Services

- National Park Service, Bering Land Bridge National Preserve, 179 Front St, Nome, AK 99762; (907)443-2522.

- Nome Convention & Visitors Bureau, Front St, PO Box 240, Nome, AK 99762; (907)443-5535. This visitors center has printed information on virtually every aspect of Nome, including ivory carving.

KIFY Expedition Tours

Storyteller Marilyn Koezuna, a "summer baby" (born to King Island parents during their summer stay in Nome), spoke Inupiat until she entered kindergarten. She learned to gather greens from the tundra at her mother's and grandmother's side. Koezuna offers storytelling in her home as well as tours of the tundra and surrounding villages. With her husband, Hank Irelan, a non-Native who pilots the couple's boat, she also offers a tour up the Snake River and around Sledge Island.

For visitors who are interested in stories, Koezuna narrates "On Thin Ice," a show-and-tell story based on her father's harrowing tale of survival when he and a biologist were lost on Norton Sound in a severe storm with only their kayak, hunting clothes, and will to survive. Her father, Quizruna, a kayak hunter, was one of the first King Island Inupiat to use the Christian naming system of first and last names, giving his family the "last name" of Koezuna. As Marilyn Koezuna tells the story, visitors can handle her dad's hunting tools, the kayak, and the skin clothing he used to stay alive. His story saved the life of his second son when he was caught in similar circumstances. The 1½-hour-long tale provides visitors with a rare opportunity to glimpse the importance of "oral history" and to see how effective story is in passing on valuable cultural information. You'll remember this one for a long time to come.

Pilgrim Hot Springs, 60 miles from Nome by road, was used as a mission and an orphanage from the 1918 flu epidemic until 1941, housing up to 120 children. The ruins of the mission remain on the site. You can soak in a rustic hot tub (although the sulfur smell may discourage you). Ask at the Nome Convention & Visitors Bureau for directions.

Visitors may also sign up with Koezuna to escort them for several hours or days into the tundra to look for birds; gather greens such as wild celery, sour dock, and willow; visit the family's fish camp at Wooley Lagoon (directly across from King Island); and visit Native villages accessible by road.

The couple's Sledge Island tour begins in a 24-foot skiff on the pretty Snake River, where gold was first discovered in Nome. See an old steam-engine wreck, the sand spit, and the Nome turning basin before passing through a break in the jetty into Norton Sound. Pass the mouths of the Penny and Cripple Rivers, see the mountains from the Inupiat point of view (out in the water), and learn about Inupiat sea mammal hunting. Thousands of birds nest on Sledge Island; on the north shore is the village site of the Sledge Island Inupiat. Tours begin in the evening and continue through the long summer twilight, when the weather is calmest and the birds have returned to Sledge Island rookeries to nest.

KIFY Expedition Tours, PO Box 181, Nome, AK 99762; (907)443-2996. Call for details.

Inua Expedition Company of Nome

Keith and Annie Olanna Conger are both teachers in the historic Eskimo village of Brevig Mission. Keith, who has a degree in biology, has worked for Outward Bound, Vermont Bicycle Touring, and Alaska Discovery, among other outdoor programs; Annie is an Inupiat Eskimo, born and raised in the Seward Peninsula and committed to preserving Inupiat culture. Together, they bring visitors to Eskimos' summer fish camps and to reindeer corrals (and to the big Nome reindeer roundup in June). They build kayaks and teach kayaking skills to members of a local Eskimo youth group; already expert hunters and fishermen, the youth are trained to work as assistant guides. Trips, which range from kayaking to van-supported biking and road trips, are generally customized, although the company also offers two packaged tours. Trips are limited to four participants at a time.

The Pilgrim River Day Trip is a one-day kayak trip down the scenic Pilgrim River, about 14 miles of flat water through Arctic wilderness. It ends with a soak at Pilgrim Hot Springs, at the foot of the Kigluaik Mountains. The Imuruk Basin Trip is an eight-day, seven-night excursion by kayak into the Imuruk Basin. Highlights include a working reindeer corral, Alaska's only known rock painting, and numerous sites of historical and mythological significance. The trip includes kayak, gear, wet suit, and camping gear. You bring only clothes, rain gear, and rubber boots. The tour can be shorter for those with limited time.

Inua Expedition Company of Nome, PO Box 65, Brevig Mission, AK 99785; winters (907)642-4161; summers (907)443-4994. Tours offered June–Aug.

Sitnasuak Heritage Gallery

The Sitnasuak Heritage Gallery is located in a three-story, 27,000-square-foot office building on Front Street that is owned by the Sitnasuak Native Corporation. (The building also houses the offices of the Bering Land Bridge National Preserve, the U.S. Fish and Wildlife Service, and the Sitnausuak Native Corporation.) To help support the work of Native artists, the corporation sells their art and crafts in the gallery, a small room on the first floor. Look here particularly for exquisite ivory carvings from Nome, Shishmaref, and St. Lawrence Island. Bracelets, animals and figurines, and cribbage boards are carved from the fossilized tusks of walrus and woolly mammoth, whalebone, and moose horn, as well as wood. You'll also find Inupiat spirit masks made of willow and carved bone, and grass baskets from Stebbins.

Ask at the Sitnasuak Heritage Gallery whether the Native corporation has a copy of the current subsistence calendar prepared by the elders' committee. It contains great photos, anecdotes, and seasonal subsistence information.

Near the reception desk on the first floor is a showcase of pieces made by the very best carvers, many of whom have left a legacy of fine carvings in Nome. On Saturdays during the summer, the Sitnasuak corporation pays artists to demonstrate skin sewing, beadwork, and the detail work of ivory carving. Gallery buyer JoAnn

Kost is Inupiat, grew up in Nome, and is committed to providing a fair deal for both buyers and sellers. The gallery also sells T-shirts, postcards, and other souvenirs.

Sitnasuak Heritage Gallery, 179 Front St, PO Box 905, Nome, AK 99762; (907)443-2632. Open 8am—5pm Mon—Fri year-round; also open Sat in summer.

Carrie McLain Memorial Museum

The recipient of 8,000 photographs as well as 5,000 Eskimo artifacts and early Nome souvenirs (dolls and ivory carvings) made by Inupiat people living on the Seward Peninsula, this little two-room museum on Nome's waterfront is a real gem. Two of its most prized possessions are a collection of flat-bottomed birds used in the game of Tingmiujaq, from St. Lawrence Island, and chest armor made of seal ribs. Anthropologist Dorothy Jean Ray, who wrote several authoritative books on the souvenir trade in this region, identified and catalogued the majority of the collection.

The museum also has hundreds of artifacts from the gold rush era, as well as memoirs from white people who lived in Nome during the gold rush, including Carrie McLain, who documented what she saw in diaries and letters: "In the early days very few Eskimos remained in Nome during the winter months. Those who came in summer in their oomiaks with a favorable west wind were mainly from Shishmaref, Cape Prince of Wales, King and Little Diomede Islands. They pitched their tents on the beach near the mouth of the Snake River or at the upper end of the sand spit, picking berries and drying salmon to take back home, and selling their knickknacks. By fall they returned to their homes under their own power." Klondy Nelson, a contemporary of Carrie McLain, wrote, "I loved to wander the beach, watching the old men of the village carving ivory in the shelter of an upended umiak, or talking with the women as they spun reindeer sinew into thread and sewed skin garments." But some of the best comments are in Native memoirs such as Edna Wilder's book, *Once Upon an Eskimo Time: A Year of Eskimo Life Before the White Man Came as Told to Me by My Wonderful Mother Whose Eskimo Name Was Nedercook.*

Under federal law, only Native families and their corporations can own reindeer. Herds roam free over nearly 15 million acres of tundra, eating grass, sedge, flowers, and willows during the summer and foraging for lichens and "reindeer moss" in the winter. Roundups are conducted with snow machines in the winter and helicopters in the summer. About 15 active herds graze close to Nome After roundup and culling, the remaining animals are released to disperse over the tundra— a great time to view the animals from your car.

Exhibits change every summer; traveling exhibits from other museums are installed during the winter months.

Carrie McLain Memorial Museum, 200 Front St, Nome, AK 99762; (907)443-2566. Open summers daily, 10am–6pm or later; winters, Tues–Sat, 1–5pm.

More Nome Galleries

The Arctic Trading Post, across the street from the Nome Convention & Visitors Bureau, has an impressive book selection devoted to natural history and Native culture and art of the Seward Peninsula (67 Front St, Nome; (907)443-2686; open 7:30am–11pm summers, 7:30am–6:30pm winters). Owner Mary Knodel, who has been buying Native art and crafts for 22 years, carries a well-stocked inventory of ivory carvings (many made by King Island carvers living in Nome) as well as skin sewing, dolls, slippers, and hats, all made locally. At Maruskiya's of Nome, owners Marty and Patty James sell Eskimo antiquities and contemporary art and crafts made by Natives of the Seward Peninsula, St. Lawrence Island, and Bethel region, including coiled-grass baskets, dolls, skin and whalebone masks, Eskimo slippers trimmed in fur, dance fans, and other items (110 Front St, Nome; (907)443-2955; open 9am–9pm summers, noon–6pm winters). Ninety-five percent of the carvings are Native made; the shop guarantees authenticity.

Visitors are welcome at the XYZ Center, an elderly care facility in downtown Nome behind the city hall. The woodblock prints on the walls are by Inupiat artist Bernard Katexac.

OUTSIDE
ALASKA

OUTSIDE ALASKA

Most of the Alaska Native art and artifacts collected at the turn of the century are housed in museums located outside Alaska. Some of the world's largest collections are in the museums of the Smithsonian Institution in Washington, D.C., and the Museum of Anthropology and Ethnography in Leningrad. Other institutions around the world have purchased or been recipients of large, specific collections. The Field Museum of Natural History in Chicago, for example, has 1,900 Tlingit items collected in 1903 from Southeast Alaska, and 1,400 Inupiat Eskimo items collected from the Kotzebue Sound and Port Clarence region. Large museums also sponsored collections of Alaska Native art, sending professional anthropologists or knowledgeable collectors to specific areas in search of the objects that best represented the culture. Objects collected in this way are usually labeled and dated.

Some museum collections were acquired from explorers, missionaries, traders, medical professionals, educators, or others who worked closely with Alaska Natives. An example is this century's Paul Jensen, an education professor who worked with Inupiat school children from the 1940s through the 1970s. His private collection of mid-20th-century items is housed in its own small museum, the Jensen Arctic Museum, on the Western Oregon

University campus in Monmouth. Many scholars and collectors have also donated their private collections to museums. Dorothy Jean Ray, for example, an anthropologist who pioneered studies about the effects of commercial demand on traditional Inupiat, Yup'ik, and Aleut art, gave a large portion of her collection of "market art" to the University of Alaska at Fairbanks. Some museums sponsor shows and purchase contemporary fine art made by Alaska Natives, much of which incorporates traditional materials and techniques.

Recognizing the lucrative market for Alaska souvenirs after the Alaska Purchase in 1867, the Alaska Commercial Company, with its trading posts stationed in the most remote areas of Alaska, fed the demand for souvenir ivory carving and other "market art" produced by Alaska Natives. The heyday of souvenir art was during the Alaska gold rush, which brought thousands of miners to Alaska.

This chapter lists museums throughout the world with significant Alaska Native collections. Because Seattle has been a hub for Alaska-bound travelers since the gold rush days, Northwest museums and galleries are discussed in detail. Not listed in the chapter, but of considerable significance, are the number of places worldwide where contemporary Alaska Native art is commissioned, displayed, and sold. As you become familiar with the names of contemporary Alaska Native artists, you'll begin to recognize their work in sometimes-surprising places such as Santa Fe, New York City, and Tokyo.

Seattle and Tacoma

Seattle, located at the southern end of the Inside Passage waterway, which connects Washington State to Southeast Alaska, has a long history as a staging and supply stop for Alaska-bound travelers. In the 1840s, the Hudson's Bay Company supplied meat and grain to Alaska fur-trading posts from its Puget Sound Agricultural Company, located near Tacoma. When gold was first discovered in Alaska in 1858, on the upper Stikine River near Wrangell, miners shipped out from San Francisco. But by the time the big strikes were made—in Juneau in 1880, Nome in 1889, and especially the Klondike in 1896—Seattle had put its public relations mechanism to work, enticing thousands of gold seekers to buy their supplies and ship out of Seattle. Rapid new rail service from the Midwest through the mountains to Seattle, along with fast steam-powered ships going north to Alaska from Seattle's waterfront, sealed the deal. Seattle boomed; in fact, more fortunes were made by merchants and outfitters than by the gold miners themselves.

The market for Alaska Native art and craft also boomed. Souvenir ivory carvings, scrimshaw and cribbage boards, and other trinkets for the masses were in high demand. Professional collectors, missionaries, anthropologists, traders, trappers, and thieves also did a brisk business of supplying the public with Alaska Native art and artifacts—the basis of many of today's finest museum collections of Native art.

There's still a big connection between Seattle and Alaska. Most of the "Alaska fishing fleet" is berthed in Seattle, and the city continues to provide Alaska with supplies—including food, lumber, hardware, and machinery—via barge and air freight. More than 8,000 Alaska Natives live and work in Seattle. And Alaska Native art is exhibited in the city's public art collection, in museums, and in several major Seattle galleries.

Burke Museum of Natural History and Culture

Inupiat winter whale ceremonies, Arctic hunting, and community sharing of whale meat are topics explored in just one of the 18 exhibits in the Burke Museum of Natural History and Culture's spectacular new Pacific Voices exhibit, drawn from its extensive collection of over 3 million items. Of these, more than 6,500 items have been collected from Arctic Alaska. Alaska Natives participated in the assembly of Pacific Voices, which is dedicated to cultures of the Pacific Rim.

The University of Washington Press has published many scholarly works about Alaska and Northwest Coast art, including six books by anthropologist Dorothy Jean Ray, whose Aleut and Eskimo Art *is a classic study of the Alaska Native souvenir trade and "market" art. The press has also published books by Ann Fienup-Riordan, including the extraordinary* The Living Tradition of Yup'ik Masks *and the ever-popular* The Wolf and the Raven: Totem Poles of Southeastern Alaska. *For a catalog of titles, call (800)441-4115.*

Recent acquisitions by the museum include a bronze and glass sculpture, *Last Chance,* by Larry Ahvakana (Inupiat), and a sealskin painting by Florence Malewotkuk (Yup'ik). The museum also has outstanding Yup'ik masks collected at the turn of the century (including the mask on the cover of this book, so large that it takes two men to hold it up, which is from Goodnews Bay on Alaska's west coast). The museum's store carries a large selection of books on Alaska Native art and culture and Alaska natural history. You might also keep an eye out for original pieces, such as masks, that have been made by Alaska Natives; sold through the store, most are purchased as soon as they are displayed.

Burke Museum of Natural History and Culture, University of Washington, DC-10, Seattle, WA 98195; (206)543-5590; Web site: http://www.washington.edu/burkemuseum. On the northwestern corner of the campus, at NE 45th St and 17th Ave; park on campus. Admission $5.50. Open daily, 10am–5pm. Gift shop and cafe.

Seattle Art Museum

The Native American exhibits at the Seattle Art Museum are based on the collection of John H. Hauberg, who spent four decades at the turn of the century collecting masks, sculpture, textiles, and household objects in an area extending from Southeast Alaska to the northern tip of Washington State. Included from Southeast Alaska's Tlingit and Haida cultures are Chilkat and button blankets; appliquéd, beaded, and woven shirts; carved headpieces inset with abalone shell; and masks. The most spectacular Alaskan piece in the collection is an original large house screen, carved about 1820, from the Frog clan house in the village of Klukwan (see "Old Village Sites" in the Haines section of the Southeast Alaska chapter), obtained by the museum in 1979. Alaskan objects are interspersed with a wealth of art from British Columbia tribes, and are carefully labeled. You can hear Tlingit oratory and songs in an audio installation in the Native American gallery.

The Spirit Within: Northwest Coast Native Art from the John H. Hauberg Collection is a 304-page volume with full-color photos and several essays, including one by Tlingit poet and writer Nora Dauenhauer, available in the museum gift shop and bookstores nationwide.

Seattle Art Museum, 100 University St, Seattle, WA 98122; (206)654-3100. Downtown between 1st and 2nd Aves, 2 blocks south of Pike Place Market. Admission $6 adults. Gift shop, cafe, library. Open Tues–Sun.

Seattle Art Galleries

Contemporary Alaska Native artwork is permanently installed at Daybreak Star Indian Cultural Center, located in Discovery Park (W Government Way at 36th Ave, Seattle; (206)285-4425). On the center's west wall is a large Tlingit house screen by artist Nathan Jackson. Entitled *Man and the Killer Whales*, it is made from Western red cedar boards, doweled together and hand-adzed on the unpainted areas. In the lounge area are six cedar panels, *Ancestor Spirit Boards*, by John Hoover (Aleut). Each panel is carved, hand-adzed, and polychromed in salmon, green, and white, and represents a single totem figure: Wolf, Eagle, Raven, Killer Whale, Salmon, or Bear. The center also hosts dance presentations by Alaska Native traditional dance groups whose members live in the Seattle area. Daybreak Star's Sacred Circle Gallery of American Indian Art sponsors one-person shows of contemporary artists such as Chilkat weaver Anna Brown-Ehlers (Tlingit) and multimedia artist Larry Ahvakana (Inupiat), as well as group shows.

Several other Seattle galleries specialize in contemporary and traditional Alaska Native art.

Hands of Creation (Pier 70, at the north end of Seattle's waterfront; (206)448-0610) is an artists' cooperative gallery with adjoining studio space. More than 50 artists living in the Northwest, including many Alaska Natives, show their work here. It's best to call for an appointment before visiting.

The Legacy (1003 1st Ave, Seattle; (206)624-6350) carries both historic and contemporary Alaska Native work, including that of totem carver David Boxley (Tsimshian, from Metlakatla), carvers Richard and Michael Beasley of Juneau, and mask maker Wayne Price of Haines. They also buy and sell Alaskan Eskimo antiquities from individual collections; many of these items came from schoolteachers and others working in Alaska between 1900 and 1930. Watch for special exhibits throughout the year.

The Snow Goose Gallery of Indian and Eskimo Art (8806 Roosevelt Way NE, Seattle; (206)523-6223) carries the work of more than 200 Native artists, many of them Arctic carvers of ivory, whalebone, jade, and soapstone.

The Stonington Gallery (2030 1st Ave, Seattle; (206)443-1108) features the work of contemporary Alaska Native artists such as painters Thomas Stream and Alvin Amason and carver John Hoover, all Aleut. They also carry the work of Inupiat whalebone carvers Melvin and Richard Olanna, of Shishmaref; John Sinnok; Tony

Weyiouanna (and other family members); reindeer herder Victor Ongtowasruk; and King Islander Sylvester Iyek.

Well-known Alaska Native artists with studios in the Seattle area include sculptors Larry Ahvakana (Inupiat) and John Hoover (Aleut); painter Thomas Stream (Aleut); totem and mask carver David Boxley (Tsimshian); glass blower Preston Singletary (Tlingit); mask maker Jerry Laktonen (Alutiiq); Chilkat and Ravenstail blanket weaver Evelyn Vanderhoop (Haida); and basket weaver Lisa Telford (Haida).

Two hours from Seattle, in Port Townsend, two galleries specialize in Indian and Eskimo art: Ancestral Spirits and North by Northwest, both on Water Street downtown.

Tillicum Village

Boats leave daily from Piers 55 and 56 in Seattle for lunch and dinner theater at Tillicum Village, a longhouse-style performance center on the northern point of Blake Island in Puget Sound. Tillicum Village was the brainstorm of a chef and Boy Scout leader who was looking for a way to combine traditionally prepared salmon and Indian crafts with Boy Scout "Indian" dancing. This dancing was all the rage in the 1950s and 1960s, when mostly non–Native Boy Scouts competed nationally for dance titles. (See "Chilkat Dancers" in the Haines section of the Southeast Alaska chapter.) Although Blake Island is a traditional fish camp of the Suquamish Indians, a Puget Sound Salish tribe, Tillicum Village presents a Southeast Alaska/British Columbia "Raven Stealing Daylight" creation story, among other tales.

The boat ride to Blake Island from Seattle's waterfront takes about 30 minutes. Native people, costumed in traditional blue and red wool button blanket capes and carved headpieces worn by Southeast Alaska and British Columbia tribes, greet passengers with cups of steaming clam broth on the walkway to the longhouse. Inside, diners line up at the buffet for an all-you-can-eat salmon dinner. The salmon is cooked in the traditional way, on alder skewers in front of open fire pits. After everyone is seated, Dance on the Wind, a choreographed stage performance showcasing legends, masked dancing, and song, begins with a drumbeat.

Over the years. Tillicum Village has become more authentically Native. Today, the attraction hires Native staff to greet visitors, cook, and perform in the stage show. At the gift shop in the longhouse, check with the store clerks to confirm the authenticity of items.

Tillicum Village & Tours Inc., 2200 6th Ave, Suite 804, Seattle, WA 98121; (206)443-1244. Call for reservations and brochures. Ticket booths are on the Seattle waterfront between Piers 55 and 56. Boats leave twice a day during most months; tours are 4 hours long.

Paramount Hotel

The Paramount Hotel, one of Seattle's newest, is owned by Tanadgusix (TDX) Corporation, the Native village corporation of St. Paul Island in the Pribilof Islands. TDX shareholders are Aleut (see the Pribilof Islands section of the Southwest Alaska chapter). Although the 11-story boutique hotel's exterior resembles that of a small European hotel of the last century, the Paramount is located in the heart of Seattle's downtown: 2 blocks from Westlake Center, Nordstrom, the Paramount Theatre, and Niketown and 1 block from the Washington State Convention and Trade Center. It seems only appropriate, given the location of the Pribilof Islands in the Bering Sea—midway between Asia and the North American continent—that the hotel's first-floor restaurant is the Blowfish Asian Cafe, specializing in pan-Asian cuisine (and, thankfully for hotel guests, American breakfasts).

Paramount Hotel, 724 Pine St, Seattle, WA 98101; (800)426-0670 or (206)292-9500. Guest rooms feature king- and queen-size beds, two telephones with data port and voice mail, a separate work area, in-room coffeemakers, hair dryers, an iron and ironing board, private bar, and a state-of-the-art movie and game system. Two Grand Suites have oversize whirlpool tubs and parlors with views of the city or the Space Needle. Barrier-free guest rooms are available. Meeting space, fitness center, covered valet parking. The hotel is managed by WestCoast Hotels. Rooms $180–$219 per night; Grand Suite from $395. Guests receive 500 Alaska Airlines miles per stay. Major credit cards accepted.

Oregon

Jensen Arctic Museum

The Jensen Arctic Museum at Western Oregon University in Monmouth has one of the largest collections of objects from Arctic Alaska in the United States. What's it doing in this little Oregon town? Dr. Paul Jensen was born and educated in Denmark. Eskimo schoolmates from Greenland sparked his interest in the Arctic at an early age. As a university professor at what was then called Western Oregon College, he taught bilingual education in Inupiat and Yup'ik villages in Alaska in the 1950s and 1960s, collecting more than 3,000 objects.

This collection eventually became the foundation of the Jensen Arctic Museum, which was established after discussion with Alaska Native elders in the 1970s. More than 70 donors, many of whom worked in Native villages, contributed items ranging from children's parkas to exquisite ivory carvings from the early 1900s. On display is a 27-foot umiak, covered with walrus hide and filled with everything needed for whale hunting, that Jensen and his St. Lawrence Island (Siberian Yup'ik) friends used for a trip around the island; it was flown to Oregon by the Alaska Air National Guard. Also impressive is a 12-foot wood-frame kayak from Kotzebue, made for and used by a missionary family in the 1950s. Unique articles of clothing include a seal intestine parka and woven-grass socks, all worn on a trip around Kodiak Island in the spring of 1900, and a cormorant skin parka and salmon skin mukluks from St. Lawrence Island. There is also a large ethnographic collection of tools, toys and cooking utensils, dolls and baskets, and large animal mounts: polar bear, musk ox, caribou, and wolves.

The collection is housed in a 1930 bungalow that's been enlarged with a large exhibit gallery and smaller outbuildings. A permanent exhibit displays modes of transportation in the Arctic: skin boats, snowshoes, dogsleds, and even an old ice crampon carved from walrus ivory.

The museum hosts shows of contemporary and traditional Alaska Native art all year, along with an annual exhibit of masterworks from mid-June through August. The permanent collection includes ink drawings on sealskin from the 1930s by Florence Nupak and Ahgupuk, as well as contemporary prints and drawings by Alaska Native artists. Art Oomittuk and Larry Ahvakana, both Inupiat, are museum board members.

Jensen Arctic Museum, 590 W Church St, Monmouth, OR 97361; (503)838-8468; e-mail: macem@wou.ed; Web site: www.edu/offices/advancement/jensen/jensen.html. Monmouth is about an hour south of Portland, off Interstate 5. Free; tours available on request. Open Wed–Sat 10am–4pm.

Indian Art Northwest

You can meet Alaska Native artists and buy their work in person at Indian Art Northwest, a huge four-day festival celebrating Native American traditional and contemporary art, held every Memorial Day weekend in Portland. The festival includes Tlingit, Tsimshian, and Inupiat dance and drumming performances (dancers wear traditional regalia) throughout the four days, contemporary films and music, and a juried art show and sale showcasing the work of more than 400 Native American artists.

On Saturday and Sunday during the festival, artists sell their work from tented booths in Portland's historic Park Blocks, adjacent to the Portland Art Museum and the Oregon History Center. The event includes a collectors' seminar on how to determine the quality and value of Native art, followed by a preview of award-winning work, at which collectors may make purchases prior to the public show and sale.

The pedestrian-friendly city of Portland gears up for the estimated 50,000 visitors with walking maps that help you locate participating art galleries and shops, bookstores, the monumental sculpture exhibit in Pioneer Courthouse Square, and hotels offering special rates during the festival.

Indian Art Northwest, 911 NE 11th Ave, Portland, OR 97232; (503)230-7005; Web site: www.columbian.com/indianartnw.

Santa Fe

Using traditional art as a springboard for personal creativity, the Institute of American Indian Arts in Santa Fe, New Mexico, has tutored at least three generations of Native American and Alaska Native artists. Some of Alaska's best artists are graduates of the school—and several have made their homes and studios in Santa Fe. Among them are metal and stone sculptor Bill Prokopiof (2200 W Alameda, Santa Fe, NM 87501; (505)982-9361) and fine-arts jeweler Denise Wallace. Wallace holds an open house each year during the Santa Fe Indian Art Market and throughout the year represents Alaska Native art at her Santa Fe showroom (DW Studio, 815 Early St, Suite A, Santa Fe, NM 87501).

Simon Paneak produced more than 97 drawings—with text, annotated pictures, and maps; in pen and ink and crayon—illustrating Nunamiut old ways of traveling, hunting, fishing, and building houses, as well as traditional utensils, hunting materials, and village life. He drew the illustrations for Dr. Jack Campbell in the 1960s while traveling with the anthropologist while he was doing field research in the Arctic. The collection is housed in the Maxwell Museum of Anthropology on the University of New Mexico campus in Albuquerque, (505)277-4404.

Other Cities

Most of the artifacts and art of Alaska Natives collected at the turn of the century are housed in museums located outside of Alaska. The following museums have significant collections of Alaska Native art and artifacts:

United States

- Heard Museum, Phoenix, Arizona
- Phoebe & Hearst Museum of Anthropology, Berkeley, California
- Robert H. Lowie Museum of Anthropology, Berkeley, California
- San Diego Museum of Man, San Diego, California

- Field Museum of Natural History, Chicago, Illinois
- William Hammond Mathers Museum, Bloomington, Indiana
- Eiteljorg Museum of American Indians and Western Art, Indianapolis, Indiana
- Peabody Museum of Archaeology and Ethnology, Cambridge, Massachusetts
- Institute of American Indian Arts, Santa Fe, New Mexico
- National Museum of the American Indian, New York
- American Museum of Natural History, New York
- New York Metropolitan Museum of Art, New York
- University of Oregon Museum of Natural History, Eugene, Oregon
- Moravian Historical Society, Nazareth, Pennsylvania
- National Museum of the American Indian, Smithsonian Institution, Washington, D.C.

Canada

- Glenbow Museum, Calgary, Alberta
- Manitoba Museum of Man and Nature, Winnipeg, Manitoba
- Agnes Etherington Art Centre, Queen's University, Kingston, Ontario
- Canadian Museum of Civilization, Ottawa, Ontario
- Canadian Museum of Civilization, Quebec, Quebec

Europe

- Museum of Mankind, Vienna, Austria
- National Museum of Denmark, Copenhagen, Denmark
- British Museum, Museum of Mankind, London, England
- Museum für Völkerkunde, Berlin, Germany
- Ubersee Museum, Bremen, Germany
- Staatliche Museum für Völkerkunde, Dresden, Germany
- Museum of Anthropology and Ethnography, Leningrad, Russia
- Academy of Sciences, Moscow, Russia

APPENDICES

Buying Authentic Native Art: Look for the Silver Hand

A unique artistic heritage is reflected in Alaska Native art—from the Yup'ik coil baskets woven of wild grasses, to the Tlingit totem poles carved from towering cedar trees, to the intricate glass-bead embroidery of the Athabascans, adapted from the decoration of ceremonial regalia with dyed porcupine quills, elk teeth, and beads made of bone.

For those of you who want more than just an Alaskan souvenir—who want to take home Native art to remind you of the land and the people you met—it's important to make sure the item is authentic. In Alaska, authentic Native work is marked with a tag bearing the "Silver Hand" trademark. The Alaska State Council on the Arts, (888)278-7424 or (907)269-6610, maintains a registry of approved artists and agents licensed to apply the Silver Hand to authentic work. Only Alaska Natives can legally market work as Alaska Native–made.

> *In Alaska, authentic work is marked with a tag bearing the Silver Hand trademark. If you're still not sure whether the item is authentic, call the Alaska State Council on the Arts, (888)278-7424 or (907)269-6610, which maintains a registry of approved artists and agents licensed to apply the Silver Hand to authentic work.*

And Alaska Native traditional and village corporations, like any government or country, decide who their citizens are.

Don't be fooled by works that simply look "Native," are called "Native-style" or "in the tradition of," or that are marked with phrases describing the artist as having Native "heritage." Do not be confused by labels that say an item is "Native Alaskan" (which means only that it was made by someone who was born in Alaska). These descriptions are often used to get around the federal Indian Arts and Crafts Act, enacted by Congress to protect the buyer from knockoffs. The law imposes stiff fines upon those caught selling or promoting non-Native products as Native-made.

No one can blame non-Native artists who are drawn to Native images and art—the bold forms and intricate designs would capture any artist's imagination. In fact, some non-Natives have taught Natives traditional skills. However, these works, no matter how good, are only replicas of the real thing. Non-Indian artists with integrity do not claim that their work is authentically Native.

Native artists draw inspiration from a continuity of culture. Even the most modern art is often guided by custom and culture. An Eagle clan Tlingit artist would not carve the story of the Raven clan without special permission. A basket maker would not weave another family's designs without their approval.

The ability to determine the quality of art comes with time and observation. At first, all totems and masks may look the same. After a while, differences among various artists' works and styles become more evident. Some galleries provide free printed materials that explain the art or discuss the artists and motifs. Most galleries can also recommend books for those who want to learn more.

When buying a piece of art from a gallery or a vendor, ask for the name of the artist and his or her tribal affiliation. Good gallery owners know this information or can find out. The best mark each piece with the name of the artist and tribal affiliation. If the sellers don't know, there's a chance it's not Native-made. If they say it was made by Natives, that's not good enough. (When we admired a rug with a Tlingit motif and questioned its authenticity, we were told it was made by Natives. When we pointed out that its label said it was made in Nepal, the gallery owner shrugged and said, "Well, it was made by Nepal natives.") Ask for information in writing; many shops provide certificates of authenticity, even for the smallest items. And, of course, look for the Silver Hand trademark.

A caution for Canadians: Alaska Native art and crafts are sometimes made of ivory, bone, or fur that only Natives can legally harvest and use. Most gift shops will mail these items to your home so you need not risk having them confiscated at the border due to endangered species regulations.

If you are going to invest in a major piece of art, buy a few books or magazines to learn what to look for. *Native Peoples, Indian Artist,* and *American Indian Art* magazines have good articles on Native arts and cultures. Another way to buy art is from the artists themselves—at art markets or special events such as the biennial Celebration in Juneau, a week-long gathering of Tlingit, Haida, and Tsimshian Natives (see Southeast Alaska chapter). Don't be disquieted if the artist is reserved. Artists are not always accustomed to selling their work, and feel more comfortable discussing how a piece is made or how they learned their craft.

To learn more about the ivory carvings and other items made and sold in Nome for the tourist trade during the summers in the 1950s, see Eskimo Art: Tradition and Innovation in North Alaska, by Dorothy Jean Ray (University of Washington Press, 1977).

Don't be surprised by innovation and contemporary works. Remember that culture is a living thing. Many Alaska Natives have acquired fine arts degrees from universities throughout the United States or at the Institute of American Indian Art in Santa Fe. Keep in mind that there's no such thing as "Alaska Native art"—only art in traditional or contemporary forms that is produced by an Alaska Native artist.

Alaska Native Claims Settlement Act and Native Corporations

—By Patricia J. Petrivelli

The Alaska Native Claims Settlement Act (ANCSA) was passed by Congress on December 18, 1971. The purpose of the law was to settle the 100-year-old question of aboriginal land rights of Alaska Natives. When Alaska was "purchased" from Russia in 1867, the land conveyed to the United States was the acreage the Russians had claimed around their outposts, as well as the "right to claim territory."

The Russians had recognized Alaska Natives' right to occupy and use land, and this right was thought to have been ensured through provisions in the treaty governing the Alaska Purchase, which required the U.S. government to negotiate with Alaska Natives as it had with other U.S. aboriginal tribes in cases where the government recognized the tribes' title to the land. In question were 375 million acres of land in the new Alaska Territory. In fact, these land issues were not resolved until 1971, over 100 years later; meanwhile, Alaska Natives watched their lands being homesteaded, mined, and drilled, and their resources taken, with no legal recourse. The impetus for the settlement of the land was the discovery of rich oil deposits on Alaska's Arctic Slope and the need to build the trans-Alaska oil pipeline through disputed lands.

Before passing ANCSA, Congress held hearings to determine the amount of land necessary for Alaska Natives to continue their subsistence way of life, the appropriate vehicle to manage these lands, and the amount of money that needed to be awarded for settlement of the acreage retained by the state and federal government.

Under ANCSA, the titles to 44 million acres, spread throughout the state, were issued to Alaska Natives. A payment of close to a billion dollars was made to compensate for the loss of the remaining 331 million acres. The act created 13 regional corporations and more than 230 village corporations to receive the federal money and manage the land on behalf of the new Alaska Native corporation shareholders.

After determining that corporations would be the right entities to manage the land and the money, Congress made some modifications to this structure. Ownership of stock was restricted to Alaska Natives. A complicated balance of surface and subsurface rights was set up to allow for the sharing of resources among the corporation and shareholders. Village corporations were given ownership of the surface rights to the land surrounding their villages based on their population. A minimum of 25 individuals in a village was necessary to claim land and incorporate. Over 200 village corporations were originally recognized. Ownership of the subsurface rights to these lands was given to 12 of the regional corporations; the 13th corporation, representing Native Alaskans living outside the state, was awarded cash. The regional corporations were also allowed to select a certain number of acres based on enrollment in the region and to select available lands relating to cemeteries and historical sites.

In addition to the 13 regional corporations, today there are 79 for-profit village corporations and 138 nonprofit, traditional village councils. The village corporations invest money in various economic development enterprises, from timber cutting and road construction to office buildings and hotels, while the village councils handle social services and other matters.

The formation of private corporations to handle the land claims settlement was perceived by Congress as a social experiment to encourage economic development in Alaska and to benefit Alaska Natives. To qualify for enrollment in an ANCSA corporation, an individual must have been born on or before December 18, 1971, be a U.S. citizen, and possess at least one-quarter Alaska Native blood. While the ANCSA corporations are like private corporations in most aspects, ownership of the corporations is wholly in Native hands because sale of the stock to those who do not meet the Native requirement has not been permitted.

Following are the 13 regional corporations formed under the act.

- Ahtna Inc., PO Box 649, Glennallen, AK 99588; (907)822-3476; fax (907)822-3495. Represents Athabascan shareholders of the Copper River region.

- Aleut Corporation, 4000 Old Seward Hwy, Suite 300, Anchorage, AK 99503; (907)561-4300. Represents Aleuts of the Aleutian Chain.

- Arctic Slope Regional Corporation, PO Box 129, Barrow, AK 99723; (907)852-8633; fax (907)852-5733. Represents Inupiat shareholders of the Arctic region.

- Bering Straits Native Corporation, PO Box 1008, Nome, AK 99762; (907)443-5252. Represents Inupiat shareholders of the Nome, King Island, and St. Lawrence Island region.

- Bristol Bay Native Corporation, PO Box 3310, Dillingham, AK 99576; (907)842-5257; fax (907)842-3904. Represents Yup'ik, Aleut, and Athabascan shareholders of Southwest Alaska and the Alaska Peninsula.

- Calista Corporation, 601 W 5th St, Suite 200, Anchorage, AK 99501; (907)279-5516; fax (907)272-5060. Represents Yup'ik shareholders of the Kuskokwim and Yukon Delta region.

- Chugach Alaska Corporation, 560 E 34th Ave, Suite 200, Anchorage, AK 99503; (907)563-8866; fax (907)563-8402. Represents Aleut and Alutiiq shareholders of the Kenai Peninsula and Prince William Sound.

- Cook Inlet Region Inc., PO Box 93330, Anchorage, AK 99509; (907)274-8638; fax (907)279-8836. Represents Natives from all over Alaska who live in the Anchorage municipality.

- Doyon Ltd., Doyon Building, 201 1st Ave, Fairbanks, AK 99701; (907)452-4755; fax (907)456-6785. Represents Athabascan shareholders of Interior Alaska.

- Koniag Inc., 4300 B St, Suite 407, Anchorage, AK 99503; (907)561-2668; fax (907)562-5258. Represents shareholders of the Kodiak archipelago.

- NANA Corporation, 1001 E Benson Blvd, Anchorage, AK 99508; (907)265-4100; fax (907)265-4311. Represents Inupiat shareholders of the Kotzebue region.

- Sealaska Corporation, One Sealaska Plaza, Suite 400; Juneau, AK 99801; (907)586-1512; fax (907)586-9214. Represents Tlingit and Haida shareholders of Southeast Alaska.

- The Thirteenth Regional Corporation, 631 Strander Blvd, Suite B, Seattle, WA 98188; (206)575-6229. Represents 5,000 Alaska Native shareholders who live outside of Alaska—in the United States, Canada, and foreign countries.

For a complete, current list of regional and village corporations and traditional village councils, contact the Bureau of Indian Affairs, Juneau Area Office, PO Box 25520, Juneau, AK 99802-5520; (800)645-8397 or (907)586-7177. The free 44-page booklet "Mailing List of Tribal Entities Served by the Alaska Bureau of Indian Affairs" lists the names, addresses, and telephone numbers of the regional corporations, village corporations, and traditional and IRA tribes.

The Complex Issue of Subsistence Hunting, Fishing, and Gathering

—By Patricia J. Petrivelli

Subsistence—hunting, fishing, and gathering wild plants—has been a way of life for Alaska Natives for centuries, and subsistence practices continue today. Various studies have documented that in Alaska villages, the inhabitants depend upon subsistence resources for from 10 percent to as much as 90 percent of their nutritional intake. For many of these villagers, subsistence is necessary for their physical well-being; for the majority of Alaska Natives throughout the state, subsistence is necessary for their cultural and spiritual well-being.

The customary and traditional use of subsistence resources by Alaska Natives is based on skills and tools developed thousands of years ago. But the issue of subsistence is complicated, and marked by conflict. The term is used to describe several different things: a way of life, an economic system, and a regulatory category for the allocation of renewable resources and land uses. Say the word "subsistence" in Alaska, and you can expect to encounter the sort of heated emotions that are aroused whenever access to resources is limited to a specific use by particular users, be they Native or non-Native.

Before contact with the Russians in the early 1700s, Alaska Natives were completely dependent on resources that were available locally or through trade. The necessities of life were obtained in defined territories for each village and through defined rules of conduct for the harvesting of animals and plants. The following statements are from Paul Williams, a Gwich'in Athabascan currently living in Beaver, Alaska. The statements were gathered during research for an exhibit on moose and the Athabascan cultures:

"Here in the Interior, the Athabascan people used the moose quite extensively. Their life depended on it in the early days. . . . They had really stringent laws that people had to follow. The law according to what you can't take during each season, like in summer time or fall time. You had to get permission from the council or the chief or the elders in order to go out and get a moose a certain time of the year. All these are tribal laws and moose is part of it: How to butcher the moose. How they sing songs before they hunt. And after they kill, who gets to eat it and in which manner. All that had laws. But now you could go out and get any moose any time. I know that is not right. We are breaking our own laws. We are not really going back to our Native way."

The laws in Native culture governing the indigenous harvest of resources were undermined by contact with non-Natives. The first wave of Russians to visit Alaska after 1741, the *promyshlenniki* (fur traders) came in search of fur-bearing animals. The commercialization of trapping and the temptation of iron and beads overrode the indigenous hunting laws that Alaska Natives had followed for thousands of years. New practices by the Russians resulted in the near extinction of sea otters and the endangerment of other species.

By 1799, the Russian American Company had been formed. This company was granted a monopoly by the Russian monarchy for the harvesting of resources and was given government-like authority to regulate the use of resources by others. Recognizing the dependency of Alaska Natives on subsistence resources and the necessity of sustaining this economy, the company regulated and restricted the settlement of Russians in Alaska.

After the Russians left in 1867, Alaska went through another period of unrestricted access to the resources, this time by Americans. Again sea otters came close to extinction—so close that regulators were forced to end the harvest in 1910. Other species, such as whales, were also threatened by overhunting. Early in this century, the salmon population was nearly wiped out by the canneries, which placed fish traps at the mouths of creeks, preventing salmon from reaching their spawning grounds. As a result of these near-extinctions, many Alaskans believe that sensible management of fish and game resources in the American period did not occur until statehood.

The most significant action affecting subsistence harvests after statehood was the Alaska Native Claims Settlement Act (ANCSA), passed by the U.S. Congress on December 18, 1971. Before passage of ANCSA, Congress held extensive hearings and debated the amount of land to be left in Native title as "private" land. Throughout the hearings, witnesses raised the point that the subsistence resources on which Alaska Natives depended were not limited to a small amount of acreage such as a typical homestead site. Instead, because the caribou, salmon, and other resources migrate, Alaska Natives had migrated with them until the middle of this century. The refrain of Alaska Natives throughout these hearings was "Take Our Land— Take Our Life."

In the end, ANCSA legislation did extinguish aboriginal claims to fish and game. However, the U.S. Congress also chose to recognize the importance of protecting subsistence use of resources on public lands:

"In order to fulfill the policies and purposes of the Alaska Native Claims Settlement Act and as a matter of equity, it is necessary for the Congress to invoke its constitutional authority under the property clause and the commerce clause to protect and provide the opportunity for continued subsistence uses on the public lands by Native and non-Native rural residents.

"The Congress finds and declares that . . . the continuation of the opportunity for subsistence uses by rural residents of Alaska, including both Natives and non-Natives on the public lands and by Alaska Natives on Native lands is essential to Native physical, economic, traditional and cultural existence and to non-Natives physical, economic, traditional, and social existence." (From *Village Journey, The Report of the Alaska Native Review Commission,* by Thomas R. Berger. New York: Hill and Wang, 1985.)

As a follow-up to the ANCSA, in 1980 the U.S. Congress passed the Alaska National Interest Lands Conservation Act (ANILCA). In the hearings in the late 70s that led up to this legislation, Congress dealt with the significance of subsistence resources to Alaska Natives and tried to accommodate those uses. But what emerged from the hearings was a clash between the federal government and the state of Alaska. In the past, in legislation and treaties with other countries, the U.S. Congress had recognized the legitimacy of "Alaska Natives only" use of resources and had provided for Native use of whales and sea mammals. But the state of Alaska argued that the state constitution calls for equal access for all users of fish and game resources (except, of course, for the Limited Entry Law for salmon commercial fishing), so the state should continue to regulate hunting and fishing on all lands in Alaska—private and public, state and federal.

Throughout the ANILCA hearings, the state of Alaska asked Congress for conditions to be attached to the federal law. The state wanted the priority for subsistence use to be granted as a preference for "rural" users, not for Native users. So the U.S. Congress used language in ANILCA that noted the dependence of Natives *and* non-Natives, and called for a "rural" subsistence priority on federal lands.

The state of Alaska passed a subsistence priority in 1978. However, the subsistence priority in the state's law was based on customary and traditional use, dependence, and lack of alternative resources only, not on rural residency—so that any Alaskan resident, Native or non-Native, could potentially qualify as a subsistence user on state lands.

In 1981, this priority was used to restore the harvesting of king salmon by the Denaina in Tyonek. In 1982, sport hunting and fishing groups spearheaded an effort to repeal the law by a statewide initiative. The initiative failed, with the voters in Alaska overwhelmingly supporting the priority for subsistence use of fish and game resources.

In 1986, the Alaska State legislature amended the law to grant the priority to rural residents only, in order to comply with the federal law. But in 1989, the Alaska Supreme Court overturned this change and ruled that the rural provision was not permis-sible under the Alaska constitution. This meant that once again every Alaskan resident could qualify as a subsistence user on state lands. It also resulted in the federal government stepping in to take over management of game resources on federal lands. (Currently, the federal government is threatening to take over management of fish resources also.)

> It is important to understand that subsistence is more that a matter of protein intake for Native people. The closest corollary is the concept of "kosher" in Jewish society—the concept that an item was obtained and prepared according to certain rules and procedures. Alaska Natives have customary ways of obtaining fish and game, preparing it for consumption, and using parts of it for clothing or tools. Just as in Orthodox Jewish society certain procedures must be followed for killing and butchering an animal, there are customary Alaska Native ways of killing and butchering an animal.

What are the differences between management by the federal government and management by the state? Both systems are based on the principle of sustained yield, a principle under which the managers look at the health and abundance of the resource to determine the allowable numbers that can be harvested without jeopardizing the health of the resource. This seems as though it should be simple and straightforward. The rub comes after the numbers of allowable harvest are determined: deciding who will harvest those resources and when. Although the user groups are in basically five categories—commercial, sport, subsistence, personal consumption, and viewing (nonconsumptive)—the federal government provides for a stronger Alaska Native/rural voice in management decisions, much to the ire of other users. The federal management system has set up regional subsistence councils and a statewide subsistence board. The function of this network is to ensure that subsistence use is recognized and the priority for the use in regulatory decisions is respected.

After the federal government threatened to take over management of fish resources, Alaska governor Tony Knowles set up a seven-member task force, which created a compromise plan that attempts to recognize the importance of subsistence and acknowledge the state's role in management. Beginning in August 1997, hearings about this proposal have been held throughout the state. One common reaction has been "What's the problem? The state wouldn't prosecute people if they really needed the meat they were hunting." But in fact, in the past both state and federal governments have prosecuted or attempted to prosecute people for the taking of resources for subsistence purposes.

In 1961, for example, there was an incident in Barrow that generated considerable media attention. Federal officials arrested two men for hunting ducks out of season. According to the migratory bird treaty between the United States, Canada, and Mexico, no one can hunt ducks from May to September (the nesting season). But the ducks are in Arctic Alaska only from May through September, and in the spring, migratory waterfowl constitute a major source of fresh meat for residents after the long winter. Needless to say, the residents of Barrow stood behind the two men. Each one killed a duck and demanded to be arrested as well. The symbolic action caused officials to release the men and ease off on enforcement of those regulations. (Thirty-six years later, the United States, Canada, and Mexico are close to amending the migratory bird treaty to account for the subsistence use in the Arctic regions of both the United States and Canada.) On the state level, misunderstandings and arrests have occurred in response to the hunting of moose out of season for funeral potlatches, the taking of fish above a catch limit to share with extended family members, and numerous instances of a similar nature.

In an attempt to reach a compromise on the issue, a number of alternatives have recently been proposed, some of which address the issue of "need." When Alaska Natives and non-Natives attempt to discuss this issue, they often end up talking past each other. Sports fishers, for example, in an offer they see as accommodating the need issue, will often volunteer to give their catches to villagers. Or they will suggest that subsistence users can catch all the fish they want at the tail end of the salmon season. Subsistence users will respond that at the end of the season, the prime fish have already been caught and the remaining fish are spawned out, and that while the remaining fish might be fine for mounting on a wall, they no longer make good eating. The sport users then charge that the subsistence users are not willing to take what is offered.

However, it's important to understand that while meat and fish are important to most users, subsistence is more than a matter of protein intake for Native people. The closest corollary is the concept of "kosher" in Jewish society—the understanding that an item was obtained and prepared according to certain rules and procedures. Alaska Natives have customary ways of obtaining fish and game, preparing it for consumption, and using parts of it for clothing or tools. Just as in Orthodox Jewish society certain procedures must be followed for killing and butchering an animal, there are customary Alaska Native ways of killing and butchering an animal. The procedures sports hunters follow are generally quite different from those of Alaska Natives.

Another problem is the type of animal hunted. The sports user hunts for "trophy" animals, which tend to be unusually large. Subsistence users hunt for meat animals, avoiding the large animals because their meat is tough. When Alaska Natives say that they prefer not to obtain their meat supply through sports hunters, but through the customary and traditional practices that have been followed by their ancestors, they are depicted as not willing to compromise on the issue.

Alaska Natives know that resources are finite and that use must be regulated; but they must be a part of the process of determining the regulations and have a voice in this process so that subsistence ways of using the resources are recognized. In the early 1970s, a Bethel Native organization posed the question: "Does one way of life have to die so that another can live?" This issue is still before the state of Alaska fish and game resource managers.

Subsistence Hunting and Fishing in the 1950s

—By Alex Muktoyuk

It was no everyday occurrence when the hunters of Ugiuvok (King Island), off the coast of Nome, woke up in the morning to the sounds of their seasonal prey. The muffled roar of the migrating walrus herds on the ice was an unabridged chorus in the otherwise silent spring. Accompanied by the squeals of the three primary species of hundreds of thousands of auklets, the walrus herds made no secret of their arrival. They were migrating to the north, resting on scattered chunks of ice from the spring breakup. Catching a ride on the ice, they would drift on the Bering Strait's current from the Pacific Ocean to their summer home in the Arctic Ocean.

An abundant walrus harvest was fortunate for the village, providing more than enough meat for that year. The surplus would be stored in a deep cave on a cliff a half mile east of the village. There, the meat would remain frozen year-round, in case it was needed to soften the severity of famine in following years, when bad weather and poor ice conditions might prevent successful hunting of any kind—for polar bear or seals during the winter, or walrus in the spring.

Great herds of hundreds of thousands of these animals passed King Island each spring, drifting north on ice floes. Many times when the walrus came, the weather would be ideal for hunting, but the ice would be too dense, with little or no open leads of water between the ice floes to allow umiaks (large skin boats), or even kayaks, safe passage toward the herds. One year a herd was estimated to be two miles long, but because there was no open water where they could navigate safely, the villagers could only watch the reddish brown *nunavalliq* ("streak of mainland") drift by freely.

In the 1950s, authorities of Alaska's newly created state wildlife division began to warn the hunting villages to limit their takes of the walrus. Each hunter was limited to five animals per season, a drastic cut in harvest. It was difficult for the Ugiuvokmiut (*miut* at the end of a word means "the people of"), who had observed the walrus migration for at least 6,000 years, to believe the state's warnings that the walrus population could be depleted by a few hunters. Natives knew that nature's cycles, and the rhythm of the Native lifestyle, were all that were needed to naturally protect the walrus from excessive predation.

Alex Muktoyuk, an Inupiat Eskimo from King Island, Alaska, has lived in Portland, Oregon, since 1967. He teaches Inupiat singing and dancing to Inupiat Natives living in Western Washington and Oregon. His dance group, Northwest Inupiaq Dancers, performs throughout the region. He is currently working on a memoir of traditional and transitional Inupiat life.

When herds were in abundance and surplus meat needed to be stored, villagers stopped hunting in order to process the animals they had taken. Nothing was wasted. The raw hides, each a half inch thick, had to be split in half in order to make them thin enough to sew. The outer split hide, used as a covering for the wooden frame of kayaks and umiaks, was stretched onto a wooden rack to dry before storing. The inner half was also dried for other uses: to make protective cushions for the floor of a umiak and to cover fresh meat when taking it home after butchering.

Much of the meat had to be cut into pieces so it could be sun-dried on the roofs of houses, provided the sun shone for enough days to do the job. (When rain or heavy fog enveloped the island, we covered the drying meat with the inner half of a walrus hide.) Other parts of the walrus had to be dried as well: the intestine, for instance, had to be cleaned inside and out with extreme care so as not to puncture holes in it, then mouth-blown into a 300-foot air tube; to dry the intestine, one end was tied to a pole, and the other to another pole at a distance equivalent to the length of a football field. When it was dried to the translucence of alabaster and almost paper-thin, it would be cut into small rectangular pieces (smaller than a dollar bill), which were then sewn together with tiny stitches and waterproof seams to make raincoats for the hunters to wear over their parkas.

The walrus stomach was also split into two thinner halves and mouth-blown into huge oblong "balloons" to dry. Once dried, they were custom cut and used as drumheads, stretched flat across a wooden frame and used to accompany songs and dances.

Every physically fit man, woman, and child had jobs to do at walrus-processing time. The older children helped carry meat home in backpacks made of *oogruk* (large bearded seal) and walrus hide, with a carrying strap worn across the shoulders and chest. Still more meat was salted in airtight wooden barrels to be preserved and sold.

Spring brought other chores besides hunting walrus. At certain times of the evening and early morning, auklets flew from their feeding grounds in the sea to King Island to roost and claim territory, where they would lay their eggs. Village boys climbed up to a rock quarry to gather stones for ammunition, which they put into cloth bags with shoulder straps. This was early in the migratory season, before the birds tucked their eggs into the shadow of rocks or on King Island's precipitous cliffs; the birds were left alone when the time neared for them to lay eggs.

The two species of puffins, horned and tufted, also arrived to hatch eggs and rear their young. Murres, cormorants, seagulls, and guillemots laid their eggs on small ledges of granite cliffs. The Natives always enjoyed the fresh eggs—a welcome change in diet—not to mention the fun, excitement, and challenge of climbing the cliffs to gather the eggs.

At least three species of edible leafy greens grew on the treeless island. They were picked primarily by women and girls, although men also gathered them when they were not hunting. Rich in vitamin A, they were used to complement meals such as fresh walrus meat; eggs; and dried or boiled meat of various animals, auklets, and other seabirds.

Thus, throughout the spring everyone was busy working together. Much of this work was in preparation for summer, when the whole village packed up and went to Nome to earn needed cash and trade for goods. Much of the dried and salted meats, as well as the skins and hides, would be traded to mainland tribes for nonmarine goods such as reindeer and caribou meat and hides, dried salmon, wolverine skins and other furs, and a variety of other products the Ugiuvokmiut could not acquire otherwise. Walrus ivory carved by the men and boys was sold to curio shops in Nome and to the summer tourists from "outside." Sealskin slippers, *kamiks* (fancy dress boots, also called mukluks), Eskimo yo-yos, and dolls made from reindeer and sealskin sewn by the women and girls were sold to shops and tourists. Much of the money from the sale of these products was used to buy provisions for the next fall, winter, and spring. Dry goods such as clothing, rifles, and ammunition were bought in Nome or ordered by mail from the Sears, Montgomery Ward, or Spiegel catalogue. Some villagers worked summer jobs to earn money to buy their provisions.

So the cycle went around for the Ugiuvokmiut: summer on the mainland in Nome, then back to the isolation of King Island for the next nine months. The great majority of the Ugiuvokmiut were happy to return to their island after three months in Nome. Although their lives on the island were physically demanding, they were bonded by their hard work together, and they were glad to leave behind the city life and cash economy to again live off the sea, faithful to their Native culture.

Afterword

Villagers abandoned King Island after the Bureau of Indian Affairs closed the island's school in 1959, forcing families to relocate and effectively destroying the continuity of traditional Ugiuvokmiut culture. They have not returned because no one can survive on the island alone; it takes a close-knit community, working together with the natural cycle of animal, bird, and fish migrations, to survive there.

As for the walrus that the hunters were restricted from taking by the wildlife authorities, the Natives' skepticism of the newcomers and their scientific reports proved prophetic: in the 1970s, after nearly 20 years of hunting restrictions, the authorities declared the existence of a serious overpopulation of walrus.

Index

About the Authors

Jan Halliday has written news, features, and travel articles for Northwest newspapers, magazines, and national publications for 25 years. Formerly on the editorial staff of *Alaska Airlines Magazine,* she is a contributor to Sasquatch Books Best Places guidebooks, and co-author of *Native Peoples of the Northwest, A Traveler's Guide to Land, Art, and Culture,* published by Sasquatch Books in 1996.

Patricia J. Petrivelli is the Cultural Programs Director at the Alaska Native Heritage Center in Anchorage. She was formerly the Executive Director of the Institute of Alaska Native Arts, and she has worked with numerous Native associations and institutes throughout the state. She is currently on the board of directors of *Tundra Times* as well as of several Native arts commissions and organizations. An Aleut from Atka in the Aleutian Islands, she holds a Masters in Anthropology from the University of Alaska, Fairbanks.